Soviet Studies in Mathematics Education

Volume 1

Sets of Mathematics Teaching Aids

Editor of the Soviet Edition

V. G. Boltyanskii

Soviet Studies in Mathematics Education

Volume 1
Sets of Mathematics Teaching Aids

M. Ya. Antonovskii, V. G. Boltyanskii, M. B. Volovich,
E. Yu. Krass, and G. G. Levitas

Volume Editor,
English Language Edition

F. Alexander Norman
The University of North Carolina at Charlotte

Translator

Joan Teller

National Council of Teachers of Mathematics
Reston, Virginia
1990

Survey of Applied Soviet Research in School Mathematics Education

Izaak Wirszup, Principal Investigator
Department of Mathematics
The University of Chicago

Series Editorial Committee

Jeremy Kilpatrick, Chairman
The University of Georgia

Izaak Wirszup
The University of Chicago

Alphonse Buccino
The University of Georgia

Robert Streit
The University of Chicago

Financial support for the *Survey of Applied Soviet Research in School Mathematics Education* has been provided by the National Science Foundation.

Originally published in 1971 by Pedagogika, Moscow, as *Kompleksy uchebnogo oborudovaniya po matematike*.

English Translation © 1990 by the National Council of Teachers of Mathematics
1906 Association Drive
Reston, Virginia 22091
All rights reserved

Set in Adobe Postscript Times Roman with Helvetica display.

Printed in the United States of America

94 93 92 91 90   5 4 3 2 1

Library of Congress Cataloging-in-Publication Data

Kompleksy uchebnogo oborudovaniĭa po matematike. English
    Sets of mathematics teaching aids / M.Ya. Antonovskii . . . [et al.] ;
volume editor, English language edition F. Alexander Norman ;
  translator Joan Teller.
        p.   cm. — (Soviet studies in mathematics education ; v. 1)
    Translation of: Kompleksy uchebnogo oborudovaniĭa po matematike.
    Includes bibliographical references.
    ISBN 0-87353-290-2 (v. 1). — ISBN 0-87353-289-9 (set)
    1. Mathematics—Study and teaching (Elementary)—Soviet Union.
    2. Mathematics—Study and Teaching—Audio-visual aids.
    I. Antonovskiĭ, M. IA. (Mikhail IAkovlevich) II. Norman, F.
Alexander. III. Title. IV. Series.
    QA135.5.K64513   1990   90-5516
    372.7'044—dc20   CIP

Contents

Series Preface ix

Introduction to the English Language Edition xv

Preface to the Soviet Edition 1

1 **Instructional Media and Their Role in the Educational Process** 5

The Concept of Visuality in Pedagogy 5

Two Aspects of Visuality: Isomorphism and Simplicity 7

The Mathematical Definition of the Concept of Isomorphism 12

Perceptual Simplicity—An Essential Feature of Visuality 20

Biotechnological Properties of Instructional Media; Rubber Stamps 27

Instructional Orientation; Written Materials 32

Individualization; Sets of Problem Cards 35

Using Charts in Mathematics Lessons 38

Film Media in Mathematics Lessons 45

The Overhead Projector	56
Magnetic Instructional Media	63
Devices and Models	66
Optical Units of Educational Materials	71
The Definition of an Optimal Instructional Unit	76

2 The Psychological Theory of Mastery As One of the Theoretical Preconditions for Creating Instructional Units — 84

Mathematical Concepts As the Result of Abstraction	84
Mental Activity in Establishing What Belongs to a Concept	87
Mental Activity in Establishing Membership in a Concept	95
Adequate Manipulative Activity	108
Must Adequate Activity Be Performed?	116
Educational Materials—The Material Basis for Performing Adequate Activity	121

3 The Concept of Volume in Modern Mathematics and Its Formation in Grade 4 — 132

The Axiomatic Definition of Volume	132
Formation of the Concept of Volume	140
Dimension Theory and "Concrete Qualities"	148
Text of a Handbook on the Topic "The Rectangular Parallelepiped and Its Volume"	156

Contents vii

4 Description of the Instructional Unit for the Topic "The Rectangular Parallelepiped and Its Volume," and the Methodology of Using It — 183

Development of the Unit—Practical Application of the Theory — 183

Description of the Single-Concept Films — 188

Methodology of Using Single-Concept Films — 199

The Filmstrip — 202

Slides — 216

The Workbook — 225

The Set of Problem Cards — 272

Rubber Stamps, the Arithmetic Kit, and the Framework Model of a Rectangular Parallelepiped — 323

5 Lesson Plans for the Topic "The Rectangular Parallelepiped and Its Volume" — 336

Notes — 371

References — 375

Series Preface

The series *Soviet Studies in Mathematics Education* is a collection of translations of books from the extensive Soviet literature on research in the psychology of mathematics instruction. It also includes works on teaching methods directly influenced by this research. The series is a product of the Survey of Applied Soviet Research in School Mathematics Education at the University of Chicago and is funded by the National Science Foundation. The final editing and preparation of manuscripts was a cooperative undertaking by the Survey and the Department of Mathematics Education at the University of Georgia, with the valuable collaboration of a team of leading scholars from around the country. The *Soviet Studies* series comprises outstanding works selected for their value to the American mathematics educator and translated for the first time into English.

In view of Soviet social and political doctrines, several branches of psychology that are highly developed in the U.S. have scarcely been investigated in the USSR. On the other hand, because of the USSR's emphasis on education and its function in the state, Soviet research in educational psychology and teaching methods has received considerable moral and financial support. Consequently, this Soviet research has attracted many creative and talented scholars who have made remarkable contributions.

Even prior to World War II the Soviets had made great strides in educational psychology. The creation in 1943 of the Academy of Pedagogical Sciences helped to intensify research efforts and programs in this field. Since then the Academy has become the Soviet Union's chief educational research and development center. One of the main aims of the Academy is to conduct research and train research scholars in general and specialized education, educational psychology, and the methods of teaching various school subjects. Members of the Academy (51 in 1987, with another 85 associate members) are chosen from the ranks of distinguished Soviet scholars, scientists, and educators.

The Academy of Pedagogical Sciences comprises 15 research institutes, most of them in Moscow and Leningrad. Many of the studies reported in this series were conducted at the Academy's Institute of General and Polytechnical Education and Institute of Psychology. In 1987 the research institutes had available some 15 laboratory schools in which experiments were conducted. Developments in foreign countries are closely followed by the Bureau for the Study of Foreign Educational Experience and Information.

The Academy has its own publishing house, which produces hundreds of books each year as well as a number of periodicals, including *Proceedings of the Academy of Pedagogical Sciences of the USSR* (Izvestiya Akademii Pedagogicheskikh Nauk SSSR), the monthly *Soviet Pedagogy* (Sovetskaya pedagogika), the bimonthly *Topics in Psychology* (Voprosy psikhologii), the journal *Special Education* (Defektologiya), and the remarkable enrichment monthly for secondary school mathematics and science students (Grades 6-10) *Quantum* (Kvant).

Soviet psychologists have concerned themselves with the dynamics of mental activity and the principles of the learning process. They have investigated such areas as the development of mental operations; the nature and development of thought; the formation of mathematical concepts and the related questions of generalization, abstraction, and concretization; the mental operations of analysis and synthesis; the development of spatial perception; the relation between memory and thought; the development of logical reasoning; the nature of mathematical skills; and the structure and special features of mathematical abilities. Over the years, they have created a vast and impressive body of research.

This research has had a notable impact on the recent Soviet literature on methods of teaching mathematics. Experiments have shown the student's mathematical potential to be greater than previously assumed. Consequently, Soviet psychologists have advocated various changes in the content and methods of mathematics instruction. They participated in designing the revolutionary Soviet mathematics curriculum of the late 1960s and have been actively involved in more recent school reforms. Studies conducted with the assistance of the Survey of Applied Soviet Research in School Mathematics Education and the University of Chicago School Mathematics Project show that Soviet and American elementary school mathematics textbooks differ strikingly, with the Soviet books featuring many more types of word problems, treating a more even distribution of problem types, a much higher percentage of problems whose solution requires more than one operation, more varied sequences of problems, earlier introduction of multidigit addition and subtraction, and an emphasis on methods of mental calculation for single-digit operations. Furthermore, Soviet elementary school mathematics texts contain a continuous treatment of intuitive geometry, which by mandate comprises at least 20% of the mathematics curriculum in grades 1-5. The Soviet textbooks have clearly been constructed to reflect careful analyses of learning tasks and students' responses to them.

The USSR's apparent successes in the mathematics classroom, especially in the lower grades, have spurred American interest in Soviet research in educational psychology. One of the first opportunities to examine that research came with the appearance of the 14-volume series *Soviet Studies in the Psychology of Learning and Teaching Mathematics*. A joint publication of the Survey of Recent East European Mathematical Literature at the University of Chicago and the School Mathematics Study Group at Stanford University, that series had a broad and beneficial impact on mathematics education research in the United States and elsewhere and led directly to a great number of influential research projects.

At the time the earlier *Soviet Studies* series was published, American educational research was beginning to turn from its strong quantitative-experimentalist orientation toward the qualitative-interpretivist view so prominent today. The *Soviet Studies* helped bring to the attention of American researchers a tradition in which case studies and intensive work with small groups of children were the norm rather than the exception. Of particular interest to Americans was the *teaching experiment*, in which children were studied in the process of learning mathematical concepts, usually in ordinary classroom settings over a substantial period of time, and the teaching was continually modified in the light of the children's responses to it.

American researchers were interested not only in the approaches Soviet researchers used in their research but also in the topics they studied. One volume in the series concerned the structure of mathematical abilities. It brought the seminal work of V. A. Krutetskii to the attention of English-speaking mathematics educators. Subsequent publication of Krutetskii's landmark book *The Psychology of Mathematical Abilities in Schoolchildren* by the University of Chicago Press stimulated a variety of investigations into children's memory for the problems they have solved and how they perceive problems as being related. A subsequent book by Krutetskii is included in the present series.

Another volume in the earlier series dealt with studies in the perception of three-dimensional space. In the United States this ability had long been considered relatively static and little influenced by school instruction. The Soviet research demonstrated clearly that spatial abilities could be developed; again, that work is represented in the present series.

The earlier series was drawn primarily from journal articles published prior to the mid-1960s. The present series picks up where that one left off and consists entirely of translated books, for the most part monographs, all of which underwent thorough review by experts before they were originally published. Each manuscript was recommended by a scholarly committee or editorial council of either a university, a research institute of the Academy of Pedagogical Sciences, or the Ministry of Education.

The aim of the present series is to acquaint mathematics educators and teachers with directions, ideas, and accomplishments in the psychology of mathematical instruction in the Soviet Union. This series should assist in opening up avenues of investigation to those who are interested in broadening the foundations of their profession, for it is generally recognized that experiment and research are indispensable for improving the content and methods of school mathematics.

We hope that the volumes in this series will be used not only for research by individuals but also for study, discussion, and critical analysis in teacher-training programs and in institutes for in-service teachers at various levels.

Series Preface

It goes without saying that a publication project of this magnitude requires the commitment and cooperation of a network of institutions and individuals. In acknowledging their contributions, we would like first of all to express our deep appreciation to the National Science Foundation. Without the Foundation's generous long-term support of the Survey of Applied Soviet Research in School Mathematics Education, these books might never have become accessible to the American education and research communities.

The Survey at the University of Chicago is very pleased that the *Soviet Studies in Mathematics Education* are being published by the National Council of Teachers of Mathematics. It has always been a major goal of the Survey to disseminate its translations to a wide audience at minimal cost. We believe that the NCTM's recognized leadership, publishing expertise, and steadfast support and encouragement have assured us of reaching that goal. We are particularly indebted to the NCTM Educational Materials Committee and the Board of Directors. Special thanks are due Ms. Cynthia Rosso, NCTM Publications Business Manager, whose expertise, counsel, and energetic efforts were critical to the publication of this series.

The Editorial Committee would like to acknowlege the special assistance provided by Steven Young and George Fowler, who made a meticulous review of the translations; Jack Kirkman of the University of Georgia, who supervised the preparation of the edited manuscripts for publication; and Birute Tamulynas, who worked tirelessly on the manuscripts at the University of Chicago. We gratefully acknowledge the dedicated efforts of the volume editors and translators whose names appear on the title pages, as well as the valued contributions of the many language editors, typists, proofreaders, and production specialists who helped bring this extraordinary research to the English-speaking public.

> Jeremy Kilpatrick
> Izaak Wirszup
> Alphonse Buccino
> Robert Streit

Introduction to the English Language Edition

F. Alexander Norman

This volume is the result of a serious attempt to provide a theoretical foundation for the development and use of instructional media in mathematics lessons. These instructional media include a wide variety of objects from simple models and manipulatives to the most recent technology made available for classroom use. The primary goals of the book are two-fold. In addition to describing a rather elaborate theoretical basis, the authors illustrate the efficacy of this theory through their development and application of an instructional unit in several third- and fourth-grade classes. (It should be noted that few details of the research experiment and subsequent analysis are reported.) In fact, the authors have set themselves a formidable task in trying to craft a book that is both interesting and useful to a wide circle of readers including classroom teachers, mathematicians, mathematics education researchers, curriculum developers, methodologists, and authors of educational materials and texts.

Two decades ago Begle[1] called for a more scientific approach to mathematics education research, pointing to the lack of theoretically grounded experimental studies. In Moscow, at precisely this time (1969), the experiment forming the core of this volume had been completed and follow-up analyses were underway. For many years prior to Begle's remarks, such research had been commonplace in the Soviet Union, where socio-political factors placed (and still place) considerable emphasis on educational research.[2] The theoretical framework of the experiment has a strong, but not unexpected, psychological component, based primarily in the work of Vygotsky,[3] but also strongly influenced by the Swiss reformer Pestalozzi. However, some of the authors' analyses of instructional materials incorporate a mathematical perspective drawing on fairly sophisticated results in information theory.

The first chapter addresses two broad areas of concern. The first is a development of didactic and biotechnological aspects of instructional media. Visuality and didactic orientation are the major didactic aspects discussed here. The role of visuality in the development of concepts is similar to that of Bruner[4] and reflects the importance the Soviets place on emphasizing concrete and pictorial models (see, for example, Gibsh[5]). The visuality of a given object in an instructional medium is mathematized by characterizing it along two dimensions—its degree of isomorphicity and its perceptual simplicity. Isomorphicity, the basic prerequisite for a "good" model of an abstraction, supposes that between an abstract concept and a representation of that concept (be it concrete, pictorial, or symbolic) there should exist an isomorphism which maps the abstraction to the model in such a way that relevant attributes and relationships are preserved. The idea of the perceptual simplicity of a model is a more pragmatic aspect relating to the complexity of the representation. It is here that the authors inject mathematical entropy as a measure of the perceptual complexity of representations. Didactic orientation is simply a strict sequence of operations, made by pupils and imposed by a particular instructional medium, which lead to concept acquisition. Thus, in developing an optimal collection of instructional materials, the didactic orientation of each item in the collection becomes a critical factor for consideration.

Biotechnological aspects of instructional media deal with factors which address the ease of implementation, time- and labor-saving properties, efficiency, individualizability, and so forth. Limited resources and support, which the authors describe as critical, make these aspects

Introduction xvii

important factors in the use of a particular medium. The second principal area of concern in this chapter is the application of instructional media in classrooms. The authors go to great lengths to describe and recommend various uses of rubber stamps, overhead projectors, magnets, films, manipulatives, and more. Explicit connections are made between these applications and the theory described earlier in the chapter.

Chapter 2 opens with a psychological perspective of the definition and nature of abstraction. The remainder of the chapter deals with the necessary activity (both mental and material) for establishing whether an object, situation, or set of conditions is sufficient for inclusion in a given concept. Much of the chapter is devoted to a development of mathematical descriptions of conjunctive, disjunctive, and conditional statements.

Chapter 3 includes an extensive (if not always precise) mathematical description of volume. The formation of the volume concept, focusing on fourth-graders, and a discussion of concrete quantities are also considered. The chapter closes with a detailed exposition of the necessary ideas required for fourth-graders to adequately understand the concept of a rectangular parallelepiped and its volume.

Chapters 4 and 5 present an application of the theory built up in the first three chapters to the topic of the rectangular parallelepiped and its volume. Chapter 4 consists of complete descriptions of the substance and use of films, filmstrips, slides, workbooks, and other instructional media. Detailed sample lessons for the entire sixteen lesson unit comprise the final chapter.

This volume, while limited in some respects, presents several valuable perspectives to mathematics educators and researchers in mathematics education. In particular, the research methodology, psychology of learning and teaching, pedagogy, and specific content provide areas for examining historical/cultural comparisons of the research and education in the Soviet Union with that in the West. As mentioned earlier, the research methodology represents the typical systematic experimental investigation firmly grounded in theory that was well-established in the Soviet Union by the 1960's. An addition to the methodology that is not commonplace in the Soviet research (at least not in earlier volumes of this series) is the inclusion of a significant mathematical component. The mathematization of various properties of instructional media is innovative and fits well with the scientific approach taken by the Soviets to educational and psychological research.

The prevailing Soviet view of a child's development of mental operations is that it is directly related to the content of knowledge. Furthermore, the importance of visuality and the emphasis placed on content as the principal factor in the systematic presentation and mastery of material[6] makes quantification of instructional media a natural avenue to follow in the characterization of an optimal set of instructional materials. The fact that both instruction and learning are viewed as very closely bound to content is reflected in the authors' detailed delineation of the content and the form it should take, the precise sequencing of that content, and the best way to present it.

The specific content presented here provides, perhaps, the most startling contrast with contemporary instruction in the United States. The unit on a rectangular parallelepiped and its volume suggests a much closer attention to developing a relational understanding of the volume concept than exists here. Certainly the time allotted for instruction is considerably greater. The unit integrates the laws of arithmetic operations into the lessons and exemplifies these laws during the development of formulas for area and volume. In general, the mathematical content, especially in view of the considerable time spent developing an understanding of geometric relationships, is much more sophisticated than that given to most eighth- and ninth-graders in the United States—and these lessons were planned for fourth-grade students. Furthermore, perhaps most importantly in view of the research reported in this volume, the laboratory approach involving manipulatives and alternatives to expository instruction alone was carefully developed and implemented successfully in the classrooms. The parallels with our own research in alternative instruction and appropriate application of new technology might well prove valuable.

In closing, consider the following examples (from the unit test) of the types of problems a student might be expected to solve:

Introduction

> The dimensions of a hayloft are 15 m x 20 m x 40 dm. Hay is kept in the loft. There are 60 kg of hay for every cubic meter of the loft's capacity. One cow will eat 16 kg of hay in a day. How many days will this hay feed 40 cows?
>
> The volume of a cube is equal to 343 cubic cm. One dimension is doubled. Find the sum of the lengths of the edges, the surface, and the volume of the resulting rectangular parallelepiped.

It is clear from these problems that students are expected to understand clearly the geometric relationships among the components of rectangular parallelepipeds and to make intelligent use of this and other knowledge in solving complex problems.

Notes

1. Begle, E. G. (1969). Research in the improvement of education. In *Proceedings of the first international conference on mathematical education.* Dordrecht, Holland: D. Reidel.

2. Brozek, J. (1966). Contemporary Soviet psychology. In *Present-day Russian psychology* (Ch. 7). Pergamon Press.

3. Vygotskii, L. S. (1962). *Thought and language.* E. Hanfmann & G. Vakar (Trans.). Cambridge: MIT Press.

4. Bruner, J. S. (1960). *The process of education.* New York: Random House.

5. Gibsh, I. A. (1975). Principles, forms and methods of mathematics instruction. In J. Kilpatrick, I. Wirzsup, E. G. Begle, & J. Wilson (Eds.), *Soviet studies in the psychology of learning and teaching mathematics* (Vol. 8, pp. 1-76). Stanford: School Mathematics Study Group. (Original work published in 1958.)

6. Ibid.

Preface to the Soviet Edition

The purpose of this book is to show, using a specific topic from a mathematics course, the composition of instructional media for mathematics lessons, how these media should be constructed, and how to use them in a lesson. This is a timely and crucial issue since mathematics as a school subject is very poorly equipped with instructional media. Many recently approved topics in the mathematics curriculum are completely new to our schools and have no supporting educational materials. Moreover, the availability of new forms of educational resources such as slides, transparency sets, written materials, and others is minimal. In addition, many of the visual aids previously issued (and even those being issued now) are outmoded.

The implication is that, with regard to mathematics as an academic subject in schools, we should be concerned essentially with recreating an entire system of educational resources—of course, involving a critical use (possibly in modernized form) of those few mathematics instructional resources available now. A well-grounded scientific approach is clearly a critical component in creating a system of school resources in mathematics.

This book, which was written by a group in the mathematics laboratory of the Scientific Research Institute for School Materials and Technical Instructional Media of the USSR Academy of Pedagogical Sciences, is a response to the issues, touched upon above, of the pedagogical possibilities of various forms of educational materials, of constructing instructional media, and of using them in mathematics lessons. We intended to write this book so that it would be useful to a wide range of readers: mathematics teachers, researchers in mathematics education, authors of textbooks and creators of educational materials. Therefore, we have not restricted ourselves to considering theoretical issues alone, but have also included in the book a set of educational materials we devised for use with fourth-graders. This set of materials, a complete instructional unit, addresses the topic "The Rectangular Parallelepiped and Its Volume," and includes a detailed exposition of methods of working with the materials. How well this design has succeeded we leave to the reader to judge.

The work on creating the instructional unit described in the book was done in the following way. After developing the school materials for the first variant of the unit, a pilot study was carried out. It had the following objectives:

> 1) To uncover flaws in the instructional materials — flaws that might have remained unnoticed when the school materials were constructed, but that showed up during class work.

> 2) To describe the basic issues involved in a methodological description of the instructional unit (Chapter 5 takes into account the results of the experiment).

> 3) To discuss guidelines for the total evaluation of the unit as a means of raising the level of instruction in the given topic.

Following the pilot study, an experiment was conducted with several classes—a total of 5 classes from 5 schools. These were the grade 4 classes in Moscow schools No. 52, 82, 527, and 625, and the grade 3 class in school No. 52, all of which had worked on the particular curriculum. The experiment was carried out in April and May of 1968. Each class was assigned a research assistant from the mathematics laboratory who directed the lessons. The classroom teachers were given only the most general directions for the use of the instructional unit so as not to stifle their initiative with overly detailed instructions. In addition, teachers' imagination and creativity might give rise to alternative uses of the materials. The teachers did not have the detailed lesson descriptions cited in Chapter 6. These lesson descriptions are based on the experiment into consideration.

During the course of the experiment, the laboratory research assistants attended the lessons in all classes. They recorded the lessons on tape, timed them, noted the extent of activity in the classes, and jotted down remarks and suggestions about methods of presenting the unit and using the various materials, including ways in which the teachers might use the instructional materials. After the lessons they exchanged ideas with the teachers.

The results of an analysis of the records resulted in improvement of individual components of the instructional unit and clarification of the structure and content of the methodological descriptions. The teachers' remarks were also taken into account in revising the instructional materials in the unit.

The teachers who worked in the experimental classes noted that using the unit promoted a sharp increase in the students' interest in mathematics lessons. This was evidenced in their generally active approach to the lessons and in the quality of preparation of the homework assignments the (students liked working at home with cards and with a printed workbook). The teachers who worked in 1968-69 with fifth-graders who had participated in the experiment the previous year noticed that the students showed a thorough mastery of the topic "The Rectangular Parallelepiped and Its Volume."

Formal test results indicated almost no change. Average marks for individual students were not significantly different from the expected level. However, considering the depth and richness of the material, we can claim to have genuinely raised the level of schoolwork in the experimental classes (see Chapter 5). All the teachers noticed that the students learned the concept of volume much more deeply than through traditional instruction. In particular, there was actually no confusion of linear, square, and cubic measures, while such confusion is a characteristic phenomenon in ordinary instruction. It is indisputable that the creation of similar instructional units for every topic in the school mathematics curriculum will substantially improve the quality of instruction.

In conclusion, we should like to take this opportunity to express our sincere appreciation to all those who assisted in the development and editing of this manuscript; to A.G. Gleikh, N.L. Karpovich, N.P. Platonova, R.A. Zaitseva, and V.M. Krainyuk, the teachers who conducted lessons in the experimental classes; and to S.G. Shapovalenko, an active member of the USSR Academy of Pedagogical Sciences, and S.I. Shvartsburd, a corresponding member, who made a number of suggestions for improving the text. In addition, V.N. Tolyarov was especially helpful by painstakingly and lovingly constructing a number of manipulatives in our laboratory's small workshop, which were then used with other instructional materials, thereby contributing to the experimental work with the instructional unit and our theoretical conclusions.

1

Instructional Media and Their Role in the Educational Process

The Concept of Visuality in Pedagogy

The term "instructional media" has come into use comparatively recently, superseding the term "visual aids." This latter term (as we shall soon see) is narrower both methodologically and with respect to the scope of the concept of visuality (i.e., the supply of objects encompassed by this concept).

The role of visuality in instruction is of exceptional importance. Ya.A. Komenskii, K.D. Ushinskii, and many other prominent educators have emphasized it in the past. Thus, Pestalozzi wrote:

> "Friend, when I look back now and ask myself, what, properly speaking, have I done for the education of humanity?—I find the following: I have established the highest basic principle of education by acknowledging sensory-perceptual observation (visualization) to be the absolute basis of all cognition" [14:329].

Moreover, not only did Pestalozzi elevate visuality to the rank of the highest principle of instruction, he also contrasted it with other methods of instruction—verbal methods in particular. We read in his work:

> "Truth originating in observation makes superfluous both the tedious utterances of speech and various machinations, although these do protect us from delusions and prejudices, as a bell's sounding protects us from calamity."[1]

Of course this contrast, making the visual method into an absolute, is a methodological error on Pestalozzi's part, as Lesgaft quite rightly pointed out.[2] In essence, Komenskii and Pestalozzi hypothesized and raised to the rank of an absolute principle, the first part of Lenin's brilliant formulation for the process of cognition: "from lively contemplation to abstract thought, and from it to practice..."[3]

K.D. Ushinskii goes further in his understanding of visuality. He writes: "The child generally thinks in shapes, in colors, in sounds, in sensations. Hence, the necessity for children to have visual instruction, which is built not on abstract concepts and words, but on concrete forms, perceived directly by the child."[4] From this and from a number of other statements, it is evident that Ushinskii attributes to visuality not only what a student contemplates directly, but also, for example, artistic reading and narrative. In other words, Ushinskii interprets visuality considerably more broadly than his predecessors. He no longer makes the direct etymological connection between "visuality" and the possibility of "vision."[5] Thus, he approaches a more modern interpretation of visuality.

A number of interesting investigations of visuality and its role in the process of instruction have been conducted by Soviet educators and psychologists, including P.R. Atutov,[6] A.P. Gromov,[7] L.V. Zankov,[8] S.G. Shapovalenko,[9] N.P. Konobeevskii,[10] and others.

However, no satisfactory definition of the concept of "visuality" has been given by these authors (or others). For example, G.G. Rozenblat writes:

> "So far as visuality in a epistemological sense is concerned (i.e., reliance on the students' sense perceptions and notions), teaching visually does not necessarily mean using only 'objects' as visual aids. But it does mean, first and foremost, designing the educational process to always rely on the students' sensations, perceptions, and, above all, concepts."[11]

Especially apparent here is the desire to interpret "visuality" in instruction significantly more broadly than simply the phenomenon of direct visual perception. Still there is no definition. But from the statement quoted, it is clear that the pedagogical interpretation of visuality in instruction is somewhat different from an epistemological one. Therefore, before discussing what "visual aids" are and which instructional media are included, we should clearly define the conception of visuality that corresponds to the present level of pedagogical science.

Two Aspects of Visuality: Isomorphism and Simplicity

The concept of "visuality" and its role in the educational process have recently been changed and significantly expanded. We now believe that a chalk notation on a blackboard, or even a teacher's oral account can sometimes be more visual than a demonstration of a phenomenon in its natural form. Thus, with respect to molecular structure, the formula

$$H_2SO_4$$

written on the blackboard is more visual than simply contemplating sulfuric acid in a beaker. Even more visual is a structural model (Fig. 1) of a sulfuric acid molecule (regardless of whether it is represented in chalk on the blackboard, prepared as a poster,[12] made up of colored circles on a magnetic board, or executed in the form of a spatial model). A structural model or even a formula for a compound, tells a student considerably more about the chemical properties of a compound than the actual object. For instance, it reveals the chemical composition of the molecule and the valence connections between individual atoms, makes it possible to find the molecular mass easily, and so forth.

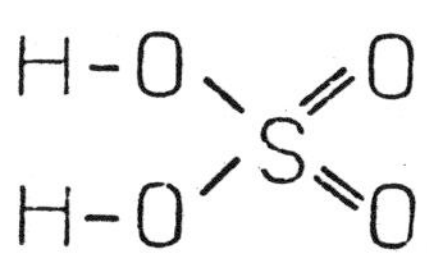

$$\begin{matrix} H-O & \diagdown & \diagup O \\ & S & \\ H-O & \diagup & \diagdown O \end{matrix}$$

Figure 1.

Even with respect to the chemical reaction (such as the reaction when sulfuric acid is combined with a metal), a model made of colored circles on a magnetic board is far more visual than direct observation of the phenomenon itself, since the student can see the essence of the reaction immediately: the substitution of metal atoms for hydrogen atoms. This is what is called *symbolic* visuality.

Taking this example, let us analyze the advantages of formula notation for understanding a compound and its reactions. A real object (a chemical compound) has innumerable attributes. However, we are interested in only one aspect: the number and nature of the atoms in one molecule of the compound. We then ignore the other aspects of the phenomenon. In precisely the same way, in studying a reaction we are interested in only one thing—the regrouping of atoms in the molecules of the compound. Representing atoms by colored circles on a magnetic board (sulfur by a yellow circle, oxygen by a red one, and hydrogen by a blue one), we obtain a model of the phenomenon. In this model we have removed the nonessential features. It reflects only one thing—the quantity and nature of the atoms (represented by circles) in the chemical compound. This is the single aspect connecting our model with the real object. But, on the other hand, this aspect is an *adequate isomorphism* of our model with the object being studied. In the present case this means that the model on the magnetic board contains one yellow circle (representing the one sulfur atom in a molecule of sulfuric acid), four red circles (representing oxygen atoms), and two blue circles (representing hydrogen atoms). In other words, a real molecule and our model are *isomorphic* in their composition. Similarly, for a chemical reaction, such a model reflects the isomorphic regrouping of atoms; the atoms in the molecules are regrouped during the reaction exactly as the circles are regrouped in the demonstration model.

Since only one aspect of the phenomenon being studied is reflected in the model, the model greatly simplifies the processes underlying the phenomenon, thus making it cruder. By giving up features of the phenomenon, the model acquires simplicity in the way it is perceived. In the present case this occurs because, as distinct from atoms of matter (which we are in no position to observe), the model contains colored circles, which are easily accessible to students' immediate visual perception. These two characteristics of a model (the isomorphic reflection of essential features of the phenomenon, and simplicity in perceiving the model) express what, in our opinion, is meant by the *visuality* of a model.

Suppose a model did not reflect isomorphically the essential features of a phenomenon. If it reflected a distortion of those features (e.g., if the number of circles did not correspond to the number of atoms in the actual molecule), we would not get a proper notion of the phenomenon being studied, nor could there be a discussion of visuality. Furthermore, suppose a model could not be perceived simply—for example, if it were based on concepts not yet adequately learned by the students or too difficult for them to grasp. This model might not make it easier for the students to acquire a proper notion of the phenomenon they are studying; it would not be visual. Both aspects—the *proper, isomorphic reflection* of the essential features of a phenomenon and *simplicity of perception*—are integral components of visuality.

The models of solids used in school are visual. For example, consider the rather complex concept of the rectangular parallelepiped. Acquisition of the concept presupposes the ability to abstract from the solid's surface various features—its color, temperature, texture, etc.—which students rarely manage right away. A real object such as a wooden bar (Fig. 2) is not, of course, a rectangular parallelepiped in the mathematical sense; it serves only as a model. However, this model reflects isomorphically the basic properties of a rectangular parallelepiped as a solid: it has the same number of faces, edges, and vertices as an abstract parallelepiped and shares the same connection scheme (for example, three edges are joined together at each vertex). Thus, this is an isomorphism. At the same time, a wooden bar is easy to perceive and is familiar to students. We see that a model of a rectangular parallelepiped (just like a model of other solids) has the property of visuality.

Finally, one more example. In studying the properties of a rectangular parallelepiped the concept of a *frame* presents a certain difficulty for students. A frame of a solid is a figure composed of just the edges and vertices of a solid. For parallelepipeds, it is not so easy to "see" the structure of its frame simply by studying a wooden bar. Therefore a framework model of a rectangular parallelepiped is used in lessons (Fig. 3). Of course, this model does not coincide with the mathematical concept of a frame (represented in Fig. 4). The edges, which we imagine as "absolutely thin" line segments, are represented in this model by pivots with readily apparent thickness.

Nevertheless, isomorphism is present here as well. We see that the number of vertices and edges, as well as the connection scheme and the parallelism of the model correspond precisely to analogous components of the abstract mathematical frame. Simplicity of perception is likewise indisputable. The invisible edges and vertices, which are not easy for students to imagine by examining a solid wooden bar, are quite apparent in this model. Thus, in the study of a frame, a framework model is *simpler* to perceive than a solid wooden bar, and consequently *more visual* as

Figure 2.

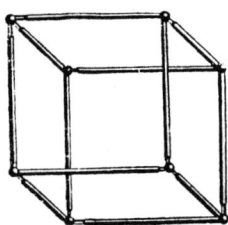

Figure 3.

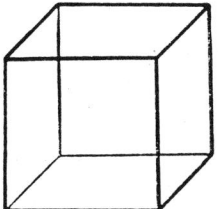

Figure 4.

well. At the same time, for an initial introduction to a rectangular parallelepiped, a framework model is less visual than a solid wooden bar. Indeed, despite the ease and simplicity in perceiving a framework model, it lacks the faces of a rectangular parallelepiped and the solid matter itself. There is no complete isomorphism between the model and the concept being studied. Therefore, in beginning the study of the topic, a framework model will not be a model for a parallelepiped for the students. Consequently, it will still be hard for students to identify the wooden bar with the framework model. This reconfirms that an absence of isomorphism implies an absence of visuality.

As students become acquainted with the concept being studied, they will be able to extend the framework model mentally, imagining the faces of a parallelepiped. Through this extension, the *partial isomorphism* (i.e., partial reflection of properties) inherent in the framework model becomes a complete isomorphism for the student, and thus the framework model becomes a visual model not only of the frame, but of the entire rectangular parallelepiped as well. Now the isomorphicity is evident, and a number of properties are simpler to perceive (for example, four parallel edges, the equality of opposite faces, etc., are clearly apparent). Moreover, from this moment on, the framework model (like the model of the whole rectangular parallelepiped) will become *more visual* for students than the bar. The foregoing means that the very concept of visuality (like that of simplicity) changes as students acquire knowledge, while at each stage the meaning of visuality remains the same: isomorphism and simplicity.

The Mathematical Definition of the Concept of Isomorphism

The preceding definition of visuality would be descriptive only if there were no precise definition of isomorphic mapping and simplicity of perception. In this section we shall examine the concept of isomorphism (well known in modern mathematics).

First let us introduce the concept of a *predicate*, which pertains to mathematical logic, and, for greater clarity, let us begin with some examples.

Example 1. We designate by N the set of all natural numbers. We then designate by $e(a)$ the following statement:

$$e(a) \equiv \{\text{the number } a \text{ is even}\}.$$

For some values of a this statement will be true, and for others, false. For example, the statement $e(8)$ (i.e., "the number 8 is even") is true, but the statement $e(23)$ is false. Thus, $e(a)$ is a statement that depends on the variable a (which in this case is a natural number).

Such "variable statements" (or, more precisely, statements containing variable quantities) are called predicates in mathematical logic. In the present case, $e(a)$ is a predicate of one variable a.

Now let us consider examples of predicates depending on more than one variable.

Example 2. Let A be a set of people. Let us consider the following statement:

$$p(a, b) \equiv \{\text{person } a \text{ is one of the parents of person } b\}.$$

This is a predicate of two variables, a and b, which can assume values in set A. If we indicate specifically whom we mean by a and b, we can determine whether the statement $p(a, b)$ is true or false. In this case, the

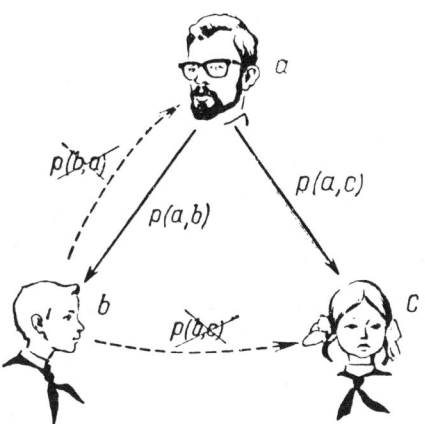

Figure 5.

predicate $p(a, b)$ expresses the parenthood relationship. If, for example, b and c are a brother and sister, and a is their father, then the statement $p(a, b)$ is true, as is $p(a, c)$, whereas the statements $p(b, a)$ and $p(b, c)$ are false (Fig. 5).

Example 3. Let us again designate by N the set of all natural numbers. Consider the following statement:

$$d(a, b) \equiv \{\text{the number } a \text{ is a divisor of the number } b\}.$$

Then d is a predicate of two variables for the set N. The statements $d(2, 6)$, $d(4, 4)$, and $d(1, 7)$ are true, but $d(3, 2)$ and $d(6, 3)$ are false. Now let $m(a, b)$ be the following statement: the number a is less than the number b. Then m is another predicate for the same set N. For example, $m(2, 4)$ is true, but $m(5, 2)$ is false. Now two predicates have been introduced in N: d, m.

Example 4. Let us again consider the set N of all natural numbers. We designate by $s(a, b, c)$ the following statement: the number a is the sum of the numbers b and c. Then s is a predicate (of the three variables a, b,

c) in N. If we substitute natural numbers for a, b, and c, we obtain different statements. For example, the statements $s(5, 2, 3)$ and $s(7, 6, 1)$ are true, but $s(4, 2, 3)$ is false.

Example 5. Let L be the set of all straight lines in the plane. Then

$$q(l, m) \equiv \{\text{line } l \text{ is parallel to line } m\}$$

is a predicate of two variables, which assume values in set L.

Example 6. Let Q be the set of all positive real numbers. Let $t(a, b, c)$ represent the following statement: a triangle can be constructed from segments of lengths a, b, c. Then t is a predicate of three variables in set Q.

In the general case, *q is said to be a predicate of s variables in set A if, for any elements $a_1, a_2, \ldots, a_s$ of the set A, the truth or falsity of the statement $q(a_1, a_2, \ldots, a_s)$ can be determijed.*

A set for which one or more predicates are specified will be called a *model*.[13] The notation $<A; \alpha, \beta, \gamma>$ will designate a model consisting of a set A for which the predicates α, β, and γ have been defined. For example, recalling Examples 1, 3, and 4, we can say that $<N; e, d, m, s>$ is a model, where e a predicate in one variable, d and m are predicates in two variables, and s a predicate in three variables.

Now let $<A; \alpha, \beta, \gamma, \ldots>$ and $<A'; \alpha', \beta', \gamma', \ldots>$ be two models. We say that these two models are similar if:

1) the number of predicates in the first model is equal to the number of predicates in the second model, and

2) predicate α depends on the same variables as predicate α', predicate β depends on the same variables as predicate β', and so forth.

For example, the model $<N; s$ of Example 4 is similar to the model $<Q; t$ of Example 6, but the models $<N; s$ and $<L; q$ (Example 5) are not similar. The models $<N; d, m$ (Example 3) and $<L; q$ are not similar either, since they do not have the same number of predicates.

Now let us define isomorphism. We shall explain it first through three examples.

Example 7. Let A be the set of all atoms constituting one sulfuric acid molecule (so that A is a seven element set). We designate by $\alpha(a, b)$ the following statement: *atoms a and b are identical* (e.g., both are oxygen atoms). Then $<A; \alpha$ is a model with one predicate in two variables. Now let A' be a set composed of two blue circles, one yellow one, and four red ones. We consider the predicate

$$\alpha'(a', b') \equiv \{\text{circles } a' \text{ and } b' \text{ are the same color}\}.$$

Then $<A'; \alpha'$ is also a model with one predicate α' in two variables. Hence the models $<A; \alpha$ and $<A'; \alpha'$ are similar. By matching a red circle to each oxygen atom in our molecule (Fig. 6) (so that different circles correspond to different atoms), a blue circle to each hydrogen atom, and a yellow one to the sulfur atom, we then obtain a *one-to-one correspondence between atoms and circles. Let us designate this correspondence as f.* The notation $f(a) = a'$ will mean that the circle a' has been matched to the atom a. In addition to the fact that f is a one-to-one correspondence, it has another important property—it leaves predicates invariant. That is, if $f(a) = a'$ and $f(b) = b'$, then $\alpha(a, b)$ is true if and only if $\alpha'(a', b')$ is true. In other words, atoms a and b are identical if and only if the circles corresponding to them have the same color. *A one-to-one correspondence that preserves the truth value of corresponding predicates is called an isomorphism.* Thus the mapping f described in this example is an isomorphism. In this case, where the molecular structure is under consideration, this means that the model of a sulfuric acid molecule composed of colored circles is an adequate representation of the actual molecule.

Example 8. Let us consider the following 27 symbols:

$$(0, 0, 1), (1, 0, *), (*, 0, *), ..., (*, *, *),$$

each of which represents a triple (x, y, z), where any of the variables x, y, and z can take the arbitrary value 0, 1, or $*$. The triples not containing stars will be called vertices; triples with exactly one star are called edges; triples with exactly two stars are called faces; and the triple $(*, *, *)$ is called a solid. In addition, we can obtain various relations among the triples. We can say a vertex belongs to an edge if the vertex can be

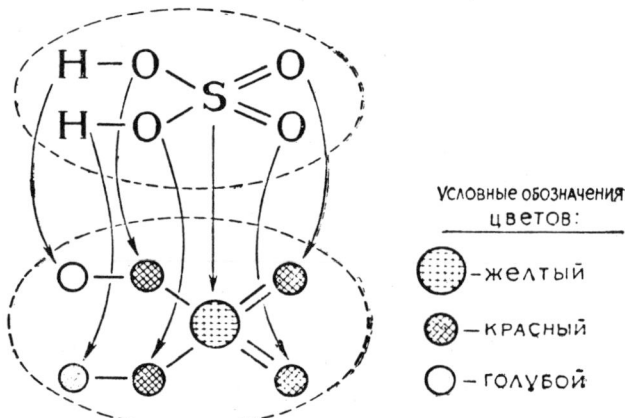

Figure 6.

obtained from the edge by replacing the edge's * component with a 0 or a 1. For example,

$$\text{vertex } (0, 1, 1) \text{ belongs to edge } (0, *, 1,),$$

since replacing the * with a 1 results in the designation for the vertex. The relations "a vertex belongs to a face" and "an edge belongs to a face" are defined analogously. For example,

$$\text{vertex } (1, 0, 0) \text{ belongs to face } (*, 0, *);$$

$$\text{edge } (0, 1, *) \text{ belongs to face } (0, *, *).$$

Finally, we will consider two edges (or two faces) parallel if their stars are in the same position. For example,

$$\text{edge } (0, 1, *) \text{ is parallel to edge } (0, 0, *);$$

$$\text{face } (*, *, 0) \text{ is parallel to face } (*, *, 1).$$

The symbol system just described can easily be transformed into a model. We designate by A the set of the 27 ordered triples, and define a set of predicates.

There are three predicates of one variable:

$$b(a) \equiv \{a \text{ is a vertex}\},$$

$$r(a) \equiv \{a \text{ is an edge}\},$$

$$g(a) \equiv \{a \text{ is a face}\};$$

There are two predicates of two variables:

$$l(a, b) \equiv \{a \text{ belongs to } b\},$$

$$n(a, b) \equiv \{a \text{ is parallel to } b\}.$$

For example, the statements $b((0, 0, 1))$, $r((0, *, 0))$, $g((*, *, 1))$, $l((0, 0, 1), (0, *, 1))$, $l((0, 1, 0), (0, *, *))$, $n((0, *, 1), (1, *, 1))$, and $n((*, 0, *), (*, 1, *))$ are true, whereas the statements $b((*, *, 0))$, $r((0, 0, 0))$, $g((0, *, 1))$, $l((0, 0, 0), (1, *, *)$, and $n((0, *, 1), (*, 0, 0))$ are false.

Thus, the model $<A; b, r, g, l, n$ is defined. Let A' be the set of components of an ordinary rectangular parallelepiped (edges, vertices, etc.) and introduce the corresponding predicates b', r', g', l', and n' (so that, for example, if the statement $b'(a')$ is true, it means that a' is a vertex, and if the statement $n'(a', b')$ is true, it means that $a' \parallel b'$ have the model $<A'; b', r', g', l', n'$, similar to the model $<A; b, r, g, l, n$. It is easy to see that these two similar models are *isomorphic*, since a one-to-one correspondence can be established between the sets A and A' such that all the predicates will be preserved (Fig. 7).

Examples 7 and 8 should help clarify the general definition of isomorphism.

Let $<A; \alpha_1, \alpha_2, \ldots, \alpha_s>$ mand $<B; \beta_1, \beta_2, \ldots, \beta_s>$ be two similar models. The mapping f of set A onto B is said to be an *isomorphism* of these models if it has the following two properties:

1) f maps set A one-to-one onto the entire set B;

2) the mapping f preserves all predicates.

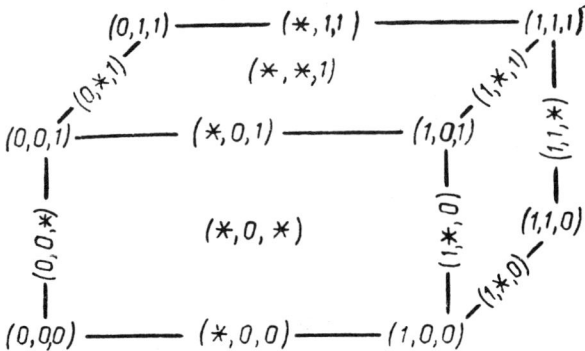

Figure 7.

The latter condition means that if $k \in \{1, 2, ..., s\}$ and the predicate α_k (hence β_k, as well) depends on m_k variables, then for any elements

$$a_1, a_2, ..., a_{m_k}$$

of the set A, the statement

$$\alpha_k(a_1, a_2, ..., a_{m_k})$$

is true if and only if the statement

$$\beta_k(f(a_1), f(a_2), ..., f(a_{m_k}))$$

is true. Roughly speaking, two models are *isomorphic* if, ignoring all properties of these models that are not related to the predicates under consideration, we can say that they are "identically organized" (they are, in essence, indistinguishable).

The value of the concept of isomorphism as one of the two essential aspects of visuality is difficult to overestimate. Indeed, before constructing a manipulative, a poster, or any other kind of instructional material which represents a visual phenomenon, we must isolate the basic properties of the phenomenon being studied. These properties should be properly and adequately reflected by the instructional medium. The properties selected can be reflected in terms of predicates (see Examples 7 and 8). In other words, by singling out the basic properties and discarding the nonessential ones, we transform the phenomenon under consideration into a *model*. The requirement for an adequate representation of a phenomenon being studied with the aid of manipulatives, a poster, or any other aid is that this instructional medium should be an *isomorphic* model.

After examining the examples given above and becoming familiar with the general definition of an isomorphism, the reader may have formed the opinion that isomorphism is the principal property in the concept of visuality, and that the property of simplicity is of secondary importance. The authors by no means share this view. Indeed, let us reconsider Example 8. It describes a model of a rectangular parallelepiped, consisting of 27 triples (x, y, z) *isomorphic* to an ordinary rectangular parallelepiped with respect to a number of properties (including how the vertices, edges, and faces belong to and are parallel to one another). This model makes it possible to answer a number of questions about a rectangular parallelepiped: how many edges adjoin each vertex? how many edges are parallel to a given edge? and so forth. And yet it cannot be claimed that this model is visual (from a fourth-grader's vantage point) since it does not have the property of simplicity. The concept of a triple is new, unusual, and the abstractness of the model is not appropriate to the level of the students. Without perceptual simplicity there is no visuality. Therefore, we cannot discard the property of perceptual simplicity in the definition of visuality and simply limit ourselves to isomorphism.

At the same time, at a higher level of development, the model of an n-dimensional cube (constructed as in Example 7) is extremely visual. This is because familiarity with finite sequences and facility in abstract thinking make the model very simple and therefore visual (for isomorphism is present). This example shows that the concept of simplicity constantly changes in proportion to the students' development. What was not simple at earlier stages of instruction and development becomes so at later stages. Consequently, the concept of visuality, including simplicity as one facet, is transformed as the students develop intellectually.

Perceptual Simplicity—An Essential Feature of Visuality

Let us stipulate at the outset that this section presents only a mathematical approach to the concept of simplicity—that is, we discuss merely the theoretical possibility of a precise quantitative evaluation of the concept of perceptual simplicity of a model. Some elementary concepts of information theory serve as a basis for the mathematics employed.

Recently the *binary number system* has begun to find increasing application. This is due to developments in computing technology and information theory. The binary number system provides us with an introduction to the concept of the complexity of a model.

Let us consider a finite sequence in which two kinds of elements alternate: red and white balls lined up in a row, for example, or magnetized and unmagnetized strips on a film. We will represent them with strings consisting of zeros and ones. The number of symbols (zeros or ones) in the string is referred to as the *number of binary digits*. Thus, there are five binary digits in the string 01101, there are seven binary digits in the string 1100110, and so on. There exist, in all, $2n$ different strings consisting of zeros and ones containing n binary digits. If we add another binary digit, the number of strings obtained (that is, strings containing $n + 1$ binary digits) will be doubled. To each of the strings consisting of n binary digits we can append either a zero or a one, thus doubling the number of possibilities.

Therefore, adding a single binary digit doubles the total number of possibilities. This is an obvious lack of correspondence: in the first instance it is a matter of adding; in the second it is one of multiplying. To eliminate this lack of correspondence, we examine, not the total number of possibilities itself, but its logarithm. We shall use, as is traditional in information theory, base-2 logarithms. If N denotes the total number of of objects in a set, then the number $H = \log_2 N$ is the entropy for the set.[14] Thus, if we consider all possible sequences of zeros and ones containing n binary digits, then the total number of possibilities (the number of all such sequences) is equal to n, and thus the entropy H assumes the value

$H = \log_2 2^n = n$ Consequently, the addition of one binary digit adds one unit to the entropy, and the lack of correspondence noted above is eliminated.

Of course, not every set of objects can be described precisely by strings of binary digits. However, any finite set can be described using a sufficient number of binary digits. Suppose that a set consists of 27 elements. We can divide the elements of this set into two approximately identical groups (13 elements in one and 14 in the other). We assign the number 0 to the elements in the first group and the number 1 to the elements in the second. We now take the first group of elements and again divide it roughly in half. To each of these new halves we assign a second binary symbol. The two halves of the first half of the set will then be designated by the strings 00 and 01. Taking the second half of the set, we shall also divide it into halves and designate these two "quarters" of the original set as 10 and 11. (It is sufficient to indicate one of the four strings 10, 11, 00, 01 in order to precisely determine which quarter of the original set contains the element we want.) We then divide each of the quarters roughly in half, and to distinguish the parts obtained we use a third binary digit. Continuing the division, we realize that after we have written out five binary digits, the original set has been divided into one-element sets. Thus, five binary digits are sufficient to distinguish the elements of the original set. In other words, all the elements can be numbered as strings containing five binary digits. This is not surprising, since there were a total of 27 different elements in a set, and there are $2^5 = 32$ strings containing 5 binary digits. We note $\log_2 H \approx 4.756$. This means that four binary digits are insufficient to describe all the set's elements, but that five are sufficient:.

The example above can be generalized so that the elements of any (finite) set can be described by some number of binary digits according to the same scheme. Here, if N is the number of elements in a set and k is a natural number such that $k - 1 < \log_2 N < k$, then $k - 1$ binary digits are insufficient to "number" all the elements in a set, but k binary digits are sufficient to do so. These considerations show that the entropy $H =$

$\log_2$ "measure of the complexity" of a set. In other words, the smaller the entropy of a set, the simpler its organization.

Let us consider a few simple examples. Suppose we are considering a chart on which five simple pictures are arranged in a row (Fig. 8). How complex is this chart? To answer this question, we must examine the chart as one element in a set of analogous charts. More precisely, we must consider all five-picture charts consisting of pictures of circles, triangles, or squares. There will be 35 distinct charts of this kind. Therefore, the entropy of the set of these charts has the value

$$H = \log_2 3^5 = 5 \log_2 3 \approx 7.925$$

This number also characterizes the complexity of the chart being considered (that is, the difficulty in distinguishing this chart from among the set of all of those analogous to it).

As a second example, consider the chart shown in Figure 9. Here either of two figures, a circle or triangle, can occur in each place. The set of all such charts (that is, charts containing seven pictures, each representing a triangle or a circle) consists of 27 charts. Therefore the entropy is $H = \log_2$ complexity of the chart shown in Figure 9 is somewhat less than for the chart shown in Figure 8.

Figure 8.

Figure 9.

These considerations apply to the calculation of the complexity of charts, models, and so forth, consisting of *homogeneous* elements.

The foregoing obviously does not assume that the perceptual complexity of a chart (or any other instructional medium) is *typical* for the set of all analogous charts, nor that it is not distinguished by any individual features that essentially simplify its internal structure and therefore make perception easier. Among the features that simplify a system's internal structure, a definite *organization* of the system's elements is identified. By the organization of a system we mean here a rule limiting the chaotic quality of arranging elements with respect to one another and which essentially permits the nature of the entire system to be established by knowing a specific number of elements.

To determine the influence of a system's organization on its perceptual complexity, let us consider the chart in Figure 10. What is the perceptual complexity of this chart? If we regard it as one of the 2^7 seven-picture charts (see Fig. 9) of the previous example, then we conclude that the perceptual complexity, represented by the entropy, has the value $H = \log_2$ conclusion is incorrect, since the *internal organization* of the elements in Figure 10 was not taken into account. Indeed, this chart has internal organization because objects of one kind (circles) are shown first, followed by objects of a second kind (triangles). Consequently, this chart must be compared not with all 27 charts, but only with those in which the same internal organization is inherent. There will be 12 such charts (beginning with 1, 2,..., or 6 circles, followed by triangles, or the other way around—triangles followed by circles). The perceptual complexity of the chart shown in Figure 10 has the value

$$H = \log_2 12 = 2 + \log_2 3 \approx 3.585.$$

This calculation provides a precise verification of the intuitive conclusion that the chart in Figure 10 is "simpler" than the one in Figure 9.

The considerations presented above have been constructed using very simple examples—linear diagrams containing elements of two types (circles, triangles). However, these considerations are generalizable to more complex cases for which the calculations, of course, will be more

Figure 10.

complex. In this case of Figure 10, the internal organization lessened the entropy of the system. This occured because we compared a system possessing an internal organization not with all systems having a chaotic arrangement of elements, but only with systems possessing the same kind of internal organization. This decreased the number of systems with which the given system was compared, and consequently also decreased the entropy.

In the preceding discussion we have dealt only with systems composed of perceptually homogeneous (equally easy to perceive) elements. Nevertheless, we will more often have to deal with models composed of heterogeneous elements, some of which are simple to perceive, others more complicated. We can consider a signed number as an elementary example. For the sake of simplicity, we shall limit ourselves to three-digit integers (positive or negative): +576, -382, -957, etc. Each signed number consists of four components: the sign (+ or -) and three digits from the set $\{0, 1, 2, ..., 9\}$.

It is easy to understand that the entropy in the present case has the value

$$H = \log_2 2 + 3 \log_2 10 \approx 11.$$

The first term in the right side corresponds to the two possible choices of sign (therefore the number 2 appears as the argument in the logarithm), and the second term arises because we have three digits with ten possible choices for each. In the general case, if a system contains s distinct types of components, with k_1 instances and N_1 possible choices for type i, then the entropy formula can be expressed in the following form:

$$H = k_1 \log_2 N_1 + k_2 \log_2 N_2 + \ldots + k_2 \log_2 N_2$$

Instructional Media in the Educational Process

In this discussion all the elements are assumed, for the time being, to be equally simple to perceive, and heterogeneity only arises in the different number of possibilities for elements of different types. For instance, in the preceding example there were two possibilities for the choice of a sign, and ten for each digit. Consequently, in the general case an expression of entropy, which represents from our point of view the measure of a model's perceptual complexity, contains not simply a logarithm (with the base 2) of the number of possibilities, but a linear combination of such logarithms based on dissimilar components of a model. In formula (1) the coefficients $k_1, k_2, ..., k_s$ expressed the number of elements of a certain type that were included in the model. In the example of a signed number $k_1 = 1$ since only one sign is chosen, and $k_2 = 3$ since three digits are chosen.

There is, however, another reason for the appearance of the coefficients in the general formula for entropy—a reason that appears to be more essential—namely, that there are differences in the degree of ease with which one perceives the individual elements. Consider the following example: In studying geometry in grade 4, students learn the following definition: *a solid bounded by six rectangles is called a rectangular parallelepiped.* In this definition students encounter three types of heterogeneous elements: the number 6, which describes the number of faces, the rectangular shape of each face, and elements of spatial geometry ("solid," "bounded"). Let N_1 designate the number of choices for the first of these elements (i.e., the number of faces); N_2—the number of choices for selecting the faces themselves; and N_3—the number of spatial elements. Then it might be expected, by virtue of the foregoing argument, that the entropy formula in the present case will take the form:

$$H = \log_2 N_1 + \log_2 N_2 + \log_2 N_3$$

(Without going into detail about how to find the numbers N_1, N_2, and N_3, simply note that a value of 10 is reasonable for N_2 since students are likely to know about ten plane geometric figures: square, rhombus, sector, and so forth). But this formula will not be correct in that form. Indeed, students have mastered the concept of "number" in the primary grades.

This concept is familiar to them and therefore easily perceived. The concept of a "rectangle" is less commonplace, but still familiar. Students have encountered it early in grade 4, but it is somewhat more complicated to perceive. Finally, spatial elements are new to the students, and are therefore the most complicated to perceive.

It is advisable to characterize the degree of perceptual complexity of a model's different elements by weighted numerical coefficients. As a result, for the case under consideration, we obtain the following corrected formula for entropy:

$$H = k_1 \log_2 N_1 + k_2 \log_2 N_2 + k_3 \log_2 N_3$$

From the foregoing observations, the coefficient k_1 will have a lesser value than k_2 (by virtue of the more easily perceived digits), while k_2 will have a lesser value than k_3 (since the elements of plane geometry are more familiar and also simpler to perceive).

This example shows that the coefficients k_1, k_2, ..., k_s in the general formula for entropy can appear not only on account of a difference in the number of possible choices for elements of different types, but also as the result of a difference in the simplicity of perception of these elements. We shall not touch upon the question of what the numerical values of the coefficients are—that determination requires a large number of experiments. Here it is only a matter of the theoretical possibility of a precise mathematical evaluation of the perceptual complexity of a model. It is essential that the coefficients characterizing the ease of perception of specific elements be non-constant quantities which change over time and experience (e.g., in connection with the presence or absence of instruction).

In other words, the concepts with which we frequently operate become simpler to perceive over time. Thus, the concept of "number," which students in primary grades have difficulty perceiving, becomes quite easy to perceive in the upper grades. The same applies to the use of literal symbols and, properly speaking, to any other knowledge as well. And since simplicity of perception is one of the two essential features of visuality, the following general principle, which must be followed in constructing visual models, becomes clear:

In constructing a model (isomorphic to the phenomenon being studied, of course), one should strive to use as elements such concepts which, as a consequence of their repeated and prolonged use, have become familiar to the students, and therefore simple to perceive.

The earlier the stages of instruction at which students master the concepts from which a model is constructed, the simpler and more visual this model is. Modern science deals with abstractions at various levels. The principle formulated above recommends, for constructing a visual model of a phenomenon studied at a given level of abstraction, using objects related to lower levels of abstraction.

Biotechnological Properties of Instructional Media; Rubber Stamps.

The two properties considered above constitute the basic content of visuality. In addition to them, a number of others can be pointed out—psychophysiological properties (e.g., the color, size, and shape of letters and signs in a poster, the contrast in a representation, fatigue from perceiving a model, and the like), aesthetic properties, and many others. There is no doubt that while some of the psychophysiological and aesthetic properties of models are related to visuality, they are not crucial to it. For this reason, in describing visuality, we have focused on only two main properties: the *isomorphicity* of a model with the phenomenon being represented, and *simplicity* in perceiving the model.

However, there are instructional media in which visuality is not a critical component—that is, for which isomorphicity and simplicity does not play a fundamental role. This observation points out the narrowness of the term "visual aid" and the natural need to introduce the new terms "instructional medium" and "educational materials," which are broader and more general. To confirm this idea let us give a few simple examples.

Rubber stamps were used in experimental lessons on the topic "The Rectangular Parallelepiped and Its Volume." A drawing of a cube in relief was reproduced on one of them (Fig. 11), and a drawing of a rectangular parallelepiped on another. It was sufficient to press the stamp onto a sheet of paper (first applying it to a stamp pad) to obtain an accurate representation of a cube or rectangular parallelepiped (incorporating parallel edges, visible and invisible edges, and so forth) (Fig. 12). These rubber stamps were used in two ways in the classroom.

Figure 11.

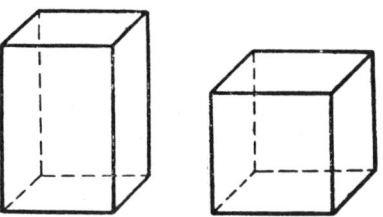

Figure 12.

First, in solving problems involving cubes or rectangular parallelepipeds, the students could rapidly produce suitable drawings in their workbooks. This was an immense time-saver. In addition, every student had identical and correct representations of parallelepipeds, which is also of no small importance. Of course, the use of rubber stamps should not prevent acquisition of skill in drawing figures (in particular, representations of a rectangular parallelepiped). Therefore, the teacher should initially demonstrate how to draw a rectangular parallelepiped and help students gain skill in doing so themselves. But the trouble is that even when students know how to draw the figure, they spend a lot of time on its execution. Frequently (especially in the primary grades) the time spent making a drawing is as time-consuming as solving the problem itself. Under these conditions the rubber stamps can be invaluable since, by saving time, students will succeed in solving a significantly greater number of problems.

Second, the teacher can use the rubber stamps at home to prepare tests. Making 40 drawings of a rectangular parallelepiped and writing in the dimensions (so as to obtain a set of individual assignments) is doubtless very laborious and unprofitable for the teacher. It is immeasurably easier to make stamp impressions on 40 sheets of paper. Of course, rubber stamps can be used in other topics of the mathematics course as well. As long as the templates for the stamps are carefully selected, stamps are one of the most valuable instructional media.

Can rubber stamps be called a visual aid? We think not. Although the concept of isomorphism plays a definite role in the construction and use of stamps (e.g., a representation of a cube should be isomorphic to a mathematical cube or a model of one), the property of isomorphism is not fundamental for a stamp. The same can be said for the simplicity of the template on a stamp. What is fundamental is that the rubber stamp saves us time. In other words, the basic property characterizing a stamp as an instructional medium is its biotechnological advantage, its value for the organization of the work of teacher and student.

This property of a rubber stamp we call its *efficiency*. A variety of control systems (sometimes called, not altogether correctly, programmed instructional media[15]) are used for the the purpose of improving efficiency. From the simplest kinds of punch cards to complex interactive communications systems and sometimes possessing a memory, these systems yield a biotechnological effect—saving time that would otherwise be spent questioning students. We do not wish to say that control systems are created just for the purpose of saving this kind of time. They also quickly convey information to the teacher, making it possible to observe how all of the students are doing the work at a given time. But still, saving time is an essential feature in the use of control systems, for if a control system required spending more time on questioning than in traditional instruction, no teacher would use it.

Describing instructional media according to their efficiency has another aspect as well. An instructional medium can be characterized by the time it takes to implement the particular medium. For example, to show the educational slides that go with "The Rectangular Parallelepiped," the classroom has to be darkened (at least partially), one has to put a slide into the projector, turn on the projector, and focus the picture. All of this takes time. As a result the students' attention wanders, and the pedagogical effect of using this instructional medium is reduced. Therefore, each piece of educational material should also be evaluated from the standpoint of how quickly and smoothly it can be introduced into the general course of the lesson.

The circumstances just noted have nothing in common with visuality. They simply describe certain biotechnological aspects of instructional media. At least two constants can be seen to characterize the temporal properties of instructional media:

1) economy of time, which is achieved while the instructional media under consideration are used; and

2) economy of implementation, measured by the rapidity in preparing the instructional media for use. Both lend themselves easily to precise quantitative time measurements.

A discussion of the biotechnological properties of instructional media is by no means limited to the preceding points. This discussion is only just beginning. A simple and inexpensive device for displaying charts (Fig. 13) is doubtless very important for proper scientific organization of the teacher's work. Questions of the storage of charts, models, and other instructional media also pertain to biotechnology. Dozens of issues concerning the organization of teacher's and students' work could be cited. This problem requires more research; no single monograph could deal comprehensively with the issue. We limit ourselves to one conclusion here: *the concept of visuality is far from the only property characterizing an instructional medium, and therefore the term "visual aid" is too narrow and outmoded.*

Another reason why the term "visual aid" is inadequate has been observed and described by A.I. Markushevich, academician of the USSR Academy of Pedagogical Sciences. The word "aid" obviously, or not so obviously, reflects the external, purely illustrative and auxiliary role of the objects that are called visual aids. Yet the modern tendency is for instructional media to play an essential and interactive role in the instruc-

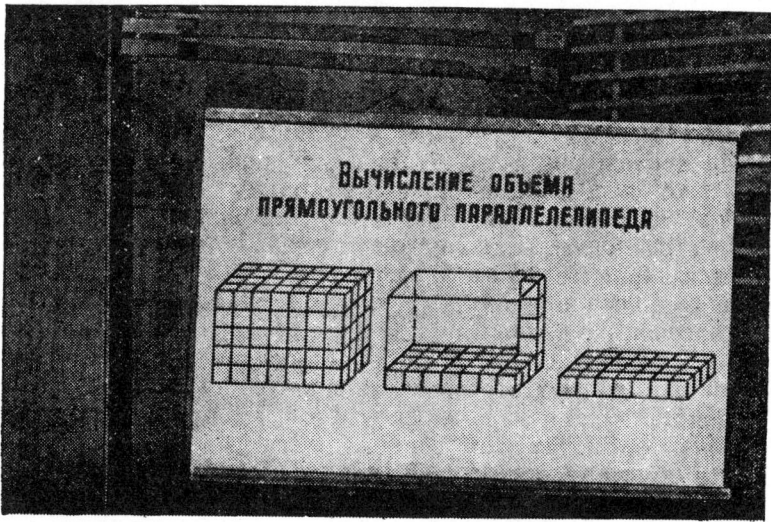

Figure 13. Calculating the Volume of a Rectangular Parallelpiped

tion process. Instructional media should be one of the basic means of pedagogical influence. Thus, the term "visual aid" is not only too narrow, but is also methodologically outmoded.

Instructional Orientation; Written Materials

Now let us consider another example of an instructional medium—a *workbook based on written material* for the topic "The Rectangular Parallelepiped and Its Volume." The workbook is described in detail in Chapter 4 of this book. Here we give several examples of exercises included in the workbook.

Assignment 67. *Write in the missing numbers:*
a) 2 + 13 = 13 + _____ [commutative law of addition]

b) 23 + (7 + 24) = (23 + _____) + 24 [associative law of addition]

(We break off the text of the assignment here, since its nature is now totally clear.)

Assignment 13. *Complete the drawing of the cube* (Fig. 14). (This assignment is not cited in full either.)

Assignment 14. *How many centimeters of wire went into making the frame of this rectangular parallelepiped* (Fig. 15)? *Solve the problem by two methods.*

First method:
1) _____ cm were used in the edges of the lower base.
2) _____ cm were used in the edges of the upper base.
3) _____ cm were used for the vertical edges.
4) _____ cm in all were used for the frame.
Second method:
1) _____ cm were used in the three unequal edges.
2) _____ cm were used for the frame.

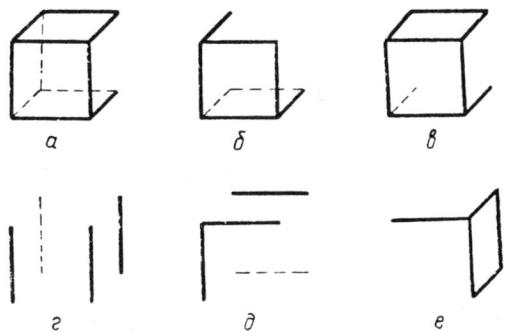

Figure 14.

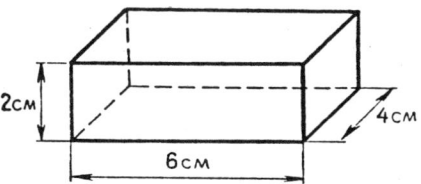

Figure 15.

Each assignment requires students to follow a prescribed plan. As a result of doing a series of similar exercises, they acquire the necessary skills. Thus, in Assignment 67 they must apply a specific field axiom for addition, and they are even reminded of the name of the axiom. When they do a series of exercises of this nature, they master the meaning and remember the names of these axioms, learning to apply them properly. Assignment 13 has the same instructional focus—the student is required to complete existing sketches of a cube (taking the visible and invisible lines into consideration). The complexity of the assignment gradually increases from sketch to sketch, but the important point is to rigorously follow a specific order in carrying out the problem. This provides the student with substantial practice in drawing a cube.

The strict sequence of the student's operations imposed by this instructional medium can be characterized as the *instructional orientation* of the medium. It is obvious that Assignment 14, cited above, also has a high degree of instructional orientation. The student is obliged to follow a prescribed course in solving the problem and a specific method of writing out the solution. After performing a series of individual exercises of this type (in which the degree of prompting is gradually reduced), the student becomes proficient in the suggested method of problem-solving and at the same time learns the required form for writing out the solution.

The majority of programmed materials also have an instructional orientation. They normally contain a strict sequence of operations, selected so that the student has to follow the basic line of the curriculum while receiving alternative explanations in the event of wrong answers.[16] The orientation intrinsic to a certain instructional medium is one of its important pedagogical characteristics. However, like biotechnological properties, this orientation is in no way related to visuality, but is an independent property that characterizes the instructional medium and helps to enhance the teaching process.

It would be incorrect to require a general answer to the question of whether the orientation of a particular instructional medium is a positive or a negative quality. If, for example, it is a matter of acquiring algorithmic skills, then the application of this instructional orientation can often be quite advisable. In other cases, particularly when it is a matter of forming the students' creative skills, the orientation can be detrimental. It may result in cliches and unoriginal thinking.

Instructional Media in the Educational Process

Individualization; Sets of Problem Cards

Another important property of instructional media related to biotechnological questions is the *individualization* of instructional media. A modernized arithmetic kit was used for investigating the topic "The Rectangular Parallelepiped and Its Volume." In contrast to the arithmetic kits issued by Uchtekhprom, it contained graduated solids of more or less complex shape (Fig. 16) which served as material for distribution in the initial study of the volume concept. Considering each student's individual capabilities, the teacher can give the students graduated solids of various shapes, thus providing similar problems of varying complexity.

Problem cards are another example of instructional media that take the students' individual abilities into account. They currently enjoy great popularity among teachers and most frequently are made by the teachers themselves. Sometimes they are used with other written materials. Using cards promotes an easy adaptation to a student's individual abilities, lessens the likelihood of copying, and simplifies the conduct of tests. (The

Figure 16.

set of problem cards on the topic "The Rectangular Parallelepiped" is described in detail in Chapter 4.)

Clearly, the individualization of an instructional medium is another property pertaining to biotechnology since it characterizes the scientific organization of work. Nevertheless, individualization is a property completely unrelated to visuality. This is especially apparent in the example of problem cards. The problems might have simply been available in the problem book, but their use in card form is purely an organizational strategy.

We have considered a number of properties of instructional media: visuality (combining the isomorphicity of a representation and perceptual simplicity), instructional orientation, biotechnological properties (including such factors as time-saving, rapid implementation, individualization), and others. Of course, not all the aspects of instructional media are among the properties listed above. Their economic properties, such as cost, amortization, the use of scarce materials, ease of reproduction, and others are also essential. We already have mentioned the psychophysiological and aesthetic properties of instructional media. What has been said to this point can be summarized in the following Table 1.1.

Table 1.1 Basic Properties of Instructional Media

Diadactic				Biotechnological					
Visuality			...	Efficiency			...		
Isomorphicity of a representation	Simplicity of perception	Didactic orientation		Saving Time	Rapid starting	Individualization		Pshychophysiological	Aesthetic	Economic

In the authors' opinion this table is certainly incomplete, as is indicated by the dots. Nevertheless, we will confine ourselves to these properties, above all the didactic and biotechnological ones. What interests us primarily are the principles for devising and applying instructional media in the classroom. We therefore will not focus on economic properties, which are chiefly related to the production of instructional media. Similarly, we will not consider, for example, their aesthetic properties.

Any instructional display can undoubtedly be done in various ways. One version may attract attention by brightly-colored letters, neatly arranged formulas, or an elegant typeface that harmonizes with the display's content. Another version of the display may be done in a mediocre, unoriginal typeface, may be distracting because of garish colors in its letters and symbols, or may suffer from careless placement of formulas. Of course, these two displays will affect us differently, enhancing or weakening mathematical inclination or interest. This has a rather strong influence on the mastery of the material presented by the teacher. In other words, the authors are not at all inclined to underestimate the importance of aesthetic properties in instructional media. If we ignore them anyway, it is only because this book concerns the content of instructional media and the methods of using them, and not what is involved in producing them.

One more remark in connection with the table given above. We would like to emphasize that some of these properties can be characterized in precise *quantitative* terms, while other properties are purely *qualitative*. Thus, it is shown in Section 3 that obtaining a rigorous quantitative assessment for the *perceptual simplicity* of a model can be substantiated, in principle, by methods of information theory. *Time-saving* and *rapid implementation* can easily be quantified, and so can a number of economic properties of instructional media. At the same time, the *isomorphicity of a representation* is a qualitative property of a model: it either is or is not isomorphic. It is hardly reasonable to characterize numerically the "greater or lesser isomorphicity" of a model. This would give a distorted representation of the phenomenon studied. In precisely the same way, *instructional orientation, individualization*, and other properties are qualitative. The difference between qualitative and quantitative properties is considered in Section 13, dealing with *instructional units of educational materials*.

Using Charts in Mathematics Lessons

Until recently only a few kinds of instructional media were used in mathematics lessons. These were chiefly charts, various models of solids, a few portable devices (a school trigonometer, the solid geometry constructors of Ranev and Sereda, and others), as well as a few movies. In recent years this inventory has been supplemented by filmstrips, single-concept films, and several sets of slides. Of course, we will not discuss such objects as a slide projector, the class blackboard, room-darkening devices, and so forth, which are *general school materials*. We are concerned with the specific instructional media pertaining to mathematics. In addition to the instructional media enumerated above, several other types are beginning to become available and will be issued in the near future. Such items as workbooks based on printed material, problem cards, magnetic tapes, rubber stamps, transparencies for direct demonstration or for showing on an opaque projector, and others fall into this category. Therefore, we must offer a pedagogical description of the various kinds of instructional media in mathematics, indicating the best methods of implementing these media.

First let us consider charts. Up until recently we had only one kind of chart in mathematics (not counting portraits of prominent scientists, which might be considered charts of a sort): illustrative charts. As a rule, they include a large number of formulas, drawings, and inscriptions, which distract students and reduce the effectiveness of this instructional medium. Two different charts were often encountered (sometimes even included in different series) with the same representation (e.g., graphs of trigonometric functions), but displaying different formulas. Teachers, as a rule, have no need for the formulas in the charts. The point of these charts is that they are well drawn, easily visible, and contain graphic material that is hard and time-consuming for the teacher to draw on the blackboard. As for the formulas in the charts, the teacher can easily put them on the blackboard in a form suitable for his method of presenting the topic. The formulas printed in a chart impose a specific methodology, distract the students, and, in essence, create no additional convenience for the teacher.

Let us cite another example of overloading margins of charts with superfluous material. In grades 4 and 5 there are charts, both printed and homemade, that illustrate properties of arithmetical operations (Fig. 17). Besides the basic properties, we can also find secondary ones, as well as numerical material illustrating these properties of operations. This leads to an overloading of the charts, as well as to students' confusing basic properties of operations with secondary and numerical examples. The charts of the properties of arithmetical operations in the set of materials described in this handbook can serve as a model in this respect.

Note: The text in this figure reads "1. Commutative law;" "2. Associative law;" "3. Distributive law of multiplication."

Figure 17. Laws of Operation for Addition and Multiplication

For example, the chart of properties of addition (Fig. 251) contains only basic laws, constituting, in essence, the *axioms of a commutative group*. This agrees completely with the didactic principle of scientific exposition: the concept of a group is a major achievement of mathematical thought. Moreover, when the chart is exhibited for a long time, the notation of the basic properties of addition in one chart will promote a more lasting and integrated understanding of them.

Overloading charts with material can also be seen in the fact that charts which are issued or made independently contain the solution of just one typical problem. As a rule, such charts are not necessary in the educational process. They are most frequently made for "showing off," so that the walls of the mathematics study room will be decorated with something.

What is the proper use of charts in mathematics lessons? What material should be selected for them? To answer, let us first note that it is best for the charts used in mathematics lessons to be divided (tentatively) into two large classes: *working charts* and *charts for memorization (reference charts)*.

Working charts are used in the classroom to aid in elaborating and reinforcing skills. Let us give several examples. The chart shown in Figure 18 may be necessary in the classroom, but it is certainly not a working chart. Rather it is used for reference. It helps students memorize how angles are labeled and read. However, the chart provides no practice in reading angles. On the other hand, Figure 19 shows a working chart. Using it, the teacher can motivate the entire class, showing certain angles and requiring students to read them. This chart also can be used when working on other topics such as vertical angles, adjacent angles, and others. What properties in Table 1.1 are essential for the chart in Figure 19? First, efficiency should be noted. It takes the teacher less time to hang it up than to make an analogous drawing on the board. Classwork using this chart can continue for 5 or 10 minutes. Thus, the biotechnological advantage of this instructional medium is evident. In a psychophysiological sense, the chart is undoubtedly much more effective than a chalk drawing on a blackboard. The monotonous appearance of chalk figures inhibits the cortex of the student's brain. On the other hand, moving from

Instructional Media in the Educational Process

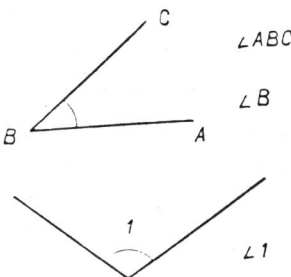

Figure 18.

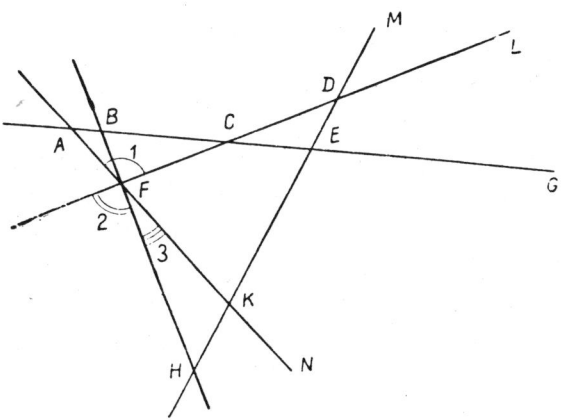

Figure 19.

writing on the blackboard to a vivid chart stimulates students' attention and improves their retention.

Consider another example of a working chart: the graph of the function $y = 10^x$ shown on a large sheet of graph paper (Fig. 20). Using this chart, students can easily find the values of this function accurate to two or three

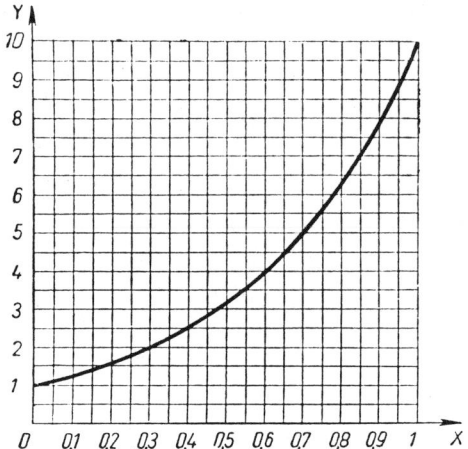

Figure 20.

places. This gives them an opportunity to realize that any positive number can be written as a power of 10, and that multiplication and exponentiation reduce to simpler operations when numbers are so represented. If the teacher spends class time working with this chart, actually anticipating the definition, properties, and application of logarithms, then subsequent study of the topic "Logarithms" will be significantly easier and more effective. Of this chart's properties, its visuality comes first. A simple visual image accompanied by simple numerical material (without actually introducing the notion of a function) clearly has the property of perceptual simplicity. At the same time, the associations between numbers that arise in working with this chart are the same (i.e., isomorphic) as those between the argument and the functional value in a logarithmic relationship, which the students have not yet studied.

It should be particularly noted that considerations of visuality or biotechnology alone still do not solve the question of the feasibility of including certain material in the chart. Economic considerations also play a significant role.

Instructional Media in the Educational Process 43

We have already noted that it is inadvisable to use a chart containing the solution of just one problem (Fig. 21). But we cannot say that the creation of such a chart is pedagogically inadvisable. On the contrary, it can be covenient to use the chart in solving that very problem, and sometimes in solving similar problems. It may be handy to use the chart before solving a problem to stimulate the students' thinking and sometimes, afterward, to review and clarify the proper method of solving the problem. But in any event, the use of a chart such as this will be short-term. Therefore, making such a chart may not be practical (it requires considerable labor and a lot of paper).

In contrast to constructing a chart, making a *slide* containing a detailed solution of a typical problem is fully advisable. In the first place, a slide is much less expensive than a chart; second, by the simple means of darkening the room and the comparatively inexpensive "Svet" slide-pro-

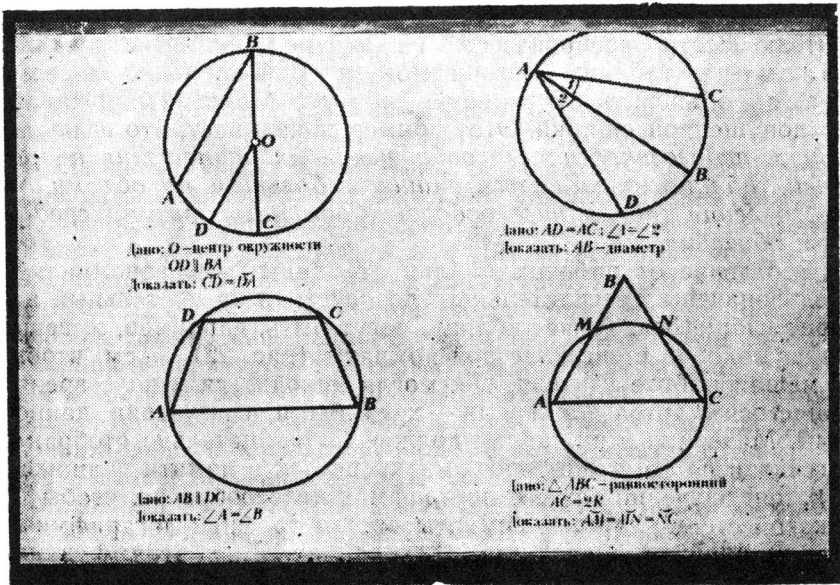

Figure 21.

jector (see Fig. 117 in Chapter 4), this material can easily be shown to the students. Moreover, it is easy to show solutions for similar problems on slides, but demonstrating several charts in one lesson is not always convenient.

In this connection let us consider the following question: Is it advisable to prepare the material collected in the students' logarithm tables in the form of wall demonstration charts? The instructional utility of this kind of chart would be unquestioned: it is much easier for the teacher to show the whole class at once how to find mantissas, to interpolate, or to work with the chart in other ways. But making this series of charts is not practical in biotechnological or, especially, economic terms. It is sufficient to say that 15 or 20 demonstration charts would have to be made in order to accommodate all the material in the logarithm charts, and operating with them during a lesson would be difficult. However, making a series of slides containing all the material in the logarithm charts is definitely a good idea: a small box of slides allows the teacher to quickly reproduce on a screen or the blackboard the requisite portion of the logarithm chart and at the same time explain to the entire class the proper way to work with the chart or the nature of a mistake that was made. This example shows that *if instructional material to be included in a working chart is too great in volume, then it is better to replace charts by other instructional media.*

In contrast to working charts, reference charts for memorization are intended to have a protracted visual influence on students. Such charts can be posted on a wall in the classroom (see, for example, Fig. 22), so that they can be in the student's field of vision for a long time during the study of a given topic without hindering the teacher's work. The material for these charts should be chosen carefully and designed to be firmly established in the students' minds. Thus, in studying the unit on logarithms, it is advisable for graphs of logarithmic functions with various bases to hang on a classroom wall. The appearance of such a function should be firmly "engraved" in the student's memory. In the study of the unit "The Rectangular Parallelepiped and Its Volume," instead of geometric charts, it is best to have charts on the wall summarizing the basic

Instructional Media in the Educational Process

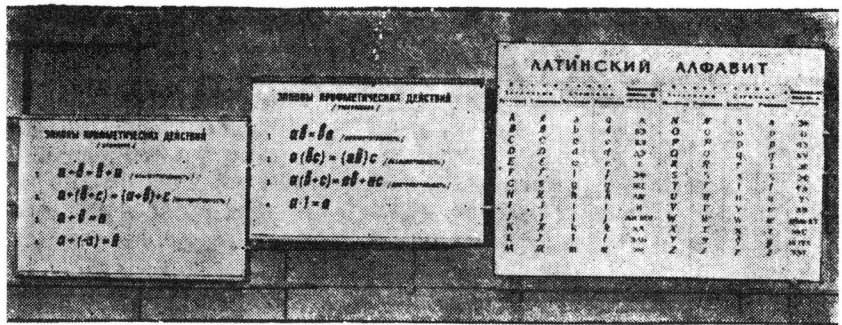

Figure 22.

laws of operations. In addition to the algebraic notation of laws of operations (using geometric content in problem-solving), these charts will help the students to remember terms that are new to them: commutative, associative, distributive. We note that a basic property of reference charts is their instructional orientation (rather than visuality, which undoubtedly also plays an important role in many instances). These charts are intended to have a positive influence on the student's memorization of basic facts, formulas, or graphs.

Film Media in Mathematics Lessons

Instructional film media (motion pictures, single-concept films, filmstrips, slides, and others) have been used comparatively infrequently to the present in mathematics lessons. Many teachers prefer to use various wooden and wire models, small cardboard and paper figures, and other objects. There are several reasons for this: first, schools are still inadequately equipped with movie and slide projectors; second, educational movies, filmstrips, and slides are not issued in sufficient quantity; third, unfortunately, even today there are too many relatively long movies for mathematics (15 minutes and longer), and long films often have an essential flaw—the abundance of material makes perception of a long film difficult during the *initial study* of a topic, and it often makes the *review* of material that has already been covered boring.

Of course, we are not opposed to long films, but they should be used either in extreme necessity or if methodologically indicated. For example, the unit on "How People Counted in Ancient Times and How Numbers Were Written" is quite acceptable for a film. The material is not too tiresome for the students, it is interesting, and it cannot be grasped in a short fragment. Films on Lobachevskian geometry, on the role of mathematics in our practical life, and others are also good to use. But we find the 1961 film "Trigonometric Functions" unsuccessful. It is unacceptable for the initial study of the topic since it contains much new material, which cannot be grasped by students in a short time. It is likewise inappropriate for review, for it contains many explanations that are then unnecessary. The possibility remains of using it in fragments—showing individual segments of the film while covering various parts of the unit. But in this case a long film makes it inconvenient for the teacher. It is sufficient to say that, as a rule, a film fragment must be shown repeatedly (in the same or a parallel class). But rewinding a long film is a great inconvenience. This again confirms that several separate film segments, as a rule, are handier than one film made up of fragments.

We have indicated above the reasons for the current sparse distribution of film media in the schools. Film media are highly effective, nevertheless, and they have a promising future. They play a particularly important role in mathematics. Indeed, mathematics is the most abstract of all subjects studied in school. While a large number of natural objects can be demonstrated in physics or biology, mathematics lacks this possibility. It is impossible to show a logarithm, a derivative, or a tangent in natural form. For just this reason schematic drawings and graphs are used in large numbers in mathematics. But graphs and drawings provide only a static notion of the abstract concepts they represent. Still, such concepts as the function, transformation, derivative, etc., which are always included in the school mathematics curriculum, are profoundly dynamic in nature and can be properly perceived only as they change and move.

It is much easier for a student to imagine an electrical current in a conductor as the movement of electrons than to master the abstract concept of a limit; it is easier to master the rule of a gimlet or the right-hand rule than to determine a scalar product of vectors. Thus, the abstractness of mathematical concepts makes the use of film media, primarily movies and single-concept films, especially important in teaching. Considering the shortcomings of long movies, as described above, as well as the fact that a shift in instructional media activates students' attention and diminishes fatigue, it should be acknowledged that brief single-concept films (2-5 minutes) are best for use in mathematics lessons. Such films should be shown in a partially darkened classroom so that the students can make notes if they need to. The film itself should enter actively into the lesson's structure, supplementing the teacher's explanations or preceding the introduction of a difficult concept.

Some people feel that only a few topics in mathematics can be filmed, and then in a very limited scope. Such an opinion is fundamentally in error. Let us cite several examples from various sections of the mathematics curriculum to illustrate the great effectiveness of single-concept films in mathematics lessons.

A cube appears on the screen. Its visible edges are outlined, and the invisible edges show slightly through the translucent material. The front face of the cube, which is visible on the screen without distortion, is transferred to a vacant spot to the right of the cube. Then three visible edges are drawn somewhat obliquely, perpendicular to the plane of the front face. Next the other visible faces appear on the screen, and the invisible faces appear with dotted lines. All this is accompanied by a commentary, clarifying the outlining of the representation of the cube. Finally the plane view of the cube appears a second time on the screen, again with commentary, but without the model of the cube being shown on the left.

This single-concept film lasts a total of two minutes. But it provides a vivid rudimentary notion of the planar [two-dimensional] representation of a cube, which is difficult for students. Indeed, the resources of cinematography, which permit the steps in a construction to be reproduced sequentially and focus (for example, through highlighting) students' attention on necessary segments and points, significantly simplify the mastery of skills in the planar representation of a cube. A cube is itself seemingly stationary; no dynamics can be detected in it. But the planar representation of a cube is a dynamic process, taking place in time. And the mastery of this process is difficult without the aid of cinematography. Neither the teacher's drawing nor a chart nor a model of a cube can completely replace this brief two-minute single-concept film.

Such geometric topics as basic geometric concepts, geometric transformations, and many others also lend themselves nicely to filming. It can be stated with confidence, for example, that a topic as difficult to comprehend as solving construction problems by the similarity method can become accessible to most students only through the resources of cinematography. For example, in solving problems on inscribing a square in a triangle, the dynamics of enlarging the square (Fig. 23) will help the student understand clearly how an auxiliary straight line arises from the triangle's vertex, and why it is a key to solving the problem.

In addition to geometric topics, many other areas are clearly suited to cinematography. They include, for example, the change of a function, the

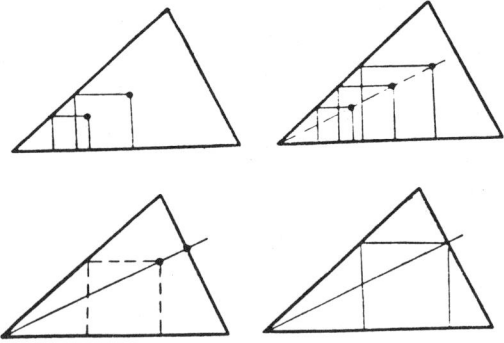

Figure 23.

graphic solution of equations, the concept of a limit and a derivative, geometric transformations, and so forth. But are there topics in which it would not make sense to use cinematography? Is it correct, by way of illustration, to assert that material in algebra hardly ever needs to be filmed? We consider this claim erroneous. The use of cinematography, above all animation (as well as such devices as highlighting, fade-ins, fade-outs, and so forth) can help students see the dynamics of a process that they would not notice in ordinary instruction. The transfer of terms from one side of an equation to the other, the reduction of like terms, the order in which operations are performed, the appearance of extra terms when both sides of an equation are squared, and many other matters urgently *demand* the use of the media and resources of cinematography for a complete explication of the topic.

Filmstrips can often be used as an instructional medium, to a certain extent replacing motion pictures and single-concept films. The dynamics inherent in motion pictures are partially compensated by the ease of changing filmstrips. Furthermore, a filmstrip projector is considerably cheaper and simpler to handle than movie projectors. But the educational value of filmstrips is not limited to partially replacing motion pictures and single-concept films. They have their own didactic features and purpose. Indeed, the basic form for working on a lesson, when new theoretical material is being presented, is (and will remain for the foreseeable future) the teacher's explanation (narration, discussion, lecture), which utilizes a variety of drawings, diagrams, and illustrative material. It is not always advisable to use charts for this purpose since they are relatively expensive, and using five or six charts for explanation in one lesson alone is an excessive luxury. Moreover, charts are cumbersome, and working with them, replacing them several times, is not very convenient. It is not always possible or a wise use of time to make the necessary pictures and drawings on the blackboard. If, on the other hand, we note that the internal logic of presenting theoretical material generally requires the display of illustrations in a strictly defined sequence, then it becomes clear that a filmstrip is a very important instructional medium which can illustrate the teacher's account during the explanation of new material. A movie, even a silent version, would often be significantly less useful for this purpose. The speed of the teacher's account and the detail in the presentation depend on a great many things: the teacher's skill, the class's preparation, the level of success in earlier topics, and so forth. While showing a filmstrip which parallels his explanation, the teacher can change frames as he wishes to match the tempo of the lesson. The use of a silent film for this purpose forces the teacher to confine himself to the Procrustean bed of an externally imposed tempo, which can lower the quality of instruction.

Figure 24 shows the first several frames of the filmstrip "The Rectangular Parallelepiped and Its Volume," which fits into the instructional unit. Let us give a sample version of the teacher's narrative that accompanied the showing of these frames:

> "Children! This is the title of the topic we are beginning to study. These words are probably not familiar to you yet. Let's learn to read them. Let's read together: The Rectangular Parallelepiped.'
>
> "These objects are alike in shape. If we pay no attention to the handle on the suitcase, the sides that stand out on the box's top, the bookbinding's edges sticking out, the basket handle, the television control knobs, then these objects will seem to us to be even more alike.
>
> "This is how the things we are talking about will look if we get rid of their protruding parts—handles, knobs, and so on. The solid shown here is called a rectangular parallelepiped. It has rectangular faces. There are six of these faces. Three of them are visible to us, and the other three are hidden from us.
>
> "How many faces does this rectangular parallelepiped have? What is the shape of these faces?" The teacher gets answers to these questions. "The segments along which the faces touch each other are called *edges*. The points at which the edges come together are called *vertices*. In a rectangular parallelepiped there are 6 faces, 12 edges, and 8 vertices.

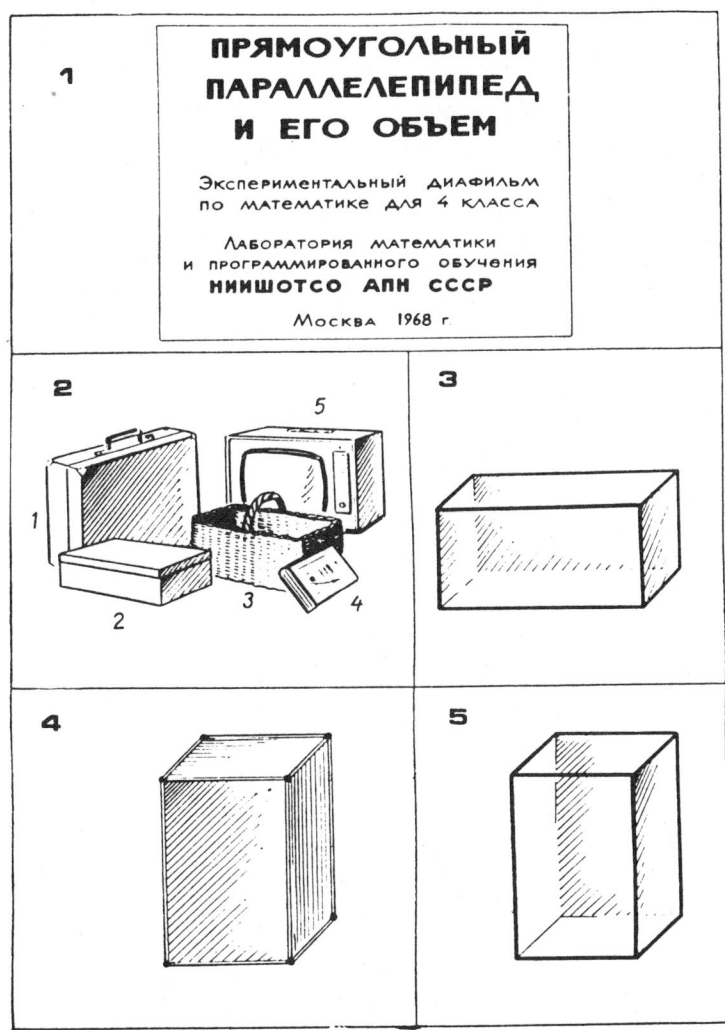

Note: The first panel of this figure reads "A Rectangular Parallelepiped and Its Volume; Experimental filmstrip in mathematics for grade 4; Laboratory of Mathematics and Programmed Instruction; Scientific Research Institute for School Materials and Technical Instructional Media of the USSR Academy of Pedagogical Sciences; Moscow, 1968"

Figure 24.

"How many faces, how many edges, and how many vertices are in view, and how many vertices are poorly visible? ..."

The teacher's account would have been considerably poorer and less descriptive without the use of the filmstrip frames.

Let us note a second feature of the filmstrip we are considering: there are no captions to the pictures in the frames. In a filmstrip intended to illustrate the teacher's account, like the present one, captions would only divert the students' attention, without introducing any supplementary content into the teacher's more detailed account. This method has been used successfully by L.P. Pressman in his excellent filmstrips on the Russian language for grades 5 and 6. This is a new trend. Until now it has been traditional to issue filmstrips with captions for each frame. Although we do not deny the merits of captioned filmstrips (or even filmstrips in which the text occupies a large part of the frames), we want to direct the reader's attention to the fact that filmstrips without captions have an undisputed right to exist, and in many cases they are considerably more convenient.

The foregoing discussion is sufficient explanation why illustrative material should be organized in the form of a filmstrip when the logic of presenting a topic requires arranging the material in a definite sequence—for example, in presenting new theoretical material.

In contrast to filmstrips, *slide series* consist of individual frames which are easily arranged in a particular order, possibly with some frames omitted. Therefore, one must select material for a slide series which, depending on the methods chosen by the teacher and the class's readiness, can be changed around—with respect both to the order of the illustrations and their composition. *Problem material* is most appropriate for slide series in mathematics. The foregoing in no way means that it is totally inadvisable to include problem material in filmstrips; a certain number of problems can legitimately be included in filmstrips, especially model problems meant to illustrate theoretical material. But problems meant for training the students or for practicing skills are more appropriate for slide series, based on the considerations outlined above.

Supplementary theoretical material, variants of the exposition of a topic, and other material are also more appropriate for slide series. This material can be used as the teacher wishes, and it would be inconvenient in a filmstrip. For example, if it is decided to omit the supplementary material included in a filmstrip, one would have to "skip" a few frames.

In certain cases it is preferable to use slides as a supplementary medium during oral computation related to the study of a topic in the curriculum. Making drawings (even rough, schematic ones) requires more time than the oral computation itself, and the interruptions caused by the drawing reduce the students' activity and divert their attention. Once again slides come to our aid. By quickly replacing a slide, the teacher instantly obtains on the screen or blackboard a drawing or the conditions of a new problem for oral computation. It is particularly convenient to use the special slide cartridges designed by S.F. Kabanov (Fig. 25). Selecting in advance slides containing the material needed for the lesson, the teacher arranges them in the necessary order in one or two cartridges of this kind. Then the slides can be changed during the lesson literally in an instant by simply sliding the cartridge 5 cm in the projector (see Fig. 26).

As an example, Figure 27 shows some slides in the series "The Rectangular Parallelepiped." In concluding the section on instructional film media and their use in mathematics lessons, let us note that a fundamental, determining property of motion pictures, single-concept films, and filmstrips is their *visuality*.

In a visually perceptible form, they provide an isomorphic, correct representation of the phenomena being studied. Of course, other properties mentioned in Section 7 are also present. Thus, the single-concept film entitled "The Representation of a Cube," which was briefly described above, undoubtedly has a high instructional orientation. But the visuality still remains fundamental. With respect to slide series, visuality recedes into the background, and the biotechnological properties move to the forefront. This was shown in the discussion of the slide series related to oral calculation (Fig. 27).

Figure 25.

Figure 26.

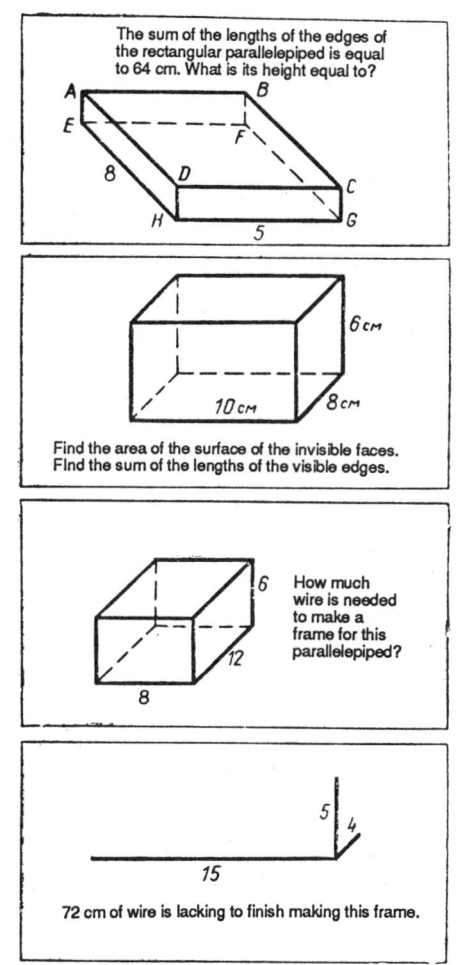

Figure 27.

And finally, filmstrips and slide series require little expenditure of scarce materials (film) and are relatively cheap.

The Overhead Projector

Although our industry has not yet implemented mass production of overhead projectors, the teacher should nonetheless be contemplating the possibilities of this medium now and preparing to use it.

A few words about this medium, which is related to slide projectors. At present, in a number of countries, including the USSR, work is proceeding toward the design and mass production of relatively cheap and lightweight *overhead projectors*. An overhead projector (Fig. 28) is an optical system permitting images of comparatively large size, to be projected from transparencies onto a screen. In existing overhead projectors, the images are made on transparent film, each frame having dimensions on the order of 20 x 20 cm. This permits the teacher (or the students) to write or make diagrams on the polyethylene film, the image appearing magnified on the screen. In addition to the long, easily rewound tape on which writing and diagrams can be done, other especially designed instructional media can be shown with the aid of an overhead projector. For example, a chart inscribed on cellophane or polyethylene can be displayed to the entire class on an overhead projector. Moreover, the high-powered lighting used in overhead projectors makes it possible to view material in a classroom that need not be completely darkened.

Materials designed for an overhead projector are rather similar to slides. Additionally, there exist instructional media meant for use only with overhead projectors. One of the examples is shown schematically in Figure 29. The base transparency (marked *a*) contains is diagram—one illustrating the statement of a theorem, for example. Overlays containing auxiliary lines and inscriptions to be made in the course of the proof are connected at the sides. Because the film is transparent, when overlay *b* is bent and placed over base transparency *a*, the students see the lines

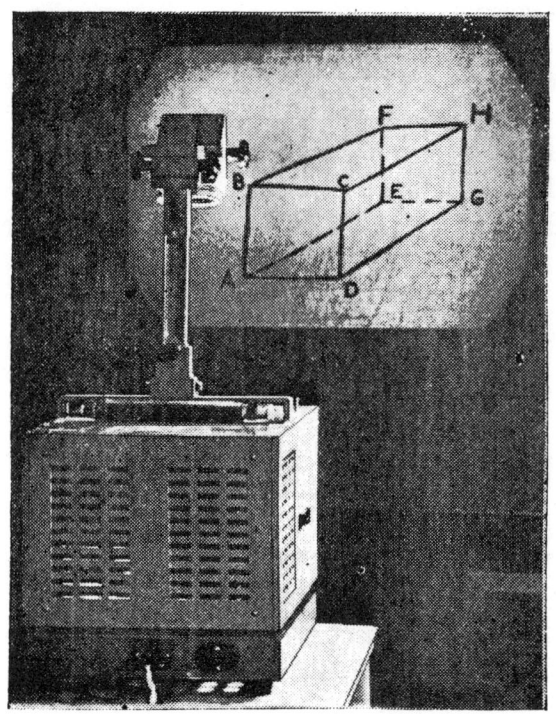

Figure 28.

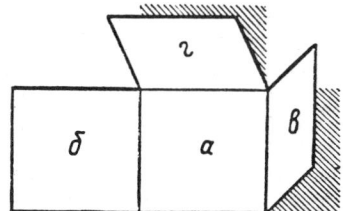

Figure 29.

both in base transparency *a* and in overlay *b*. For example, auxiliary lines necessary for doing a proof can be added to a base transparency. Then frame *c* can be overlaid, with the notation of the basis of the proof, followed by frame *d*. Of course, not all of the overlays can be placed on the base transparency simultaneously, but rather sequentially in certain combinations.

The materials meant for demonstration on an overhead projector have not yet come into extensive use and do not have a definite name. For brevity we will call them *transparencies*. A mathematics transparency is shown in Figure 30. For convenience, its frames are represented separately, and only the letters *T, U, V*, and *W* show how they should actually be connected. For example, the bottom frame *d* should be glued to base transparency *a* along line *TW*— that is, frame *d* must be placed upside down on a chart, its edge *TW* must be brought close to edge *TW* of the

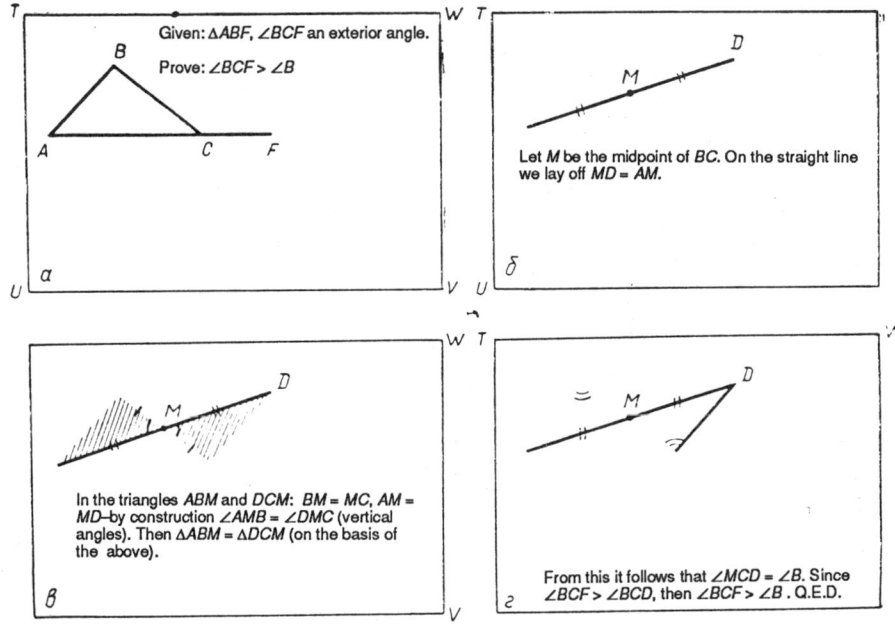

Figure 30.

Instructional Media in the Educational Process 59

base transparency, and then glued together with a cloth strip (Fig. 31). However, the text in frame *d* will be upside down, and it will be inconvenient to read in that position (therefore, the frames are shown separately in Figure 30). However, when frame *d* is turned up so as to cover base frame *a*, the text will be reversed and will now be in a normal position with respect to the base, which also assures proper projection onto the screen.

Frame *a* contains a diagram to go with the theorem stating that an exterior angle of a triangle is greater than an opposite interior angle, along with a written summary of the theorem's conditions and conclusion. Frame *b* contains an auxiliary construction. Equal elements of triangles

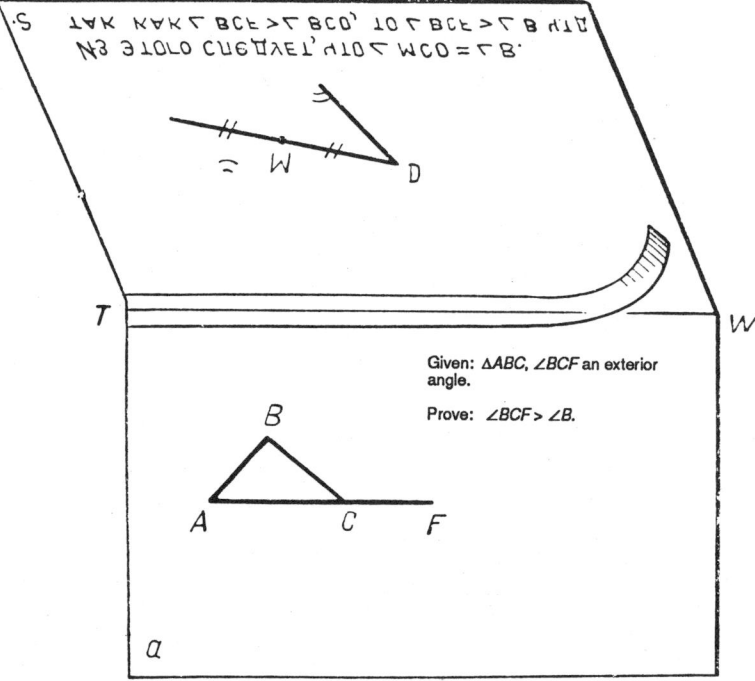

Figure 31.

ABM and *DCM* are noted in frame *c*, and it is shown that these triangles are equivalent. Finally, frame *d* indicates a consequence of fact that triangles are equivalent ($\triangle ABM = \triangle DCM$) which also assists in completing the proof.

The convenience of the transparency, as shown in Figure 30, is that the teacher can reproduce the proof of a theorem step by step, just as it is presented on the blackboard, but now the teacher can still face the class. He can also use a small pointer to focus attention on a certain part of the diagram: the pointer's location will be very visible on the screen. The teacher can use various black-paper masks, which permit everything except the required part of a screen to be covered. If the teacher needs to return to an original diagram without auxiliary lines, it is easily done by turning back the overlays and leaving only the base transparency on the overhead projector lens. It is considerably harder to erase part of a blackboard diagram and then to reproduce it.

The transparencies shown in Figure 30 can be used according to the following method. The teacher shows the base transparency *a* covered with a mask (a sheet of black paper). He discusses the formulation of the theorem, achieving a clear understanding of the theorem's conditions and conclusion. Then the written notation is uncovered by removing the mask. The students transfer this to their workbooks along with the diagram for the problem. Afterwards the teacher places overlay *b* on the base transparency *a* (possibly again covering the caption on the right with a mask), and discussing the auxiliary construction at the same time. Then the students copy the description of the construction into their workbooks. Then the question is resolved as to which equal segments and angles can be found in the diagram, and which triangles are best to consider for this purpose. Now, placing overlay *c* on transparencies *a* and *b*, the teacher shows how the equal segments and angles are labeled, and concludes that triangles *ABM* and *DCM* are equal. The students copy the appropriate notation in their workbooks. Now overlay *c* must again be folded back and replaced by overlay *d*. Here the number of lines to distract the students' attention is decreased, but, on the other hand, a consequence of the equality of the triangles is added: $\angle ABM = \angle DCM$

(it is also noted that segments *AM* and *MD*, lying opposite these angles, are equal). The teacher has finished the proof of the theorem, and the students write out the ending to the proof. Finally, superimposing frame *c* again, the teacher proposes that they check the whole proof. The entire proof and its steps can readily be repeated with the students as desired, again folding back all the frames except *a*.

Let us give one more example. The instructor has two transparencies, which are not fastened together. On one of them (Fig. 32) a coordinate system—done, say, in blue—is plotted onto a rather dense grid. A red line diagram of the graph of parabola $y = x^2$ is made on another sheet (Fig. 33), but without the coordinate system. If we place one transparency on another so that the vertex of the parabola falls at the point (0, 0), then the entire parabola will be situated above the *x*-axis, and the students will see the parabola $y = x^2$ in the coordinate system on the screen (Fig. 34). By simply translating the upper transparency, a graph of the function $y = x^2 + px + q$ appears on the screen. By selecting the translation in a certain way, we can obtain the graph of any such function. This provides an opportunity, for example, to illustrate the graphic solutions of quadratic equations and second-degree inequalities. If a third sheet is added, on which a green straight line is drawn (Fig. 34), we can illustrate the graphic solution of the system

$$\begin{cases} y = x^2 + px + q, \\ y = ax + b \end{cases}.$$

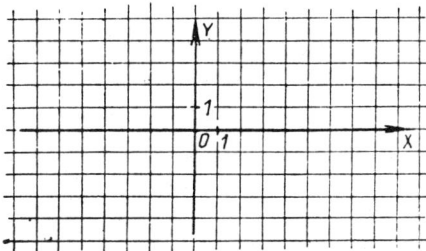

Figure 32.

Figure 33.

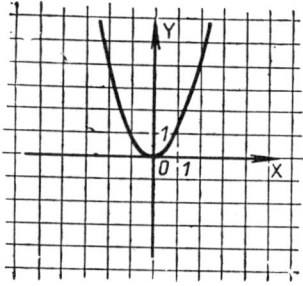

Figure 34.

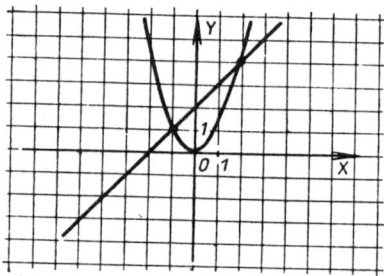

Figure 35.

Instructional Media in the Educational Process

In general, ten or fifteen sheets marked off as graphs form an indispensable aid for the course in algebra and the theory of functions. This aid can be used not only to illustrate the teacher's explanation, but also for exercises and in questioning the students. For example, a student can do the exercises on the topic "Constructing the Graph of the Function $y = x^2 + 4x - 5$" with the aid of an overhead projector. Thus, the whole class can see whether it is done correctly or not.

Magnetic Instructional Media[17]

Let us now examine the so-called magnetic instructional media. These include a number of items that are affixed by means of magnets to a painted steel sheet or other flat surface with magnetic properties. Research is going on in developing special dyes with ferromagnetic materials sprayed on them. When the class blackboard is covered with such a dye, it acquires ferromagnetic properties. The part of the board that is covered with a steel sheet (or dyed as described above) is called the *magnet board*. Soviet industry is turning out a ceramic magnet in the form of a thin round disk with a hole in it (Fig. 36). Using these magnets, various figures (triangles, circles, certain letters, and so forth) cut from cardboard or other material can easily adhere to the magnet board in a variety of positions, if magnets are attached to the back sides of these figures. The front part of the figure, which faces the class, can be painted or covered with colored paper (Fig. 37). In some cases it is convenient not to stick magnets to figures, but rather to attach a piece of paper, cardboard, etc., to a magnet board, first placing the sheet itself on it, then putting a ceramic magnet on it, firmly pressing the sheet onto the board.

The educational materials used in the method described above are called *magnetic instructional media*. Here it is a matter only of a specific, purely technological feature—a method of affixing various plane figures to the class blackboard. Nevertheless, this technological feature of the magnetic media, the ensuing ease with which figures are attached to the

Figure 36.

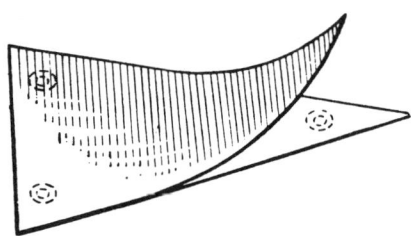

Figure 37.

Instructional Media in the Educational Process 65

board, and the free interchange possible among them create several specific instructional possibilities. In this connection, the magnetic aids have their particular method of application, and the instructional possibilities they give rise to are often very important.

As an example, let us consider a kit containing 10 charts that can be attached to the magnet board by simply pressing on ceramic magnets (as will become apparent, 12 magnets will suffice for this purpose). There are two different types of charts involved. Three charts represent a coordinate system on a sheet of paper, with a unit segment equal to 10 cm in one, and unit segments of one-half and one-third that size on the other two charts. In all three cases a rather finely scaled system of coordinate lines is represented (at every 0.1 units on the first sheet, at every 0.5 on the second, and at every 0.5 on the third). The other charts exhibit various curves marked in color on transparent material (cellophane or polyethylene). Thus, it is necessary to have two transparencies, each displaying one straight line (for example, a blue line on one sheet, a red line on another), and two or three transparencies, each displaying a parabola (for example, parabolas in the smallest coordinate system with the equations $y = x^2, y = 2x^2, y = 1/2\, x^2$. It is also useful to have on separate transparencies an equilateral hyperbola, two circles with different radii, and, as far as possible, other curves.

When this device is used in the classroom, a sheet of paper with a coordinate grid is first attached to the magnet board by means of four magnets at the corners. Then one or two transparencies with curves drawn on them are placed on top of it and attached to it by individual magnets. Holding the paper with one hand and pulling the transparency by the edge, one can easily move the curves on the transparencies without removing the magnets. The possibilities for using this device are abundantly clear. Actually, it creates approximately the same opportunities as the overhead projector overlays described above. True, their economic characteristics are rather different. The overhead projector is an expensive device, whose presence in every classroom or study room is a matter of the distant future. But the magnetic apparatus described above can easily be made by any teacher at the present time. All the materials are available in educational lending departments and dime stores.

Another example is made from a sheet of paper displaying a coordinate grid, several letters cut from, e.g., cardboard and equipped with ceramic magnets glued on to them, and several small colored circles (representing points) to which magnets are also glued. With this device the teacher can explain the material and propose various exercises related to coordinates. For example, after posting a few colored circles and affixed letters on the magnet board, he can ask: What are the coordinates of point A? of point B? and so on. With a few changes, the points with the letters are shifted to a new position and the students get a new exercise.

Of course, an assignment of this kind can be given to students using the ordinary blackboard and chalk, but the magnet board has a number of advantages: it is not necessary to draw a coordinate system, changing the problem does not require erasing it and spoiling the figure, and so forth. Moreover, the transition from explanations using the blackboard to consideration of vivid circles and letters enhances activity, attentiveness, and the like.

No less rich in possibilities is the application of magnetic aids to geometry (moving figures around, deducing formulas for areas by cutting and shifting parts of figures, and so forth).

Devices and Models

We have considered above a number of different instructional media: film media (motion pictures, single-concept films, filmstrips, slides, transparencies), charts, magnetic instructional media, printed workbooks, problem cards, and rubber stamps. This large group of instructional media has the common, unifying property that they are all meant for reproducing various plane representations.

Several demonstration devices in mathematics belong here: a demonstration slide rule (Fig. 38), a school trigonometer (Fig. 39), various

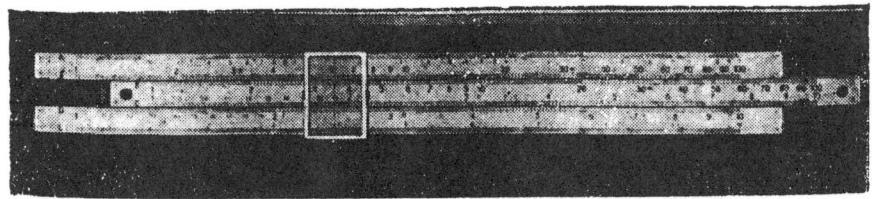

Figure 38.

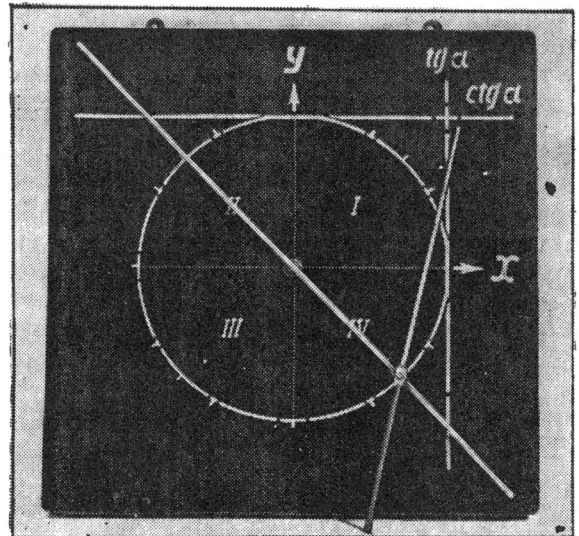

Figure 39.

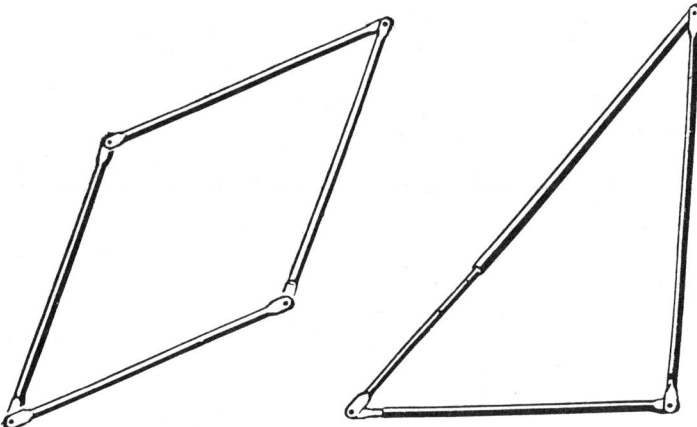

Figure 40.

diagrams with movable parts, plane hinged triangles and quadrangles (Fig. 40), and others. Many devices of this sort are made by teachers as "do-it-yourself equipment" for mathematics study rooms. In most cases these devices have visuality as their sole objective: they provide a proper, isomorphic reflection of the phenomena being studied, and at the same time they are simple to perceive. Sometimes biotechnological elements also play a role in the devices (e.g., folding hinged triangles of various kinds).

We have yet to consider another large group of instructional media in mathematics which combines different kinds of three-dimensional models and devices. These are models of solids and various stereometric construction sets which make it possible to reproduce prisms, pyramids, and various sections of them, as well as curved solids. Other devices can illustrate the properties of parallel and perpendicular planes, hinged dihedral angles with the sides of a linear angle drawn on their faces, and others. All of the instructional media included in this group are used primarily for purposes of visuality. Spatial concepts are not immediately absorbed by students, or only with great difficulty. Therefore visual models, yielding a simple, vivid, and yet correct isomorphic representation of abstract geometric figures in space, play a large role in the study of solid geometry.

We shall not cite examples, as these aids and their roles are well known to every mathematics teacher. We would only caution against excessive enthusiasm for showing these models. Sometimes a teacher, aided by interested students, will make framework spatial figures for literally every theorem and every solvable problem in solid geometry. The mathematics study room, in which many dozens of these models are displayed, looks very imposing. In reality, however, the benefit from such excessive enthusiasm for visuality is very dubious. Pupils accustomed to working with prepared spatial models are sometimes incapable of solving a problem without a ready-made model. Indeed, in real life they will solve problems for which no one will have made models in advance.

This does not mean that the teacher should completely avoid using models to directly illustrate a certain problem or theorem. These models are sometimes absolutely justified (for example, in solving two or three problems of a completely new type, related to difficulties in spatial concepts).

Some teachers opt to create complex general-purpose stereometric construction sets, which permit them, when necessary, to reproduce a model for almost any theorem or problem. Such universality is most often achieved by virtue of essential flaws in the construction set that is obtained. For example, when a pyramid is constructed on a device, the parts needed to construct a model of a prism or a sphere are left over (Fig. 41), and this distracts the students. Moreover, all-purpose fastenings, hinges and other contrivances may be complicated and technically unreliable. A model assembled from a construction set sometimes falls apart, and is not easy to reassemble. Moreover, as a rule, assembling a given model from an all-purpose construction set requires no small amount of time, and sometimes virtuosity. A pyramid, before it is fully assembled, must be held at several connection points at once, and the assembler literally does not have enough hands. All of this compels one to doubt

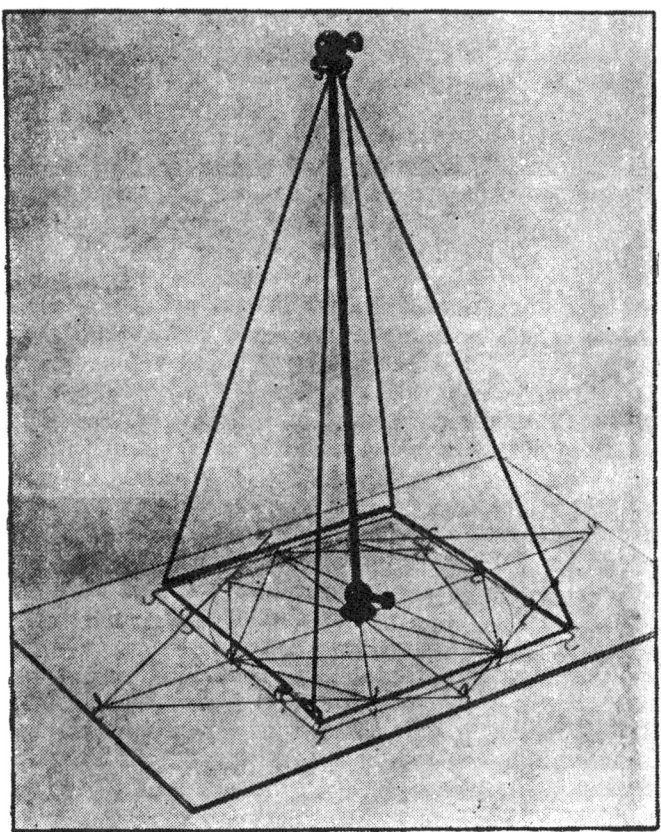

Figure 41.

the advisability of creating *all-purpose* stereometric construction sets. It is better to have several specialized devices, one for building a triangular pyramid showing various plane sections rapidly and without superfluous details, another for demonstrating a triangular prism, and so forth.

We note in conclusion that there are almost no *natural objects* in school mathematics instruction. Indeed, although in science classes the teacher might exhibit a vial of sulfuric acid or an electric motor, in a mathematics lesson it is impossible to "show" the students a derivative, a logarithm, a limit, or to let them "touch" them. In mathematics lessons we study almost exclusively abstract concepts. Of course, there are abstract concepts in other school subjects as well: suffice it to name the concepts of mass, center of gravity, potential, and work in physics. But in addition to these abstract concepts, natural objects—e.g., an electric motor, a volt meter, a lens—are studied in physics. There is almost none of this in mathematics. Among natural objects there are only a few devices: the slide rule, adding machine, abacus. In only a very few schools are students able to acquire a concept of other mechanisms—electronic computers, say. A well-made educational movie can provide an idea of the working of these very complex mechanisms.

Among natural objects there are a variety of manipulatives for laboratory and practical work in mathematics lessons. True, few such practical assignments arise in mathematics lessons. However, they should be carefully designed and equipped with well-prepared manipulatives so that the students can be led, as they perform these assignments, to the important realization that mathematical concepts are borrowed from life and are reflections of real-world processes. Thus, in an experimental unit on the topic "The Rectangular Parallelepiped and Its Volume," manipulatives were prepared in the form of a variety of graduated solids. Having such a graduated solid and comparing it with an individual cube (for more detail see Fig. 269 in Chapter 4), a student acquires a notion of the interrelationships between actual solids in space, of which the mathematical concept of volume is a reflection.

Optimal Units of Educational Materials

As a rule, every piece of educational material has its own special purpose. An instructional orientation is intrinsic to some of them, a high degree of visuality to others, a biotechnological advantage, i.e., efficiency to others, and individualizability to yet others. A lesson will be fruitful, clearly, only if it utilizes a wide range of instructional media, each of which performs its own function. Of course, all educational material used in the study of a given topic should constitute a unique *unit of educational materials* and not a collection of individual items unrelated by a common topic and orientation. This means that the objects in an instructional unit should share a common content and methodological approach (i.e., a common method of presenting the topic). Furthermore, they should embrace every aspect of the learning process, that is, if necessary, they should have the property of visuality, as well as essential biotechnological properties that promote the scientific organization of work for both teacher and student. It might be said that *an instructional unit for a given topic should maximize the effects of teaching.* In view of the importance of this concept let us consider in more detail the following conditions, which ensure that an instructional unit for a given topic is really capable of yielding a close to the maximum possible pedagogical effect.

1) The unit should contain instructional objects that share a common content and methodology.

2) The material in the unit should fully correspond to the modern scientific concepts related to the given topic and should also take into account (in planning the depth of exposition of a topic) the students' age-level; of course, in these respects the material must correspond to the established curriculum.

3) The objects involved in the unit should be coordinated methodologically.

4) The objects involved in the unit should have a high degree of visuality in all necessary respects.

5) The unit should contain materials that ensure a high instructional orientation whenever it is a matter of developing students' algorithmic or nearly algorithmic skills.

6) The unit should contain material that permits the acquisition of skills in problem-solving, to be individualized as necessary.

7) The material in the unit should provide for highly scientific organization of work for teacher and students—in particular, it should be sufficiently efficient, so that a minimum of time is spent unproductively.

8) The instructional unit should ensure a high degree of student attentiveness and activity, which can be achieved through bright colors and a well-designed sequence of objects to be used in the unit's lessons.

9) The material in the unit should satisfy the necessary psychophysiological requirements (the size of letters and symbols in charts, the lighting for the screen, etc.).

10) The material in the unit should meet the necessary aesthetic requirements. The coloring and arrangement of parts of the objects of instruction, their external appearance and shape, as well as the possibilities for arranging them on the classroom walls and on the teacher's chart, should be envisioned so that, upon entering a mathematics study room equipped with items from the unit, the students naturally take on a frame of mind conducive to composed, fruitful classwork.

A nearly maximal pedagogical effect can be achieved in the study of a given topic by many different methods, not just one. For example, it is conceivable that the classroom might have closed-circuit television, a videotape recorder with tapes of the lessons conducted on a certain topic by superior teachers, or that a teacher would have a large stock of films at his disposal including copies of single-concept films. Of course, these possibilities currently seem excessive, involving a cost that is totally out of proportion to the not very significant improvements in teaching they can yield. In this connection, we must introduce a definition of an optimal set of materials for a given instructional unit. By optimal instructional unit we mean a unit that yields a nearly maximum pedagogical effect with tolerable economic indices: the cost of the unit should correspond to the planned level of media for public education, the use of scarce materials should be kept to a minimum, and so forth.

In the next section we shall discuss this definition of the optimal, but now let us turn to the question of how an optimal instructional unit can be created.

Until now educational materials have been created individually by various curriculum developers—some specializing in making up charts, others constructing devices and models, still others in the making of movies, and so on. This has resulted in a haphazard process of equipping schools with educational materials in mathematics. As a result of such haphazard "production", many areas of the mathematics curriculum are unequipped (or almost so) with instructional media. A collection of various instructional media in other topics can in no way be considered an optimal instructional unit: the individual objects are not coordinated (and sometimes even contradict one another) with respect to the content, teaching methods, principles of organizing the lesson, etc. Furthermore, a randomly supplied collection of educational materials for a given topic does not satisfy the list of conditions cited when we defined an optimal unit (see pp. 63-64). Principal attention has been given to visuality alone, with an unnecessary duplication often observable in these collections.

To create an optimal instructional unit it is best to employ a group of developers who are experienced in teaching a given topic and have varied interests in the construction of instructional media (charts, devices, film media, etc.). *Group work on developing an optimal instructional unit of educational materials in mathematics is the most progressive trend in supplying schools with educational materials.*

One such instructional unit to accompany the topic "The Rectangular Parallelepiped and Its Volume" has been devised by a group in the Laboratory for Mathematics and Programmed Instruction in the Scientific Research Institute for School Materials and Technical Instructional Media of the USSR Academy of Pedagogical Sciences. We regard this unit as optimal: it costs little and can yield a high pedagogical effect, as shown in Chapter 5.

Before turning to a description of the items included in this unit, let us briefly focus on how the work to create it was done. This might interest groups of authors who intend to develop other units.

The topic "The Rectangular Parallelepiped and Its Volume" was not chosen at random. According to the new curriculum, this topic in the grade 4 mathematics course comes under the authority of the mathematics specialists, for whom it is new. On the other hand, geometry and the elements of algebra (properties of arithmetic operations) are successfully integrated into the treatment of this topic. If one takes into account, moreover, that in the existing standard textbooks it was presented very poorly, then the interest in elaborating the topic is clear. Moreover, the topic's simplicity creates an opportunity to explain to the broadest possible range of teachers the concept of an optimal unit. All of this has determined our choice of topic.

The inadequate treatment of this topic in the existing textbooks provided the empetus for us to elaborate the materials for the unit. Our laboratory group discussed the topic thoroughly from the standpoint of modern mathematics, methodology, and teaching methods. This stage of work—working out a single scientific and methodological pespective—seems to us now to be essential in planning other units.

Of course, as we devised our point of view, we discussed the possible nature of future educational materials. It gradually became clear what should be included in a slide series or left for a single-concept film. We then wrote sample lesson plans, which were replete with concrete problems, remarks on the use of workbooks based on printed materials, and other educational materials. Several discussions and conferences were held with experienced teachers. Only toward the end of this rather lengthy period of study and discussion did the nature of the future unit become completely clear to us. It was crucial that these discussions be conducted by the entire group of laboratory workers. We gradually worked out common points of view, and the subsequent elaboration of materials by individual workers resulted in the creation of a unit in which everything was as closely interconnected as possible.

The materials in the unit reflect modern scientific concepts, are united by a single content and methodology, promote the students' acquisition of knowledge and skills in this topic, and are coordinated with respect to methods of teaching. We envisioned that the items in the unit could be substituted for one another, and that it would be possible to shift frequently from traditional work at the class blackboard to using the objects in the unit.

As for the other conditions listed , whether they were satisfied can be judged by the following chart (Table 1.2; pluses indicate the presence of each property).

In addition to the materials listed in the table (and properly constituting the unit), many items of general equipment were used, which did not strictly belong to the unit: the class blackboard, a darkening device, movie and slide projectors, devices for hanging up charts; a set of solids, measuring cups (1 liter and 0.5 liter), measuring glasses, set squares, a ruler, and so forth.

The table shows that the unit as a whole satisfies all of the requirements (thus enabling us to consider it optimal). There is no point in requiring all properties for every item. For example, it would be strange to require individualization of single-concept films which are intended for simultaneous showing to the whole class. This again shows that only the creation of units of materials (and not individual materials) can solve all of the problems posed.

The Definition of an Optimal Instructional Unit

It might seem that the general definition of an optimal instructional unit (based on a topic taken in isolation) is inadequate. Thus, the authors have often heard the following sentiment expressed in discussions: one must learn to quantify various aspects (visuality, instructional orientation,

Table 1.2

Material in the Complex	Visuality	Didactic Orientation	Individu-alizability	Saving of Time Spent Unproductively
1. Single-concept film: "A Rectangular Parallelepiped"	+	+		+
2. Single-concept film: "Representing a Rectangular Parallelepiped"	+	+		+
3. Single-concept film: "The Concept of Volume"	+			+
4. Single-concept film: "The Volume of a Solid"	+	+		+
5. Single-concept film: "The Volume of a Rectangular Prallelepiped"	+	+		
6. Fimstrip: "A Rectangular Parallelepiped and Its Volume"	+	+		+
7. Slide Series (same title)		+		+
8. Rubber Stamps: "A Cube" and "A Rectangular Parallelpiped"			+	+
9. Arithmetic Box	+		+	
10. Framework model of a rectangular parallelepiped	+			
11. Table of the Latin alphabet		+		
12. Series of tables: "Laws of Arithmetic Operations"		+		
13. Series of tables: "Volume of a Rectangular Parallelepiped"	+	+		
14. Notebook based on printed material		+	+	+
15. Assignment cards			+	+

biotechnological and economic properties, etc.) of the instructional unit (regardless of whether this is easy or difficult to do). We obtain as a result a sequence of numbers $a_1, a_2, ..., a_s$ (let us say that the numbers a_1 and a_2 characterize the *visuality* of objects in the unit, expressed in certain sets; the number a_3—the *instructional orientation*; the numbers a_4, a_5, a_6—the *biotechnological properties* of the unit, and so on). We can then agree to regard a unit as optimal only on the condition that all of its characteristics $a_1, a_2, ..., a_s$ assume the largest possible values. For example, if one author prepared a unit characterized by the values

$$a_1 = 3.2;\ a_2 = 4.0;\ ...;\ a_s = 3.7,$$

and another composed for the same topic a unit characterized by larger values, e.g.,

$$a_1 = 3.5;\ a_2 = 4.3;\ ...;\ a_s = 4.0,$$

then it is clear that the second unit should be acknowledged as better. A unit will be optimal if it is better than any other unit.

Unfortunately, such an attempt at defining an optimal unit is doomed to fail. And not because it is difficult to quantify visuality, instructional orientation, etc., but rather from theoretical considerations.

The difficulties in quantifying the various properties of a unit are certainly great. But they can be overcome, at least in theory. It is possible, in principle, to provide precise quantitative methods for evaluating simplicity (see Section 3), efficiency, and the other quantitative properties considered above. Qualitative properties can also be quantified (isomorphicity, instructional orientation, individualizability, and others). For example, in the presence of a didactic orientation we might agree to let $a_3 = 1$, and, in its absensce, $a_3 = 0$. This is not simple in practice, but these difficulties can in principle be surmounted.

Now let us assume that all difficulties in finding quantitative evaluations have been solved, and we have precise, objective, and scientifically sound methods of evaluating the numbers $a_1, a_2, ..., a_s$, which together characterize all aspects of the instructional unit. Let us imagine that we have two units composed by two individuals on a single topic and characterized by the data in Table 1.3.

Table 1.3

	Number of objects in complex	Visuality		a_3—didactic orientation	Biotechnological Properties		a_6	Economic Properties	a_8	a_9
		a_1—isomorphicity	a_2—simplicity		a_4—individualizability	a_5—saving of time		a_7—cost	...	...
Complex 1	12	1	5.3	1	1	9.8	1	-50	...	...
Complex 2	9	1	3.7	0	0	2.1	1	-25	...	...

It is apparent from the table that Unit 1 has a number of higher indices. For example, it saves significantly more time than Unit 2; it has an instructional orientation and individualization (of which Unit 2 is devoid); and so forth. But it is twice as expensive as Unit 2. (Cost is shown in the chart with a minus sign because an increase in this quantity, that is, a reduction in the price of the unit, means an improvement of the economic indices.) In other words, Unit 1 is better by a number of indices but costs more, while Unit 2 is inferior to Unit 1 in a number of respects but is cheaper. Which unit is better? In the light of the constraints expressed above, neither will be "better"—they are incomparable, since Unit 1 is better in some indices and Unit 2 in others. And this is entirely reasonable. By increasing the number of objects in a unit one can increase the number of its pedagogical indices, but the economic indices (cost, use of scarce materials) deteriorate. Another analogous consideration is that when the number of written materials and problem cards is increased, the indices of the instructional unit can be improved with respect to individualization and instructional orientation, but some biotechnological indices decline (keeping and finding the necessary cards is more involved, and checking the work will be harder).

Thus, units composed by different developers (on the same topic) will as a rule be incomparable from the standpoint of the constraints expressed above, and we cannot choose (or even precisely define) the "best" of them. This is not surprising from a mathematical point of view. Each instructional unit is characterized by several numerical indices—that is, by a *vector* $a_1, a_2, a_3, ..., a_s$, and it is impossible to introduce the concepts of "more" and "less" as completely as for numbers into a set of vectors. Therefore, any idea of choosing the "greatest" of several vectors is doomed to failure.

It might appear that the way out of this difficult position will be provided by the (at first glance very tempting) idea of a quantitative description of "optimal" following from the above considerations. Since the properties of the instructional unit are described not by one but by several numbers $a_1, a_2, ..., a_s$, then the *sum* of all these numbers can be taken as a quantitative characterization of optimization. This question can also be approached in a slightly more general way. We must have valid reasons for choosing several coefficients $k_1, k_2, ..., k_s$ and composing the expression

$$H = k_1 a_1 + k_2 a_2 + \ldots + k_2 a_2,$$

which becomes a "measure of optimization" of the unit. (If each of the coefficients $k_1, k_2, ..., k_s$ is equal to 1, then H will be the sum of the numbers $a_1, a_2, ..., a_s$. Now we will have only one number H, and the instructional unit with the greatest value of H should be acknowledged to be "optimal." Suppose the coefficients have the values $k_1 = 3$, $k_2 = 6$, $k_3 = 1$, $k_4 = k_5 = k_6 = 0.5, \ldots$. acknowledged to be half as important a property as simplicity, but three times more important than instructional orientation, and so on. Increasing the number a_1, which characterizes isomorphicity, by one unit adds three units to the value of H, while increasing the number a_3 by a unit adds only one unit to H.)

This is roughly the sort of approach offered by Strezikozin [19]. Instead of the numbers $a_1, a_2, ..., a_s$, he used the signs "-," "×," and "+," corresponding approximately to the values 0, 1/2, and 1, respectively. Each individual item in the unit could be marked by these signs. For example, using these symbols we can characterize the presence of individualization by the "+" sign in the appropriate column, its absence by "-," and the partial possibility of individualization by "×." In essence, this approach means considering approximately the same table as Table 1.3, but with "-," "×," or "+" instead of pluses and empty spaces.

Unfortunately, this approach cannot lead to success since there is no an objective method of choosing the coefficients $k_1, k_2, ..., k_s$. Indeed, let us assume that two teachers have received the same unit for evaluation and attempt to resolve the question of finding the coefficients $k_1, k_2, ..., k_s$. The first considers visuality a basic property, and the second—individualization. The first teacher will clearly be inclined to increase the coefficients k_1 and k_2 in the expression for H, while the second will strive to increase the coefficient k_4 and decrease the others. They will not arrive at a consensus. This problem will arise because they have different views of the role and purpose of instructional media; this difference in views is apparently a consequence of a divergence in teaching methods. In other words, the choice of coefficients $k_1, k_2, ..., k_s$ will always besubjective.

Finally, we note a third approach to determining whether a unit is optimal—an approach that is frequently suggested: a statistical method of evaluating the effectiveness of a unit based on a large number of experiments. The idea is to conduct a broad experiment in teaching a single topic, using the proposed unit for some classes (the experimental group) and not using it for others (the control group). However, this method (despite the well-developed mathematical apparatus of probability theory and statistics which can be applied) cannot serve as a basis for determining what is optimal. The fact is that in the study of each topic the students generally acquire a considerable amount of diverse knowledge and skills. Thus, in the unit on "The Rectangular Parallelepiped" they should:

1) learn to distinguish the elements of a parallelepiped (the vertices, edges, and faces) and remember their combinatorial properties;

2) acquire rudimentary spatial concepts;

3) learn to represent a rectangular parallelepiped on paper (or on the blackboard);

4) acquire a basic concept of the volume of a solid;

5) study and remember the formulas for the volume of a rectangular parallelepiped;

6) learn to solve problems on computing the volume of a rectangular parallelepiped; and so forth.

If we wish to study the influence of an instructional unit in detail, we must evaluate each student according to all of these points, giving not one but several evaluations. In other words, the students' knowledge should be characterized not by one number or rating, but by several—that is, this knowledge takes the form of a *vector*. But then we run up against the same difficulty as before: if one of the proposed units is much better for the acquisition of spatial concepts, and a second unit (on the same topic) is better for a basic understanding of volume, then it is impossible to say which of these units is more nearly "optimal."

Moreover, there is another circumstance which makes a statistical method (even with the most rigorous mathematical treatment of data) unconvincing. The rating that the teacher proposes is not an objective quantity corresponding to a certain standard of knowledge and evaluation, but is largely determined by the level of success of the class as a whole. In any class there are the more and the less capable, or better and more weakly prepared students. And even if the weak students in the experimental class know the subject no better than the average students in the control class, the teacher *cannot* give only grades of A and B to the experimental class. In most experimental classes there will be strong, average, and weak students. This means that grades will be relative, that is, attributable to the average level of knowledge in that class. And since the percentages of the more and the less capable students should be approximately identical in the experimental and the control classes, then, considering the relativity of the grades, we can expect approximately identical success in the experimental and the control classes. This result was found by the authors in an experiment (a very small one, to be sure) conducted to check the unit to accompany the topic "The Rectangular Parallelepiped and Its Volume." Despite a manifestly higher quality of knowledge in the experimental classes, the (relative!) progress was approximately the same.

Of course, the non-objectivity of relative grades is easily overcome by well-known methods (tests or written work with a standardized treatment of the results). However, in this case all the knowledge and skills related to the topic must be considered; that is, the vector nature of the problem reappears.

Finally, let us note a third circumstance which impedes the application of the experimental statistical method. Different teachers will surely use a given unit in different ways—depending, for example, on the teaching methods. Therefore, the statistical data will reflect in the experimental classes the compound effect of the influence of both the unit itself and the methods of using it. For the first several years, the method of employing a new unit will be less complete and elaborate, despite the teacher's interest in new instructional media. Thus, objective statistical data characterizing the effectiveness of a unit can be obtained only over several years, when imperfect and underdeveloped teaching methods will cease to have a negative effect on the indices of success.

The foregoing discussion shows that a "descriptive" definition of an optimal unit is entirely justified, and in essence the only one possible (although it may be that something has been omitted from these ten points, or something should be made more precise and detailed). Utterly conscientious consideration of all ten conditions may not lead unilaterally to an optimal unit. Two different groups of authors, working along parallel lines on the same topic, might present two entirely different units as optimal.

2

The Psychological Theory of Mastery as One of the Theoretical Preconditions for Creating Instructional Units

Mathematical Concepts as the Result of Abstraction

Mathematics studies the material world. More precisely, it studies the spatial forms and quantitative relationships of the real world. However, mathematics is distinguished from other natural sciences by its abstractness; mathematical concepts are the result of multi-level (at least two-step) abstractions.

When a person mentally combines several objects with common characteristics and associates this class of objects with a certain word (e.g., "house"), he has acquired an abstract concept. This concept has arisen as a result of an elementary form of abstraction—*abstraction by identification*. We mentally identify several objects with one another, according to their common characteristics (all these objects have been created by human hands and are capable of serving as human dwellings) and we associate the whole class of objects with a certain word ("house").

Elementary mathematical concepts, primarily the concept of number, arise via this form of abstraction. The child repeatedly observes various sets consisting of two objects: two eyes, two apples, two cubes, two chairs, etc. In doing so he hears adults say the word "two," which gradually becomes associated in his mind with the number of objects observed. "Two" is what all those sets have in common. The child mentally combines all such sets and associates this class of sets with the word "two." All secondary, nonessential features are discarded (it is irrelevant what two objects belong to the set: two apples, two hands, etc.), and only one essential feature remains, by which all of these sets are combined into one class—the number of objects in a set. Thus, as a result of abstraction by identification the concept of number arises—two, three, etc..

Another form of abstraction that contributes to the development of mathematical concepts is *abstraction by idealization*. Dimensionless points, lines without thickness, and many other elementary geometric concepts arise through this form of abstraction. We do not simply combine in one class a line drawn on a sheet of paper, a thread, a wire, and other objects whose extent in one direction far exceeds their extent in other directions. We do create in our minds an *idealized* image of a line devoid of thickness (although a thread or a wire does have an insignificant but still absolute thickness). The word "line" is thus related, not simply to combining a series of objects into one class, but to creating a certain ideal image. There are houses in the real world around us, but there are no mathematical lines. The concept of a "line" not only generalizes or combines a number of objects, but it also *idealizes* their properties. In this instance we are indeed dealing with abstraction by idealization. Many elementary mathematical concepts are formed through this form of abstraction, including the cube, rectangular parallelepiped, and sphere.

It is essential that, once having arisen, these abstract concepts become a reality for the mathematician. Combining mathematical concepts by their common characteristics and ignoring any secondary features, we complete a second step in abstraction. Many mathematical concepts arise in this way. For example, by examining the set of all quadrilaterals and combining them (according to their properties) into various classes, we arrive at the concepts of parallelogram, rhombus, trapezoid, etc. This is again abstraction by identification, except that here, instead of objects from the real world, we are combining abstract mathematical concepts that we have formed into a single class.

The essential uniqueness of mathematics as a science lies in this independence, in the fact that mathematics forms its concepts by proceeding from previously formed concepts (which of course reflect reality) rather than directly from objects taken directly from the real world.

> "Mathematics studies the material world from a particular point of view; its immediate object is the spatial forms and quantitative relations of the real world. These forms and relations themselves in their pure form, and not concrete material bodies, are the reality that is studied by mathematics."[1]

But mathematics does not stop at the second stage of abstraction. Many mathematical concepts are the result of subsequent abstractions. Among them are the concepts of equivalence (for plane figures or solids in space) and volume. Such fundamental concepts of modern mathematics as groups and fields, vector spaces, and others are also the result of multi-level abstraction.

Volume as a mathematical concept is thus obtained as a result of at least a two-level abstraction. Does this mean that the concept of volume, like other multi-level mathematical abstractions, is so far divorced from reality that it cannot be applied in practical activity? Absolutely not. It is well known that two- and multi-level mathematical abstractions find practical applications every day.

Returning to the concept of volume, let us note that besides the mathematical concept of volume (which will be described precisely in Chapter III), there is another, purely practical notion. This idea is a matter simply of the place occupied by a certain object in space. For example, suppose that six children's blocks can be packed in one box and 15 blocks of the same size in another. The second box clearly occupies a larger place in space than the first. These words suggest a rudimentary practical notion of volume. The abstract mathematical concept of volume is a reflection of this practical concept. This makes for the great practical applicability of the abstract mathematical concept of volume.

We have focused especially upon the concept of volume, since its formation is one of the basic purposes of the instructional unit described in this book.

Mental Activity in Establishing What Belongs to a Concept

Let us now turn to the question of the formation and mastery of concepts and show that this question is very closely related to the use of instructional materials. Moreover, we will see that a psychological theory of learning concepts (discussed below) is one of the basic theoretical premises for creating complete instructional units. We will illustrate this position primarily with material from the unit entitled "The Rectangular Parallelepiped and Its Volume."

Before starting work on the unit, we attempted to ascertain just what the students should learn in the course of 16 hours,[2] and what abilities and skills they should acquire. It is indisputable that, in the first place, they should master the concept of a "rectangular parallelepiped."

Besides a mastery of this concept, the instructional unit should familiarize students with volume as a property of objects occupying space and with the computation of volumes, which reduces to finding a number that shows how many volume units (liters, cubic centimeters, or some other units) are contained in a given object. Next the range of practical problems for the students was determined. It remained only to ensure that the material in the instructional unit brings each of these problems to the students (by the way, the textbook is undoubtedly a type of instructional material and should be regarded as part of the unit).

Let us begin with issues related to organizing the mastery of the concept of "rectangular parallelepiped." According to the work by P.Ya. Galperin[3] and his colleagues, "mastering a concept" means primarily learning to establish by means of a definition whether an object belongs to a given concept.

The following definition of the concept of a "rectangular parallelepiped" is suitable in grade 4: a rectangular parallelepiped is a solid bounded by six rectangles. Using this definition, the students should learn to establish whether or not an indicated object (e.g., a polyhedron) is a rectangular parallelepiped.[4]

Let us analyze how membership in a concept can be established. Suppose that someone who has mastered the definition above is shown a rectangular-shaped bar and is asked whether this solid is a rectangular parallelepiped. Naturally, the answer would follow: "Yes, it is." Here well-established operations are performed mentally in an instant, often unconsciously. The person would note that:

1) the given solid has not just any number, but exactly six faces;

2) all of these faces are rectangles.

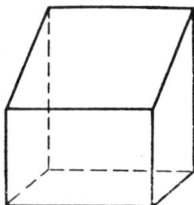

Figure 42.

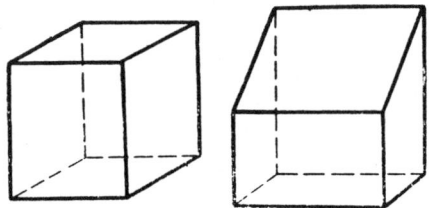

Figure 43.

This aggregate of mental "baby steps," which establish inclusion in a concept, is called "mental activity" by psychologists. This activity always boils down to checking whether or not an object has the relevant properties.

If an object does not have one of the properties, it is concluded at once that it is not a rectangular parallelepiped. For example, a person who has mastered the definition sees a "spatial cross." Instantaneous, often unconscious processes are going on in his mind. (Psychologists say that these processes are "condensed" or "automatic.") The person checks whether this solid has six faces. He notes that it does not have six faces and, not at all concerned that all the faces are rectangles (squares), he concludes that this is not a rectangular parallelepiped.

Mental activity proceeds analogously in establishing whether the solid shown in Figure 42 is a rectangular parallelepiped. Someone who has mastered the definition either notices at once that there are faces which are not rectangles, or first checks how many faces it has, and then determines that there are six, whereupon, without rushing to a conclusion, he checks that all the faces are rectangles.

We repeat that the whole process is automatic and condensed. Therefore, it seems to the person that he has looked and seen at once, without checking, that the solid is (or is not) a true rectangular parallelepiped. In some instances the proper response to the question whether a solid is a rectangular parallelepiped is that we do not know. For example, suppose it is clear from the statement of a problem that a polyhedron has six faces, but nothing more is known about this polyhedron. In solving the problem, a student notes the six faces, but does not jump to a conclusion. He tries to determine whether all the faces are rectangles. However, if it is impossible to determine this from the problem, then he concludes that it is unknown whether the given solid is a rectangular parallelepiped. In other words, both a rectangular parallelepiped and a solid that is not a rectangular parallelepiped can satisfy the conditions of the problem (Fig. 43).

This activity corresponds directly to establishing membership in the concept of a "rectangular parallelepiped" using the definition cited above—or, as psychologists say, it is *adequate* to the given definition.

It is remarkable that precisely such an activity is adequate not only to the definition of the concept of a "rectangular parallelepiped" but to many others as well, not just in mathematics, but in other sciences, too. For example, if it becomes clear to us from a problem that the two opposite sides of a quadrilateral are not parallel, we conclude at once that this is not a parallelogram. Our mental activity proceeds along the following lines. We break down the definition of the concept of a "parallelogram" into two requirements:

1) In a quadrilateral that we can call a parallelogram, two opposite sides must be parallel.

2) The other two opposite sides in this quadrilateral must also be parallel.

Then we must check each of these requirements. If we establish that the first condition is not fulfilled, we conclude that the quadrilateral is not a parallelogram (Fig. 44a).

Once it becomes clear from the problem that two of the quadrilateral's sides are parallel, the presence of requirement 2 is checked (Fig. 44b, c). Only after it is established that the other two sides are also parallel (Fig. 44c) can we conclude that the quadrilateral is a parallelogram.

In order to obtain a general scheme combining the examples considered above, let us reconsider our definition of a rectangular parallelepi-

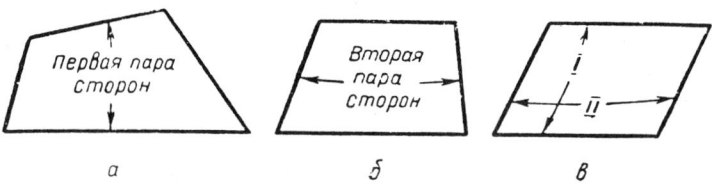

Figure 44.

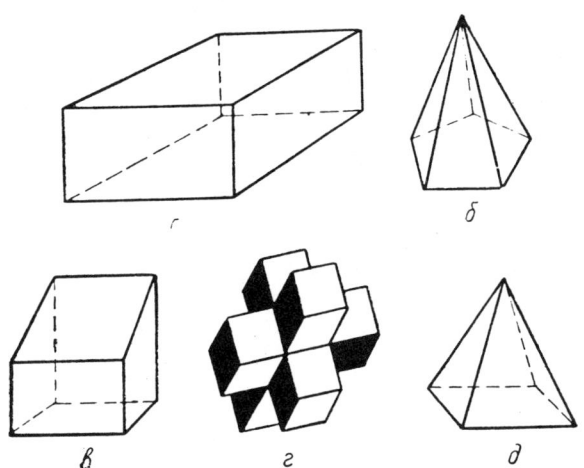

Figure 45.

ped. We designate by M the set of all polyhedra. Polyhedra will be designated by lower-case letters. Then let $\alpha(x)$ denote the following statement: *Polyhedron x has six faces.* In other words, the statement $\alpha(x)$ is true if polyhedron x has exactly six faces; otherwise $\alpha(x)$ is false. (Thus, α is a predicate in one variable for the set M). For example, for the polyhedra shown in Figure 45, the statements $\alpha(a)$, $\alpha(b)$, and $\alpha(c)$ are true, but the statements $\alpha(d)$ and $\alpha(e)$ are false.

Let β denote the property of having only rectangular faces. In other words, $\beta(x)$ is true if all faces of polyhedron x are rectangular, and false if any face is not a rectangle. For the polyhedra shown in Figure 45, the statements $\beta(a)$ and $\beta(d)$ are true, and the statements $\beta(b)$, $\beta(c)$, and $\beta(e)$ are false.

Finally, let us agree to designate (as in mathematical logic) the conjunction "and" by the sign $\wedge$. In other words, the statement $\alpha(x) \wedge \beta(x)$ will be true if polyhedron x has both properties α and β (i.e., it has six faces, each of which is a rectangle). But this, according to the definition, means that polyhedron x is a rectangular parallelepiped. Thus, using the symbols we have introduced, we can formulate the definition in this way: a polyhedron x is a rectangular parallelepiped if the statement $\alpha(x) \wedge \beta(x)$ is true.

The definition of a parallelogram, as we have seen, and a number of other definitions of mathematical concepts, can be formulated in terms of the conjunction of two predicates. In the general case, a definition of this kind can be described in the following way. We wish to define a concept P (e.g., as above, the concept of a rectangular parallelepiped). For this purpose, we consider a set M (in this case the set of all polyhedra), from which those elements belonging to P are singled out (here, simply all rectangular parallelepipeds). To this end, we consider two properties α and β of the elements of M, that is, two predicates of one variable for M.[5] An arbitrary element x of M either has property α (i.e., $\alpha(x)$ is true) or does not (i.e., $\alpha(x)$ is false). Similarly, x does or does not have property β. Now we formulate the definition that interests us: an element x of the set M belongs in P if it has both properties α and β—that is, if the statement $\alpha(x) \wedge \beta(x)$ is true.

Figure 46 illustrates what has just been said. Points lying interior to the heavy line are elements of set M. The left (shaded) region represents elements with property α, and the lower region (shaded differently) represents elements with property β. The elements with both properties α and β (that is, belonging to the concept P) are situated in the lower

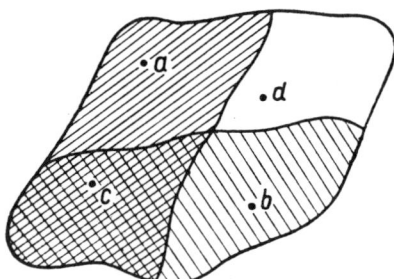

Figure 46.

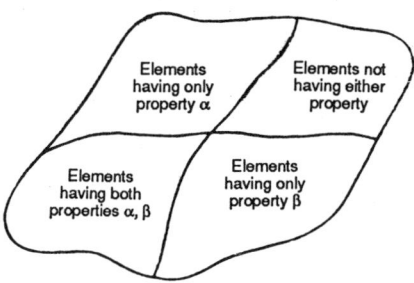

Figure 47.

left-hand corner of the figure, marked by double shading. For example, the element represented by the point a has property α, but not property β. Moreover, the element b has property β, but not property α. Finally, the element c has both of these properties (thus, belonging to the concept P), whereas the element d does not have either of them. Figure 47 illustrates these possibilities.

Suppose that we are given some element x of set M. What must we consider in order to determine whether element x belongs or does not belong to the concept P? First, we attempt to establish whether element x has property α. If it does not, we conclude at once that x does not belong to the concept P. But suppose x does have property. On this alone it is impossible to claim that x belongs to the concept P. (For example, both the elements c and a in Figure 46 have the property, but one of them belongs to the concept P and the other does not). If x does not have the property, it does not belong to the concept P. (In Figure 48 the elements without the property lie in the dotted region.) Only if x has not only property α, but property β as well can we assert that it belongs to the concept P.

Many mathematical definitions can be obtained by this general scheme. We have seen this above with examples of definitions of a

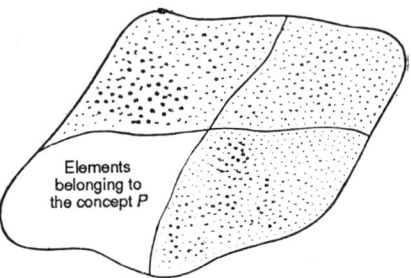

Figure 48.

rectangular parallelepiped and a parallelogram. Let us give two more examples.

A pair of numbers (x_0, y_0) is said to be a solution to the system of linear equations

$$\begin{cases} ax + by = P \\ cx + dy = Q, \end{cases}$$

if both equations reduce to an identity under the substitution $x = x_0$, $y = y_0$. This definition has the structure of the previous examples. Indeed, let us designate by M the set of all possible pairs (x, y) of real numbers. We shall say that the pair (x_0, y_0) has property α if it satisfies the first equation in the system, and has property β if it satisfies the second. In other words, the statement $\alpha(x_0, y_0)$ is true if $ax_0 + by_0 = P$ (and analogously for the statement $\beta(x_0, y_0)$). The concept of "a solution of a system of linear equations" is now defined in this way: a pair (x_0, y_0) belongs to this concept (that is, it is a solution of the system) if it has both properties α and β, that is, if the statement $\alpha(x_0, y_0) \wedge \beta(x_0, y_0)$ is true.

Another example. Two straight lines l and m in space are said to be *parallel* if they lie in the same plane and have no points in common. This definition also has the structure of the examples above. Let M be the set of all possible pairs (l, m) of straight lines in space. We say that the pair (l, m) has property α if the lines l and m lie in the same plane, and property

The Psychological Theory of Mastery

β if the lines l and m do not have common points. The concept of "a pair of parallel straight lines" is now defined in the following way: a pair (l, m) is a pair of parallel lines ($l \parallel m$) if the statement $\alpha(l, m) \wedge \beta(l, m)$ is true.

In both examples it is readily apparent that the simultaneous fulfillment of both properties α and β is essential for membership in the concept. Thus, if we know only that the pair (l, m) satisfies property α (that is, l and m lie in the same plane), then we cannot further assert that $l \parallel m$, for the lines might intersect. In exactly the same way, if we know only that the pair (l, m) satisfies property β (that is, the lines l and m have no common points), then the statement that $l \parallel m$ is incorrect, for the lines might cross.

Mental Activity in Establishing Membership in a Concept

Definitions of concepts are not formed with the aid of the logical connective $\wedge$ alone. Another logical connective that is used no less often is "or" (or *disjunction*) and is represented by the symbol $\vee$. Let us clarify its meaning by means of the following definition: *a quadrilateral is said to be a trapezoid if at least one pair of opposite sides are parallel.*[6] In other words, quadrilateral $ABCD$ is a trapezoid if $AB \parallel CD$ or $AD \parallel BC$. We note that a parallelogram is considered a special case of a trapezoid, that is, if both $AB \parallel CD$ and $AD \parallel BC$, then quadrilateral $ABCD$ is considered a trapezoid (that it is a parallelogram does not interest us here). In other words, quadrilateral $ABCD$ will be a trapezoid in the following three cases:

$AB \parallel CD$, but $AD \nparallel BC$ (Fig. 49*a*),

$AB \nparallel CD$, but $AD \parallel BC$ (Fig. 49*b*),

$AB \parallel CD$ and $AD \parallel BC$ (Fig. 49*c*).

In order to justify this definition, we designate by M the set of all plane quadrilaterals, assuming for convenience that the vertices in each quadrilateral are designated by the letters A, B, C, D. We say that a quadrilateral has property α if $AB \parallel CD$, and property β if $AD \parallel BC$. Thus the quadrilateral shown in Figure 49a has property α but not property β; the quadrilateral in Figure 49b has property β but not property α; in Figure 49c, the quadrilateral has both properties α and β; and in Figure 49d, it has neither property.

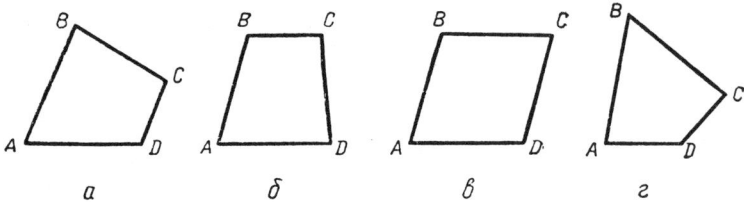

Figure 49.

Now the definition of a trapezoid can be formulated as follows: *a quadrilateral ABCD is said to be a trapezoid if it has at least one* of the properties α or β. If we agree for simplicity's sake to designate quadrilaterals by single lower-case letters, then membership in the concept "trapezoid" can be described in the following way: a quadrilateral x is said to be a trapezoid if at least one of the statements $\alpha(x)$ or $\beta(x)$ is true. This is a typical situation in which the logical connective $\vee$ ("or") can be used to make the notation simpler. It means: *the statement $\alpha(x) \vee \beta(x)$ is considered to be true if at least one of the statements $\alpha(x)$ or $\beta(x)$ is true.* The statement $\alpha(x) \vee \beta(x)$ is considered to be true in the following three cases:

1) object x has property α but not property β;

2) object x does not have property α but does have property β;

The Psychological Theory of Mastery

3) object x has both properties.[7]

The statement $\alpha(x) \vee \beta(x)$ will be false only if object x has *neither* of the properties α or β. Now we can formulate the definition of a trapezoid as follows: *a quadrilateral x is said to be a trapezoid if the statement $\alpha(x) \vee \beta(x)$ is true* (where property α means that $AB \parallel CD$, and property β means that $AD \parallel BC$).

A definition of this kind can be described in a general form. Some set M is considered (in our case the set of all plane quadrilaterals), from whose elements we wish to select those belonging to the concept Q (here, the concept of a "trapezoid"). For this purpose we consider two properties α and β of the elements of M (that is, two predicates in one variable for M) and formulate the definition in the following way: *an element x of set M is said to belong to the concept Q if it has at least one of the properties α or β, that is, if the statement $\alpha(x) \vee \beta(x)$ is true.*

If we turn again to Figure 46 (where the left half represents elements that have property α and the lower half elements that have property β), then we say that the concept Q includes, in the present case, all the points in any shaded region. Figure 46 shows visually that the scope of the concept defined by the formula $\vee$ is broader than the concept defined by the formula $\wedge$ (Fig. 50). For example, the scope of the concept of a "trapezoid" is broader than the scope of the concept of a "parallelogram" (the set of all parallelograms is a subset of the set of trapezoids).

What mental activity does a person carry out in establishing whether an object x belongs to the concept Q defined by the formula $\alpha \vee \beta$ (e.g., in establishing whether a quadrilateral $ABCD$ belongs to the concept of a "trapezoid")? First, he determines whether object x has property α. If it does, he can quickly conclude that object x belongs to the concept Q regardless of whether this object has property β. For example, if $AB \parallel CD$, the conclusion quickly follows that $ABCD$ is a trapezoid. If, on the other hand, it is found that object x does not have property α (in this case, $AB \times CD$), he does not jump to a conclusion, but attempts to establish whether object x has property β. If x has this property, then he again concludes that x belongs to the concept Q (if $AD \parallel BC$, then $ABCD$ is a trapezoid). Only when he finds that object x has neither property α nor

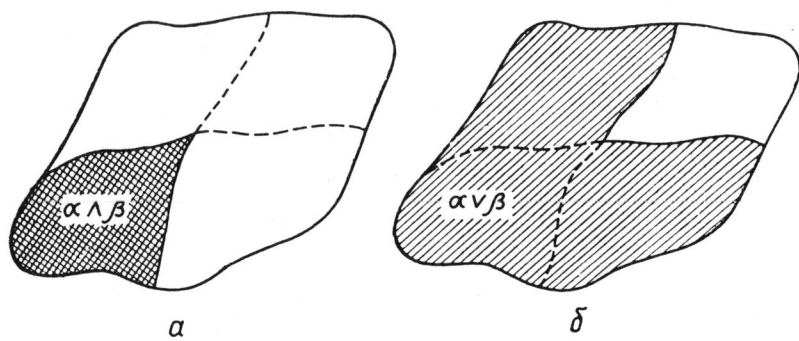

Figure 50.

property β does he conclude that x does not belong to the concept Q (if $AB \times CD$, and $AD \times BC$, as well, then $ABCD$ is not a trapezoid).

Again, as in the case of the concept defined by the formula α ∧ β, all this work is carried out, as a rule, in a condensed and automatic way. It therefore seems to the person that he sees immediately whether or not $ABCD$ is a trapezoid.

More complex definitions also arise, in which more than two properties are joined by the logical connectives ∧ and ∨. Consider the following definition: *the equation $ax^2 + bx + c = 0$ is said to be an incomplete quadratic equation if $a \neq 0$ and at least one of the coefficients b or c is zero.* Let α, β, and γ be the following properties of a quadratic equation:

property α: coefficient a is not zero;

property β: coefficient b is equal to zero;

property γ: coefficient c is equal to zero.

Designating the set of all quadratic equations by M and an arbitrary quadratic equation by q, we can define the concept of an "incomplete quadratic equation" by the formula α ∧ (β ∨ γ). Then *q belongs to this concept if the statement* α(q) ∧ (β(q) ∨ γ(q)) *is true.*

The Psychological Theory of Mastery

What mental activity does a person perform when he establishes membership in the concept of an "incomplete quadratic equation"? He observes that the equation q should have two properties joined by the connective "and"— namely, the properties α and $\beta \vee \gamma$. Therefore, he attempts to verify whether equation q has property α. If it does not have property α (that is, equation q is not quadratic), then it follows at once that the equation does not belong to this concept. If equation q has property α, the analysis continues. He must then check whether it has the property $\beta \vee \gamma$. If equation q has property β, then q belongs to the concept "incomplete quadratic equation." If not (that is, $b \neq 0$), he has to go on and check property γ. If q has property γ, it again belongs to this concept. Only when q does not have property γ can he conclude that q does not belong to the concept of an "incomplete quadratic equation."

In concluding this section, let us note that the logical connectives $\wedge$ and $\vee$ are not the only logical means used to define concepts. *Negation* is often used. If α is some property, then its negation is designated by $\neg\alpha$: if the statement $\neg\alpha(x)$ is true, it means that object x does not have the property α. We have already encountered definitions in which it would have been convenient to use negation. In defining an incomplete quadratic equation, it would have been better to use the following properties:

property σ: coefficient a is equal to zero;

property β: coefficient b is equal to zero;

property γ: coefficient c is equal to zero.

Then the definition of an incomplete quadratic equation takes the following form: $(\neg\sigma) \wedge (\beta \vee \gamma)$; that is, an equation q should not have property σ, but should have at least one of the properties β or γ. As another example, in order to define parallel lines in space it is convenient to use the following properties:

α: the lines lie in the same plane;

σ: the lines have at least one common point.

Then the definition of parallel lines l and m in space takes the form $\alpha \wedge (\neg \sigma)$; i.e., the lines lie in the same plane and have no common points.

Let us give another example: the concept of an "extraneous root" of an equation. In solving an equation $f(x) = 0$ (e.g., the irrational equation

$$x + \sqrt{6-x} = 0,$$

the student must simplify (for example, by isolating the radical sign and squaring), so that the original equation is transformed into a new, equation $g(x) = 0$ (in this case, $x^2 = 6 - x \;[\Rightarrow x^2 + x - 6 = 0]$). The number x_0 is said to be an *extraneous root* if it is a root of the equation $g(x) = 0$, but it is not a root of the original equation $f(x) = 0$ (in this example, $x = 2$ is an extraneous root found by squaring both sides of the original equation). In order to establish a formula for this definition, let us introduce the following two properties:

property α: the number is a root of the derived equation $g(x) = 0$;

property β: the number is a root of the original equation $f(x) = 0$.

Then membership in the concept of an "extraneous root" is specified by the formula $\alpha \wedge (\neg \beta)$, that is, the number x_0 is an extraneous root if the statement $\alpha(x_0) \wedge (\neg \beta(x_0))$ is true.

Essential to many definitions are the words *all*, *any*, or *arbitrary*, which are replaced by the sign $\supset$ in mathematical logic, and the expressions *there is found*, *there exists*, *at least one*, which are replaced by the sign $\exists$. Thus, the definition of a composite number takes the following form: a natural number n is said to be composite if there exists a natural number k, distinct from 1 and n, which is a divisor of the number n. If we let $\alpha(k, n)$ be the property $1\ k\ n$, and let $\beta(k, n)$ be the property "k is a divisor of n," then the definition can be written in the form

$$(\exists^k)\; \alpha\,(k, n) \wedge \beta(k, n).$$

In other words, n is composite if there exists a k such that the statements $\alpha(k, n)$ and $\beta(k, n)$ will be true.

Using this definition, what mental activity must a person carry out in order to determine whether $n = 539$ is a composite number? According to property α, he would have to test integer values from 2 to 538, checking each time to see whether the number is a divisor of 539. When he finds that 2 is not a divisor of 539, he still cannot draw any conclusion since it is possible that he may find a divisor among the remaining numbers. Trying the number 3, he determines that it is not a divisor either. Once again, he should not jump to a conclusion. However, when he tests 7, he finds that it is a divisor: $539 \div 7 = 77$. He can immediately conclude that 539 is a composite number. Thus, if just one divisor is found, it can be immediately stated that a number is composite. If we make one trial after another and find no divisor, we have to continue our attempts to the end. Only after we are convinced that sifting through all the numbers will not yield a divisor can we conclude that a number is not composite.[8] This is the meaning of the symbol $\exists$.

We invite the reader to analyze on his own a definition containing the sign $\supset$. For example, we can take the following definition: *a sequence $a_1, a_2, a_3,...$ is said to be increasing if the inequality $a_{n+1} > a_n$ holds for any natural number n.*

The logical symbols considered above—$\wedge, \vee, \neg, \exists$, and $\supset$—in essence permit us to write most definitions used in mathematics (and some beyond mathematics). Another symbol $\rightarrow$ ("implication") is used considerably less often in definitions. We will become acquainted with the meaning of this logical symbol when we consider the features of concepts.

Conclusion

We cannot establish what belongs to the concept of a "parallelogram" in the same way as indicated on previously. When the properties of a parallelogram are studied in school, it is ascertained that it is not necessary to check whether both pairs of opposite sides in a quadrilateral are parallel. It is sufficient, for example, to determine that one pair of opposite sides are congruent and parallel. Or it is possible to establish that two pairs of opposite sides are congruent, or determine that the intersecting diagonals of the quadrilateral bisect each other, and so forth. Moreover, if it is clear that all the angles of the quadrilateral are right angles, or that all of its sides are equal, we also conclude that we have a parallelogram. In geometry such assertions are called *sufficient criteria* for a given concept.

What, in general, is a sufficient condition for a concept? In mathematics (and other sciences) it is often said that one statement "follows" or "proceeds" from another. The sign $\to$ is used to signify this. The notation $\alpha \to \beta$ means that statement α follows from β. For example, suppose that $\alpha(x)$ is the predicate "*in convex quadrilateral x all sides are equal*" and $\beta(x)$ is the predicate "*in quadrilateral x the diagonals are mutually perpendicular.*" Then $\alpha(x) \to \beta(x)$.

The logical operation $\to$ is the basis for introducing the concept of a "sufficient condition." Let σ be a definition of some concept P. An object x belongs to a certain concept P if it has property σ (i.e., if $\sigma(x)$ is true). Then let α be a property such that $\alpha \to \sigma$ (i.e., if $\alpha(x)$ is true, then so is $\sigma(x)$). Then α is said to be a sufficient condition for the concept P. For example, if all the sides of a quadrilateral are equal, that is a sufficient condition for the concept of a "quadrilateral with mutually perpendicular diagonals."

Let us analyze a number of sufficient conditions, using the example of the concept of "parallelogram." We designate by M the set of all plane convex quadrilaterals, assuming for convenience that in any quadrilateral the consecutive vertices are labeled A, B, C, and D, and that diagonals AC and BD intersect at point O. Now we introduce the following properties of the elements of the set M (that is, predicates in one variable for M):

α: $AB \parallel CD$;

β: $AD \parallel BC$;

γ: $AB = CD$;

δ: $AD = BC$;

ε: $AB = BC = CD = AD$;

η: $\angle A = \angle B = \angle C = \angle D = \pi/2$;

ξ: $AO = OC$;

λ: $BO = OD$.

Then the property $\sigma = \alpha \wedge \beta$ is a definition of the concept of a "parallelogram." Accordingly, from the indicated properties, we can compose a whole series of sufficient conditions for this concept. Thus, if $AB \parallel CD$ and $AB = CD$, then $AD \parallel BC$. In other words, $(\alpha \wedge \gamma) \to \sigma$; this means that $\alpha \wedge \gamma$ is a *sufficient condition* for the concept of "parallelogram." Similarly, $(\beta \wedge \delta) \to \sigma$, showing that $\beta \wedge \delta$ is also a sufficient condition. These two conditions combine in the following statement: *in order for a quadrilateral to be a parallelogram, it is sufficient that its two opposite sides be equal and parallel*. Then, as we know, $(\gamma \wedge \delta) \to \sigma$, so $\gamma \wedge \delta$ (pairwise equality of opposite sides) is another sufficient condition for a parallelogram. Noting that $\varepsilon \to \sigma$, we obtain another sufficient condition (for a quadrilateral to be a parallelogram, it is sufficient that all of its sides be equal). The property η is also a sufficient condition ($\eta \to \sigma$), since a quadrilateral with four right angles is a parallelogram. Finally, $(\xi \wedge \lambda)$ is another sufficient condition (for a quadrilateral to be a parallelogram, it is sufficient that its diagonals bisect each other).

In order to establish membership in a concept, we can use not only the initial definition of the concept, but any sufficient condition as well. Thus, if we have succeeded in establishing that at least one of the sufficient conditions $\alpha \wedge \gamma$, $\beta \wedge \delta$, ε, η, or $\xi \wedge \lambda$ is satisfied, then quadrilateral $ABCD$ is a parallelogram. This can be written symbolically in the form

$$[(\alpha \wedge \beta) \vee (\alpha \wedge \gamma) \vee (\beta \wedge \delta) \vee (\gamma \wedge \delta) \vee \varepsilon \vee \eta \vee (\xi \wedge \lambda)] \to \sigma.$$

If any one of the seven sufficient conditions *or* the original definition $\alpha \wedge \beta$ can be established, then property σ is satisfied and it follows that the quadrilateral belongs to the concept of a "parallelogram."

Note that some of the sufficient conditions indicated are *equivalent* to the definition, or, as we say, are *necessary and sufficient conditions*. Thus, the condition "the diagonals of a quadrilateral bisect each other" is both necessary and sufficient; i.e., it is equivalent to the definition. Indeed, not only is the conclusion $(\xi \wedge \lambda) \to \sigma$ correct, but also its converse, $\sigma \to (\xi \wedge \lambda)$: if a quadrilateral is a parallelogram, then its diagonals must bisect one another. Other conditions, however, such as η, are sufficient but not necessary, and therefore they are not equivalent to the definition. Indeed, the conclusion $\eta \to \sigma$ is correct (four right angles in a quadrilateral imply a parallelogram) but the converse $\sigma \to \eta$ does not hold (given a parallelogram, it is impossible to conclude that all of its angles are right angles).

The activity providing for the use of sufficient conditions of a concept (along with the definition) differs significantly from the activity involved in establishing membership in a concept using only the definition.

Suppose that we must establish, using a definition and a number of sufficient conditions, whether a certain quadrilateral is a parallelogram. For this purpose we can attempt to use the first group (the definition $\alpha \wedge \beta$) to check whether a pair of opposite sides are parallel. Let us assume that we have managed to establish that the quadrilateral has this first group of properties (i.e., $\alpha \wedge \beta$). We conclude at once that it is a parallelogram.

If it is not clear from the problem's conditions whether the quadrilateral has the first group of properties, we examine the second group (the sufficient condition $\alpha \wedge \gamma$). In other words, we check if it can be established whether the pair of sides *AB* and *CD* are a) equal and b) parallel. If we cannot obtain a positive answer even using the second group, we consider the third group $\beta \wedge \delta$, and so on.

Thus, the activity that should be performed by someone who is using a definition to establish whether an object belongs to a concept depends entirely on the connecting principle for the individual properties that make up the definition and the sufficient conditions, and not on the specific content of these properties. To establish what activity should be performed and in what sequence, one must dissect the definition and the relevant sufficient conditions into individual properties and establish which logical connectives relate these properties.

The foregoing discussion describes the mental activity carried out by a person who hopes to obtain a positive answer. But often, while attempting to obtain a positive answer, a person begins to wonder whether he

The Psychological Theory of Mastery

can obtain a negative answer to the question of membership in a concept. The *necessary conditions* of a concept are used for this purpose. Let us define precisely what this means. Again let σ be the definition of some concept P (i.e., object x belongs to concept P if it has property σ). Then let α be a property such that σ → α, so that if σ(x) is true, then α(x) will also automatically be true (in other words, if object x belongs to concept P, then it immediately has property α). Then α is said to be the *consequence* of membership in the concept P or a necessary *condition* of concept P. For example, it is a necessary condition of the concept of a "parallelogram" that opposite angles be equal (Fig. 51).

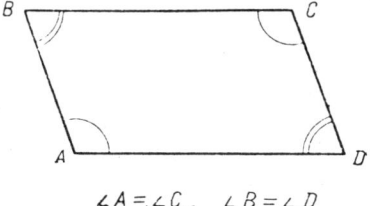

∠A = ∠C., ∠B = ∠D

Figure 51.

Clearly, if an object x has no necessary condition of a concept, it does not belong to the concept. For example, if a quadrilateral x does not have the property γ, i.e., the statement ¬γ(x) is true (so that $AB \neq CD$), then x is not a parallelogram.

A condition that is simultaneously necessary and sufficient is *equivalent* to the definition of a concept. In other words, if σ is a definition of concept P, and μ is both a necessary (σ → μ) and a sufficient (μ → σ) condition for P, then an object x belongs to concept P if and only if it has the property μ (that is, μ(x) is true). In this case, instead of two relations σ → μ and μ → σ, we write one: μ ↔ σ. This means that property μ is equivalent to the definition σ. For example,

$$(\gamma \wedge \delta) \leftrightarrow (\alpha \wedge \beta)$$

indicates that the property $\gamma \wedge \delta$ is equivalent to the definition of a parallelogram $\alpha \wedge \beta$ (thus, for a quadrilateral to be a parallelogram, it is necessary and sufficient for its opposite sides to be pairwise equal). On the other hand, δ and ϵ are sufficient but not necessary conditions for a parallelogram.

How can we obtain the various properties equivalent to the definition of a concept? One possible way is to take the simplest and most elementary necessary conditions of a concept. For a parallelogram, these conditions are $\alpha, \beta, \gamma, \delta, \xi$, and λ, (and possibly a number of other conditions (for example, equal opposite angles). Note that any conjunction of necessary conditions is a new necessary condition for the concept. If each of the properties α, β, γ, etc., is necessary for membership in the concept, then pairwise conjunction of the properties (e.g., $\alpha \wedge \beta, \alpha \wedge \gamma, \gamma \wedge \beta, \beta \wedge \delta$, etc.) will also be necessary. Therefore, to obtain necessary and sufficient conditions for a concept, we can keep forming new necessary conditions by composing multiple conjunctions of elementary necessary conditions (i.e., examining conditions $\alpha \wedge \beta, \alpha \wedge \gamma, \beta \wedge \gamma$, etc.). As soon as a condition sufficient for membership in the concept is obtained, we will then have a necessary and sufficient condition. Here it is desirable that the necessary and sufficient condition thus obtained not contain superfluous properties. For example, the condition $\beta \wedge \gamma \wedge \delta$ will of course be necessary and sufficient, but it contains a superfluous property since discarding β leaves the simpler necessary and sufficient condition $\gamma \wedge \delta$. Thus, among these properties of a parallelogram $\alpha, \beta, \gamma, \delta, \xi$ (each of which is a necessary condition), the following are examples of equivalent combinations defining a parallelogram:

$\alpha \wedge \gamma$: two opposite sides are equal and parallel;
$\beta \wedge \delta$: the other two opposite sides are equal and parallel;
$\gamma \wedge \delta$: the opposite sides are pairwise equal;
$\xi \wedge \lambda$: the diagonals bisect each other;
$\xi \wedge \alpha$: two opposite sides are parallel and one diagonal bisects the other.

The Psychological Theory of Mastery

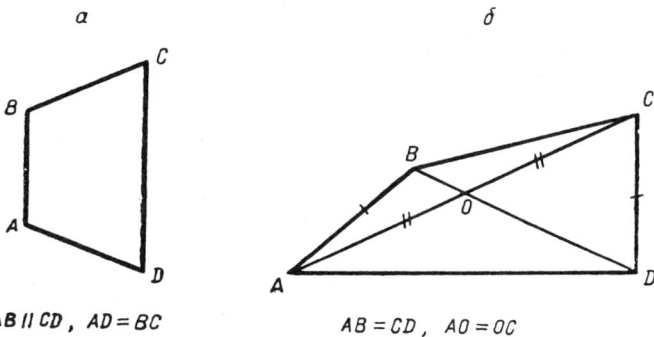

Figure 52.

Of course, not every conjunction of necessary conditions is certain to be necessary and sufficient. For example, the conditions $\alpha \wedge \delta$ and $\gamma \wedge \xi$ are not sufficient (Fig. 52a, b).

We have noted above two ways of using necessary conditions: (1) failure to satisfy any one necessary condition enables us to conclude non-membership in the concept; (2) a combination (more precisely, a conjunction) of necessary conditions can result in finding a necessary and sufficient condition (that is, properties equivalent to a definition).

It is essential to understand that there is a third, perhaps most important way of using necessary conditions. The point is that attributing an object to a concept is not always the final goal of reasoning. More frequently, membership in a concept is established in order to use some *consequence* of including an object in a concept. Mastery of the consequences (the necessary conditions) is a mandatory condition for mastery of a concept, since these consequences can be applied during the solution of a number of problems. Here, for example, is a partial list of the consequences of the fact that an object is a rectangular parallelepiped: opposite faces are equal; there are 12 edges; each edge has three other edges parallel to it; there are 8 vertices; three edges meet at each vertex; two faces meet at each edge; etc.

After establishing that an object belongs to a concept, the subsequent mental activity consists in choosing from the known consequences the one that can be useful in solving the given problem. And again, with some training this activity proceeds in a condensed and automatic way—that is, it seems to the person that he saw at once, without recalling anything, the conclusion that is the key to the solution of the problem.

Adequate Manipulative Activity

It is no accident that we have dwelt in such detail on the various forms of mental activity. The point is that, as Galperin's research has shown, [9] the most effective form of learning is *organization for performing activity adequate to this knowledge.*

For example, suppose we want a fourth-grader to master the definition of the concept of a "rectangular parallelepiped," and that mastery means correctly establishing whether or not a certain solid belongs to this concept. The best way to check whether a solid belongs to the concept of a "rectangular parallelepiped" is for the student to have to (1) check whether there are six faces, and (2) determine that all the faces are rectangles. According to the definition, the student can conclude that "yes, this is a rectangular parallelepiped" if and only if both answers are positive. To check mastery, it is necessary to have a collection of solids, including solids which:

> have both properties (1) and (2) (i. e., rectangular parallelepipeds);
> have only property (1);
> have only property (2); and,
> have neither property (1) nor property (2).

It is a good idea to have several solids of each type. Sorting out these solids and checking for each one whether conditions (1) and (2) are satisfied is adequate manipulative activity. The student accomplishes the activity in an external, material form: he holds a real object in his hands (a model of a solid), fingers its edges and faces, and so forth. But this activity corresponds precisely to the mental activity that a person carries out in establishing membership in the concept of a "rectangular parallelepiped." A set of geometric solids is important for controlling proper performance of this activity.

After a preliminary introduction to the definition, students are asked to determine whether certain solids are rectangular parallelepipeds. Here the teacher requires that the students not simply state, "Yes, it is a rectangular parallelepiped," or "No, it is not a rectangular parallelepiped," but also count the faces and check whether all the faces are rectangles.

This "external" form of activity permits control over the course of performing each "baby step." It is important for the students to encounter every possible case. Some of the objects given for identification should have all the specific differences included in the definition: they are rectangular parallelepipeds. Others should have none of the specific differences included in the definition: they are not rectangular parallelepipeds.

Thus, if a new activity is in principle adequate to certain knowledge, learning theory dictates creating a completely distinct class of instructional manipulatives. Their purpose is to ensure that both the student and the person regulating his activity can see how each operation is carried out. In other words, school materials should ensure that an activity is performed so that all the condensed and automatic mental operations are evident to everyone, especially the learner.

Manipulative object activity (counting the faces on a model, etc.) should gradually give way to mental activity. In the case under consideration, this means asking the student at this latest stage to state immediately whether or not a solid is a rectangular parallelepiped. Only in some instances should it be suggested that he refer to the definition.

At the same time students should begin solving problems in which a solid is described verbally. They can be asked to determine whether a solid is a rectangular parallelepiped. Such problems familiarize the students with yet another kind of conclusion—the indefinite answer. (Unfortunately at present, students almost never have to give an indefinite answer. Problems are selected so that they can always state whether or not an object belongs to a concept.)

Suppose, for example, that a problem tells us that one of the faces of a solid is a rectangle. If, when asked whether the solid must be rectangular parallelepiped, a student answers either "Yes, it is" or "No, it isn't," this suggests the student should return to manipulative activity. The student can be shown a model that contradicts the conclusion, and he has another opportunity to count the faces and check whether they are all rectangles. In this way students realize that they must answer: "It is unknown whether this solid is a rectangular parallelepiped."

Thus, one of the basic tenets of the psychological theory of learning is that an operation that we want to teach someone to perform mentally should first be presented in an external, material form. Then the knowledge is mastered without special efforts at memorization; it is learned in the process of concrete, manipulative activity.

In the approach that we have described for organizing mastery of the definition of the concept of a "rectangular parallelepiped," the students' activity is always directed towards using the definition. However, the students learn not only the definition of a concept, but something larger as well—a general method of working with definitions. This is demonstrated when a student who needs to establish whether something belongs to a concept given by a new definition grasps the essence of what he is doing more readily. The teacher needs less time and effort to explain why he must check all the properties that make up the definition and to explain what conclusion should be drawn in which case.

Clearly, when beginning the topic "The Rectangular Parallelepiped and Its Volume," the students can be introduced to activity directed at using the definition—for example, while they are learning the definition of the concept of a "rectangle." In this case they will require less practice to learn the definition of the concept of a "rectangular parallelepiped."

Let us give another example of adequate manipulative activity. Consider the concept of labelling angles with three letters. If, for example, an angle is designated as "angle *MON*," this means that the property $\alpha \wedge$

The Psychological Theory of Mastery

$\beta \wedge \gamma$ is satisfied, where the "elementary" properties α, β, and γ have the following meaning:

α: the middle letter (in this case, O) designates the vertex of the angle;

β: the initial letter (M) designates a point on one side of the angle;

γ: the last letter (N) designates a point on the other side of the angle.

The activity adequate to this portion of knowledge consists in correlating the points (the vertex and the points on the sides) with the letters included in the angle designation.

Making the activity concrete can consist, say, in correlating letters and points with an external image that everyone in the class can see. An example of this correlation is provided by two assignments that might be incorporated into a written workbook (Fig. 53a, b).

Fill in the blanks.

1) To designate angle 1 by three letters, we must place the letter _____ in the middle. We can put the letters _____ and _____, or _____ and _____, on the sides.

Answer: Angle 1 can be designated by the letters _____.

2) Angle 2 can be designated by three letters: _____, _____, or _____.

The external form is only one way of organizing activity adequate to knowledge. What is more, it is very important gradually to lessen and finally to eliminate concrete, manipulative activity (external visuality), translating it into an internal framework. The teacher can gradually make this transition by using oral identification of operations (the "talking aloud" stage in Galperin's terminology). This idea can be illustrated by Figure 19. Using this figure, the teacher can ask the students to find the angles as he names them orally, as well as naming the angles that he indicates visually. We recommend not just performing the appropriate mental activity and giving an answer, but performing adequate manipulation of objects. For example, upon being asked to "indicate the angle

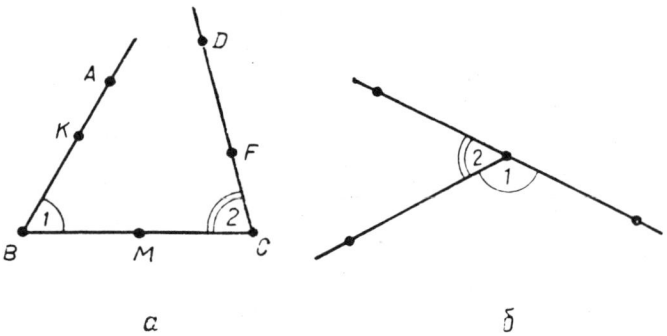

Figure 53.

MKN," the student should explain every "baby step" and every operation leading to the answer. The student should respond in roughly the following way:

> 1) Since the letter *K* is in the middle, this means that we must find an angle with its vertex at point *K*;
>
> 2) the letter *M* comes first so one side should pass through point *M*—that is, ray *KM* is one side of the angle;
>
> 3) since the letter *N* is last, the second side passes through point *N*—that is, ray *KN* will be the second side;
>
> 4) therefore, rays *KM* and *KN* are the angle's sides; here is the angle (the student points it out).

When the activity is organized in this way, students very quickly learn to read and find the necessary angles.

In conclusion we should like to emphasize that external, concrete activity is preferred primarily in those instances when new activity is in principle appropriate to the knowledge. If activity that students have already mastered is appropriate for new knowledge, then the activity can

The Psychological Theory of Mastery

be organized in other forms (based on the existing knowledge), including purely mental activity. Suppose we have to teach students the conditions for parallel vectors. One problem that may have to be solved is the following: *given the coordinates of the four vertices of quadrilateral ABCD, determine whether this quadrilateral is a trapezoid.* The solution to this problem (that is, establishing membership in the concept) is based on the definition of a trapezoid, which takes the form $\alpha \vee \beta$. For comparison, let us give three numerical variants of this problem, indicating in each instance the appropriate activity to be performed. In order to check whether the straight lines are parallel, we will use the proportionality of vectors directed along these lines. We note that in the problems cited below the numbers are sufficiently large that a graphic solution, checking for parallelism using a set square and a ruler, will not be convincing (Figs. 54-56 illustrate these problems).

Problem 1. $A(-15, 8)$, $B(22, 73)$, $C(66, 18)$, $D(-8, -112)$.

We check for property α (i.e., is it true that $AB \parallel CD$). $\vec{AB}$ has the coordinates: $x = 22 - (-15) = 37$; $y = 73 - 8 = 65$; i.e., $\vec{AB} = \{37, 65\}$. $\vec{CD}$ has the coordinates: $x = -8 - 66 = -74$; $y = -112 - 18 = -130$; i.e., $\vec{CD} = \{-74, -130\}$.

It is easy to see that the vectors are proportional ($\vec{CD} = -2 \times AB$), that is $AB \parallel CD$. Property α is satisfied; so, without checking further, we can state that $ABCD$ is a trapezoid.

Problem 2. $A(-20, 3)$, $B(23, 74)$, $C(67, 19)$, $D(28, -57)$.

We check for property α (i.e., is it true that $AB \parallel CD$). We find that $\vec{AB} = \{43, 71\}$; $\vec{CD} = \{-39, -78\}$.[10]

These vectors are not proportional, so $AB \nparallel CD$. Though property α is not satisfied, we cannot yet say anything about membership in the concept; we must check for property β.

We have: $\vec{BC} = \{44; -55\}$; $\vec{AD} = \{48, -60\}$. These vectors are proportional ($\vec{AD} = (12/11)BC$) so $BC \parallel AD$ and property β is satisfied. Thus, although α is not satisfied, β is, and so $ABCD$ is a trapezoid.

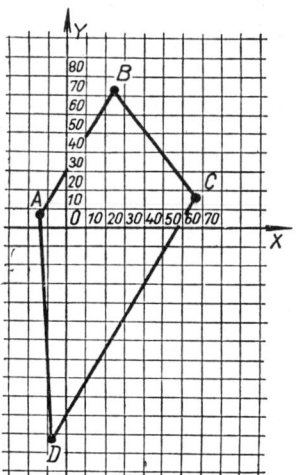

Figure 54.

Problem 3. $A(-10, 5)$, $B(27, 70)$, $C(71, 15)$, $D(33, -49)$.

We check for property α ($AB \parallel CD$). We find that $\vec{AB} = \{37, 65\}$; $\vec{CD} = \{-38, -64\}$.

These vectors are not proportional, so $AB \not\parallel CD$. Thus property α is not satisfied, and we cannot yet say anything about membership in the concept; we must check for property β.

We have: $\vec{BC} = \{44, -55\}$; $\vec{AD} = \{43, -54\}$. These vectors are not proportional so $BC \times AD$ as well. Since neither property α nor property β is satisfied, $ABCD$ is not a trapezoid.

These problems include all possible cases of appropriate activity for establishing whether a quadrilateral given by its coordinates belongs to the concept of a "trapezoid." Of course, these problems are inapplicable as exercises for learning this concept, since proportional vectors come considerably later in the curriculum.

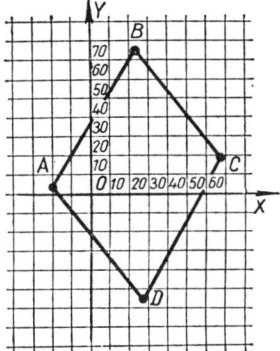

Figure 55.

In solving these problems, students deal not with objects of the real world, but with numbers and points, i.e., with mathematical abstractions. This by no means contradicts the idea of adequate "external, manipulative" activity. We cited above A.N. Kolmogorov's statement to the effect that abstract concepts are reality for the mathematician. Therefore, the term "adequate manipulative activity" should be interpreted conditionally when applied to mathematics. The objects actively manipulated can be abstract concepts that have been thoroughly mastered (i.e., abstractions from previous levels). It is in this sense that we must often view the somewhat unsuccessful term "adequate manipulative activity" adopted in Galperin's theory when it is applied in mathematics (and sometimes in other fields).

Must Adequate Activity Be Performed?

Doubts may arise about the necessity for conducting special work and selecting special material for implementing adequate manipulative activ-

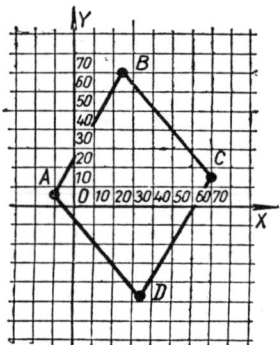

Figure 56.

ity. Some teachers may regard all this as superfluous, thinking that all they have to do is make it clear to students what they are to do and how they should do it. In this sense "understanding" can be identified with what in reality might be called "learning" (in the sense that what is said does not evoke negative emotions in the students, and they are prepared to agree with the conclusions drawn by the teacher). But this identification is inappropriate.

Understanding is a necessary and essential condition for successful learning. But understanding is not enough for students to operate with their knowledge successfully and perform the necessary activity.

The following situation is probably familiar to every teacher. The lesson has been going well and actively. In the teacher's opinion, his explanations have been understood well by the class. But the next day a seemingly elementary question proves to be beyond their powers. One after another the students either fail to answer or do so altogether unsatisfactorily.

What does a teacher do in this case? Most frequently he accuses the students of laziness and inattentiveness, or suggests reviewing a defini-

The Psychological Theory of Mastery

tion. The students review, but err repeatedly in establishing membership in a concept, or ascribe properties to objects which they do not have.

What are the reasons for the mistakes? Many investigators have attempted to answer this question. It has been established that mistakes are often related to deficiencies in the preliminary introduction to a concept. For example, the literature describes cases where a teacher, in introducing his students to the definition of the concept of a "straight angle," demonstrates only those angles whose sides are parallel to the lower edge of the blackboard and whose vertices are marked off in the middle of the segments that serve as the sides of the straight angles. As a result, a student may literally quote the definition correctly, but actually supplement it with properties it does not include.

However, deficiencies in the preliminary introduction are far from the only reasons for failure. As a rule, the reason is that although the students may have understood the material, they have not learned to perform activity that is adequate to the knowledge—they have not mastered the concept. As a result the assignments offered by the teacher, which ask students to determine whether objects belong to a given concept, do not always achieve their goal. The students formulate the definition but actually use something quite different for establishing membership in the concept. We will show below what this "something different" is.

If a teacher demonstrates a model or a diagram, the students often draw a conclusion about membership in a concept, not because they have checked whether all the requirements of the definition have been satisfied, but simply because it is "similar." The mental image of the model or diagram has become in their minds a standard by which to compare new models and diagrams.

Is it good or bad that the students appeal to established standards? In our view, it is good. However, in order to preclude mistakes, it is essential in the initial development of a concept for students to consider basic visual examples for which membership in the concept is to be established. Second, in difficult cases they must be taught to use a definition or other sufficient evidence of membership in the concept.

Unfortunately, students generally do not know how to do this. Let us give an example. We asked a large group of good or excellent students in grades 8 and 9 who had studied in various schools under different instructors to establish whether the angles in a drawing were adjacent or vertical angles, and to substantiate their conclusions. Most of the group could not manage the substantiation (558 out of 680 responses, or 82%, were incorrect). As a reason for why the specified angles could be regarded as vertical, about 70% of the students wrote that "the angles are vertical because they are equal." About 90% asserted that the angles were adjacent "since the sum of the angles is equal to 180°."

Some of the answers to the question "Why can the given angles be regarded as vertical?" suggest that students do not always focus on the properties that they report using in establishing membership in a concept. Many students cited the standard textbook definition: "Two angles are said to be vertical if the sides of one angle are extensions of the sides of the other." And here, right under the definition, we might read: "I check opposite angles with a protractor: if the angles are equal, they are vertical."

Thus, many students indicated one reason for verticality when they in fact used another. This is well illustrated by the transcript of a conversation with Sasha K., a ninth-grader making excellent progress. The response is quite characteristic, and we will cite it in full.

Experimenter: Why do you believe that vertical angles are represented in the figure? (Indicates the angles that the student has identified.)

Subject: They are equal.

Experimenter: Take some instruments and check whether they are really vertical angles. I see you have used some instruments.

Subject: No, I haven't. It is so obvious.

Experimenter: Can you still check whether these angles are vertical, not just because "it is obvious," but by using some instruments?

Subject: I can. (Uses a rules and realizes that the sides of the angles lie on the same line.)

The Psychological Theory of Mastery

Thus the student asserted that he used equal angles as an indication, when in reality he used another property—"the sides of the angles lie on the same line."

The students' explanations show that they do not understand what conditions are essential for establishing membership in a concept. Moreover, the poorly selected problems that are usually given students in school yield a primary orientation only towards individual properties. This has been noted and discussed in the works of V.I. Zykova[11] and N. F. Talyzina.[12]

For example, in establishing whether given angles are adjacent, students are usually given only contiguous angles. To obtain an answer, they therefore need only to check one thing—whether the sum of these angles is 180°. Exclusive orientation toward this property means that the other properties necessary for adjacent angles (a common vertex and a common side) are not considered at all. This stands out with particular clarity in solving problems involving groups of properties that are insufficient for establishing whether objects belong to the concept.

Let us cite one such assignment as an example: *two angles are equal to 100° and 80°. Are these angles adjacent?*

The proper conclusion ("it is impossible to tell") to asssignments such as this one is likely only if the students are oriented toward the entire set of necessary conditions. Almost no participant in our study was able to cope with this or similar tasks. Out of 450 students, only 35 solved it correctly (less than 8%); the remaining 415 gave incorrect answers.

It is interesting that most students drew the conclusion that "the object does not belong to the concept" primarily only when they made a diagram for the problem and obtained a figure that was unlike the one demanded in the problem. For example, in stating whether the 100° and 80° angles were adjacent, some students constructed the angles separately (Fig. 57). This is the reason why 40% of the students said that the angles in this problem were not adjacent.

Even faced with the fact that a certain set of properties was insufficient for relating an object to a given concept, the students still used it as sufficient in other problems. For example, of the 42 who noted that

Figure 57.

knowing that the sum of the angles was 180° is insufficient to establish that they are adjacent, 35 still used this property in the next problem. They claimed that the angles were adjacent since their sum was 180°.

Let us give the transcript of a conversation with Nadya S., an eighth-grader who was making good progress.

Experimenter: Why do you believe that the angles in [the problem] are adjacent?

Subject: Their sum is 180°.

Experimenter: And why do you believe that the angles of 100° and 80° in the previous problem were not adjacent?

Subject: Why? Here they are (indicates Figure 57). Here is one, here is the second. They aren't adjacent.

Experimenter: What is the sum of these angles?

Subject [surprised]: One hundred eighty degrees.

Thus, in establishing whether a the figures in a diagram belong to a concept, students orient themselves toward visual images; but if the conditions indicate a system of properties possessed by an object, then they orient themselves toward specific, ordinary properties. This orientation toward individual properties is due to the nature of the problems they have encountered. In these problems they had to establish, upon discerning objects, the presence of the same properties, which were not always sufficient. This resulted in numerous mistakes by students in the above experiment.

Therefore it is utterly insufficient to teach students simply to formulate a definition, or to cite examples and non-examples of objects belonging to a concept. They must be taught to perform an activity adequate to the concept. If the students who took part in the experiment had developed skill in checking the presence in a figure of all properties constituting the definition ("subsuming under a concept"), then the number of mistakes would have been minimized.

Educational Materials—The Material Basis for Performing Adequate Activity

The most effective way to mastery of knowledge is to organize activity that is adequate to the knowledge. The instructor's first step when planning to organize activity in the class should be to determine what activity is required for learning the given concept. This work is somewhat eased because one activity is adequate to a large class of concepts: establishing membership in a concept and searching for the consequences of an object's membership in a concept. For example, in planning to teach the concept of a "rectangular parallelepiped," the instructor plans the work in: (1) identifying examples and non-examples of rectangular parallelepipeds based on the definition; and (2) finding consequences of the fact that an object is a rectangular parallelepiped.

The plan we outline can be executed successfully if the teacher himself has a secure knowledge of just what must be checked in establishing membership in a concept. Definitions are given in textbooks in a comprehensive form, without being broken down into individual properties joined by logical connectives. Thus, we must think of a list of consequences (necessary criteria) of membership in a concept—the very consequences that are most often applied in problem-solving. Naturally, before beginning to apply a number of such consequences, we must identify each of them. And again it is necessary to analyze which activity is adequate to each consequence.

All of this leads inevitably to the question of how to create activity that is adequate to knowledge. Since in many cases this activity should involve manipulatives and other tangible material, we arrive at the question of the selection of educational materials.

The above observations enable us to draw a number of conclusions about the nature of educational materials for organizing the mastery of a given topic. First, they should give the teacher an opportunity to reveal the essence of the activity that is adequate to the given knowledge. When an activity that is new in principle is adequate to some knowledge, the collection of instructional aids should: (1) provide for the students' use of external, manipulative activity; and, (2) gradually move from explicitly visual activity to activity in an internal, mental framework.

The use of educational materials under this approach is neither random nor episodic. After analyzing the knowledge that underlies mastery and establishing what activity is adequate for this knowledge, we can indicate precisely what types of instructional media should be used. Here it makes sense to speak not of individual components of educational materials, but rather an entire collection of them—a set of educational materials.[13]

In Table 1.2 we mentioned items included in an instructional unit on the topic "The Volume of a Rectangular Parallelepiped" created in the Laboratory of Mathematics and Programmed Instruction of the Scientific Research Institute for School Materials and Technical Instructional Media. The aids reinforce and coordinate with each other, performing a variety of functions. Thus, by showing models of a concept, single-concept films are the most effective for clarifying the essence of a new activity. Here the students themselves are not yet performing adequate activity, but are only becoming acquainted with it, observing how the activity is performed on the screen. The role of filmstrips is analogous. It is harder to show the dynamics of performing an activity through filmstrips. On the other hand, it is easier to focus the students' attention on its individual, basic features.

A printed workbook is quite valuable for properly directing a student in a new activity. The workbook includes written models for performing the necessary activity, which reinforce and make precise the models that have been described aloud to the students. The workbook assignments are chosen so the students will learn the material and simultaneously perform activity that is adequate to the knowledge. The workbook permits the students' work to be individualized, helping every student to perform the necessary activity. However, in many cases it is advisable to organize discussion periods during class. Slides and working charts are handy for this purpose.

The theory of mastery defines only the basic kinds of assignments. In addition, many tasks, both quite difficult and comparatively easy, are indirectly related to adequate activity, yet also require cleverness, resourcefulness, and guesswork. Such tasks are also clearly useful. Some of them are included in the workbook, others are in the slide series, and still others are on the problem cards.

It must be noted that there are essential differences in the adequate activity (and therefore the materials required for this activity) during the initial introduction to a concept and after learning the definition. Let us begin by considering the materials needed for an initial introduction to a concept.

First, the students should understand the essence of the activity. Preliminary introduction with a new activity takes place simultaneously with the initial introduction to the new content—above all, the concepts. In the educational and methods literature, special attention has been paid to preliminary introduction to concepts. For example, the well-known Soviet scientist A.Ya. Khinchin has noted the crucial importance of the nature of the first encounter with a given concept in subsequently establishing that concept.[15] Khinchin indicated that even after a person has reached maturity, mentioning certain term almost always elicits associations with the initial encounter. The entire style, effectiveness, and practical efficacy of a concept, as a rule, depend essentially on the situation or surroundings in which it first entered our consciousness.

Many investigators consider the most important aspect of an initial introduction to concepts to be prior familiarity with what is being defined. For example, before giving a definition of similarity, the teacher should show maps of various localities done in different scales, prints made from a photographic negative with a different enlargement coefficient, or other examples of similar figures.

What is the purpose of demonstrating objects belonging to the given concept? *First*, it eliminates the need for a so-called *existence* theorem to show that objects with the requisite properties can actually be constructed. To be sure, students very rarely question the existence of the required objects in any clear way, since this abstract formulation of a question is still foreign to the child's concrete style of thinking. Moreover, this formulation of the question leads away from the objectives of school instruction. Therefore, exhibiting objects to *remove* the question of existence, making new objects "palpable" and "natural," and therefore real, is exceptionally important. The question of introducing negative numbers (especially the number -1) evokes no difficulties[16] (the history of mathematics shows clearly how great they have been[17]) only because students are used to negative temperatures and scales with markings on either side of the zero—that is, they have dealt practically with objects that reflect membership in the given concept. On the other hand, introducing complex numbers almost always gives rise to the question of their existence, primarily because no objects have been exhibited to describe or reflect the concept of a complex number.

Second, displaying objects that belong to a given concept enables the teacher to prepare for introducing a definition, making the introduction to the new definition active and creative.

Third, exhibiting various objects pertaining to a given concept permits attention to be focused on the essential properties, enabling us to ignore properties irrelevant to the area of inquiry.

Fourth, this demonstration provides a model for establishing membership in a concept based on the essential properties—i.e., a model for performing adequate activity.

The theory of mastery attaches particular significance to preliminary introduction to the knowledge being studied when the activity that is adequate to the knowledge is new in principle. It is important to show the students the essence of the activity, separate the essential from the secondary, and provide a model for performing the new activity. Of course, visual media can play a great role in this process. Let us clarify what we have said using the example of an introduction to the concept of a "rectangular parallelepiped" in grade 4.

The instructor usually brings a few solids—rectangular parallelepipeds, prisms, and the like—to class. The students are shown a model of a rectangular parallelepiped and asked to select the solids that are like the model. Here it is important to direct their attention toward what is important or essential for the concept of a "rectangular parallelepiped." The shape of the solid is of primary importance.

This is not the first time students encounter the need to identify from a collection of objects those which have a certain shape. For example, they are already familiar with rectangles, circles, and triangles. Before beginning to teach them about rectangular parallelepipeds, it is advisable to ask them to identify the objects in a group that have a familiar shape—such as a rectangle. Such assignments enable them to recall that the material, color, purpose, etc., are nonessential properties of the objects called "rectangles," "circles," "squares," etc. After this preliminary work, when the students have already chosen solids that are similar in shape to a model they are shown, they can transfer what they have previously learned to the new concept.

Suppose the students have selected a number of solids that they think are rectangular parallelepipeds. Some of the selections may not be rectangular parallelepipeds, while some that are may have been left out. The teacher first calls their attention to the solids that are rectangular parallelepipeds. Examining these solids, contrasting them with those which are not rectangular parallelepipeds, enables the students to "discover" the following definition:

A rectangular parallelepiped is a solid (1) bounded by six faces, (2) with all faces being rectangles.

The solids that not all students include among the rectangular parallelepipeds can be used naturally to ask students how we can ascertain whether a given solid is a rectangular parallelepiped. Counting the faces (there should be six of them) and checking whether all the faces are rectangles provides a model of the required activity for establishing membership of an object in the class of rectangular parallelepipeds.

Various methods for acquainting students with a definition and subsequently making the definition exact have been elaborated. Of particular importance is the principle of *varying the nonessential properties* of objects belonging to a certain concept.[18]

According to this principle, the formation of concepts should proceed with varied material, selected so that only the *essential* features of the concept remain constant. For example, in forming the concept of a "rectangular parallelepiped" it is recommended that not one, but many different rectangular parallelepipeds be shown, large and small, with elongated and square faces, in various locations in space. This means that students should see, among other things, models in which one dimension is either many times greater than the other two (e.g., a ruler) or much smaller (e.g., a slab of tile), and so forth.

It is important to foresee which solids the students might erroneously take to be rectangular parallelepipeds. For example, a right non-rectangular prism, a three-dimensional cross, and a letter box (Fig. 58) should be shown as non-examples. The preceding observations pertain to the initial introduction to a concept. We turn now to the organization of adequate activity *after* introduction to the definition.

For an activity to be performed successfully, the students must be provided with models of it. The primary model may be the teacher's explanation organized using single-concept films and filmstrip frames. But this does not address the problem completely. We know how hard it

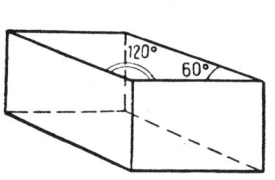 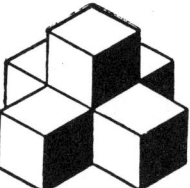 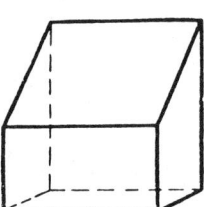

Figure 58.

The Psychological Theory of Mastery

is for students (particularly in the primary grades) to formulate their ideas clearly, and especially to relate these ideas to the execution of an activity.

Workbooks can make this task easier. This kind of workbook differs from the ordinary type in that the conditions of problems are printed in it, diagrams have already been made (where such diagrams might otherwise have been simply copied from problem books), and so forth. All of this saves a great deal of time, i.e., as we noted in Chapter 1, it solves important biotechnological questions. But another aspect of this instructional medium is much more essential for the organization of adequate activity: its high level of *instructional orientation.*

A number of the problems in the workbook come with incomplete solutions in which individual words or computations are omitted. This provides a model of an appropriate reasoning process, while also requiring specific activity adequate to the solution of this and similar problems. Solving the problems requires filling in the blanks. We have included examples of these assignments in Chapter 1. Let us give two more examples that are directly related to the concept of a "rectangular parallelepiped."

Assignment 1. *Fill in the blanks in the following sentences:*

To find out whether a solid is a rectangular parallelepiped, we must:

1) count to see how many faces it has; a rectangular parallelepiped has _____ faces;

2) see whether all the faces of the solid are rectangles; in a rectangular parallelepiped all the faces are _____.

Assignment 2. *Determine whether this solid is a rectangular parallelepiped* (Fig. 59).

Solution.

1) We count to see how many faces the solid has. This solid has _____ faces.

A rectangular parallelepiped has _____ faces. We do not need to check the second statement.

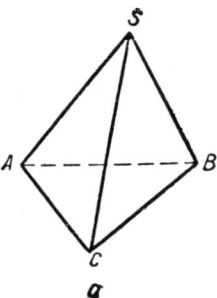

Figure 59.

Answer. This solid is not _____.

Later—e.g., when solving problems given on cards—the instructions can be reduced to writing the answer according to the following pattern:

This _____, since: 1) _____; and 2) _____.

Consider the following example showing how to choose instructional media that provide mastery of the relevant features of a concept. This example involves mastery of the property "opposite faces of a rectangular parallelepiped are equal."

To organize mastery of this property, we must first develop the concepts of an "adjacent face" and an "opposite face." To establish membership in these concepts, we check whether the two faces have a common edge. If they do, the faces are adjacent; otherwise they are opposite.

Obviously, it can be determined whether there is a common edge for two indicated faces by means of either a model or a diagram of a rectangular parallelepiped. The printed workbook can give the line of reasoning. Let us give an example of such an assignment.

Assignment 6. *Fill in the blanks* (see Fig. 60).

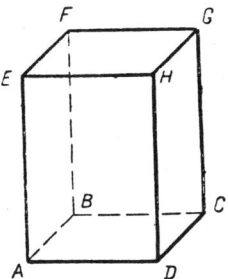

Figure 60.

Faces ____ and ____ are adjacent since they have a common edge AD.

Faces ____ and ____ are adjacent since they have a common edge GH.

Faces ____ and ____ are adjacent since they have a common edge ____.

Faces *ABFE* and ____ are opposite since they have no common edges.

It is useful to organize practice in determining whether faces are adjacent or opposite, so that the students have to establish the presence of a common edge and the teacher can easily determine whether they are performing the activity properly.

Activity promoting familiarity with the equal opposite faces of rectangular parallelepipeds can be reduced to taking a rectangle that completely covers one face and "fitting" it onto the other faces. If the student performing this activity is working with a rectangular parallelepicped in which all the dimensions are different, he easily realizes that only the opposite face is equal to the one he started with (Fig. 60). If the student

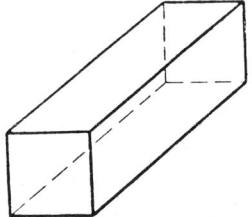

Figure 61.

Figure 62.

The Psychological Theory of Mastery 131

is given either a square prism (Figs. 61 and 62) or a cube, he can determine that there might four or six equal faces.

It is important for the students to be oriented toward searching for opposite faces when they establish the necessary equality of faces. Since this is related to the method of reasoning, model lines of reasoning are given in the workbook. Let us give one last assignment as an example.

Assignment 8. *Fill in the blanks* (Fig. 60).

The face of a rectangular parallelepiped has the shape _____. In rectangular parallelepiped *ABCDEFGH*, face *ABCD* is equal to face _____ since these are _____ faces.

Face *BFGC* is _____ to face *AEHD*, since it is _____.

3

The Concept of Volume in Modern Mathematics and Its Formation in Grade 4

The Axiomatic Definition of Volume

To describe the concept of "volume" in modern mathematics, we first identify the class of *cubable* solids. A cubable solid E is then taken as a standard for measuring volumes and called the *unit of volume*. Every cubable solid A is associated with a positive number $V(A)$, which is said to be the volume of the solid A. Here it is required that

$$V(E) = 1. \tag{1}$$

Volume is a positive *function* on the set of all cubable solids and takes on only positive values:

$$V(A) > 0 \tag{2}$$

The preceding two conditions do not, however, provide a complete definition of the concept of volume. For a function $V(A)$ to be called a volume, it must satisfy two more conditions. First, congruent solids must have identical volumes:

$$\text{if } A = B, \text{ then } V(A) = V(B) \tag{3}$$

The last condition is that if a solid A is composed of two adjacent parts B and C, then the volume of A is equal to the sum of the volumes of solids B and C:

$$V(A) = V(B) + V(C) \tag{4}$$

The Concept of Volume

This gives a complete inventory of all the conditions for stating that the function $V(A)$ is a volume for the class of cubable solids under consideration. Of course, in order to precisely formulate this definition of volume, we must not only indicate the class of cubable solids and the unit of volume, but also define clearly what is meant by "congruent solids" and "a solid A is made up of two adjacent parts B and C." Different interpretations of these terms may lead to different concepts of volume.

A simpler and more precise definition consists of the following conditions:

> a) The class of cubable solids consists of all polyhedral solids.
>
> b) The unit of volume is a cube.
>
> c) Congruence is understood as usual in elementary geometry: figure A is congruent to figure B if A can be made to coincide with B by being moved in space.[1]
>
> d) Finally, we say a polyhedral solid A consists of two adjacent parts B and C if B and C have no common interior points, and taken together they are congruent with polyhedron A [$A = B \cup C$].

On this basis we have a specific understanding of the term "volume."

A function satisfying conditions (1)-(4) described in the definition of volume is said to be *standardized, positive, invariant,* and *additive,* respectively. Using these terms, we can briefly formulate the following definition of volume. *Given a class ζ of cubable solids, one of which is taken as a unit of volume, then a standardized positive function $V:\zeta \to R^+$* given on the set of real numbers is called a volume if it is invariant and additive.

We have already mentioned that there are various methods of specifying classes of cubable solids. Let us note several classes relevant to teaching of the theory of volume in school.

A. One of the simplest classes of cubable solids can be described by a decomposition. *A solid is said to be cubable if it can be cut into several rectangular parallelepipeds.* In other words, all polyhedral solids whose

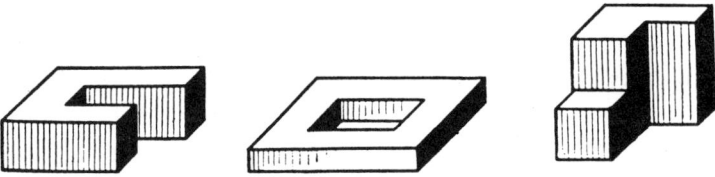

Figure 63.

Figure 64.

faces include only right angles are cubable solids. Some examples of such solids are shown in Figure 63. Given this interpretation, all solids that can be constructed from one or more congruent cubes will be cubable (Fig. 64).

B. We have already mentioned a broader class of cubable solids—the polyhedral solids.

C. We obtain an even more extensive class of cubable solids if we consider as cubable any solid A possessing the following property: given any positive number $\varepsilon > 0$, there exist polyhedral solids A', contained in solid A, and A'', containing solid A, such that $A' \subset A \subset A''$ and $V(A'') - V(A') < \varepsilon$. In other words, solid A can be sandwiched between two polyhedra (inscribed and circumscribed), which differ in volume by very little. This class of cubable solids is substantially broader than the preceding one. Any convex solid (a sphere, for example) belongs to this class.

The Concept of Volume

D. The broadest class of cubable solids is the class of all *Lebesgue measurable* subsets of three-dimensional space. In this case the volume of a solid (that is, of the measurable set) is simply its Lebesgue measure. This class of sets is rather remote from geometry instruction in the middle grades. For example, a Lebesque measurable set having a measure of 0.999, can be constructed as a subset of a unit cube, but which is *disconnected* (that is, no two of its points can be connected by a line lying within it). Such a set contains no whole piece of space, no piece of the plane, no segment, and still its volume (i.e., measure) differs by just 0.001 from the volume of the cube that contains it.[2]

E. Of course, from the standpoint of maximum generality, it would be desirable to regard as cubable (that is, as having volume) any solid, i.e., any set of three-dimensional space. Is such a point of view possible? Modern research in mathematical logic and in the foundations of mathematics (especially the work of Godel and Cohen) shows that it is indeed.

The existence of sets that are not Lebesque measurable can not be proved without appealing to the so-called *axiom of choice*, introduced into mathematics by Zermelo. An assumption about the truth (or falsity) of this axiom leads (as shown by Godel and Cohen) to *unfalsifiable* mathematical systems. Zermelo's axiom is so remote from the questions studied in school that whether or not it is satisfied in no way affects "school" mathematics, or even the so-called "higher mathematics" studied in universities. Since nothing requires us to assume Zermelo's axiom, then every subset of three-dimensional space can be assumed to be Lebesgue measurable. We will take this collection of sets as our class of cubable solids, regarding the Lebesgue measure of a set as its volume.

In all five cases we can take a cube to be the unit of volume. Then, in cases D and E the additivity of volume reflects the fact that $V(A \cup B) = V(A) + V(B)$, if sets A and B have no common points.[3]

Suppose we have selected a class of cubable solids and chosen a cube E as a unit for measuring volume. Then a function specified for the chosen class of cubable solids that possesses properties (1)-(4) is said to be the volume. What questions arise at this point? The following three important questions suggest themselves:

a) the existence of volume;

b) the uniqueness of volume; and

c) methods for computing volumes.

Let us clarify the meaning and importance of these questions. The question of existence can be posed in the following form: *Does there exist at least one function V specified for the class of cubable solids under consideration that is a volume (i.e., a standardized, positive, invariant additive function)?* The importance of this question requires no elucidation: if it is not established that such a function V exists, then it makes no sense to study the concept of volume, since there is no object to study. Mathematically, this question is solved by producing an *existence theorem*, whose proof is an integral part of a rigorous and mathematically complete theory of volume. From a practical standpoint, the possibility of a rigorous mathematical proof of an existence theorem for volume reflects the interrelationship among real material objects and the space they occupy. Different paths are taken in the proofs of the existence theorems, depending on which of the cases A-E is chosen to develop a certain theory of volume. (For details of the proof of the existence theorem, we refer the reader to Rokhlin[4] and Khadviger.[5])

Now we turn to the question of uniqueness. It is difficult to overestimate the importance of this question. Indeed, let us assume for a minute that uniqueness does not occur, so that there exist at least two functions V_1 and V_2, whose domain is the class of cubable solids under consideration and which satisfy the axioms of volume, (1)-(4). Then, for the same cubable solid A we will have two numbers $V_1(A)$ and $V_2(A)$, which do not always coincide since V_1 and V_2 are different; which of them should be taken as the "volume" of solid A will be unclear. As a rule, the absence of uniqueness means that the list of axioms describing a concept is incomplete (for example, a property distinguishing function V_1 from V_2 might be found). If uniqueness does occur, however, this means that the list of axioms (1)-(4) is complete—that is, it unambiguously determines the function V, satisfying these axioms, which should be called the

The Concept of Volume

"volume." In all of the cases A-E noted above, a *uniqueness theorem* does exist.[6]

As a consequence of uniqueness, it can be noted that since axioms (1)-(4) determine function V (the volume) unambiguously, all the properties of volume are generated by these axioms.

Finally, let us discuss the question of methods of computing volume. There is a widespread opinion among mathematics teachers that a knowledge of methods and formulas for computing volume is the fundamental question, and that this knowledge totally eliminates the problems of both existence and uniqueness. Nothing could be more erroneous.

As an example, consider case B, which takes for the class of cubable solids all polyhedral solids. Let us assume that we already know the formula for

$$V = \frac{1}{3} Sh, \tag{5}$$

Here S is the area of the base of the pyramid and h is its height. The unit for measuring the area is the square that represents one face of the cube, and the unit of length is an edge of this cube. Then we can calculate the volume of any cubable (polyhedral) solid by dividing it into pyramids with pairwise disjoint interiors (Fig. 65). Its volume is found simply by summing the volumes of the separate pyramids, each of which can be found by means of (5).

However, this line of reasoning does not eliminate the questions of existence and uniqueness of volume. Let us add the formula (5) as an *axiom* to the four conditions already established. Will this extension of the axiom system remove the questions of existence and uniqueness of volume? No, it does not! Just as every triangle can be divided into triangles in an infinite number of ways (Fig. 66), so every polyhedron has infinitely many pyramidal decompositions. Do we obtain the same value if we divide the same polyhedron into pyramids in different ways and add the volumes of the constituent pyramids, as computed by formula (5)?

There is no obvious affirmative answer to this question. However, if it were not so—that is, if different methods of division into pyramids

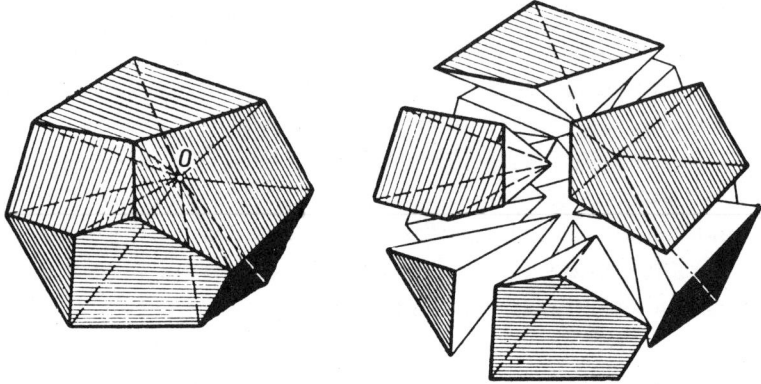

Figure 65.

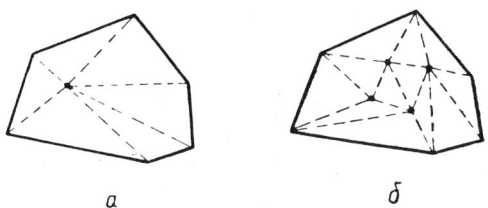

Figure 66.

yielded different values of the volume of a single polyhedron—it would mean that the volume function V did not exist, and discussions of volume would be pointless. In reality, regardless of the method of pyramidal decomposition, the summation of the volumes of the component pyramids, calculated by formula (5), will always yield the same result for a specified polyhedron. This fact is far from obvious, however, and requires proof. Such a proof (and it is by no means simple!) will be, in

The Concept of Volume

essence, a proof of the existence theorem for volume in the class of all polyhedra. A proof of this theorem is given in Khadviger.[7] Yet this proof does not eliminate the need for establishing uniqueness. In addition to the volume calculated by formula (5), there might exist some other function V' which satisfies conditions (1)-(4). In fact, as we have stated, uniqueness does occur, but it requires a specific proof.

Although schools usually restrict themselves to questions involving the computation of volume, such considerations cannot replace or eliminate questions of existence and uniqueness. A complete mathematical construction of the theory of volume should contain proofs of existence and uniqueness theorems, in addition to deriving the properties of volume, especially formulas for computing volume from axioms (1)-(4).[8]

In concluding this section, let us focus on the role of each of axioms (1)-(4) in defining the concept of volume. It can be shown that each of these axioms is essential for the concept of volume. More precisely, if we discard any one of these axioms, the uniqueness of volume is violated. This statement is most evident with respect to axiom (1). If we discard axiom (1), *infinitely many* different functions V may be found which satisfy the remaining axioms (2)-(4). In fact, any cube can be taken as a unit of measuring volume and a corresponding function V (volume) obtained. This means that, *without establishing* a specific unit for measuring volume, we can obtain infinitely many different volumes. This point, which is related to changing the unit of measuring volume, will be discussed in detail in section 24.

If, on the other hand, we discard axiom (4), we can easily obtain infinitely many different functions V satisfying axioms (1)-(3). For example, if V is an ordinary volume, the function V^k (the kth power of V) satisfies each of the axioms (1)-(3), but for $k \neq 1$ it does not satisfy axiom (4).

An analogous situation arises with axioms (2) and (3). It is rather easy to prove that axiom (3) is necessary, while that of axiom (2) is much more subtle—it calls for Cauchy-Hamel functions, which require the axiom of choice. Without discussing these matters in detail, let us formulate only a basic, definitive conclusion: each of axioms (1)-(4) are essential for the construction of the concept of volume; none can be disregarded.

Formation of the Concept of Volume

Which of the classes of cubable solids mentioned in the previous section is most appropriate for grade 4, where the concept of volume is first elaborated? Although it may appear odd at first glance, two of these classes—A and E—are equally appropriate for this purpose.

First let us consider class E cubable solids. The point of this class is simply that *every solid* (that is, every set of points in space) *has volume.* Of course, in grade 4 we cannot fully substantiate this proposition, bring up Lebesgue measure, or above all Zermelo's axiom. Rather, students are given an intuitive notion of volume as a property of a solid occupying a specific place in space. They find it easy to learn that any solid has volume (that is, it occupies space), for this is an informal, intuitive, preliminary notion of volume. (Although, as we know, to carry this point of view further involves unusually subtle questions of modern mathematics).

We will indicate below how this rudimentary concept of volume should be developed, but for the time being let us note the role this concept plays. In our view, such a basic concept of volume is exceptionally important because it *replaces the existence theorem of volume.* Therefore, students know that they are performing an intelligent activity, based on the calculation of a meaningful aspect of a real object (volume).

Let us consider, for example, the solid shown in Figure 67. If students already know the formula for the volume of a rectangular parallelepiped, they can calculate the volume of this solid by mentally breaking up the solid, perhaps in various ways, into several rectangular parallelepipeds (Fig. 68). Several questions naturally arise. Are the answers from students who decompose the solid in different ways the same? And will the same answer always be obtained for different solutions to the problem? This is a very important methodological question. For a mathematician the

The Concept of Volume

answer is clear, for the existence theorem of volume assures that the results will be identical. But what can be said on this subject to a fourth-grader? He will certainly not understand the proof of an existence theorem for volume (even for the elementary class of cubable solids considered in item A). One approach is to give the student an elementary, non-rigorous, intuitive concept of volume that will replace an existence theorem. Having such a basic notion, the student will be able to give an accurate reply when asked why different methods of solution (Fig. 68) lead to the same result. After all, we are computing just one thing—the volume of a specific solid—a volume whose meaning and existence the student does not doubt.

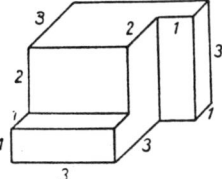

Figure 67.

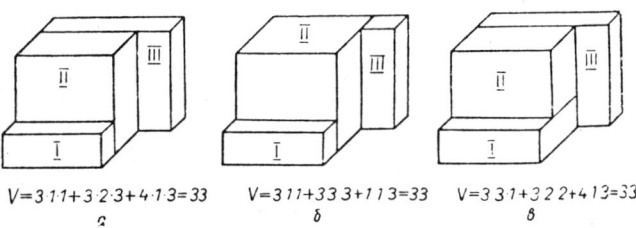

$V = 3 \cdot 1 \cdot 1 + 3 \cdot 2 \cdot 3 + 4 \cdot 1 \cdot 3 = 33$ $V = 3 \cdot 1 \cdot 1 + 3 \cdot 3 \cdot 3 + 1 \cdot 1 \cdot 3 = 33$ $V = 3 \cdot 3 \cdot 1 + 3 \cdot 2 \cdot 2 + 4 \cdot 1 \cdot 3 = 33$

Figure 68.

Thus, instead of an abstract and inappropriate existence theorem, the student should acquire a rudimentary notion of volume as the space that can be occupied by a solid. We repeat that there is no point in limiting the class of solids considered—when it is a matter of such a basic notion for a student, *all* solids have volume (class E of cubable solids correspond mathematically to this notion). The computation of volume is another matter. Here, during the preliminary introduction, the concept of volume must be simplified considerably, and the class of cubable solids must be narrowed down as far as possible. Therefore, class A is most suitable for considering the computation of volume. Even then, it is advisable to restrict class A of cubable solids somewhat, taking instead the class A' of polyhedra that can be cut into a finite number of cubes equal to a unit of volume. In other words, we agree to place a solid in class A' of cubable solids if it is made up of several small unit cubes. Examples of cubable solids of class A' are shown in Figure 69. It is this class of cubable solids that is most suitable for study in grade 4.

What ideas must be mastered by a fourth-grader who is computing the volumes of solids that belong to class A'? This should not be reduced to simply counting the cubes that make up the given solid. Counting yields, at best, only formal knowledge, with no clear understanding of the relationship between the counting and the rudimentary concept of volume

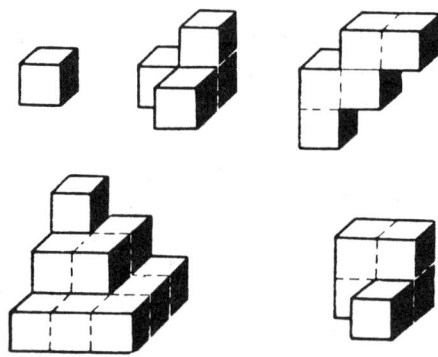

Figure 69.

The Concept of Volume

that the student has developed. It is essential that, upon counting the number of little cubes, the student must master properties (1), (3), and (4) of volume—possibly without formulating them outright, but clearly understanding the reasons for operating in just this and no other way.

Thus, in comparing the unit of volume E with solid P (a rectangular parallelepiped) in Figure 70b, the teacher and students should note that *solid P can be mentally divided into two parts* (Fig. 70c). *Each of these parts is "the same as" the unit cube E, and so each part has the same volume*[9] *as the unit cube E; but the unit cube has a volume of 1,*[10] *and so each part in Figure 70c has a volume of 1; and, since solid P is made up of two of these parts, its volume is equal to the sum of the volumes of the parts*,[11] (*i.e.*, $1 + 1 = 2$). This is a complete description of the mental activity which results in the conclusion that the volume of solid P is equal to 2. It is readily apparent in this example how properties (1), (3), and (4) of volume are used, although these properties need not be formulated outright.

If the teacher now offers the solid shown in Figure 71b, the student can mentally divide it either into two parts (Fig. 71c), saying that the volume of the solid is equal to $1 + 2 = 3$, or into three parts (Fig. 71d), computing the solid's volume as $1 + 1 + 1 = 3$. Gradually, the student reaches a stage of simply counting the number of unit cubes that make up the solid. But what is most important is that the student should explain his operations here, using properties (1), (3), and (4) of volume. (Property (2) in class A' is fulfilled automatically; it assumes an important role only when we move to broader classes of cubable solids.) With this approach, the formula for computing the volume of a rectangular parallelepiped—the

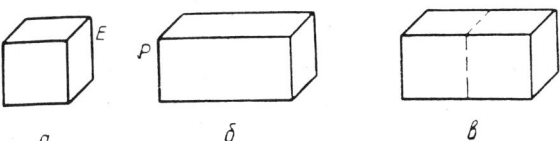

Figure 70.

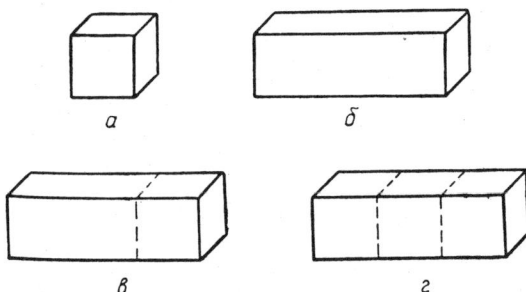

Figure 71.

ultimate objective of studying the topic—will be perceived actively and with complete understanding.

The reader has undoubtedly realized that nowhere in this exposition have we exploited the uniqueness of volume. However, it is a foregone conclusion (not formulated outright), since each time we have defined the volume of a solid unambiguously by means of properties (1), (3), and (4).

While studying this topic, students should: a) acquire a rudimentary familiarity with the concept of volume (as a substitute for the existence theorem); and b) learn to calculate the volume of solids in class A' on the basis of properties (1), (3), and (4). We feel that these conceptions are exceptionally important. Without them, memorizing the formula for the volume of a rectangular parallelepiped, $V = abc$, is of very little use.

The foregoing discussion reflects the approach we have followed in creating educational materials. Before actually producing materials, we worked to determine precisely what outcomes the teacher should strive to as obtain a result of the instruction.

During their study of the topic "The Rectangular Parallelepiped and Its Volume," students, as we noted above, should acquire: 1) a notion of volume as occupied space; and 2) a notion of volume as a number indicating how many units of volume are contained in a solid. It was

The Concept of Volume

decided only to have the students develop general notions of volume as occupied space, while pursuing the second aspect to the highest level. As a result of the instruction, the students should have learned to mentally compute the numerical volume of the solids considered and to decompose a complex solid into simpler ones (all the way down to unit cubes). This activity should take place in a condensed and automatic way. However, if necessary, students should know how to "fill it out"—to relate (in the case of a rectangular parallelepiped) what is meant by a numerical volume and why a complex solid must be decomposed into simpler ones.

It does not follow that the first aspect is less important than the second. This is the first time that students encounter the concept of volume. And the first encounter with a concept, as we have said, is always crucial. At the same time, the task of providing a rudimentary notion of volume saves us from having to organize higher-level activities corresponding to a more sophisticated and mathematically precise knowledge of volume. Therefore, explanation is "delegated" to single-concept films and filmstrips in the instructional unit. The formation of the concept of volume as a number that indicates how many unit cubes are contained in a given solid is another matter. In order to form this concept, we must establish what activity is adequate to it, for, as we have been emphasizing, the most rational course for learning lies in the organization of implemented adequate activity. It is important for us that students *associate (identify) the number obtained through calculations with the number of unit cubes into which the given solid can be divided.*

If we proceed from what we have said, then the activity adequate to the concept of "the volume of a rectangular parallelepiped" consists in counting the unit cubes into which the given solid can be cut. A convenient method of calculation can be "discovered" in the course of this activity—namely, the formula for computing its volume.

What instructional media introduce students to the computation of volume and enable them to carry it out successfully? Above all, the teacher needs materials to familiarize students with the idea of decomposing a solid and calculating the number of unit cubes that constitute the entire solid. This calls for solids (or drawings of solids) in which the eye can single out the unit cubes that compose it. These solids (Fig. 16) are included among those found in the modernized arithmetic kit, which we included in the unit.

For students, the number of unit cubes should characterize the volume of a solid, the amount of space it occupies. Suppose that a student has established that one solid in a filmstrip consists of 15 cubes, and another of 20. Can anything be said about the volumes of these solids? No; it is unknown whether the units of volume for the two solids are equal. Consequently, when there is simple counting, the number occurs as a measure of volume only on condition that the unit of measuring the volume is indicated. Therefore, educational materials should ensure not mere counting, but rather calculations in which students are constantly reminded of the specific unit of volume being used.

The number indicating how many unit cubes are contained in a given solid—the volume—should be characterized by the dimensions of the space occupied by the solid. One method of stressing this idea is to compare the volumes of solids calculated using various units. The educational materials should stimulate such a comparison. For this purpose, various unit cubes are included in the arithmetic kit, and they can be used by students to aid in determining the volume of a single solid.

Counting all the unit cubes comprising a solid can be a tiresome and not very sensible method of determining volume. Instructional media are needed that would enable us to explain the idea of intermediate steps in the calculation of the number of unit cubes that make up a rectangular parallelepiped. For this reason the instructional unit includes filmstrip frames, slides, assignment cards, workbooks, and a table entitled "The Volume of a Rectangular Parallelepiped."

Using these materials, it is easy for students to calculate the number of unit cubes constituting a given rectangular parallelepiped. It is also easy for the teacher to explain that the volume of a rectangular parallelepiped is obtained by multiplying its dimensions, that is, by multiplying the area of the base by the height. But if we confine ourselves to this and move at once to computing volumes using formulas, training the students only in the multiplication of numbers, they will very soon forget our entire

The Concept of Volume

line of reasoning. In their minds the counting of cubes will not be associated with computing volume. Therefore, the unit stresses the gradual removal of manipulatives. For example, sometimes the students should determine the volume of a rectangular parallelepiped by indicating how and why unit cubes are to be counted.

In teaching with the instructional unit, we expect the teacher to project (onto the blackboard) slides depicting parallelepipeds with their dimensions broken down into linear units. Then a student can divide one of the parallelepiped's faces into squares directly on the blackboard, easily showing how many cubes make up this face and how many layers can be stacked up.

Even after the students have successfully calculated the volume several times, using formulas, we consider it useful to return periodically to counting the unit cubes. For this purpose, slides with the dimensions indicated can be used. The students can break down the measurements by sight into the specified number of parts, construct a grid on the blackboard (the squares into which the face is broken up), and draw the layers of cubes that fill the solid. The work can be repeated for different faces.

Properties (1) and (3) are evident and are always learned without difficulty. However, for the mastery of property (4) of volume, additivity, which seems most essential to us, we envision a number of assignments (of the same kind as in Fig. 68) in the workbook and on problem cards.

And so the discussion of the question as undertaken in this and the preceding section has led us to the following conclusions. First, fourth-graders should develop a rudimentary concept of volume as a property of solids that occupy space. This creates in their minds an impression of the genuine meaningfulness of the concept of volume and eliminates the question of existence. For subsequent study of the concept of volume, especially for familiarity with the computation of volumes of specific solids, it is best to narrow the class of solids significantly, limiting it to consideration of class A' (as indicated previously). Volume in this class is a function that for each solid takes on a value equal to the number of cubes which comprise the solid. It is very essential here for the students to master the idea of additivity of volume (formula (4)). The appropriate educational materials are needed for organizing adequate activity to ensure the mastery of these concepts.

Dimension Theory and "Concrete Quantities"

However, another question has evoked incredible confusion among authors of school textbooks, creators of educational materials and manipulatives, methodologists, and teachers: how to deal with linear, square, and cubic measure—the so-called "concrete quantities"—and the best way of including them in answers and solutions in workbooks. The absence of detail on this problem in methodology literature means that students are unprepared in subsequent grades for the perception of the concept of dimension in physical quantities and the concept of systems of units. Nevertheless, in both mathematics and physics this question is fully elaborated and unambiguous.

The essence of the problem consists in the following. As we have noted, any cube whose edge is a unit of length can be taken as a unit for measuring volume (Fig. 72). If only one unit were always used to measure length, there would be no difficulty in measurement—the length of a segment would be the number showing how many units of measurement (uniquely existing units!) can be marked off along a given segment. The

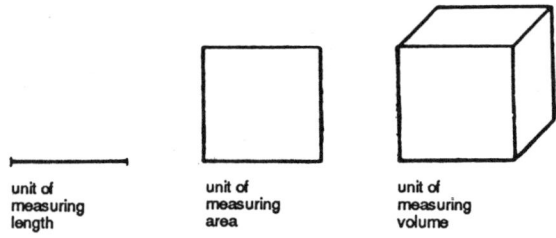

Figure 72.

The Concept of Volume

situation is analogous for measuring areas and volumes (and later, other physical quantities). But in practice not one but several units of measuring length are employed: the *centimeter*, *decimeter*, *meter*, and so forth. Accordingly, different units of measuring area and volume are used. Thus, a square with a side equal to a centimeter is called a *square centimeter*, and similarly for the other units of length and their corresponding area measure. The situation is the same for measuring volume: a cube with an edge of one meter is called a *cubic meter*, and so on.

Although various units of measuring volume are used in practice, there is nothing new or unexpected here from a theoretical standpoint. As we noted in section 22, any cube can be taken as a unit for measuring volume. That alters nothing of essence. Volume is a function assigned to a set of cubable solids, and the volume of a particular solid is a numerical value. However, in saying that the volume of a solid is a number, and the volume of another solid is another number, and so on, we assume a standard unit of volume. In other words, when the volumes of many solids (parallelepipeds, prisms, pyramids, etc.) are considered in theoretical questions, the same fixed unit of measuring volume is used. Therefore, when we write the formulas for computing the volume of a rectangular parallelepiped,

$$V = abc, \text{ or } V = Sh, \qquad (6)$$

or a pyramid,

$$V = \frac{1}{3} Sh \qquad (7)$$

or any other solid, we do not actually refer to a particular unit of volume. Whatever unit is selected for computing volume (like the units for measuring area or length) must be fixed for comparisons of volumes to make sense. Applying formula (6) or (7), we obtain (corresponding to the definition) some *number* as the polyhedron's volume. What does it mean? This number shows how many units of measure are contained in a given solid (just *which* units of measure is entirely clear: the ones involved in the very beginning of the discussion, which have not changed).

The situation becomes more complex in practical questions. To say that "the volume of a solid is equal to five" is to say nothing unless it is additionally indicated what cube is taken as the unit for measuring volume. Therefore, to give complete information about the space occupied by a solid, we must say something like: *The volume of a solid is equal to five, taking a cubic decimeter as the unit of volume measure.* For brevity's sake, let us agree to write this sentence in the following way:

$$V = 5 \text{ (cubic dm)}. \qquad (8)$$

Here the notation $V = 5$ means that the volume of the solid is equal to 5 (after all, volume is always some *number*!), and the notation in parentheses (cubic dm) should be taken as a shorthand equivalent for the following phrase: "and we take a cubic decimeter as the unit of volume."

If, say, we have to compute the volume of a rectangular parallelepiped with sides of 3, 4, and 5 cm, the volume can be written in the following form:

$$V = 3 \times 4 \times 5 = 60 \text{ (cubic cm)}. \qquad (9)$$

Here the computations are done with numbers, and the answer is also the number 60. The notation in parentheses (cubic cm) is a reminder, or supplementary information to the effect that all of these calculations were done on the condition that a cubic centimeter is taken as the unit of volume measure.

Suppose we must compute the volume of a cube with an edge of 2 dm. Clearly, the result can be written in the form

$$V = 8 \text{ (cubic dm)}. \qquad (10)$$

Note that when a cubic centimeter is taken as the unit of volume, the result will be written thus:

$$V = 8{,}000 \text{ (cubic cm)}. \qquad (11)$$

At first glance there is a contradiction here. For volume is a number, and it suddenly happens that the volume of a single cube is equal to both 8 and 8,000, as if 8 and 8,000 were the same number. In fact, there is no contradiction at all. Taking a cubic decimeter as a unit of measuring

The Concept of Volume 151

volume, we obtain a function V (volume), assigned to solids of class A'. For this solid (a cube with an edge of 2 dm), this function takes on the value 8. But if we take a cubic centimeter as the unit of measuring volume, we obtain a different function (another volume). It is true that we usually designate it by the same letter V, but this does not change things. It is another function and its value for the given cube is different (namely, 8,000)—which is not surprising. And it is not at all unusual that different functions are designated by the same letter V. After all, we typically use the letter x to denote an unknown in any problem—sometimes $x = 5$, sometimes $x = 2$, sometimes $x = -7$, and this surprises no one.

Thus, we recommend that fourth-graders always remember that the volume of a solid is a *number*, and that they perform all operations with numbers, indicating the unit of volume in parentheses. It is quite useless to repeat the parenthetical notation for the unit of measure in every part of an equation. We emphasize that this notation only reminds us of what the unit used for measuring volume in the entire calculation has been (cf. (9)). Here a transition from one unit of volume to another will evoke no difficulties for the students, as we stressed above the importance of the distinct geometric meaning in a problem on computing volume. For example, students interpret the transition from equality (10) to equality (11) in this way: *equation (10) means that the solid can be composed of eight unit cubes, taking a cubic decimeter as the unit cube. But since a cubic decimeter consists of 1,000 cubic centimeters,*[12] *our solid is made up of 8 × 1,000 =* 8,000 cubic centimeters, as indicated in equation (11).

As we have seen, the parenthetical reminder of the unit of volume measure after every equality not only makes the notations complete and meaningful; it also helps effect a transition from one unit of volume measure to others. Let us stress that a parenthetical notation, such as (cubic cm), *is not part of the equality*. It is simply supplementary information for interpreting the calculation that has been performed. Moreover, if a solution to a problem contains several lines of equalities, it is possible that the student might add an appropriate notation only at the end to indicate the unit of volume. For example, in solving a problem on finding the volume of the solid shown in Figure 67, using the method of Figure 68a, a student can set up the equations in the following way:

$$V = V_1 + V_2 + V_3;$$
$$V_1 = 3 \times 1 \times 1 = 3;$$
$$V_2 = 3 \times 2 \times 3 = 18;$$
$$V_3 = 4 \times 1 \times 3 = 12;$$
$$V = 3 + 18 + 12 = 33 \text{ (cubic cm)}.$$

The notation at the end (cubic cm) shows that the student has remembered the unit of volume and has indicated it in his final answer. We see nothing harmful in this notation. Of course, it is the teacher's business to require (if desired) a reminder of the unit of volume measure at the end of every equality. But this is really unnecessary. An indication of the units of measure will be needed if a change occurs in the units of volume measure (say, converting from cubic decimeters to cubic centimeters (cf. (10) and (11)) in the process of solving a problem.

The position described above is opposed by some methodologists and methodological handbooks with completely different (and, as a rule, totally inconsistent) views on "concrete quantities." The idea of these views is that the designations cubic cm, cubic m, and so forth, are written without parentheses and represent distinct rules about their position in equalities. Thus, some methodologists, when computing, e.g., the volume of a parallelepiped as shown in Figure 73a, require that the notation be done only in the following form:

$$V = 4 \times 5 \text{ cubic cm} \times 3 = 20 \text{ cubic cm} \times 3 = 60 \text{ cubic cm}.$$

They motivate this notation because, in computing the volume, one layer (Fig. 73b) is first considered, which contains 4×5 cubic cm, and since there are three of these layers, the quantity 4×5 cubic cm must be multiplied by 3. Therefore, the notation should take precisely the preceding form:

$$4 \times 5 \text{ cubic cm} \times 3.$$

The Concept of Volume

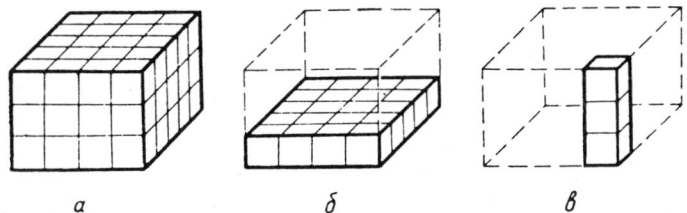

Figure 73.

Other methodologists, in solving the same problem, require the notation to be written in the following form:

$$V = 3 \text{ cubic cm} \times 4 \times 5 = 3 \text{ cubic cm} \times 20 = 60 \text{ cubic cm}.$$

This is justified by the fact that each column (Fig. 75c) contains 3 cubic cm, and since the number of these columns is equal to the number of small squares in the base (i.e., 4×5), the quantity 3 cubic cm should be multiplied by 4×5, so that the notation takes the following form (in precisely that order):

$$3 \text{ cubic dm} \times 4 \times 5.$$

There are other views as well (which there is no need to cite), and the adherents of one method of notation regard the other notations as "grossly in error" (!). All possible misunderstandings have arisen from trying to use the *theory of dimension* of geometric quantities (which is part of the theory of dimension of physical quantities in general). These attempts are positive in themselves, but the trouble is that such attempts are usually inconsistent, and the concrete quantities that appear in mathematics lessons often only vulgarize the really important and profound theory of dimension of physical quantities.

What makes up the theory of dimension of geometric quantities (our concern here)? It can be presented through the following conventions:

1) Square measures are designated by the symbol ^{2}, and cubic measures by ^{3}. For example, we write cm^2, instead of square cm, m^3 instead of cubic m, and so on.

2) To designate lengths, areas, and volumes, we write the units of measure as *factors*, with appropriate numbers. For example, instead of the words "The volume of a solid is equal to seven, taking a cubic centimeter taken as the unit of volume," we write simply $V = 7$ cm^3. The notations 5 m^3, 13 mm^2, etc., have analogous meaning. We stress that the notation 7 cm^3 is only a formal product, since cm^3 is a conventional symbol, not a number. In other words, 7 cm^3 is written in the form of a product, but this notation means nothing other than what has been stated above.

3) In computing volumes and areas from various formulas, we handle the designations of units of measure (length, area, volume) by the usual algebraic rules. For example:

$$5 \text{ m}^2 \times 3 \text{ m} = 5 \times 3 \text{ m}^2 \times \text{m} = 15 \text{ m}^3;$$
$$3 \text{ cm}^3 + 6 \text{ cm}^3 = (3 + 6) \text{ cm}^3 = 9 \text{ cm}^3, \text{ etc.}$$

4) Numerical coefficients are used in the usual way to replace units of measure. For example, since there are 10 dm in one meter, we can write:

$$1 \text{ m} = 10 \text{ dm};$$
$$1 \text{ m}^2 = (10 \text{ dm})^2 = 100 \text{ dm}^2;$$
$$1 \text{ m3} = (10 \text{ dm})^3 = 1{,}000 \text{ dm}^3, \text{ etc.}$$

These, properly speaking, are all the basic conventions underlying the theory of dimension. Of course, the question arises why we can operate in this way. Thus, this dimension theory requires substantiation. And indeed, why the symbol cm can be "multiplied" by or "added" to something, and even be squared or cubed, is not at all clear. Without touching on the question of substantiating the theory of dimension, we

The Concept of Volume

shall focus on only two related questions. 1) Should dimension theory be included in the school mathematics course? 2) If so, what notation should be regarded as correct in writing solutions to problems on volume?

The first question should undoubtedly be answered affirmatively: the geometric theory of dimension should be included in the school mathematics course. This topic (requiring 5 or 6 hours of school time) should follow the topic on the volume of a rectangular parallelepiped and, doubtless, before the general theory of dimension in the physics course. In our opinion, fourth-graders are still unprepared to apprehend the geometric theory of dimension. The material on the volume of a rectangular parallelepiped is new for them. This material must be mastered and firmly established in their minds. Apparently, the most acceptable place for studying the geometric theory of dimension is grade 5. Covering this topic in grade 5 permits the topic on area and volume to be reviewed and completed, and the question of substituting certain units for others to be definitively resolved, while laying the groundwork for the general theory of dimension of physical quantities.

When dimension theory is applied to the question of the method of notation, there is no dispute as to the correct notation. For example, in finding the volume of the rectangular parallelepiped shown in Figure 73a, the student can either use the formula $V = abc$ and write

$$V = 4 \text{ cm} \times 5 \text{ cm} \times 3 \text{ cm} = 60 \text{ cm}^3,$$

or the formula $V = Sh$, writing

$$V = (4 \times 5) \text{ cm}^2 \times 3 \text{ cm} = 60 \text{ cm}^3.$$

Nor is it terrible if he writes

$$V = 3 \times 4 \times 5 \text{ cm}^3 = 60 \text{ cm}^3.$$

It is only important that the dimensionality of every quantity involved in the formula be taken into proper consideration, and that the usual laws of algebra be used in transforming the equations. No student can say that dropping a coefficient or letter (in transferring an expression from one side of an equality to the other) is permissible. The same applies to the designations of the units of measure: "dropping" a designation in moving from one side of an equality to the other is inadmissible.

For example, the solution to the problem on the volume of the polyhedron shown in Figure 67, according to the method of Figure 68a, can be written out in this way by a student who has learned the theory of dimension of geometric quantities:

$$V = V_1 + V_2 + V_3$$
$$= (3 \text{ cm} \times 1 \text{ cm} \times 1 \text{ cm}) + (3 \text{ cm} \times 2 \text{ cm} \times 3 \text{ cm})$$
$$+ (4 \text{ cm} \times 1 \text{ cm} \times 3 \text{ cm})$$
$$= 3 \text{ cm}^3 + 18 \text{ cm}^3 + 12 \text{ cm}^3$$
$$= (3 + 18 + 12) \text{ cm}^3 = 33 \text{ cm}^3.$$

Similarly, in solving a problem on finding velocity, a fourth-grader writes a designation such as km/hr along with the number as a reminder. A fifth-grader, however, using the theory of dimension, writes the designation km/hr as a factor. No half-measures are needed; they only elicit confusion and lack of coordination.

Thus, in grade 4 it is advisable to indicate units of volume measure in parentheses after the numerical calculations, regarding this notation as unrelated to the numerical equalities. It serves merely as a reminder, a separate, auxiliary statement about the choice of a unit of volume. Repeating these parentheses in every part of the equality is totally superfluous. As for a sequentially ordered theory of dimension of geometric quantities, it has no place in grade 4.

Text of a Handbook on the Topic "The Rectangular Parallelepiped and Its Volume"

The topic entitled "The Rectangular Parallelepiped and Its Volume" is handled unsatisfactorily in existing standard textbooks (in B.G. Pchelko's arithmetic textbook, in particular). Suffice to say that the theoretical text

The Concept of Volume

on this topic (which is designed for 16 lessons!) occupies a total of only one and a half pages. Moreover, the student can receive patently incorrect notions from this theoretical exposition. For example, a cube with an edge of 1 cm is called, quite properly, a "cubic centimeter." But the volume of this cube is also regarded (without any explanation) as equal to one cubic centimeter. It turns out that this cube and its volume are identical. And since volume is a number (contained in a solid of unit cubes), one can draw the strange conclusion that the cube is that number...

Furthermore, the textbook says nothing about the geometric properties of the rectangular parallelepiped, so that if a student has missed a lesson, he cannot read in the textbook about the opposite faces of a parallelepiped, or about its measurement, or even about what a rectangular parallelepiped is.

All this has compelled us to produce a written *handbook* on this topic. This handbook, in essence, has also been included in the unit to be described in the next chapter. However, we cite the text of the handbook in this chapter for two reasons. First, it is the practical result of all of the theoretical tenets developed in this chapter. Second, textbooks and printed handbooks are not currently accepted as belonging among "educational materials." Still, the tradition of separating the textbook from a collection of educational materials, in the opinion of the authors, is outmoded. A textbook can be regarded as one of the instructional media that form a set of educational materials. Therefore, we are including the text of the handbook here, as a conclusion to the topic on volume.

I. The Rectangular Parallelepiped

1. The Shape of Objects. In real life we encounter objects of various shapes. A suitcase and a soccer ball (Fig. 74) might be the same color (say, brown), and they might be covered in the same material (leather). Nevertheless, these objects are quite unlike each other; they have a different shape. The two containers shown in Figure 75 might be the same color, but their shape is not identical.

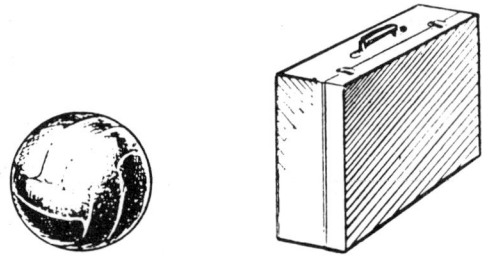

Figure 74.

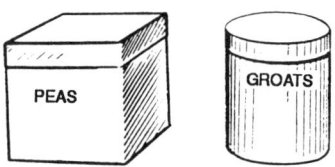

Figure 75.

We also encounter objects that have similar shapes. They might be made of different materials or painted different colors, but they resemble each other in shape. A suitcase, a television, a cupboard, and a parcel for mailing are shown in Figure 76. These objects have a similar shape. To be sure, they differ in minor details: the suitcase has a handle, the cupboard has doors. But if we disregard these minor details, we can state that all these objects have approximately the same shape. They all resemble in shape the object shown in Figure 77, which has no secondary details.

2. The Rectangular Parallelepiped and Its Faces. The solid shown in Figure 77 is called a *rectangular parallelepiped*. The side facing us has the shape of a rectangle. This is the front *face* of the rectangular

The Concept of Volume

parallelepiped. It has exactly the same kind of rectangle in back. That is the back face. We do not see it. There are two more faces above and below. The top one is visible to us. We do not see the back face, for the rectangular parallelepiped is resting on it. Finally, there are two more faces on the sides. We see the right face in the drawing, but not the left.

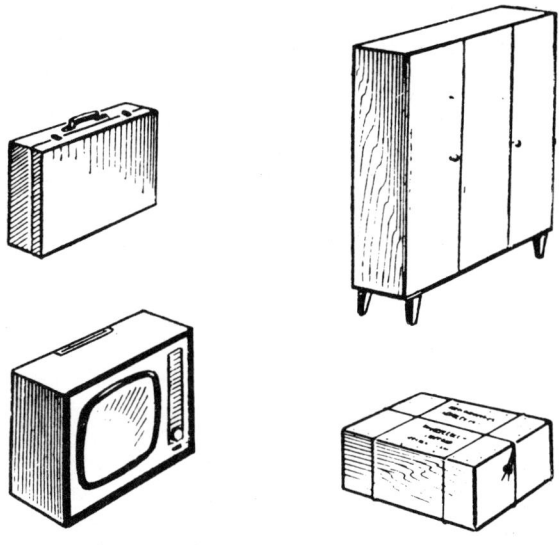

Figure 76.

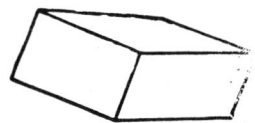

Figure 77.

A rectangular parallelepiped has a total of 6 faces, each of which has the shape of a rectangle.

A rectangular parallelepiped is also depicted in Figure 78. However, it is not resting on any of its faces; it is hanging in the air. Like the previous one, it has six faces, but we cannot call any of them upper or lower. We can speak of the lower face when the rectangular parallelepiped is sitting on a table or other flat surface. The face on which a parallelepiped is resting is usually called its *base* (or its *lower base*). The opposite face (the upper one) is called the *upper base*. Of course, since a rectangular parallelepiped can rest on any of its faces, we can treat any face as the base.

In Figure 78 the visible faces of the parallelepiped are numbered 1, 2, 3; those we cannot see are numbered 4, 5, and 6. We can agree to regard any one of these six faces as the base of the rectangular parallelepiped (removing the parallelepiped from the string, we can place it on this face). Thus, *a rectangular parallelepiped is a solid that has six faces, each of which is a rectangle.*

3. Edges and Vertices. *The sides of the rectangles that form the faces of a rectangular parallelepiped are called its edges. In Figure 79 we see several edges of a rectangular parallelepiped: AB, BC, CD, AD, AE, CG, DH, EH, GH*; the other three edges we cannot see are: *EF, BF, FG*. A rectangular parallelepiped has a total of 12 edges. They can be regarded

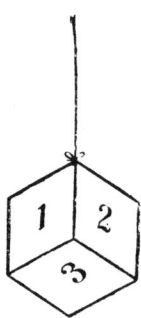

Figure 78.

The Concept of Volume

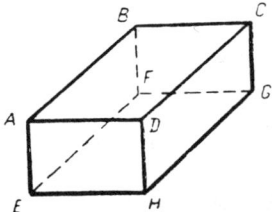

Figure 79.

in this way: 4 edges belong to the lower base, 4 to the upper, and 4 edges (in Fig. 79, edges *AE*, *BF*, *CG*, *DH*) join the upper and lower bases. Two faces of the rectangular parallelepiped adjoin each edge. For example, in Figure 79 faces *ABCD* and *ADHE* adjoin edge *AD*; faces *ADHE* and *CDHG* adjoin edge *DH*.

The endpoints of the segments which form the edges of a rectangular parallelepiped are called its vertices. For each face of a rectangular parallelepiped there are 4 *edges* and 4 *vertices*. For example, edges *AB*, *BC*, *CD*, and *DA* and vertices *A*, *B*, *C*, and *D* lie on face *ABCD* (Fig. 79). A rectangular parallelepiped has a total of 8 *vertices*—4 on the lower and 4 on the upper base. Three edges and three faces meet at each vertex of a rectangular parallelepiped. For example, in Figure 79, three edges *AD*, *CD*, and *DH* and three faces *ABCD*, *ADHE*, and *DCGH* meet at vertex *D*.

4. Adjacent and Opposite Faces. Two faces of a rectangular parallelepiped that share a common edge are said to be *adjacent faces*. For example, in Figure 79 faces 1 and 3 are adjacent. Faces 2 and 3 are also adjacent. In Figure 79 faces *ABCD* and *DCGH* adjoin edge *CD*; these faces are adjacent.

Two faces of a rectangular parallelepiped that have no edges in common are said to be *opposite faces*. For example, the lower and the upper bases are two opposite faces. Faces *ABFE* and *CDHG* in Figure

79 are opposite. A rectangular parallelepiped has three pairs of opposite faces.

Two opposite faces of a rectangular parallelepiped are *congruent*. For example, if we cut a paper rectangle that can be precisely superimposed on the front face of a rectangular parallelepiped, the same rectangle can be superimposed precisely on the back face as well. A lower base of a rectangular parallelepiped is congruent to its upper base; the front face is congruent to the back face; and the left face is congruent to the right face.

5. Groups of Four Parallel Edges. Let us look once more at Figure 79. Edges *AE* and *DH* are opposite sides of rectangle *ADHE* (the front face). These edges are congruent and parallel. Edge *DH* is congruent and parallel to edge *CG*—for these edges are the opposite sides of face *CDHG*. Likewise, *BF* is congruent and parallel to *CG*. Thus we have four mutually congruent and parallel edges: *AE*, *DH*, *CG*, and *BF*.

Similarly, edges *BC*, *AD*, *EH*, and *FG* comprise another set of four edges that are congruent and parallel to one another. However, these edges need not be either congruent or parallel to the edges in the first set of four. There is a third set of four such edges (*AB*, *CD*, *GH*, and *EF*), all of which are mutually congruent and parallel. Thus, we have found three pairwise disjoint sets of four edges in the rectangular parallelepiped. All four edges in a particular set are congruent and and parallel to one another.

6. The Dimensions of a Rectangular Parallelepiped. The three edges of a rectangular parallelepiped that meet at a given vertex belong to three *different* sets of four edges such as just described. For example, edges *AB*, *AD*, and *AE* meet at vertex *A*. In Figure 80 three edges of a rectangular parallelepiped that meet at a vertex are indicated with heavy lines. Their lengths are 3 cm, 5 cm, and 2 cm. Therefore the parallelepiped shown in this figure has dimensions of 3, 5, and 2 cm.

In Figure 79 face *EFGH* is the lower base of the parallelepiped. Edges *AE*, *BF*, *CG*, and *DH* extend from the base to its opposite face. They make up a set of four congruent and parallel edges. Each of these edges is called a *height* of the rectangular parallelepiped. *An edge extending from the*

The Concept of Volume

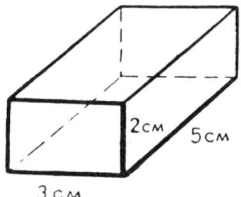

Figure 80.

base to the opposite face is said to be the height of a rectangular parallelepiped.

If, for example, we take face *ABFE* as a base in the parallelepiped represented in Figure 81, then edge *AD* (or any one of *BC*, *FG*, or *EH*) will be the height.

Let us take any vertex belonging to the base of a rectangular parallelepiped—for example, vertex *H* in Figure 79. Three edges meet at this vertex: *DH*, *EH*, and *GH*. Edge *DH* is the height, and edges *EH* and *GH* belong to the base of the rectangular parallelepiped. They are called its *length* and *width* (Fig. 82). The length, width, and height are the three edges belonging to three different sets of four edges. The lengths of these edges, also called the length, width, and height of the rectangular parallelepiped, are the three dimensions of a rectangular parallelepiped. The first two dimensions (length and width) indicate the measurements of the base.

Height is the third dimension of a rectangular parallelepiped. Again, note that both this edge and the length of the edge are referred to as the height.

7. The Surface and Frame of a Rectangular Parallelepiped. A rectangular parallelepiped is a solid, and, as such, includes its interior. For example, a wooden bar sawed in the shape of a rectangular parallelepiped (Fig. 83) will provide an idea of this solid. There is no empty space inside this bar.

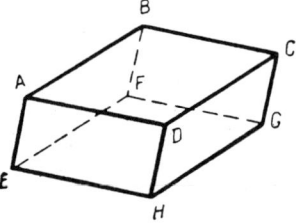

Figure 81.

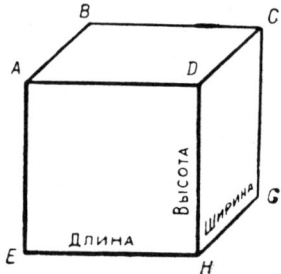

Figure 82.

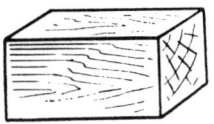

Figure 83.

The Concept of Volume

An empty shoebox, for example, contains nothing on the inside, although externally it has the same shape as the bar. It offers an idea of the *surface* of a rectangular parallelepiped. The surface is made up of the 6 rectangular faces of the box. It is like the outer shell of a parallelepiped.

The 12 edges of a parallelepiped, taken together, form the *frame* of a rectangular parallelepiped. An idea of the frame can be acquired by welding 12 small wires together (Fig. 84). If we have such a wire frame and if we cover it with 6 paper rectangles (instead of faces), we can easily imagine the surface of a rectangular parallelepiped (Fig. 85). But even without being covered in this way, the frame will give us a clear notion of the shape of a rectangular parallelepiped, its vertices, edges, and faces.

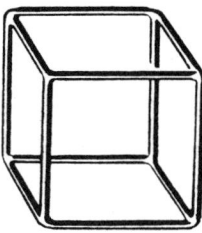

Figure 84.

Figure 85.

8. A Two-Dimensional Pattern for a Rectangular Parallelepiped.

It is not difficult to glue together six paper rectangles in the shape of a closed box representing the surface of a rectangular parallelepiped. (Adjacent faces can be attached to each other by making folds along the edges as in Fig. 86.) Of course, if we now cut the surface along all of the edges, it again falls apart into 6 rectangles. But we shall make the cut along only some of the edges.

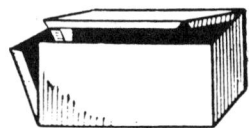

Figure 86.

First we cut the surface along the three edges belonging to the upper base. Now, the upper base can be partly opened, like a lid (Fig. 87). Then we cut the surface along the four parallel edges that form the heights (Fig. 88). The remaining surface is easily opened (Fig. 89) and subsequently transformed into the plane sheet of paper shown in Figure 90. We have now unfolded the surface of the figure.

If we were now to repeat all the folds, and then glue together the edges along which the cuts were made, then (as shown in Fig. 90) we would again obtain the surface of a rectangular parallelepiped. The figure shown in Figure 90 is called a pattern, or *evolute*, of a rectangular parallelepiped.

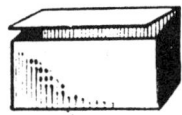

Figure 87.

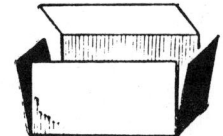

Figure 88.

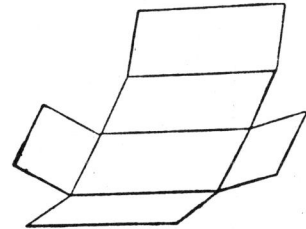

Figure 89.

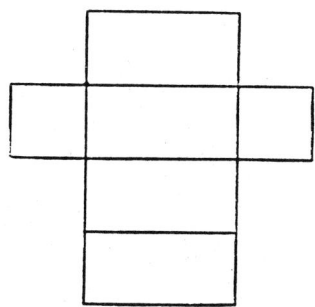

Figure 90.

9. The Cube. In the rectangular parallelepiped shown in Figure 91, two dimensions (length and height) are identical. The front face of this parallelepiped is a square. The back face is the same kind of square. The other four faces are rectangles, all equal to one another. In this parallelepiped the length and the height are identical, but the width is different (it is greater than the length).

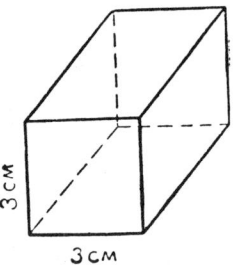

Figure 91.

Figure 92 shows a rectangular parallelepiped in which all three dimensions are identical. *A rectangular parallelepiped in which all three dimensions are identical is called a cube.*

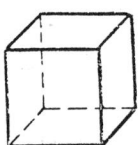

Figure 92.

A cube has 6 faces, all of which are congruent squares. All 12 edges of the cube are equal. A two-dimensional pattern of a cube is shown in Figure 93.

The Concept of Volume

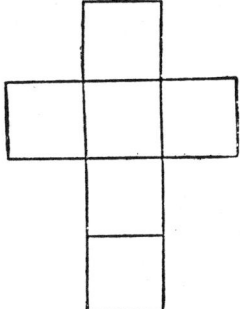

Figure 93.

II. The Volume of a Solid

10. The Basic Concept of Volume. There is more water in the carafe than in the cup (Fig. 94). It is said that the carafe's *capacity* (or cubic content) is greater than the capacity of the cup. Two cups of water have been poured into the carafe. In this case we say that the volume of the water in the carafe is equal to 2 cups. But the carafe is not filled to the brim. Altogether, it will hold 5 cups. This means that the cubic content of the carafe is equivalent to 5 cups, while the volume of the water it contains is 2 cups. Three more cups of water could be added to the carafe.

Figure 94.

If the carafe were filled to the top, the volume of water it contains would be equal to 5 cups.

Liquids are not the only things that have volume. The jar shown in Figure 95 contains salt. It has volume. Right now there are 2 cups of salt in the jar.

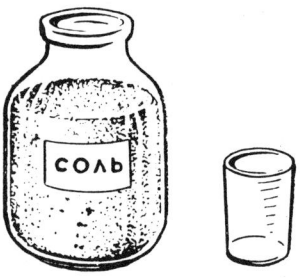

Figure 95.

To make good jam, we need to know the volume of sugar and the volume of berries. For example, in making gooseberry jam, the volume of berries and of sugar should be the same. Seven cups of gooseberries have been poured into a pan, and the sugar is still in the package (Fig. 96). How much of it do we need? We must measure the volume of the sugar. To do so, we pour it out, measuring it with cups. There turn out to be 7 cups of sugar in the package—just the amount we needed.

Figure 96.

The Concept of Volume

Figure 97 shows some children's blocks, along with a cardboard box. Six blocks can be put into the box. Can more than six blocks go into the box? No. Each block occupies a certain amount of space; it has volume. If we put six blocks into the box, there will be no room left in it. Six blocks occupy so much room that they fill the entire box. This can be stated otherwise: The volume of the six blocks is equal to the capacity of the box. *All objects around us take up room in space. All of them have volume.*

Figure 97.

11. Measuring Volume. The volume of liquid or dry substances can be measured in cups. But how can we measure the volume of a hard solid such as a small rock? We cannot pour it out in cups! To find the volume of a rock, we can proceed as follows. We take an aquarium and fill it approximately half full of water. Then we make a mark on the glass to show the level reached by the water in the aquarium (Fig. 98). Now we drop a stone into the aquarium (Fig. 99). The rock sinks in the water, and the water in the aquarium rises higher. Why? Because the rock has volume; it occupies space. Formerly this space was filled by the water, but now the rock has displaced the water. What has become of the water that was displaced by the rock? It has occupied space above the mark that we made earlier. We make a second mark on the cup to show the new level of the water in the aquarium (Fig. 99). How much water has been displaced into the space between the two marks we have made (more precisely—between the old and new levels of the liquid)? How much

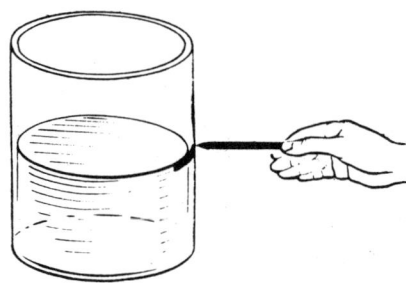

Figure 98.

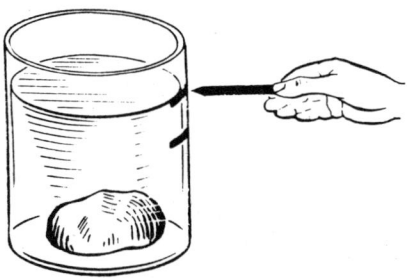

Figure 99.

space is occupied by the water displaced by the rock? It clearly occupies the same amount of space as the rock that has placed in the water. In other words, the volume of the displaced liquid is equal to the volume of the rock. *The volume of a solid submerged in a liquid is equal to the volume of the liquid displaced by it.*

Once we know this, it is easy to measure the volume of a rock. We dip the water out of the aquarium with cups. When we remove one cup of water from the aquarium, the level of the liquid lowers somewhat, but it still does not reach the lower mark. We remove another cup of water from

The Concept of Volume

the aquarium, and then another. After removing 5 cups of water, we note that the water level coincides with the lower mark. This means that the volume of the water displaced by the rock was equal to 5 cups. But then we can say that the volume of the rock is itself equal to 5 cups. By immersing hard solids in a liquid, we can find their volume.

12. Units of Volume. Cups are available in various capacities. Therefore measuring volume in cups is an imprecise method. For example, the salt in a package might fill 12 cups of one type, but 10 cups of another.

In medieval Russia, cloth was measured in cubits. This was inconvenient. A tall man would buy 10 cubits of cloth from a short salesman, would go home and, measuring it by his own forearm, find there would scarcely be 9 cubits. Nowadays, lengths are measured in millimeters, centimeters, decimeters, kilometers—all rigidly established *units* for measuring length. The centimeter in Moscow and in Leningrad, whether measured by one person or another, is identical. The situation is the same for the measurement of volume. For precise measurements we must establish rigid *standard units* for measuring volume which are the same for everything.

Milk from a tap is measured in *tankards*. When these are made at a factory, they are strictly checked so that they all have exactly the same cubic content. The cubic content of such a tankard (that is, the volume of the liquid it holds) is called a *liter*. Besides liter tankards, we also use smaller measuring cups equivalent to half of a large tankard—half a liter.

Even smaller units of measure than the liter are required in preparing medicines and in many other situations. A *milliliter*—one-thousandth of a liter—is one such unit. The volume of a liquid in milliliters can be measured by a *graduated cylinder* (Fig. 100). If liquid fills a graduated cylinder to the 5 mark, then the volume of the liquid is equal to 5 milliliters; if it goes to the 15 mark, then it is 15 milliliters.

We can use graduated cylinders and cups to measure the volume not only of liquid and dry substances, but also of small hard solids. Suppose we wish to measure the volume of a steel ball. To do so we fill a graduated cylinder approximately half full of water and note the water level. When

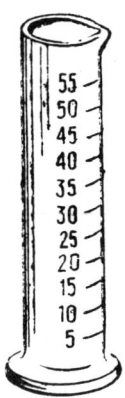

Figure 100.

we drop the ball into the water, the water rises 5 milliliters. Then we know that the volume of the ball is equal to 5 milliliters.

13. Cubic Measures. Let us select a unit for measuring length. In our country we have settled on metric measures of length—millimeters (mm), centimeters (cm), decimeters (dm), meters (m), kilometers (km). In England they use an inch—a unit of length equal to approximately two and one-half centimeters. There are other units of measuring length, too—feet, miles, etc. Moreover, we can take any segment as a unit of length. But once we have chosen a unit for measuring length, we should not change it until we finish our measurement.

A cube whose edge is equal to a unit of length is called a *unit cube* (or a unit of volume). *A cube with an edge equal to one millimeter is called a cubic millimeter. A cube with an edge equal to one centimeter is called a cubic centimeter.* A cubic meter, cubic decimeter, and cubic kilometer can be defined in the same way. *The volume of a solid is a number showing how many of the chosen units of volume are contained in the solid.*

The solid shown in Figure 101 is made up of 5 unit cubes. The volume of the solid is equal to 5. If, however, someone informs you that the

The Concept of Volume

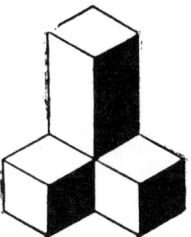

Figure 101.

volume of a solid is equal to 5, you still cannot say how much room it occupies in space. You merely know it contains 5 unit cubes. But how large is the unit cube itself? You have not been informed of this. If 1 mm is taken as a unit of length, then a cube with an edge of 1 mm will be the unit cube. A solid containing 5 of these unit cubes is rather small. But if 1 m is taken as the unit of length, then a cube with an edge of 1 m is the unit cube. A solid containing 5 of these cubes is rather large; it will fill an entire room.

This means that, to have a proper idea of how much space is occupied by a solid, we must know: 1) the volume of the solid; and 2) the unit of volume (that is, the unit cube). For example, suppose the volume of a solid is equal to 5, taking a cubic meter as the unit of volume. Here everything is explicit, but the result is a rather lengthy statement. For brevity's sake let us agree to write this idea in the following way:

the volume of a solid is equal to 5 cubic m

(which is read as: "The volume of a solid is equal to five cubic meters"). Or, even more briefly, we can write the formula:

$$V = 5 \text{ (cubic m)}.$$

The designation "cubic m" pertains to the entire equality, and is only a reminder that a cubic meter was taken as the unit of volume.

Sometimes we speak of "the volume of a solid in cubic meters," "the volume of a solid in cubic centimeters," and so forth. For example, we ask: "What is the volume of this rectangular parallelepiped in cubic meters?" In a more detailed formulation this is equivalent to asking:

"What will the volume of this rectangular parallelepiped be if a cubic meter is taken as the unit of measuring volume?"

14. The Relation between the Liter and Cubic Measures. Look again at Figure 101. It represents a solid that can be cut into 5 small cubes with an edge of 1 cm. The volume of this solid is equal to 5 cubic cm. However, the volume of this solid can also be computed in another way: we can drop it into a graduated cylinder containing water and check the volume of water displaced. Then we will learn the volume of this solid in milliliters. If we do this, we shall see that the volume of this solid is equal to 5 milliliters. This means that the volume of the solid in cubic centimeters is identical to its volume in milliliters.

In precisely the same way, the volume of a solid in cubic decimeters is identical to its volume in liters. If, for example, the volume of a solid is equal to 35 cubic dm, we can also say that its volume is 35 l.

In order to verify that a volume of 1 cubic dm coincides exactly with a liter, let us conduct this experiment. We make an aquarium out of glass in the shape of a cube whose inner edge is equal to 1 dm. The cubic content of this aquarium is precisely equal to 1 cubic dm. Now if we fill a one-liter tankard with water up to its edges and pour this water into the aquarium, we will see that the water fills it completely. Therefore, exactly one liter of liquid will fill this aquarium.

How can it be that the volume of one cubic decimeter coincides exactly with a liter? Is this a coincidence? No, of course not! It is simply that, when the mold of the tankard was made at the factory, its dimensions were calculated such that precisely 1 cubic dm of liquid would go into it. Thus, we can speak of volume in cubic dm, and we can speak of volume in liters—they are precisely the same. Most frequently the volume of liquids or dry substances is expressed in liters or milliliters, and that of solids—in cubic centimeters, decimeters, etc.

15. Computing the Volume of a Rectangular Parallelepiped. We can find the volume of a small hard solid by the method previously described—immersion in liquid. But, of course, it is impossible to find the volume of a house, or the volume of air in a room by this method. In such instances, instead of *measuring* the volume directly, we *compute* the

The Concept of Volume 177

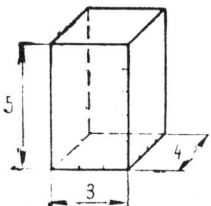

Figure 102.

volume. We should learn to compute the volume of a rectangular parallelepiped.

Let us consider the rectangular parallelepiped shown in Figure 102. The dimensions of this parallelepiped are equal to 3, 4, and 5 units. To compute the volume of this rectangular parallelepiped, we mentally cut it into unit cubes, as illustrated in Figure 103. Now we must count to see how many unit cubes there are—this number will also be the volume. Look at the lower base of the figure. It is a rectangle whose sides are equal to 3 and 4 units of length. Therefore it can be divided into 12 unit squares ($3 \times 4 = 12$). In Figure 104 the lower base is drawn in unit squares. We can place a unit cube on each of these squares. As a result we get one layer of unit cubes placed on the base (Fig. 105). How many unit cubes are in this layer? Just as many as the number of squares in the parallelepiped's base— 12. Now we place another unit cube on each of the cubes. We obtain another layer (Fig. 106). In this layer there are also 12 unit cubes. There are also 12 cubes in the third, fourth and fifth layers. When we have made 5 of these layers, we obtain the original parallelepiped, made up of unit cubes. Now it is not hard to determine the volume of this parallelepiped. It contains 5 layers, with 12 unit cubes in each layer, or a total of $12 \times 5 = 60$ unit cubes. Thus, the volume of the parallelepiped in Figure 102 is equal to 60.

16. Formula for the Volume of a Rectangular Parallelepiped. Now we take a rectangular parallelepiped of length a, width b, and height c

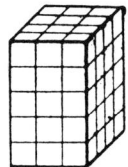

Figure 103.

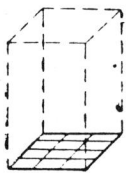

Figure 104.

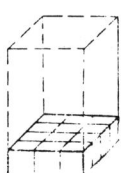

Figure 105.

The Concept of Volume

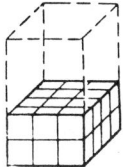

Figure 106.

(Fig. 107). The unit of length is marked off a times on edge OA, b times on edge OB, and c times on edge OC. In order to find the volume of this rectangular parallelepiped, we do just what we did before—we cut it into unit cubes. The parallelepiped's lower base has an area of ab (since it is a rectangle of length a and width b). Then we can draw in ab unit squares on the lower base (cf. Fig. 104), and therefore ab unit cubes can be placed on the base in one layer (cf. Fig. 105). There will also be ab unit cubes in the second layer, the third layer, and so on. We will have c layers of cubes in all (Fig. 108). Since there are ab unit cubes in each layer, the total number of unit cubes in our parallelepiped is equal to $ab \times c$—so it is equal to abc. Therefore, the volume of a rectangular parallelepiped is equal to abc. Let us designate the volume by the letter V. We can now write a *formula for the volume of a rectangular parallelepiped*:

$$V = abc.$$

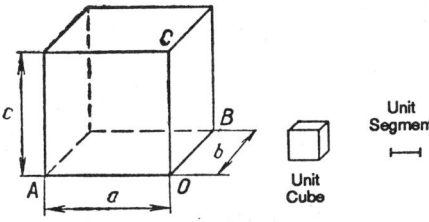

Figure 107.

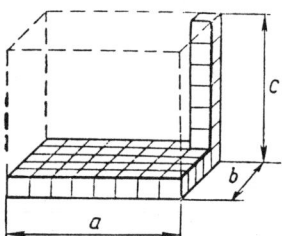

Figure 108.

The volume of a rectangular parallelepiped is equal to the product of its three dimensions.

If the lengths of the edges of a rectangular parallelepiped are measured in linear measures, then, by this formula, the volume is obtained in corresponding cubic measures. For example, if the lengths of the edges are measured in meters, the volume is given in cubic meters.

17. Second Formula for the Volume of a Rectangular Parallelepiped. The volume of a rectangular parallelepiped can also be calculated if we know the area of its base and its height. Let us designate the area of the base of a rectangular parallelepiped by S, and the height by h (Fig. 109). Then the base can be drawn in S unit squares, and therefore S unit cubes are needed for one layer of the base (see Fig. 105). There will also be S unit cubes in the second layer, in the third, and so on. We should have h layers in all, each containing S unit cubes. Therefore, the entire solid is made up of Sh unit cubes. The volume of this parallelepiped is

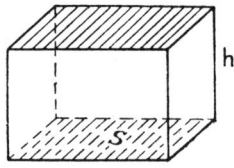

Figure 109.

The Concept of Volume

equal to Sh. Thus, we have obtained a second formula for the volume of a rectangular parallelepiped:

$$V = Sh.$$

The volume of a rectangular parallelepiped is equal to the product of its height and the area of its base.

If the height is measured in linear units, and the area of the base in corresponding square units, then the volume is given in corresponding cubic measures. For example, if the height is measured in centimeters, and the area of the base in square centimeters, then the volume is obtained in cubic centimeters.

18. The Volume of a Cube. A cube is a rectangular parallelepiped in which all the edges are identical. If the length of the edge of a cube is equal to a, then the length, width, and height of this cube are all equal to a. By the formula for volume we find that the volume of a cube is equal to $a \times a \times a$. *The product of three identical factors equal to a is called the cube of the number a, and is written a^3*:

$$a \times a \times a = a^3$$

Thus, for a cube with an edge equal to a, we obtain the following formula for the volume:

$$V = a^3.$$

19. Conversion from One Unit of Measurement to Another. Suppose that the volume of a rectangular parallelepiped is equal to 6 cubic dm. What will be the volume of the same parallelepiped in cubic centimeters? To solve this problem, we note that a cube with an edge of 1 dm has a volume of 1,000 cubic cm. This is obtained by the formula for the volume of a cube, with $a = 10$ (since there are 10 centimeters in one decimeter):

$$V = 10^3 = 1,000 \text{ (cubic cm)}.$$

This means that a rectangular parallelepiped containing 6 cubic dm will have a volume of $6 \times 1,000 = 6,000$ (cubic cm). A table for converting from one cubic measure to another is given in the workbook included in the instructional unit .

4

Description of the Instructional Unit for the Topic "The Rectangular Parallelepiped and Its Volume," and the Methodology of Using It

Development of the Unit—Practical Application of the Theory

The nomenclature, form, and content of a thematic set of instructional materials are determined by the content of the material to be taught. Therefore, before describing the set of instructional materials on the topic "The Rectangular Parallelepiped and Its Volume," let us describe the topic itself and the subtopics that comprise it.

In the grade 4 curriculum, the volume of a rectangular parallelepiped is addressed in connection with the laws of arithmetic operations. Indeed, the commutative and associative laws of multiplication, $ab = ba$ and $a(bc) = (ab)c$, are well illustrated by the formulas for volume, $V = abc$ and $V = Sh$. The student who understands the calculation of volume by these formulas and is certain that it does not depend on the method of calculation, can through this example realize that the laws of multiplication are valid.

It should also be noted that a rectangular parallelepiped is actually the first spatial solid that fourth-graders encounter. Here for the first time the problem of developing spatial concepts arises. Finally, the concept of volume itself—from a rudimentary notion up to a formula for the volume of a rectangular parallelepiped—is also new to the students. Therefore, before deriving a formula for the volume of a rectangular parallelepiped, the teacher must give the students a basic notion of volume in general, make them realize that the volume of a solid—the number—represents something real, some property inherent in objects. Without this, the concept of volume (of a rectangular parallelepiped) is identified with the formula *abc*. The concrete, geometric meaning of both the concept of volume and this formula is lost. As a result the formula for volume, $V = abc$, does not become concrete material for clarifying the laws of multiplication.

When asked why volume can be computed by the formula $V = (ab)c$, or $V = a(bc)$, the student can give only one response: because of the associative law of multiplication. This student cannot see the actual intuitive, geometric reasons why these formulas coincide (at least, traditional explanations of this material do not develop such insight).

In Chapter III we outlined various means of overcoming mere formal mastery of the formulas for the volume of a rectangular parallelepiped, where we considered various methodological questions related to the concept of volume. Given a scientifically valid and methodologically substantiated presentation, the student should conceive of volume as a reality, and should see the concrete sense in multiplying dimensions and in combining two factors in order to compute volume.

As a result we conclude that the entire topic under consideration should be divided into the following three basic subtopics:

    A. The concept of a rectangular parallelepiped.

    B. The concept of volume.

    C. Calculation of the volume of a rectangular parallelepiped (with parallel study and application of the laws of operations).

Of course, each of these subtopics can also be further subdivided. Let us consider, for example, the subtopic "The Concept of a Rectangular Parallelepiped." Fourth-graders can cope with a definition of a rectangular parallelepiped as a solid bounded by 6 rectangular faces. But the concept of a "face" is new to them. Therefore, before introducing this definition, the teacher must conduct the necessary *orientation*—using physical examples of polyhedra to teach them the concept of a "face" and help them learn to pick out rectangular parallelepipeds from among other solids shown to them.

The definition of a rectangular parallelepiped does not contain the terms "edge" and "vertex." But one of the main tasks of the topic is to teach the children to calculate the volume of a rectangular parallelepiped by multiplying its three *dimensions*. Therefore, we must not only define the concept of an "edge," but also show which edges of a rectangular parallelepiped are equal, and the lengths of which edges (those originating from one vertex) are the dimensions of a rectangular parallelepiped.

In just the same way, we must not train students simply to calculate the volume of a rectangular parallelepiped by multiplying the area of the base by the height if that student does not understand that *opposite faces are equal*. The concepts of "base" and "height" are prerequisites for complete understanding.

When solving problems on calculating volumes, we must strive to develop students' spatial thinking. In particular, they should be schooled in drawing a rectangular parallelepiped. Thus, they must understand how to represent the visible and invisible edges and faces.

A drawing of a rectangular parallelepiped is useless without letter designations for its vertices and edges. There is no point in delaying the introduction of the customary use of letters of the Latin alphabet to designate points and segments in mathematics. Therefore, we regard it as important to cultivate *Latin designations* (just as during the study of the laws of the arithmetic operations).

In section 23 we cited an approach to the concept of volume that led from a basic notion of volume as a part of space occupied by a solid to the concept of volume as a number. To achieve these most difficult objectives, we must develop the entire chain of concepts of *length-area-volume* and define a unit of volume. A mandatory requirement is the development of a scientific definition of a *cube* as a special case of a rectangular parallelepiped. Simultaneously, in order to assure fluent use of the formulas $V = abc$ and $V = Sh$, the students should thoroughly master the concepts of length and area and the formula for calculating the area of a rectangle. The concepts of a *frame* and a two-dimensional *pattern* of a rectangular parallelepiped are helpful.

As a result, we can compile the following list of concepts and skills that must be developed during the study of the first basic subtopic ("The Concept of a Rectangular Parallelepiped"):

(1) A rudimentary notion of a rectangular parallelepiped.

(2) The ability to pick out rectangular parallelepipeds from among a collection of solids.

(3) Attribution of idealized properties to solids.

(4) A notion of the face of a polyhedron.

(5) Definition of a rectangular parallelepiped.

(6) The cube as a special case of a rectangular parallelepiped.

(7) The concepts of an edge and a vertex.

(8) The equality of parallel edges.

(9) Sets of four equal and parallel edges.

(10) The frame of a rectangular parallelepiped.

(11) Adjacent and opposite faces.

(12) The equality of opposite faces.

(13) The dimensions of a rectangular parallelepiped.

(14) The base and the height.

(15) Drawing a rectangular parallelepiped.

(16) The Latin alphabet.

(17) The two-dimensional pattern of a rectangular parallelepiped.

(18) Skills for finding the sum of the lengths of the edges.

Description of an Instructional Unit and Methods of Use 187

(19) Skills for finding the area of each face and the entire surface area.

We could compile similar lists of crucial concepts and procedures for the other basic subtopics. We will not cite them, although it should be clear, however, that such lists would include several dozen entries and cover an extensive amount of material. Note that the traditional curriculum alloted 16 hours for the topic "The Volume of a Rectangular Parallelepiped." The new curriculum, although it allots significantly less time to this topic, calls for mastery of all the points listed above. This is made possible by the distribution of the material on the topic "The Volume of a Rectangular Parallelepiped." It is envisioned that mastery of the material on the concepts of the rectangular parallelepiped, the volume of a rectangular parallelepiped, and so forth, will be distributed over the entire grade 4 mathematics course. Thus, the lesson plans cited in Chapter V, which pertain to a 16-hour segment of the course, are only tentative. We regard them as a method of illustrating, with concrete material, our view on the most effective use of the materials that make up the instructional unit.

In order to successfully teach each subtopic given above, an entire arsenal of educational materials was included in the unit. Consider, for an example, the first item—*a rudimentary notion of a rectangular parallelepiped*. The presentation of this idea was "delegated" to 1) the first few frames of the single-concept film, "The Rectangular Parallelepiped;" 2) frame 2 of the filmstrip, "The Rectangular Parallelepiped and Its Volume"; 3) a collection of solids; and 4) a collection of small objects assembled on the teacher's desk. These same aids are also used for the second point—*the ability to pick out a rectangular parallelepiped from among a collection of solids*.

The third point—*attribution of idealized properties to solids*—is a matter of abstract idealization, leading to the notion of an ideal mathematical object (namely, the rectangular parallelepiped). This subtopic is demonstrated through subsequent frames of the first single-concept film. No matter how often the teacher has stated that students should ignore the colors on a matchbox, the protruding parts of a suitcase, a cupboard, etc., it will be hard for the student to achieve this process of idealization. The process of abstraction requires a protracted length of time. On the screen, however, these superfluous protruding parts *literally* vanish, just as if the student is seeing the process of abstraction on the screen.

Thus, in examining the nineteen points, we arrived at the most expedient instructional media that can be consistently applied in lessons. The question arises as to which representations should be displayed in charts, and which on frames for a projector. Moreover, of the frames meant for the slide projector, some should be selected for a filmstrip, and some for a slide series. Of course, the theoretical considerations developed in Chapter 1 were critical to our decisions. The theory developed in Chapter 2 helped us select assignments for the workbook and problem cards and construct graduated solids and other objects which enabled us to effect adequate and appropriate activity for learning the necessary concepts. In elaborating objects for the concept of volume and implementing appropriate activity for the students, the basis was, of course, the theory set forth in Chapter 3.

We do not regard it as advisable to describe in detail how the objects in the unit were obtained, and which elements of the theory developed above have been used in each individual instance. What is important is the very fact of a *theoretical* design for the unit, proceeding from the theory in Chapters 1-3. Thus, the unit described below not only serves as a collection of materials for creating effective opportunities for teaching the chosen topic but is also an illustration of the theory set forth above.

Description of the Single-Concept Films

The following 5 single-concept films are included in the unit:

1) "The Rectangular Parallelepiped";

2) "Drawing a Rectangular Parallelepiped";

3) "The Concept of Volume";

Description of an Instructional Unit and Methods of Use

4) "The Volume of a Solid"; and

5) "The Volume of a Rectangular Parallelepiped."

Below we give the scenarios of these five films.

"A Rectangular Parallelepiped""

Visual	Voiceover
A bookshelf or cabinet with a clearly-defined shape of a rectangular parallelepiped, a suitcase, and a mail package appear in sequence and remain in the frame.	These objects differ from one another.
The material of which each object is made is thoroughly illustrated. The objects are arranged on the screen so that their dimensions can be observed.	They have different purposes, different dimensions, and are made of different materials.
Zoom in on the cabinet. Its individual details (doors, handles, etc.) gradually disappear, leaving a rectangular parallelepiped in the frame. Pull back to show the parallelepiped, suitcase, and package.	But they have one quality in common.
Zoom in on the suitcase. The handle, rounded corners, latches, and other details disappear. A rectangular parallelepiped remains. Pull back to the full frame, which now shows two parallelepipeds and a package.	All of them have the shape... of a rectangular parallelepiped.

"A Rectangular Parallelepiped" (continued)

Visual	Voiceover
Zoom in on the package. The labels, stamps, string, and other details disappear. In the frame is a rectangular parallelepiped.	
All three rectangular parallelepipeds are in the frame. Their former qualities are "restored." Fade out.	
Fade in on a modern apartment house. The details gradually vanish; the building is transformed into a rectangular parallelepiped.	An apartment house also has the shape of a rectangular parallelepiped.
The house is "restored" and shrinks out of the frame. A matchbox appears from the center; zoom in on it. Its details disappear. A rectangular parallelepiped looms large in the frame.	Many objects around us have the shape of a rectangular parallelepiped.
A rectangular parallelepiped. It turns slowly. Its rectangular faces are clearly apparent each time.	A parallelepiped is bounded by rectangles.
One face is illuminated. It coincides with the plane of the screen.	They are called the faces of a rectangular parallelepiped.
The parallelepiped comes to a rest. The edges on it sparkle and are illuminated.	These segments are called the edges of the rectangular parallelepiped.
The illuminated edges form a framework model. The edges vanish. The former parallelepiped reappears in the frame. Its vertices sparkle and are illuminated in succession.	These points are called the vertices of the rectangular parallelepiped.

"A Rectangular Parallelepiped" (continued)

Visual	Voiceover
The parallelepiped with the illuminated vertices turns, gradually showing the vertices. The vertices fade out. The original parallelepiped is shown.	
The parallelepiped's upper base is illuminated. A rectangle breaks away and moves to coincide with the lower base.	The upper and lower faces are equal to each other. They are called the bases.
The front face is illuminated. A copy of it moves inside the parallelepiped and coincides with the back face.	These two opposite faces of the parallelepiped are also equal.
The right lateral face is illuminated and moves to coincide with the left.	A rectangular parallelepiped has three pairs of equal faces.
The rectangular parallelepiped is placed on one of its lateral faces.	Any face can be a base.
The parallelepiped is restored to its original form. The four equal edges sparkle and are illuminated. A copy of an edge breaks away and moves from one to another in succession, coinciding with each each of these four edges.	These four edges are equal.
Another set of four edges is similarly illuminated. It is obvious that they are equal.	These four edges are equal, too.
Finally, the remaining four edges are illuminated.	And these four edges are equal segments.
The original parallelepiped is restored in the frame. Fade out. End.	

"Drawing a Rectangular Parallelepiped"

Visual	Voiceover
A rectangular parallelepiped of translucent material appears in the center of the frame. Three faces and their edges are clearly visible. The other edges and faces are barely visible through the nearly opaque material. The camera pulls back and it decreases in size. The parallelepiped moves to the upper left corner and stays there until near the end of the film.	Let's draw a rectangular parallelepiped in a diagram.
A sheet of paper appears in the center of the frame. The parallelepiped's front face is illuminated.	The front face of the parallelepiped is a rectangle.
The upper left vertex of the front face is illuminated. This vivid point moves along the perimeter of the rectangle, leaving a distinct outline. A point appears on the sheet of paper simultaneously. It moves, leaving the outline of a similar rectangle.	
The parallelepiped's visible right face is illuminated. It is outlined brightly.	We see the right face as a quadrangle... whose opposite sides are equal and parallel.
From the front side of this rectangle a copy of the edge breaks away and moves until it is matched with the opposite side. The same occurs with another pair of sides. The segments (sides of the right face) are drawn on the sheet of paper.	Let's trace this face.

"Drawing a Rectangular Parallelepiped" (continued)

Visual	Voiceover
The upper face is illuminated. An outline is traced around it to show that the opposite faces are equal.	We see the upper face as a quadrangle in which opposite sides are also equal and parallel. Let's trace the upper face.
The visible edges of the rectangular parallelepiped are drawn on the paper.	
A finished drawing of the visible edges and faces of a rectangular parallelepiped is in the frame.	We have drawn the visible part of the figure.
One of the hidden edges stands out more vividly, sparkles, and is replaced by a dotted line on the model of the parallelepiped. A copy of it gradually moves to the picture in the center of the frame. The same thing happens with the other edges.	We will agree to draw the hidden edges of a rectangular parallelepiped with dotted lines.
A copy of the front face falls away and moves to merge with the back face. The same thing happens with the other opposite faces.	If a diagram is properly done, the opposite faces should be congruent quadrangles.
The model of the parallelepiped moves, increasing in size, until it coincides with the drawing of the parallelepiped in the center of the screen.	
The material parallelepiped disappears and the representation remains on the left. The outline of the front face is illuminated while the same rectangle is simultaneously drawn in animation.	A rectangular parallelepiped can also be drawn in the reverse order.

"Drawing a Rectangular Parallelepiped" (continued)

Visual	Voiceover
The edges sparkle and are illuminated, moving away from the vertices of the front face of the representation on the left. On the right, three segments and one dotted line appear. Animation first fills in the visible edges, then the hidden ones (with dotted lines). Fade out. End.	

"The Concept of Volume"

Visual	Voiceover
A glass and a cylindrical glass pitcher simultaneously appear in the frame. Each is filled with water. The water is poured out of the pitcher. Water from the glass is poured into the empty pitcher.	The pitcher holds more water than the glass. We say that the cubic content, or capacity, of the pitcher is greater than that of the glass.
The pitcher and the glass are again filled with water.	We also say that the volume of water in the full pitcher is greater than the volume of water in the glass.
There appears a box filled with lump sugar (with the label "Sugar" on it), and an open package filled with sugar lumps (with the same label).	There is more sugar in the box than in the package.

"The Concept of Volume" (continued)

Visual	Voiceover
The box and the package tip over simultaneously. The sugar from the box and the package spill out into piles of different sizes.	The volume of sugar in the box is greater.
In the frame are four identical molds (for playing in the sand), inserted one inside another.	These molds are identical.
The molds are placed in a single row. On them the numerals 1, 2, 3, 4 can be seen. We see the first mold filled with water, then the second with sand, then the third is levelled off.	We fill the first mold with water; we pour sand into the second; we fill the third with clay; and we leave the fourth empty—it is filled with air.
The water is poured from the first mold into the fourth.	The water in the first mold occupies the same amount of space as the air in the fourth.
The sand is poured from the second mold into the first.	The sand in the second mold occupies the same amount of space as the water in the first.
The clay is taken from the third mold and put into the second.	The clay in the third mold takes up just as much room as the space with sand.
The molds are overturned one after another, and their contents are again transferred from one to another.	In our experiment, the same amount of space is taken up by a liquid, solid, dry substance, and gas (air)...
Pan across the various molds. Fade out. End.	They all have the same volume.

"The Volume of a Solid"

Visual	Voiceover
In the frame there appear a pitcher and a glass—the same ones as in the film "The Concept of Volume." The pitcher is filled up with water from full glasses.	This pitcher contains 5 glasses of water.
In the frame there appears a glass jar; it is filled up with water from full glasses.	There are four glasses of water in the jar.
A coffee cup appears. Water is poured into it from the glass, filling it to the top. The glass remains half full.	There is half a glass of water in the cup.
There are several glasses of water with various cubic content.	These glasses are different.
A jar and the original (thin-walled) glass appear.	There are 4 of these glasses in the jar.
One by one, 4 identical thin-walled glasses are filled from the jar. The jar again is filled with water from these glasses. On the other side of the jar, 5 heavy tumblers appear in succession and are filled from the jar.	But there are 5 tumblers. So when we measure the same amount of liquid with different glasses, we obtain different results.
A tankard, labelled "1 liter," appears on the screen.	The commonly accepted measure of volume is the liter.
Two half-liter bottles of milk appear. The caps are removed. Milk is poured from them into a measuring cup, filling it.	There is a liter of milk in these two bottles, a half-liter in each one.

"The Volume of a Solid" (continued)

Visual	Voiceover
In the frame there appears a narrow glass cylinder without markings on it. Milk is poured into it from the measuring cup. A scale appears on the surface of the cylinder.	A thousandth part of a liter is called a milliliter.
The graduated cylinder is emptied and a liquid is poured into it up to the fifth mark.	With a graduated cylinder we can measure the volume of a liquid in milliliters. Here is 5 milliliters of a liquid.
Water is poured into the graduated cylinder up to the 100 ml mark. The mark is redrawn thicker. A small ball falls into the graduated cylinder. The water rises 5 ml. Fade out. End.	The graduated cylinder also lets us measure the volume of a hard solid. The ball has taken the space of 5ml of the liquid in the graduate. Then the volume of the ball is 5 ml.

"The Volume of a Rectangular Parallelepiped"

Visual	Voiceover
A unit segment appears in the frame, labelled "1." A cube is constructed on it in animation.	A cube whose edge is equal to one unit of length is called a unit cube.
The cube is filled with a white liquid.	We will take the volume of a unit cube as a unit of volume.
The unit cube moves to one side. Beside it, a staircase-shaped solid is constructed of 6 unit cubes.	This solid is composed of 6 unit cubes. Thus, its volume is equal to 6.

"The Volume of a Rectangular Parallelepiped" (continued)

Visual	Voiceover
The staircase vanishes. A framework parallelepiped appears. Duplicates of the unit cube are placed inside it one after another.	This parallelepiped's length is equal to 5.
The cubes along the edge vanish one at a time, but four marks remain along the edge. Similarly, copies of the unit cube are arranged along the width of the figure.	The parallelepiped's width is equal to 3.
The cubes along the width vanish one after another, and two marks remain along the width. Copies of the unit cube are placed along the height.	The parallelepiped's height is equal to 4.
The cubes are removed one after another. Marks remain along the height. The cubes, one by one, fill the bottom layer.	The volume of one layer is equal to the product of two dimensions—length and width...
Segments sparkle along the height. The remaining layers are filled up one at a time.	And the number of layers is equal to the height. Therefore, the volume of a rectangular parallelepiped is equal to the product of its three dimensions.
The formula $V = abc$ appears. Fade out. End.	

Methodology of Using Single-Concept Films

Each of the five single-concept films included in the unit can be viewed in only two or three minutes. Therefore, the film must be shown either directly in the classroom or in any location that can be used for conducting a normal lesson.

Each film can be used to introduce and reinforce new material, and also for asking questions. A useful strategy involves several repeated viewings of the film without the sound. For instance, after showing the film, the teacher asks the students to make up commentary on their own for a silent showing. Then the film is shown again with sound. Finally, the film is shown a fourth time with a student's accompaniment. We note that the content of all of the single-concept films is actually duplicated on the filmstrip. This is done for those instances in which there are no facilities for showing the films. (We will discuss the use of the filmstrip in conjunction with the single-concept film in the subsequent discussion of the methodology of using a filmstrip.)

The film entitled "The Rectangular Parallelepiped" is effectively broken into two separate parts. The first part promotes the formation of the concept of a rectangular parallelepiped. Here we are dealing with abstraction by idealization, whereby students should imagine the idealized properties of a figure that are imprecise in real objects. The teacher can repeat several times: "Pay no attention to the suitcase handle, its latches and rounded corners," but it is difficult for fourth-graders, with their concrete mode of thinking, to ignore these secondary details. On the screen, however, these secondary details actually fall away. The student literally "sees" that these details are not a part of the idealized figure.

The second part of the single-concept film introduces a "combinatorial design" for a rectangular parallelepiped, with its basic elements. The vivid, distinct lines and the illumination of the elements (faces, edges, vertices) as the voiceover mentions them lead to rapid and solid mastery of the material. Demonstrating the edges and faces on a model, without using the single-concept film, is undoubtedly much less visual, since a model is difficult to see from the back rows, and it may not be immediately clear what the teacher is showing with the pointer.

We do not recommend using an entire single-concept film before explaining new material or as the beginning of an explanation of new material; it contains too many new concepts. Before beginning an explanation, it is more advisable to show only the first part of the film as an introduction to the topic. After finishing the first part, the teacher should stop the film and discuss the material (best of all at this stage is the teacher's account, accompanied by filmstrip frames). Only at the end of the first lesson should the class return to the single-concept film and watch it through to the end. However, if the students have already abstracted from concrete objects to the concept of a rectangular parallelepiped (for instance, from the teacher's account plus filmstrip frames and models), the single-concept film can then be watched as a whole. In this case, the first part serves as a review and reinforcement of what has been studied, and the second becomes the beginning of a subtopic about the elements of a rectangular parallelepiped—its faces, edges, vertices.

After the second part of the film is shown, the class should work on reinforcing the concepts of faces, edges, and vertices. The chart entitled "The Rectangular Parallelepiped," models of solids, and the workbook all serve this purpose. Then a second (silent) showing of the film is recommended. The teacher can ask questions: What do we call the rectangle that is sparkling now? What is the sparkling segment (edge) called? and so forth. The final step can be (not necessarily in the same lesson) a repeat viewing of the film with the soundtrack back on.

The film "Drawing a Rectangular Parallelepiped," in our view, should *initiate* the subtopic "Drawing a Rectangular Parallelepiped." After viewing it, the teacher can proceed to work with filmstrip frames 8-11 (Fig. 110), with rubber stamps), and the workbook . A second showing of the film (silently or with the soundtrack) is desirable, but not compulsory.

The film "The Concept of Volume" is devoted to a preliminary development of the concept of volume. Because of the dynamic structure of the content, this brief, two-minute single-concept film attracts the students' attention to one central idea: each solid occupies a place in space (i.e., has volume). Simple experiments with liquid, dry, and hard substances confirm for the students that *volume is an objective property of real things*. Volumes can be discussed and compared.

Might the same effect be achieved through other means? Yes, of course—but it would not be so convincing in such a short time. Experiments that teachers can do at their desks are not as visible and are time-consuming, and thus students' attention may waver. If we consider that the students are not expected to actively participate in this approach (the main point is just familiarity with the idea of volume), then it is clear that the single-concept film we have described is needed.

It is advisable to show the film at the very beginning of the subtopic addressing the concept of volume, after which the teacher moves on to a lecture or discussion using filmstrip frames. A repeat showing of this single-concept film is possible, but not obligatory.

The film "The Volume of a Solid" should demonstrate to students that volume can be measured precisely. As in the case of the previous film, what is important here is to introduce the idea; the students are not expected to engage in adequate activity. And this once again justifies and indeed requires a vivid, dynamic single-concept film. It is methodologically advisable to begin the study of the subtopic "The Volume of a Solid" by showing the film. Despite the difference in subject matter, the third and the fourth films are tied together by a common methodological purpose—preparing the students to see the reality behind the formulas for volume, and assisting in developing a materialistic world-view.

Finally, the film "The Volume of a Rectangular Parallelepiped" is devoted to an explanation of the proof of the hardest theorem in this topic—the theorem on the volume of a rectangular parallelepiped. The resources of cinematography illustrate the meaning of this theorem with the utmost intelligibility, laying the foundation for the adequate activity to which the students must become accustomed. The dynamics of filling a rectangular parallelepiped with small cubes makes the concept of volume concrete and tangible. Moreover, the film helps to make the formula for volume and the method of deriving it understandable.

Like the film "The Rectangular Parallelepiped," this film also consists of two parts. The first part defines the concept of volume as the number of unit cubes which make up a given solid. The second part explains the proof of the basic theorem. The methodological recommendations for the use of this film are essentially the same as for the first film. It is advisable to show the first part as an introduction before beginning the exposition. Then the teacher should move on to a discussion of the material (augmented by frames 30-33 of the filmstrips) and to work with staircase solids (Fig. 269), slides, and the workbook. Only after practicing with the concept of the volume of a staircase solid should the class return to the film and view it through to the end. If, however, the subtopic "The Volume of a Staircase Solid" is studied without showing the first part of the film (which is also quite possible), then the film can be viewed as a whole. In this case the first part serves for review, and the second will provide a first acquaintance with the proof of the basic theorem.

The Filmstrip

The filmstrip "The Rectangular Parallelepiped and Its Volume" partially overlaps with the material of both the single-concept films and the textbook. In particular, the teacher who does not have such films (or a projector on which to show them) can use a filmstrip.

One feature of the present filmstrip is the nearly complete absence of text in the frames. This not only gives teachers an opportunity to follow their own methods, but also limits the problems caused by fourth-graders' slow reading. However, we provide the teacher with a sample text for each frame. Note that although the filmstrip is broken into several parts, there are no special frames bearing the titles of new sections in the filmstrip. They are unnecessary, since the teacher can communicate the appropriate title.

Description of an Instructional Unit and Methods of Use 203

Methodology of Using the Filmstrip

The filmstrip is to be shown in parts, with an average of 3 to 5 frames to a lesson. Accordingly, it is designed in segments. A complete representation of all the frames in the filmstrip is given in Figures 110-116. Here, however, let us tell how the filmstrip should be *divided* into individual segments and give a sample text of the narrative a teacher can use to accompany the frames. Of course, this is only a sample narrative, which the teacher may choose to modify (or even change completely). The version of the narrative will depend substantially on whether the film precedes or follows the showing of the filmstrip frames (if it is shown at all), on the other instructional media used, and so on. The reader will doubtless notice that the text given below corresponds exactly to the educational aid described previously. This seems quite natural to us: serious discrepancy between the textbook and what the teacher says is undesirable.

First a note about using the projection equipment. It is best to conduct a lesson involving filmstrip frames in a semi-darkened room, so that the students can make notes, if need be, without eyestrain. Of course, the picture on the screen is then faded, but the projector can be moved closer to the screen. This diminishes the picture size, but enhances its clarity. For example, the filmstrip can be shown on a "Svet-2" projector such that the picture's dimensions are 60 x 45 cm, scarcely darkening the classroom (or not at all, if the day is overcast). This picture size is quite sufficient for classwork, and the frames will be readily visible from the most remote seats in the classroom.

The first filmstrip segment (frames 1-5) tells about the shape of a rectangular parallelepiped and its component parts. A sample text for these frames was given earlier. Note only that frames 2 and 3 are connected to the first part of the film "The Rectangular Parallelepiped," and frames 4 and 5 to the second. It is possible, for example, that once the teacher has shown the first part of the film, she will move on to a lecture using frames 2 and 3 of the filmstrip, models, and various other objects. This could be followed by showing the second part of the film and frames 4 and 5 of the filmstrip. Finally, the teacher would turn to the chart entitled "The Rectangular Parallelepiped" and use the appropriate lesson plans (see the last chapter).

Frames 5-7 comprise the second segment of the filmstrip. In them, the teacher shows adjacent and opposite faces and discusses sets of four equal edges. Frame 7 is a cube. The teacher emphasizes that a cube is a special case of a rectangular parallelepiped.

The next segment contains frames 8-11. They show the process of representing a rectangular parallelepiped. Here is a sample text of the teacher's narrative for these frames.

> *Frame 8.* We can represent a rectangular parallelepiped in this way on paper.
>
> *Frame 9.* We can begin a drawing of a rectangular parallelepiped by drawing the front face.
>
> *Frame 10.* Then we can draw the edges that extend from the vertices of the front face. One of them is hidden, and it is usually represented by a dotted line. Since these four edges are congruent and parallel, they are represented as congruent and parallel segments.
>
> *Frame 11.* Now we join the endpoints of these edges. We have now obtained a representation of the back face. Two of its edges are hidden; they are represented by dotted lines.

Frames 12 and 13 constitute the next segment. They show how to glue together a cube or a rectangular parallelepiped, cutting its pattern out of paper. The teacher emphasizes that a two-dimensional pattern of a cube consists of 6 congruent squares, and a pattern of a rectangular parallelepiped consists of of 6 pairwise congruent rectangles.

Frames 14-29 make up the next segment, which introduces the concept of volume. A sample narrative for these frames is given below.

> *Frame 14.* More water can go into the pitcher than into the glass. We say that the pitcher's capacity (or cubic content) is greater than the glass's capacity (or cubic content).

Description of an Instructional Unit and Methods of Use 205

Frame 15. Two glasses of water are poured into the pitcher. In this case we say that the volume of the water in the pitcher is equal to 2 glasses. But the pitcher is not filled up to the top. A total of 5 glasses will go into it. This means that the pitcher's capacity is 5 glasses. Right now, the volume of the water it contains is a total of 2 glasses. How much water can still be added to the pitcher? What will be the volume of the water in the pitcher if it is filled to the top?

Frame 16. Liquids are not the only things that have volume. There is salt in the jar. It takes up space in the jar. It has volume. Right now there are two and a half glasses of salt in the jar.

Frame 17. One mold is empty, the second is filled with water, the third with sand, and clay is closely packed in the fourth. The clay has dried out and become hard. Let's compare how much space the water occupies and how much the clay occupies.

Frame 18. We take the clay from its mold and pour the water into it from the other mold. The water fills this mold up to the edge too, since the molds are identical. In our experiment the water and the clay occupy the identical amount of space. They have the same volume.

Frame 19. All objects around us occupy space. All of them have volume.

Frame 20. We fill the jar to the brim with water and put in the clay that was removed from the mold. We collect the water that overflows in a saucer. What will happen if all the water in the saucer is poured into the same mold from which we removed the clay?

Frame 21. The water from the saucer will fill the mold up to the brim.

Frame 22. The volume of a solid immersed in a liquid is equal to the volume of the liquid that it displaces.

Frame 23. What is the volume of the piece of clay that was removed from the mold? Half a glass. We have measured the volume of a hard substance by immersing it in a liquid.

Frame 24. But the capacity of these glasses is different. Let's pour the water from the thick glass into the thin one. The thin glass is not filled to the top. And thick glasses do have a different capacity. Therefore, it is not always convenient to measure volume with glasses.

Frame 25. How many glasses of sand are in this package? There are 12 thick glasses, but only 10 thin ones.

Frame 26. In ancient Russia material was measured in cubits. This was inconvenient, since arm length differs in different people. Now lengths are measured in millimeters, centimeters, decimeters, meters, kilometers—that is, there are standard units of measuring length that are the same for everyone. A centimeter measured in Moscow or in Leningrad, yesterday or today, by one person or another, is the same centimeter. The situation is the same for the measurement of volume. Here, too, we need identical units of measure for everyone.

Frame 27. Milk is measured in special tankards that hold one liter and or one-half liter. A liter is a generally accepted measure of volume. Smaller units of volume than a liter are required in making medicines and in many other situations. One such unit is the milliliter—one-thousandth of a liter (compare: a millimeter is one-thousandth of a meter; a milligram is one-thousandth of a gram). To measure a liquid in milliliters, we use a measuring glass the milliliters marked off on its side.

Frame 28. We have to measure the volume of a metal ball. We fill a measuring glass with water approximately halfway to the top and note how much water it contains.

Frame 29. Now we drop the ball into the glass. The water rises 10 marks. Then the volume of the ball is equal to 10 milliliters. Why did we fill the glass halfway? Could we have filled it to the brim? Could we have poured a few drops of water into it?

Frames 30-33 make up the next segment of the filmstrip. They define a unit cube and the volume of a staircase solid. A sample narrative for these frames follows.

Description of an Instructional Unit and Methods of Use

Frame 30. Six small cubes can be placed in a box. We will regard each cube as a unit of volume. Then the box's volume is equal to the number of cubes in this solid.

Frame 31. The volume of a solid is a number showing how many units of volume it contains.

Frame 32. A cube with an edge equal to one unit of length is called a unit cube. Unit cubes can be different, since units of length can be different. In the Soviet Union length is measured in centimeters, meters, and other units. In England they use feet and inches. In general, the length of any segment can be taken as a unit of length. Therefore, any cube can be considered a unit cube. But once we have chosen a unit cube, we cannot change it later. We will regard the volume of a unit cube as a unit of volume, and we will measure the volumes of solids in terms of this unit.

Frame 33. This solid is composed of 5 unit cubes. Therefore, its volume is equal to 5.

Frames 34-37 contain preparatory material for the formula for the volume of a rectangular parallelepiped, describing and illustrating the idea of counting objects by layers. How many books are in the bundle (frame 35)? How many dominoes make up the solid (frame 36)? and so forth. This segment is followed by another one in frames 38-42 devoted to deriving and interpreting the formula for the volume of a rectangular parallelepiped. A sample narrative for these frames follows.

Frame 38. How many unit cubes can be arranged on this area in one layer? in three layers? If cubes are arranged in three layers, how many cubes fill the resulting rectangular parallelepiped? What will be its volume?

Frame 39. Find the volume of this rectangular parallelepiped and make up a formula for calculating it. (The teacher helps the students derive the formula for volume: $V = abc$ or $V = 7 \times 4 \times 5$.)

Frame 40. A rectangular parallelepiped is composed of unit cubes. One edge has a length of 3. The others measure 4 and 8. These are the dimensions of the rectangular parallelepiped. Count the number of unit cubes that the given rectangular parallelepiped can contain. What is its volume?

Frame 41. By multiplying the lengths of the edges (the dimensions) of a rectangular parallelepiped, we obtain its volume.

Frame 42. The volume of a rectangular parallelepiped can also be obtained by multiplying the area of its base by the height. Why?

Finally, frames 43-46 constitute the last segment of the filmstrip. They relate to the question of the change in the volume of a rectangular parallelepiped when all of its dimensions are increased (or decreased) by the same factor.

Frame 43. If each edge of a rectangular parallelepiped is doubled, then its volume will be 8 times greater than it was. What laws of arithmetic operations are used in these calculations?

Frame 44. If each edge of a rectangular parallelepiped is tripled, its volume becomes 27 times greater.

Frame 45. By what factor has the cube's edge been increased? By what factor has its volume increased?

Frame 46. If every dimension of a rectangular parallelepiped is increased by a factor of 10, its volume becomes 1,000 times greater. How many cubic millimeters are there in one cubic centimeter? How many cubic centimeters are there in one cubic decimeter? How many cubic decimeters are there in one cubic meter? Why? How many cubic meters are in one cubic kilometer? How is this calculated?

These frames prepare the students for converting from one cubic measure to another.

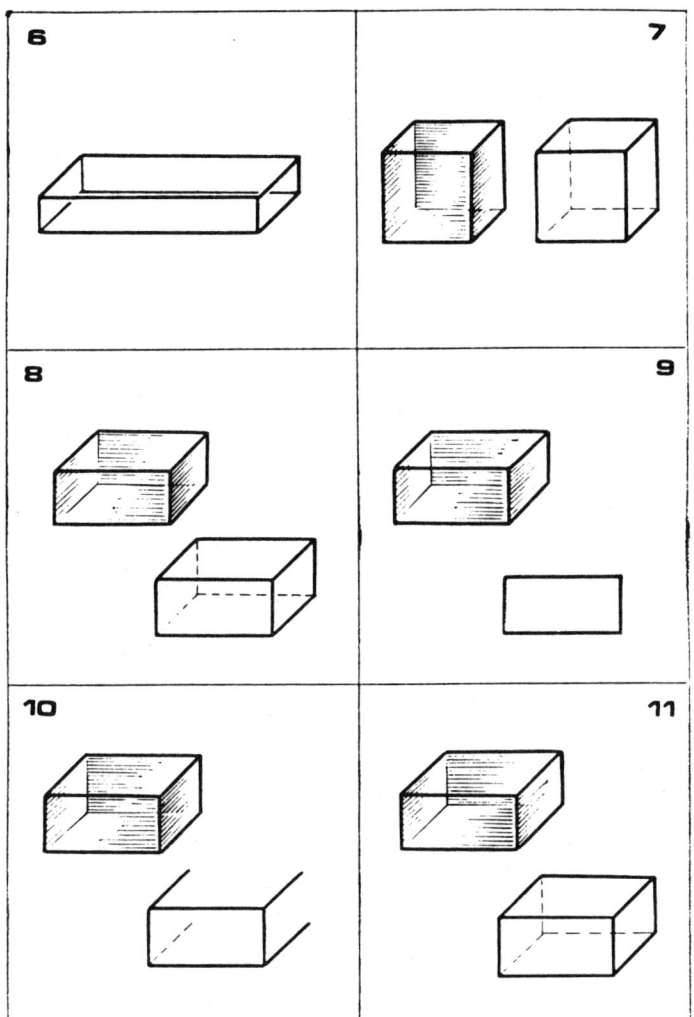

Figure 110.

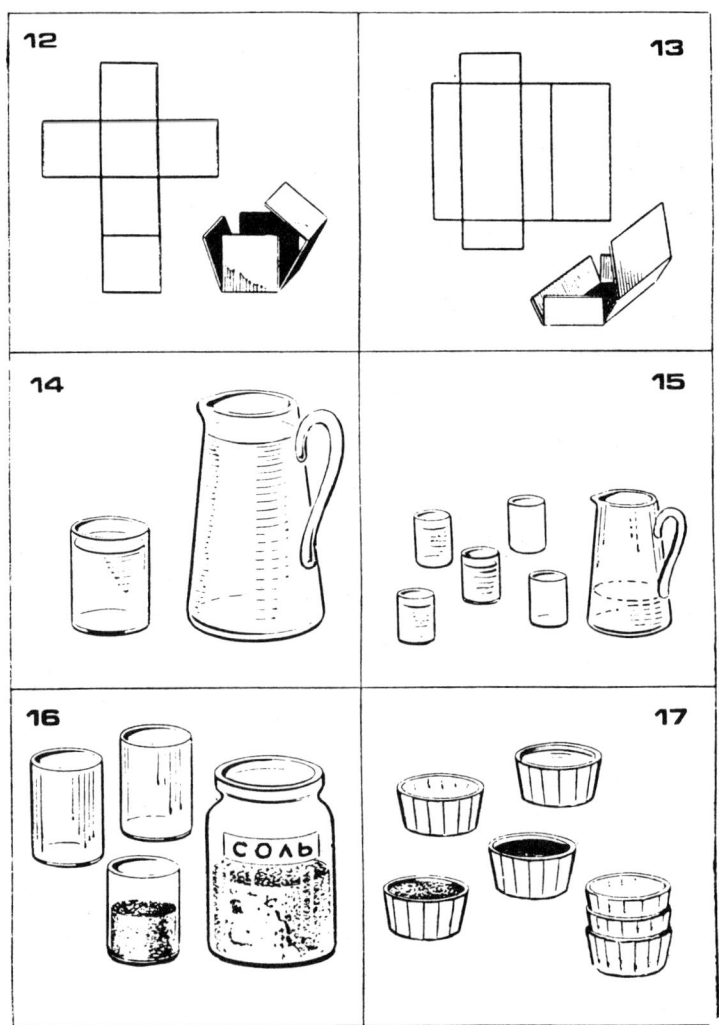

Figure 111.

Figure 112.

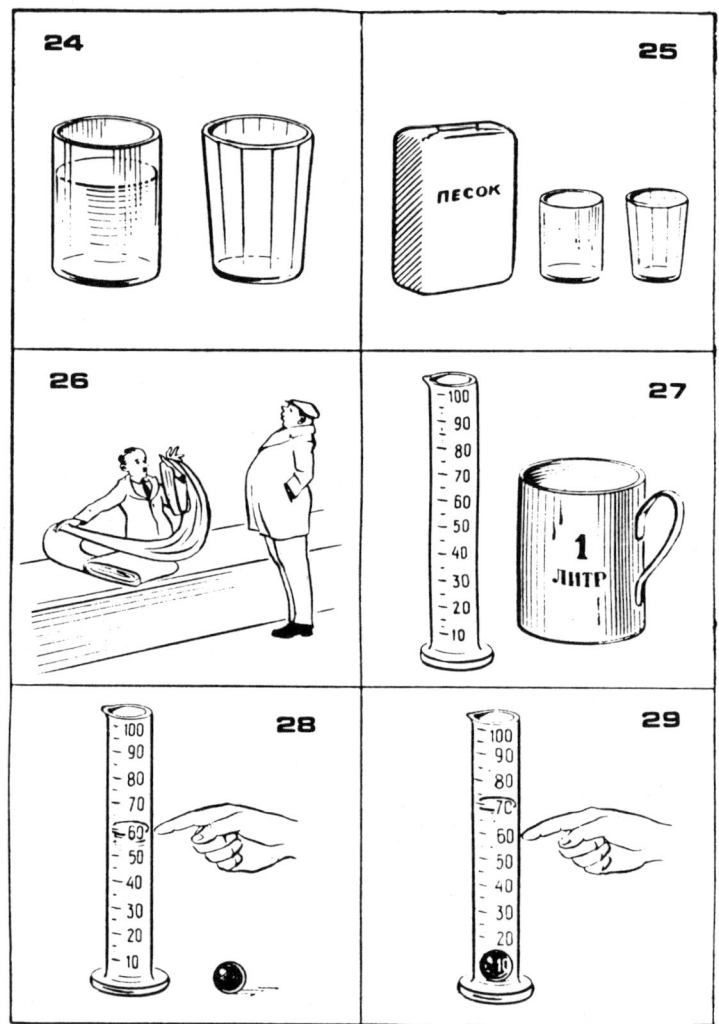

Figure 113.

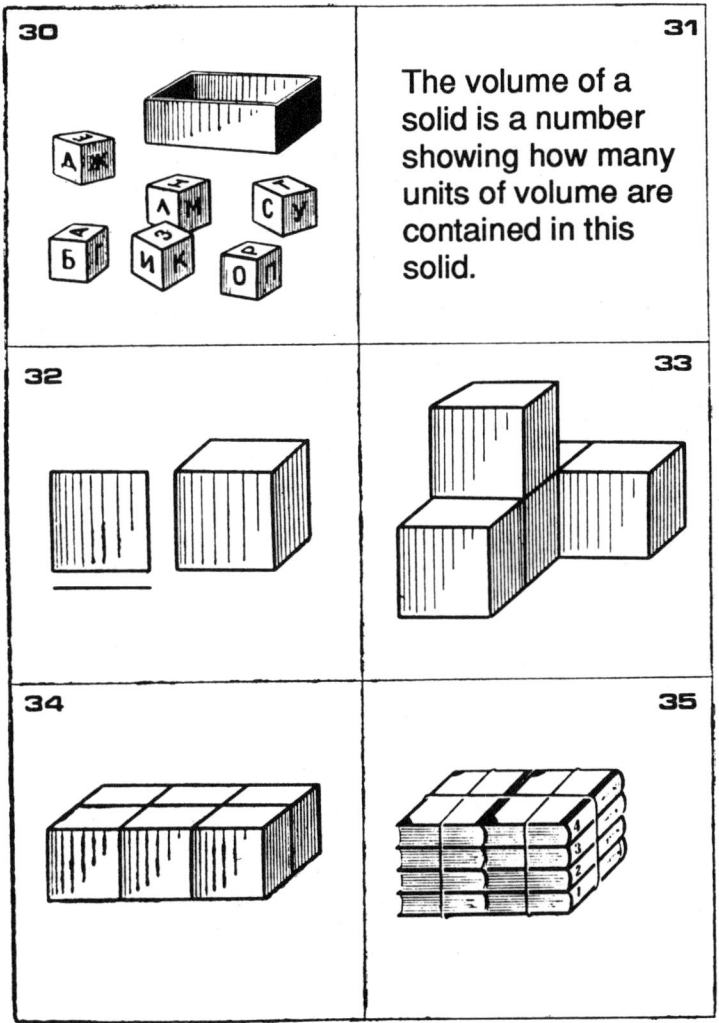

Figure 114.

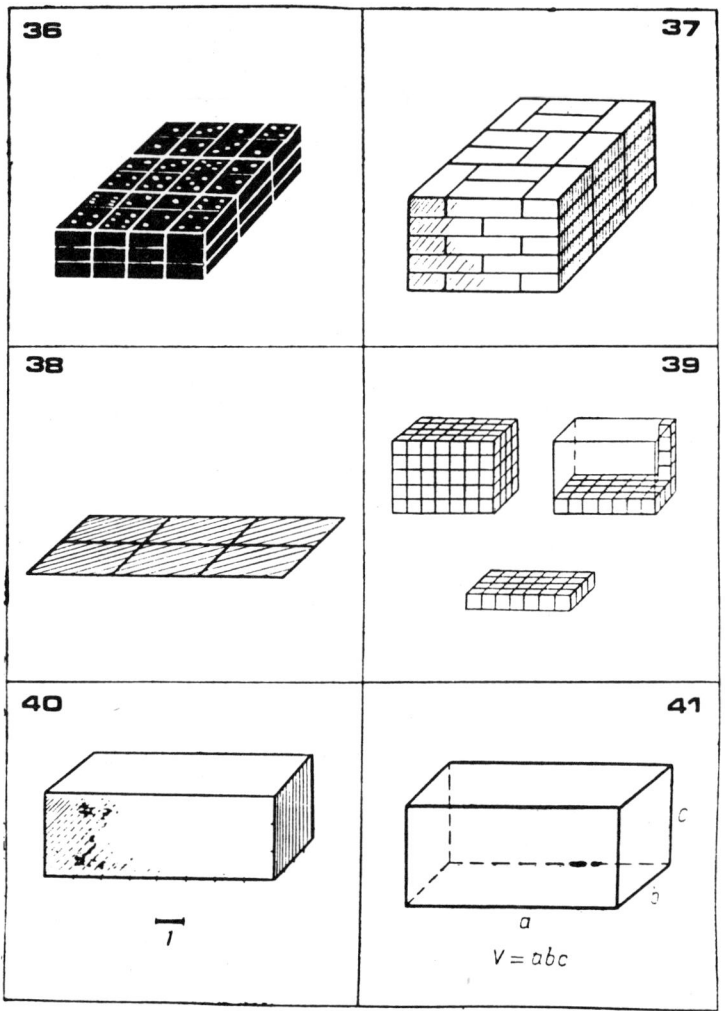

Figure 115.

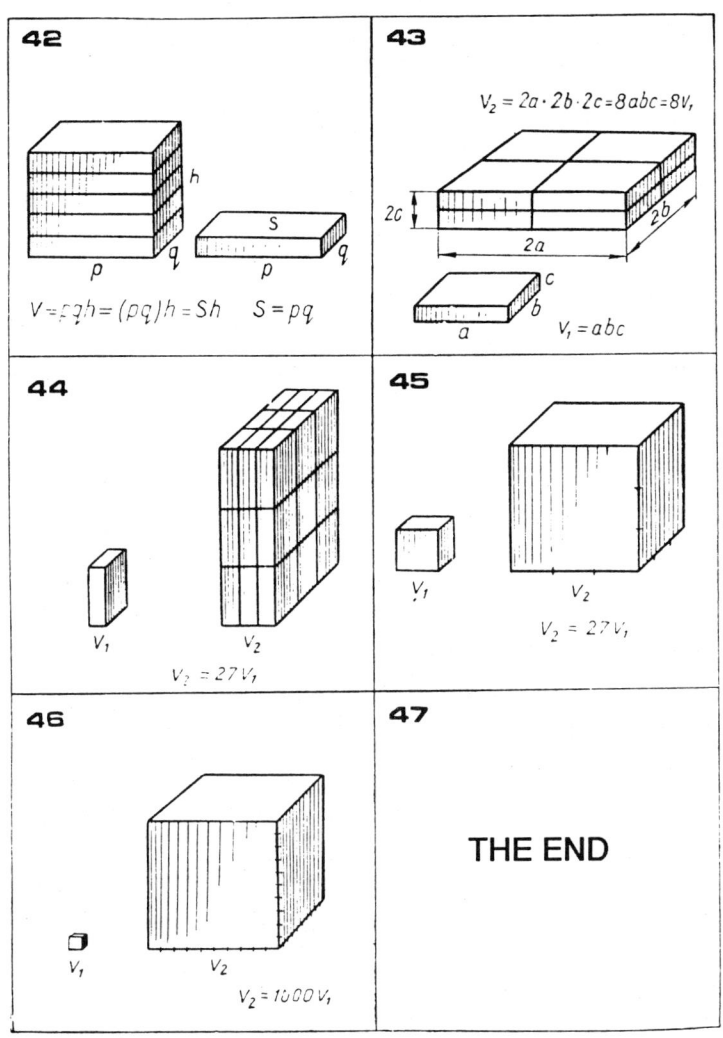

Figure 116.

Slides

The slide series includes primarily problem material. They can be shown in class using the standard frame of the "Svet" slide projector (Fig. 117), which enables the operator to show one slide while inserting the next into the second slot (Fig. 118). But the homemade device by S.F. Kabanov described earlier. All of the slides in the series entitled "The Rectangular Parallelepiped and Its Volume" are reproduced below in full. The slides (Figs. 119-123) are divided into several groups with similar assignments.

Methodology of Using the Slide Series

Although the filmstrip contains the theoretical part of the course, the problem material is included in the slides. The first task—*recognizing a*

Figure 117.

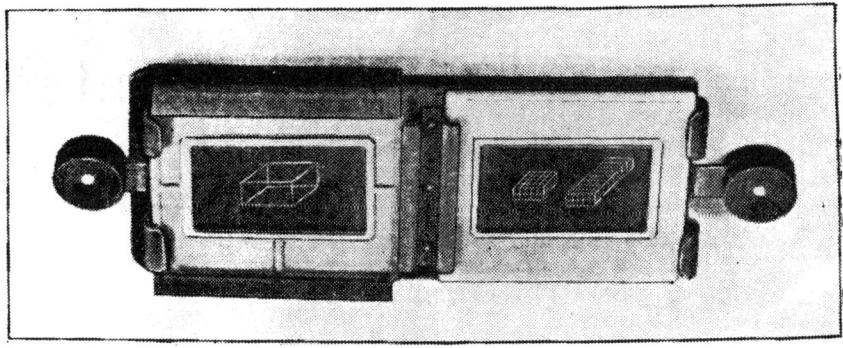

Figure 118.

rectangular parallelepiped—is given in frames 1 and 2. The students encounter several questions: Which of these objects is like a rectangular parallelepiped (frame 1)? Which of these solids is a rectangular parallelepiped (frame 2)? It is desirable for the students not only to identify the required solids, but also to reason out their answers in response to the question in frame 2. The possibility of more profound questioning is incorporated in frame 2. If, for example, a student says that solid 5 is a rectangular parallelepiped because it has 6 faces, it can be pointed out that solid 7 also has 6 faces. If the student adds that solid 5 has 8 vertices and 12 edges, the teacher can show that solid 4 also has 8 vertices and 12 edges (and, what is more, 6 faces). If the student states that every face of solid 5 is a rectangle, it can be observed that every face of solid 6 is a rectangle, too. The students should conclude that these properties, taken individually, are insufficient. They must realize that the solid fits the definition—that is, it has 6 faces *and* every face is a rectangle.

The second task—*drawing a rectangular parallelepiped*—arises in frames 3-7. Frame 3 thus provides representations of a translucent cube and rectangular parallelepiped, and frame 4 is merely a diagram of the framework. The students find the hidden edges in these two frames. Assignments for completing the drawings of rectangular parallelepipeds are given in frames 5-7. All these problems are to be done in the same

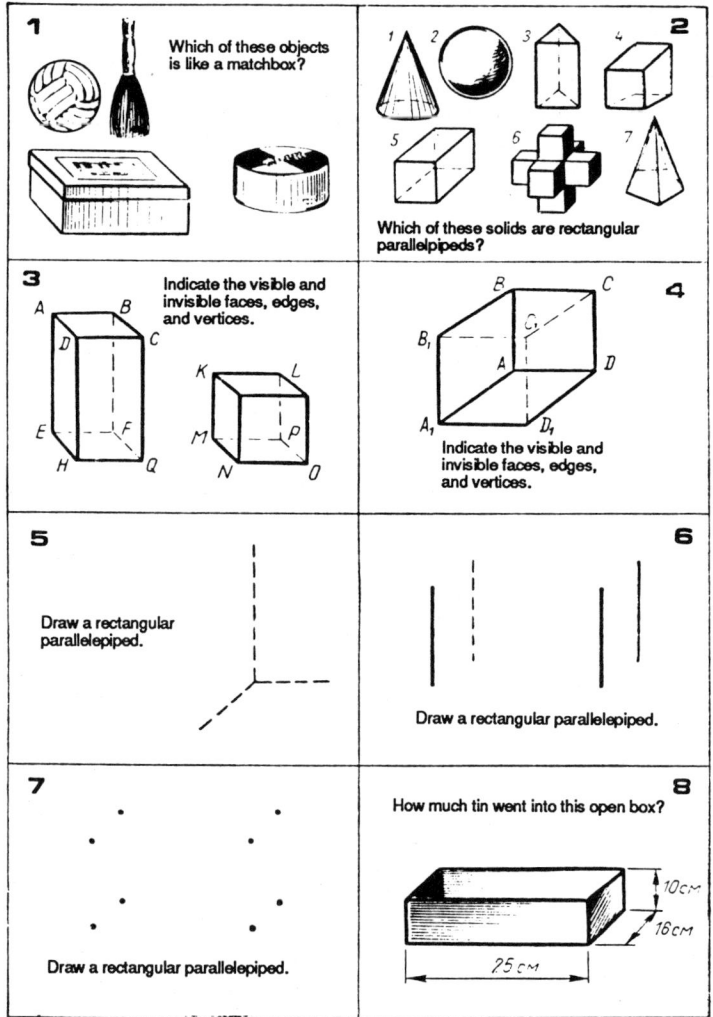

Figure 119.

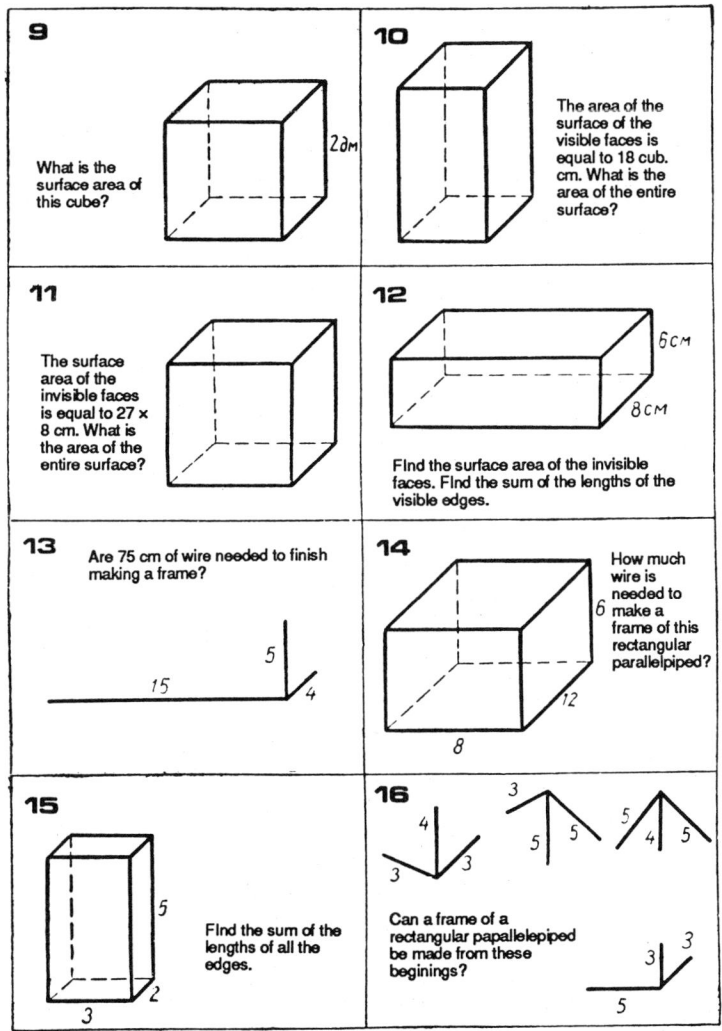

Figure 120.

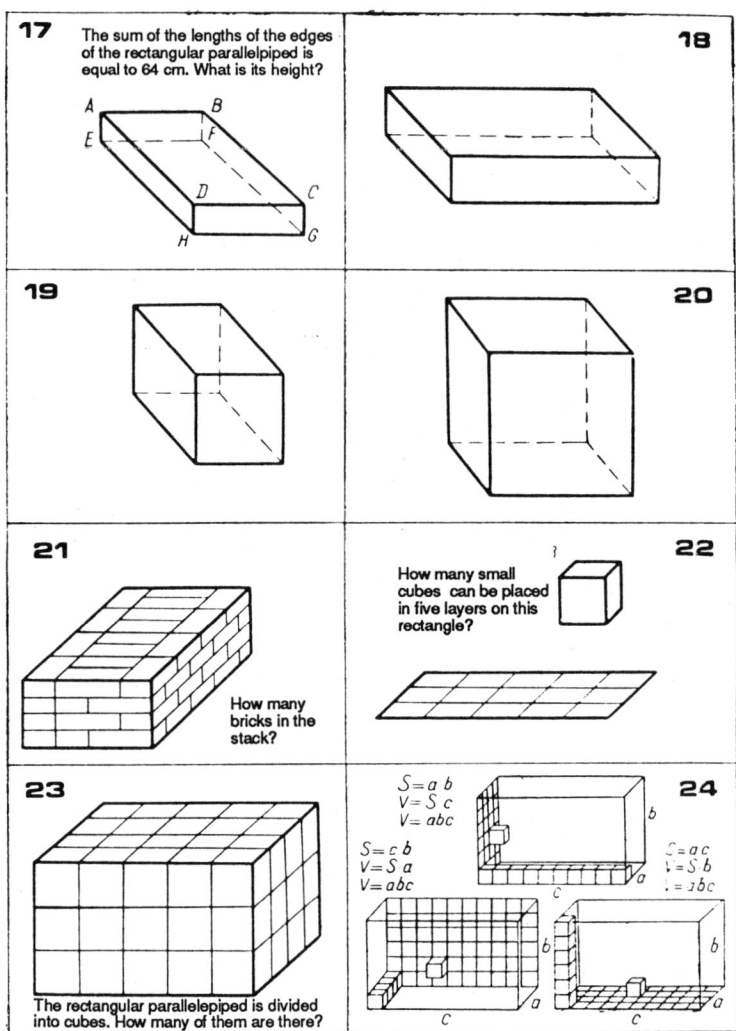

Figure 121.

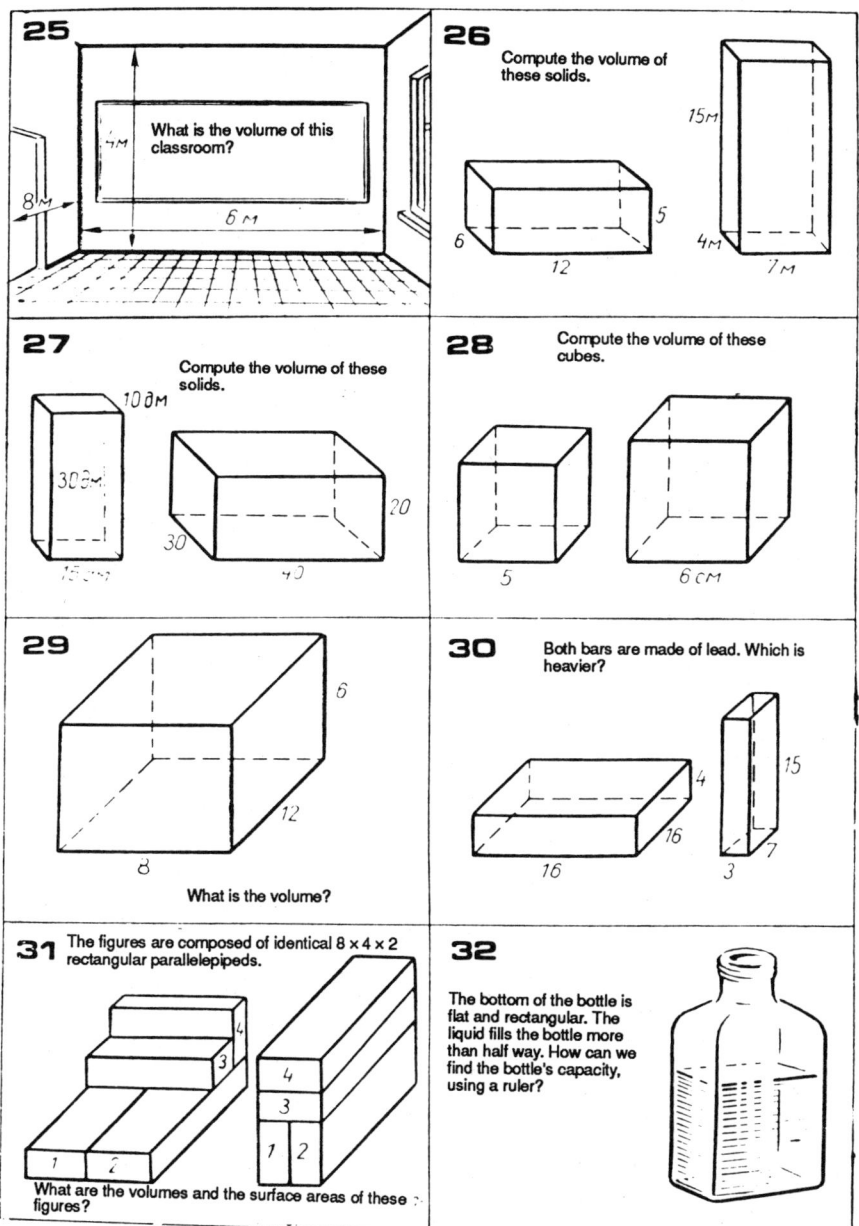

Figure 122.

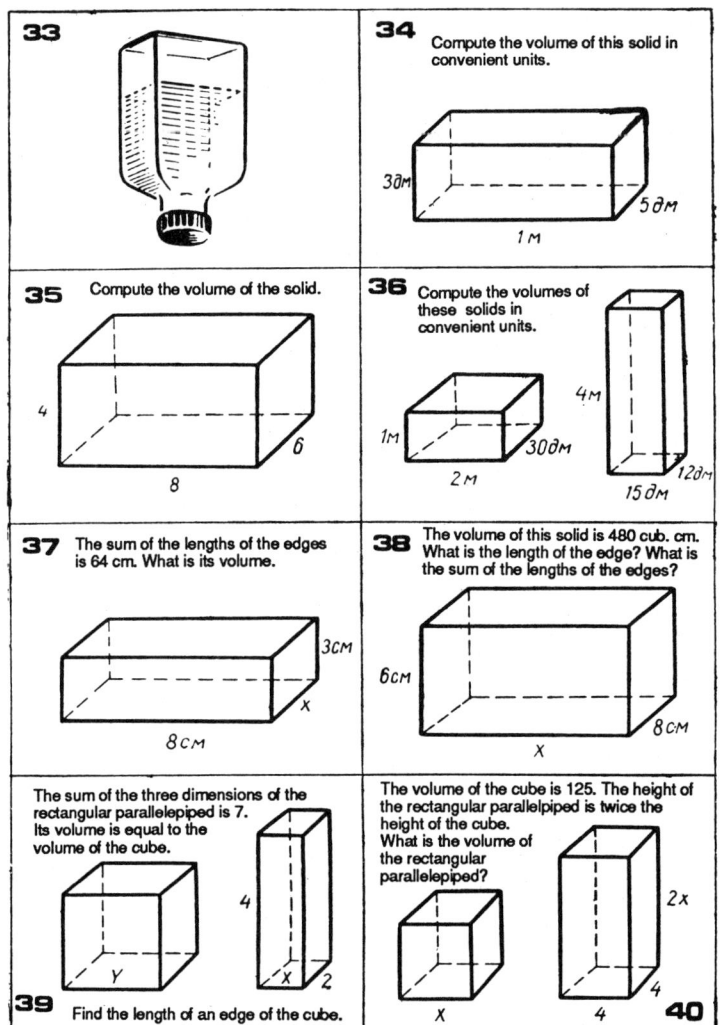

Figure 123.

Description of an Instructional Unit and Methods of Use

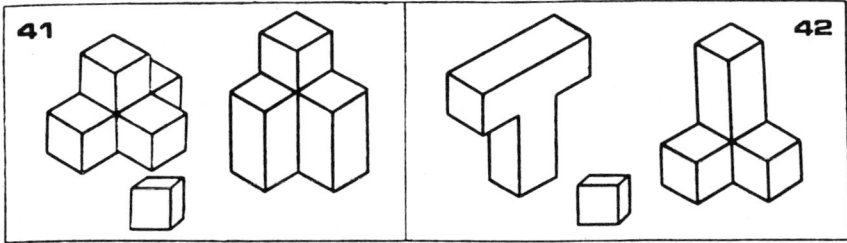

Figure 123a.

lesson. The projector should be set up so that the picture is projected directly onto the blackboard, and then the students can finish the drawing with chalk. Incorrect drawings can be erased while the projected image remains on the board. We note that the assignment in frame 7 is somewhat vague. According to the conditions set forth in the frame, it is possible to draw rectangular parallelepipeds with two different orientations, as shown in Figure 124. The teacher should direct the students' attention to this fact (asking "Who is drawing it another way?").

The third task—*finding the surface area and the sum of the lengths of the edges of a rectangular parallelepiped*—is presented in frames 8-17. We recommend that these assignments, together with frames 18, 19, and 20, be done in the same lesson. The calculations they entail are not complicated, and are essentially designed for oral calculation. It should

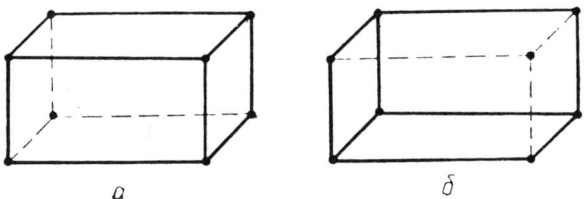

Figure 124.

take no more than one or two minutes to solve each of them. This economy of time is achieved because, given the predrawn figure, the conditions can be formulated all at once. Slides' high degree of operativity is significant here. The method of using this type of slide (and the frame for working with them) was described in detail earlier. Note the special role of frames 17-20. In frame 17 two dimensions must be established first. Teachers can use the other frames at their own discretion. The rectangular parallelepiped can be shown in various positions (the slide frame is square!), dimensions written on the board, calculational problems set up, and so forth. And the frames are different: frame 18 shows an ordinary rectangular parallelepiped; in frame 19 it has a square face; frame 20 shows a cube.

Frames 21-23 set problems that prepare for the development of the formula for volume. (Frame 22 is required for analyzing the structure of the figures in frame 23.)

Frame 24 occupies a special place in the series. It is needed if the teacher wishes to deepen the presentation of theoretical material. It supplies various ways to fill the figure with unit cubes and suggests the different formulas for volume, $V = abc$ and $V = Sh$. When this frame is used, the students' attention should be focused on the commutative and associative laws of multiplication.

Frames 25-29 introduce the problem of calculating volumes, and frames 30-31 give a more complicated version of this task. The problems in frames 30-33 are practical in nature. The teacher should encourage the students to solve problem 30 without calculations. This problem shows two figures in which one dimension is greater than the other, and asks which has the greater volume. Students may be inclined to calculate with the numerical values given in the problem, but this is unnecessary. The problem in frame 32 is clarified by frame 33. To solve it, the student must first calculate the volume of the liquid in the bottle (this is easy to do by measuring the edges of the "liquid" parallelepiped), then turn the bottle over and calculate the volume of air (in this position the empty part is also a parallelepiped). The sum of these numbers yields the desired answer.

Description of an Instructional Unit and Methods of Use   225

Frames 34-40 provide various problems for oral calculation. Note that in these last frames, as well as in the preceding ones, some problems are more concrete and others more abstract. If designations are given, commentary is unnecessary. By not indicating specific measures, we wanted to emphasize that the answer (a number) does not depend on the unit of measure. Of course, once a unit of length is chosen, all the dimensions are to be stated in these units.

Frames 41 and 42 are designed for a laboratory analysis or preparation for laboratory work. Counting the number of cubes is best done "by steps" in each instance. For example, the left-hand solid in frame 41 has 4 cubes in the bottom row and 1 cube in the top—a total of 5 cubes. The individual cubes represented in these frames are assumed to be unit cubes for the calculation of volume.

The Workbook

This printed notebook contains 71 assignments, to be done independently by the students. Stamped on the front cover is:

Workbook for the Topic

"The Volume of a Rectangular Parallelepiped"

School No. _____

City _____

Grade _____

A table of squares and cubes and the metric system are given on the back cover of the workbook (Table 4.1).

The assignments in the workbook are primarily of the fill-in-the-blanks type. The nature of these blanks varies. Sometimes (particularly in the first few problems of each topic) no more than one or two words (or numbers) have been omitted. But sometimes the blank is a free space in which students work the problem almost entirely on their own. The

Table 4.1

Tabel of Squares and Cubes		
Number	Square	Cube
0	0	0
1	1	1
2	4	8
3	9	27
4	16	64
5	25	125
6	36	216
7	49	343
8	64	512
9	81	729
10	100	1000
11	121	1331
12	144	1728
13	169	2197
14	196	2744
15	225	3375
16	256	4096
17	289	4913
18	324	5832
19	361	6859
20	400	8000
25	625	15625
30	900	27000
35	1225	42875
40	1600	64000
45	2025	91125
50	2500	125000
55	3025	166375
60	3600	216000
65	4225	274625
70	4900	343000
75	5625	421875
80	6400	512000
85	7225	614125
90	8100	729000
95	9025	857375
100	10000	1000000

Table of Linear Measures

1 m = 10 dm
1 dm = 10 cm
1 cm = 10 mm

Table of Square Measures

1 sq. m = 100 sq. dm
1 sq. dm = 100 sq. cm
1 sq. cm = 100 sq. mm

Table of Cubic Measures

1 cub. m = 1000 cub. dm
1 cub. dm = 1000 cub. cm
1 cub. cm = 1000 cub. mm

Description of an Instructional Unit and Methods of Use

assignments from the unit's workbook can be augmented with work in the students' usual working notebook. Moreover, the teacher can indicate (to all students or individuals) which assignments are to be done—possibly with omissions and changes in the order of the assignments. The complete text of all assignments included in the workbook is given below.

Assignments

A rectangular parallelepiped is a solid with 6 faces, each a rectangle.
Assignment 1. Fill in the blanks in the following sentences.
To find out whether a solid is a rectangular parallelepiped, we must:
1) count to see how many faces it has; a rectangular parallelepiped has _____ faces;

2) see whether all faces of the solid are rectangles. In a rectangular parallelepiped all faces are _____.

Assignment 2. Determine whether this solid (Fig. 125*a*) is a rectangular parallelepiped.

Solution. 1) We count to see how many faces the solid has. This solid has _____ faces. A rectangular parallelepiped should have _____ faces.

We do not need to check the second condition.

Answer. This solid is not a _____.

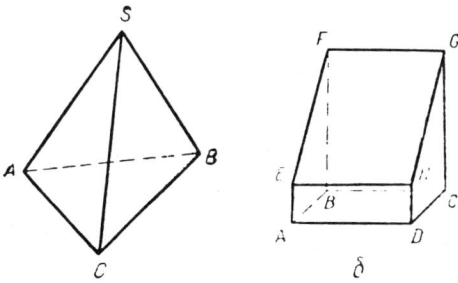

Figure 125.

Assignment 3. Determine whether this solid (Fig. 125b) is a rectangular parallelepiped.

Solution. 1) We count to see how many faces this solid has. This solid has _____ faces. A rectangular parallelepiped also has _____ faces.

2) We check whether all the faces of this solid are rectangles. Face *ABCD* is a rectangle.

Face *AEHD* is _____.
Face *BCGF* is _____.
Face *FGHE* is _____.
Face _____ is _____.
Face _____ is _____.

In a rectangular parallelepiped all the faces are rectangles. In solid *ABCDEFGH* _____.

Answer. This solid is _____.

Assignment 4. Determine which of the solids in Figure 126 are rectangular parallelepipeds.

Solution. The first condition (that there be 6 faces) is satisfied for solids _____.

The second condition (that all faces be rectangles) is satisfied for solids _____.

Answer. Solids _____ are rectangular parallelepipeds. Solids _____ are not rectangular parallelepipeds.

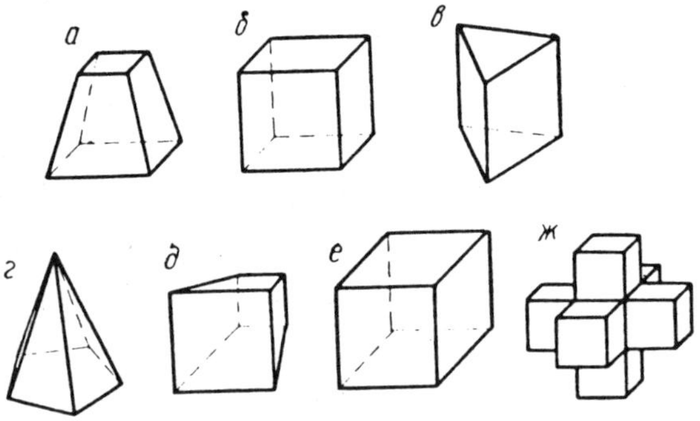

Figure 126.

Description of an Instructional Unit and Methods of Use

Assignment 5. Fill in the blanks in the following sentences.

A solid 1) with ____ faces and 2) in which each face is a ____ is called a rectangular ____.

In a rectangular parallelepiped there are 6 ____, ____ edges, and ____ vertices.

____ is a rectangular parallelepiped in which all the faces are equal squares.

Assignment 6. Fill in the blanks (Fig. 127).

Faces *AEMD* and *MFCD* are adjacent, since they have a common edge ____. Faces *AEMD* and ____ are adjacent, since they have a common edge *AE*. Faces ____ and *AEMD* are adjacent, since they have a common edge ____.

Faces *AEMD* and ____ are ____ since they have a common edge ____.

Faces *AEMD* and ____ are opposite, since they have no common edges.

Assignment 7. Which faces are adjacent or opposite (Fig. 128)?

ABCD and *EFGM* are ____.
ABFE and *BFGC* are ____.
DMGC and *EFGM* are ____.
DMGC and *AEFB* are ____.
AEMD and *BFGC* are ____.
ABCD and *ABFE* are ____.

Assignment 8. Fill in the blanks (Fig. 129).

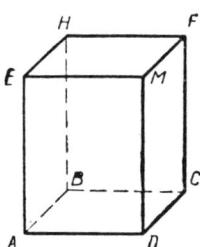

Figure 127.

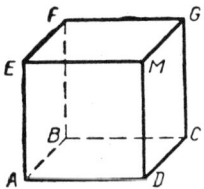

Figure 128.

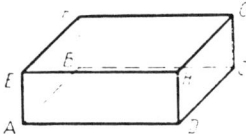

Figure 129.

The face of a rectangular parallelepiped has the shape of a _____. In the rectangular parallelepiped ABCDEFGH the face ABCD is equal to the face _____; face _____ is equal to face DHGC; face BFGC is _____ to face AEHD.

Assignment 9. Fill in the blanks.

In cube ABCDEFGM (Fig. 128) face ABCD is equal to face AEFB, and equal to face _____, and equal to face _____, and equal to face _____, and equal to face _____. All of the cube's faces have the shape of _____.

Assignment 10. Fill in the blanks (Fig. 130).

AB = DC = _____ = _____;
AD = _____ = _____ = _____;
AE = _____ = _____ = _____.

Bases: ABCD and _____. Vertices: A, B, _____, _____, _____, _____, _____, _____.

Description of an Instructional Unit and Methods of Use

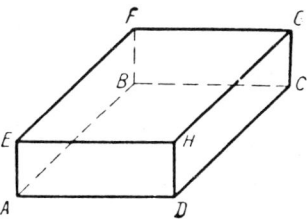

Figure 130.

Assignment 11. Outline the edges of the rectangular parallelepiped represented in Figure 131 so that the equal edges are the same color.

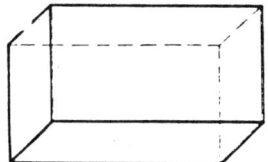

Figure 131.

Assignment 12. Fill in the blanks.
In a rectangular parallelepiped the upper face is equal to the _____, the left face is _____ to the right, and the front face _____.

Assignment 13. Complete the drawing of the cube (Fig. 132).

Assignment 14. Outline the visible faces in different colors (Fig. 133).

Assignment 15. Outline the hidden faces in different colors (see Fig. 133).

Assignment 16. Draw rectangular parallelepipeds made up of two of these cubes (Fig. 134).

Assignment 17. Draw rectangular parallelepipeds made up of three of these cubes (see Fig. 134).

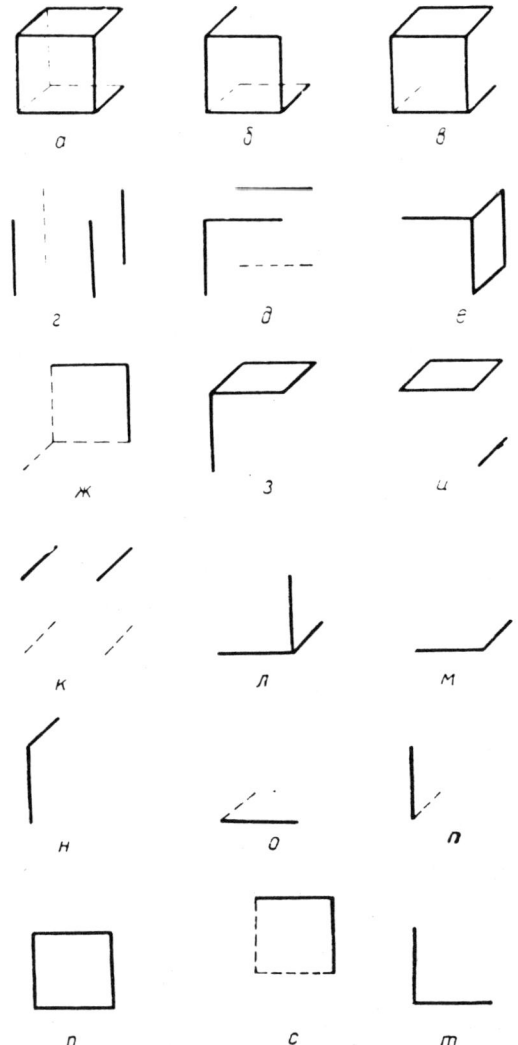

Figure 132.

Description of an Instructional Unit and Methods of Use   233

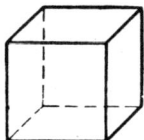

Figure 133.

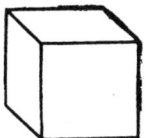

Figure 134.

Assignment 18. Which are the front faces in these representations of rectangular parallelepipeds (Fig. 135)?
Answer. In (*a*) the front face is _____. In (*b*) the front face is _____. In (*c*) the front face is _____. In (*d*) the front face is _____.

Assignment 19. Which diagrams of a cube contain errors (Fig. 136)? (Be ready to give the teacher an explanation.)
Answer. Mistakes were made in pictures _____.

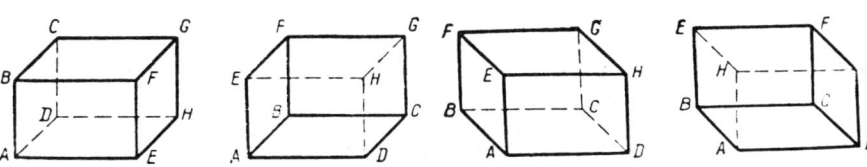

Figure 135.

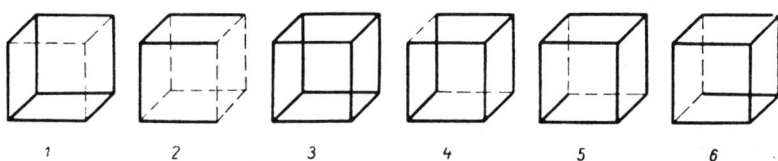

Figure 136.

Assignment 20. Can a rectangular parallelepiped be turned so that 6 faces are visible? 5 faces? 4 faces? 3 faces? 2 faces? 1 face? Draw the positions that are possible (do not draw what is impossible). 6 faces are visible _____. 4 faces are visible _____. 5 faces are visible _____. 3 faces are visible _____. 1 face is visible _____. 2 faces are visible _____.

Assignment 21. How many centimeters of wire did it take to make the frame for this rectangular parallelepiped (Fig. 137)? Solve the problem in various ways.

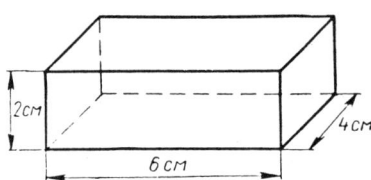

Figure 137.

Method 1.
1) It took _____ cm for the edge of the lower base.
2) It took _____ cm for the edge of the upper base.
3) It took _____ cm for the vertical edges.
4) It took _____ cm for the entire frame.

Description of an Instructional Unit and Methods of Use

Method 2.
1) It took _____ cm for the three unequal edges.
2) It took _____ cm for the entire frame.

Method 3.
A rectangular parallelepiped has sets of four equal edges.
1) It took _____ cm for the edges that are equal to 2 cm.
2) It took _____ cm for the edges that are equal to 6 cm.
3) It took _____ cm for the edges that are equal to 4 cm.
4) It took _____ cm for the entire frame.

These calculations can be written in one line:
$2 \times 4 + 6 \times 4 + 4 \times 4 = ($_____$ + $_____$ + $_____$) \times 4 = $_____$ \times $_____
$= $_____.

Assignment 22. Find the sum of the lengths of the edges of the rectangular parallelepiped (Fig. 138).

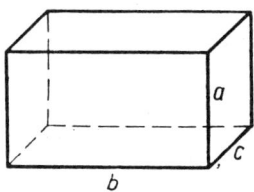

Figure 138.

Method 1.
1) There are four edges of a cm. The sum of their lengths is $4a$ cm.
2) There are _____ edges of b cm each. The sum of their lengths is _____ cm.
3) There are _____ edges of _____ cm each. The sum of their lengths is equal to _____ cm.
4) The sum of the lengths of all the edges is _____ cm.

Method 2.
1) The sum of the lengths of the three dimensions is equal to $a + $_____ $+ $_____ cm.

2) The sum of the lengths of all the edges is equal to 4(____ + ____ + ____) cm.

Explain why the answers obtained in the two cases are equal.

Assignment 23. In this cube (Fig. 139) one of the edges is doubled, and the other dimensions are not changed. Draw the resulting rectangular parallelepiped and calculate the surface area and the sum of the lengths of its edges. The length of the edge is 2 cm.

Solution. ____.

Answer. The surface area is ____ square cm. The sum of the lengths of the edges is ____ cm.

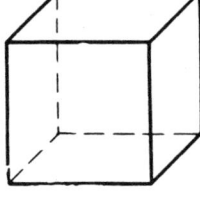

Figure 139.

Assignment 24. In this cube (Fig. 140) one dimension is doubled, another is halved, and the third is left unchanged. Draw the resulting rectangular parallelepiped. Calculate the surface area and the sum of the lengths of its edges.

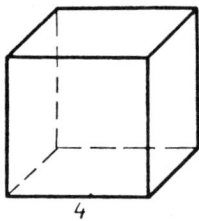

Figure 140.

Description of an Instructional Unit and Methods of Use

Solution. _____.

Answer. The surface is equal to _____ square cm. The sum of the lengths of the edges is equal to _____ cm.

Assignment 25. How many more centimeters of wire will we need to finish the frame of the rectangular parallelepiped (Fig. 141)?

Solution. _____.

Answer. _____.

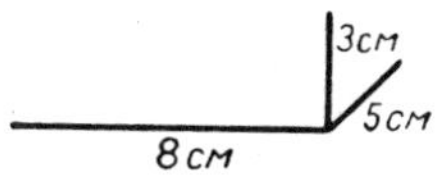

Figure 141.

Assignment 26. How many faces of the rectangular parallelepipeds shown here (Fig. 142) are squares? Which of these rectangular parallelepipeds are cubes?

Answer. How many square faces do the rectangular parallelepipeds have? Rectangular parallelepiped (*a*) has _____ square faces; (*b*) has _____ square faces; (*c*) has _____ square faces; (*d*) has _____ square faces; (*e*) has _____ square faces. Rectangular parallelepipeds _____ are cubes.

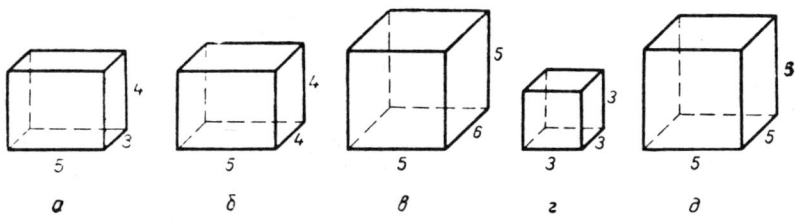

Figure 142.

Assignment 27. The length of each of the edges of the rectangular parallelepiped shown in Figure 143 is doubled. By what factor has the sum of the lengths of its edges increased?

Solution. 1) The dimensions of the new rectangular parallelepiped are $2a$ cm, _____ cm, _____ cm.

2) The sum of the lengths of the edges of the new rectangular parallelepiped is $4 \times 2a + 4 \times 2b + 4 \times 2c = 8a +$ _____ $+$ _____ $= 8 \times (a + b +$ _____ $)$ cm.

3) The sum of the lengths of the edges of the rectangular parallelepiped depicted in Figure 143 is $4(a +$ _____ $+$ _____ $)$cm.

Answer. The sum of the lengths of the edges of a rectangular parallelepiped has been increased by a factor of _____.

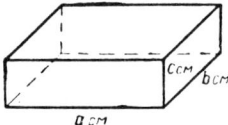

Figure 143.

Assignment 28. The length of each edge of the rectangular parallelepiped shown in Figure 144 has been doubled. Now what is the sum of the lengths of its edges?

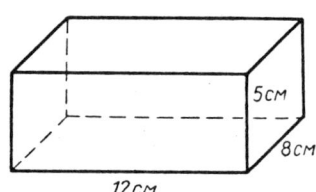

Figure 144.

Description of an Instructional Unit and Methods of Use

Method 1.
The lengths of the edges are now equal to ____, ____, ____, ____,
____, ____, ____, ____, ____, ____, ____, ____.
Total: ____.

Method 2.
The sum of all the edges of the given parallelepiped is ____. The sum of the edges of the new parallelepiped will be equal to ____ = ____ × ____.

Method 3.
The parallelepiped's dimensions are now equal to ____, ____, and ____. The sum of the edges of the new parallelepiped will be 12 × 4 + ____ × 4 + ____ × ____ = (____ + ____ + ____) × 4 = ____.

Assignment 29. Fill in the blanks (Fig. 145).
BF = ____ cm. The area of BFMC = ____ (square cm).
BC = ____ cm. The area of ABCD = ____ (square cm).
CM = ____ cm. The area of DCMN = ____ (square cm).

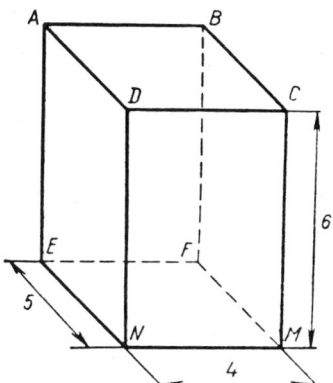

Figure 145.

Assignment 30. How many square decimeters of glass will it take to make an aquarium (Fig. 146) if the bottom is glass? What if the bottom is metal?

Solution.
A 40 × 30 face will take _____ square _____ .
All the 40 × 30 faces will take _____ square dm.
A _____ face will take _____ square _____ .
All the _____ faces will take _____ square _____ .
A _____ face will take _____ square _____ .
The entire aquarium will take _____ square _____ of glass if the bottom is made of glass.
The entire aquarium will take _____ square _____ of glass if the bottom is made of metal.

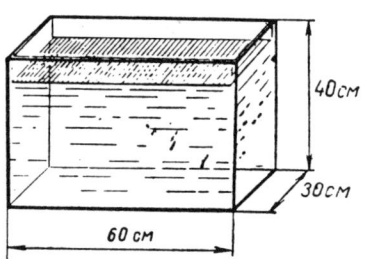

Figure 146.

Assignment 31. A cube and a rectangular parallelepiped are made from the same piece of tin (Fig. 147). Which is heavier? What if they were made from the same piece of wire?

Answer. The weight of the tin parallelepiped is _____ than the weight of the tin cube. The weight of the wire parallelepiped is _____ than the wire cube.

The number that indicates how many units of volume are contained in a solid is called the volume of the solid.

Assignment 32. Let us determine the volume of a solid (Fig. 148).

Description of an Instructional Unit and Methods of Use

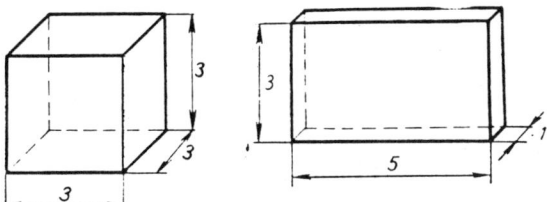

Figure 147.

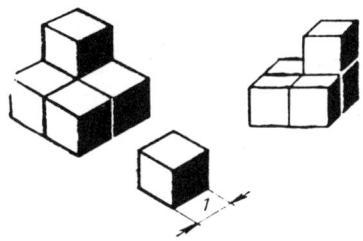

Figure 148.

Solution. To find the volume of a solid, we should count to see how many _____ are contained in this solid. _____ units of volume are contained in this solid. Therefore its volume is equal to _____.

Answer. The volume of the solid is equal to _____.

Assignment 33. In this cube (Fig. 149) one of the edges is doubled, and the other dimensions are unchanged. Draw the resulting rectangular parallelepiped. Taking the cube shown in Figure 149 as a unit, find the volume of the rectangular parallelepiped.

Solution. To find the volume of the rectangular parallelepiped, we must count _____.

Answer. The volume of the solid is _____.

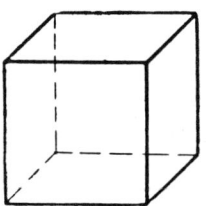

Figure 149.

Assignment 34. In this cube (Fig. 149) two dimensions have been tripled, and the third is unchanged. Draw the resulting rectangular parallelepiped. Taking the cube shown in Figure 149 as a unit, find the volume of the rectangular parallelepiped.

Solution. The volume of the rectangular parallelepiped is _____. The number obtained shows _____.

Assignment 35. Find the volume of the rectangular parallelepiped shown in Figure 150 (in cubic centimeters).

Solution. The volume of one layer is _____ cubic cm. The total number of layers is _____. The volume of the rectangular parallelepiped is _____ cubic cm.

Answer. _____.

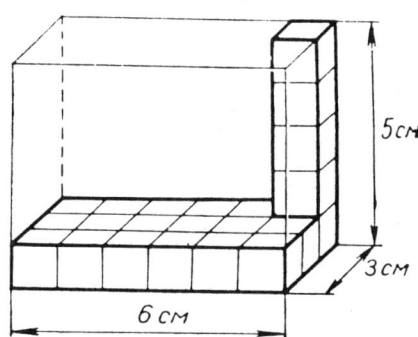

Figure 150.

Description of an Instructional Unit and Methods of Use

Assignment 36. The length of a rectangle is 5 centimeters, and the width is 2 centimeters. How many cubes with an edge of 1 centimeter can be placed in 1 layer on this rectangle? in 4 layers? Draw the resulting rectangular parallelepipeds and find the volume of these parallelepipeds.

Solution. _____ cubes can be placed on the rectangle in 1 layer. _____ cubes can be placed on the rectangle in 4 layers. The volume of the rectangular parallelepiped composed of 1 layer of cubes is _____ (cubic cm). The volume of the rectangular parallelepiped composed of 4 layers of cubes is _____ (cubic cm).

Assignment 37. Each dimension of a cube (Fig. 151) has been reduced by one-third.

1. Draw the resulting cube.
2. Divide the lower base into squares such that a small cube can be placed on each one.
3. How many small cubes will fit on the lower base of the large cube? _____ small cubes.
4. How many small cubes will fit on the front face of the large cube? _____ small cubes.
5. Taking the small cube as a unit, find the volume of the large cube. The volume of the large cube is _____.

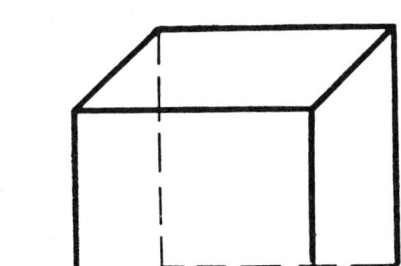

Figure 151.

Assignment 38. For brevity's sake, the dimensions of a rectangular parallelepiped can be written $a \times b \times c$. Find the volume of a rectangular parallelepiped having the dimensions: a) 30 x 40 x 50 mm; b) 4 x 5 x 6 dm.

Answer. a) _____ cubic mm; b) _____ cubic dm.

Assignment 39. Write a formula for calculating the volume of a rectangular parallelepiped (Fig. 152).

$V =$ _____ $\times$ _____ $\times$ _____

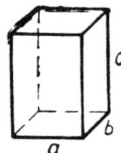

Figure 152.

Assignment 40. The dimensions of a rectangular parallelepiped are equal to 6, 3, and 2 units of length (Fig. 153).

1) Determine the volume of this rectangular parallelepiped. The volume of the rectangular parallelepiped is _____. The resulting number shows _____.

2) Draw the unit of volume used for measuring the volume of the given parallelepiped.

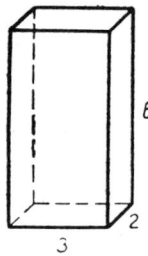

Figure 153.

Description of an Instructional Unit and Methods of Use

Assignment 41. The dimensions of some rectangular parallelepipeds are designated by the letters a, b, and c in Table 4.2. Calculate their volumes.

Table 4.2

a	4 cm	21 cm	8 dm	400 mm
b	23 cm	14 cm	38 dm	32 mm
c	250 cm	32 cm	15 dm	25 mm
V				

Assignment 42. Using the data in Table 4.3, calculate the area of the floor for each room, and then the volume of each room. Figure the total volume of all three rooms.

The sum of the volumes of the room is _____.

Table 4.3

Room Number	Length	Width	Height	Area of Floor	Volume
1	8 m	6 m	4 m		
2	7 m	5 m	4 m		
3	4 m	4 m	4 m		

Assignment 43. The edge of a cube is equal to a. Make up a formula to calculate the area of the base S and the volume of the cube V. Fill in Table 4.4.

Table 4.4

a	S	V
8		
17		
25		

Check your results, using the table of squares and cubes on the cover of this workbook.

Assignment 44. How many cubic centimeters in the box?
1) The length of the box is 8 cm, the width 1 cm, the height 1 cm.
2) The length of the box is 6 cm, the width 4 cm, the height 1 cm.
3) The length of the box is 10 cm, the width 10 cm, height 5 cm.
Answer. 1) _____ ; 2) _____ ; 3) _____ .

Assignment 45. Compare the volumes of the boxes depicted here (Fig. 154). The volume of the first box is _____ than the volume of the second box by _____ cubic dm.

The volume of the first box is _____ times _____ than the volume of the second box.

How can we solve the second part of the problem without calculating the volumes of the boxes?

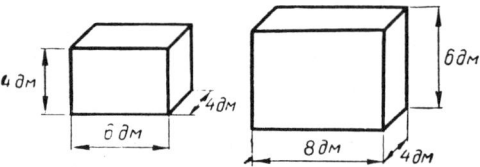

Figure 154.

Assignment 46. Make up a formula for calculating the volume of a rectangular parallelepiped based on the area of its base and its height (Fig.155): $V =$ _____ × _____ .

Using the formula you have obtained, fill in Table 4.5.

Assignment 47. The volume of the rectangular parallelepiped shown in Figure 156 is equal to 748 cubic dm. What is its height?

Solution. _____ .
Answer. _____ .

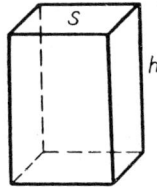

Figure 155.

Table 4.5

S	h	V
302 sq. cm	10 cm	
201 sq. mm	20 mm	
15 sq. dm	15 dm	

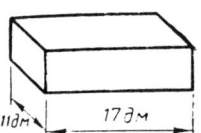

Figure 156.

Assignment 48. The length, width, and height of our classroom are _____ m, _____ m, and _____ m, and there are _____ students. How many cubic meters of air are there for each student?
Solution. _____.
Answer. _____.

Assignment 49. A solid cube is placed in an empty cubic box (Fig. 157). What is the volume of the remaining part? (Solve the problem using the table of cubes on the cover of this workbook.)

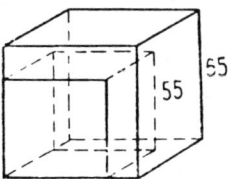

Figure 157

Assignment 50. Using Figure 158, count to see how many cubic decimeters are contained in one cubic meter.

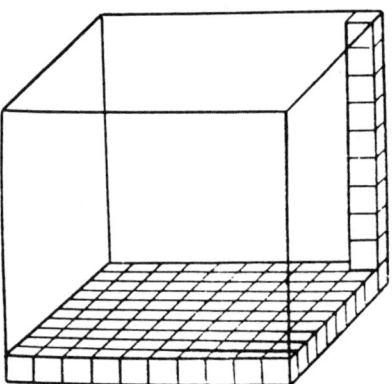

Figure 158.

Assignment 51. Find the volumes of the rectangular parallelepipeds (see Table 4.6).

Description of an Instructional Unit and Methods of Use

Table 4.6

Area of Base	350 sq. dm	400 sq. dm	31 sq. dm
Height	24 dm	50 cm	7 cm
volume			

Assignment 52. A rectangular parallelepiped is divided into two parts with base areas of 30 and 45 (Fig. 159). What is the volume of the entire parallelepiped?
Solution. Method 1. (_____ + _____) × 10 = _____.
Method 2. _____ × 10 + _____ 10 = _____.
Answer. _____.
What law of arithmetic operations guarantees that the answers will be the same? _____.

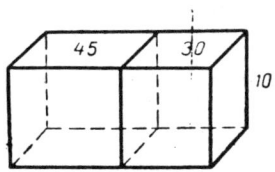

Figure 159.

Assignment 53. A rectangular parallelepiped is divided into three parts, with base areas of 13, 10, and 12 (Fig. 160). Find the volume of the rectangular parallelepiped.
Solution. _____.
Answer. _____.

Assignment 54. Using the data given in Table 4.7, calculate the volume of an apartment with a height of 28 decimeters. Fill in only those blanks in the table that you consider necessary.

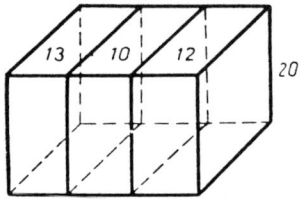

Figure 160.

Table 4.7

	1st room	2nd room	3rd room	Common access places	Total
Area of Floor	10 sq. m	15 sq. m	20 sq. m	15 sq. m	sq. m
Volume					

Assignment 55. What is the volume of each of the parts into which the rectangular parallelepiped is divided (Fig. 161)?
   Answer. a) _____ and _____; b) _____ and _____; c) _____ and _____.

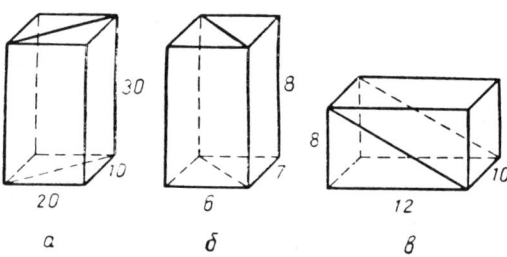

Figure 161.

Description of an Instructional Unit and Methods of Use

Assignment 56. How do we calculate the volume of this solid (Fig.162)? (Be ready to give an explanation to the teacher.)
Answer. The volume of the solid is _____ cubic cm.

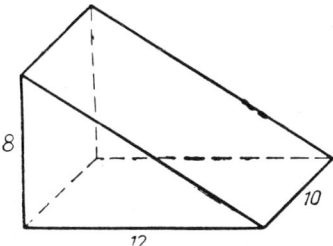

Figure 162.

Assignment 57. The thickness of a solid triangle is 5 mm, and the lengths of its sides are 30, 40, and 50 cm (Fig. 163). What is the volume of the triangle?

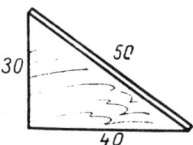

Figure 163.

Assignment 58. The volume of the first cube (Fig. 164) is equal to the sum of the volumes of the three others. What is the edge of the first cube?
Solution. According to the table of cubes (on the workbook cover), we find that:
the volume of a cube of edge 3 is _____;
the volume of a cube of edge 4 is _____;

the volume of a cube of edge 5 is _____.

Therefore, the sum of the volumes of all three cubes is equal to 27 + _____ + _____ = _____, and this is also the volume of the first cube. Using the table of cubes, we find that its edge is equal to _____.

Answer. The edge of the first cube is equal to _____.

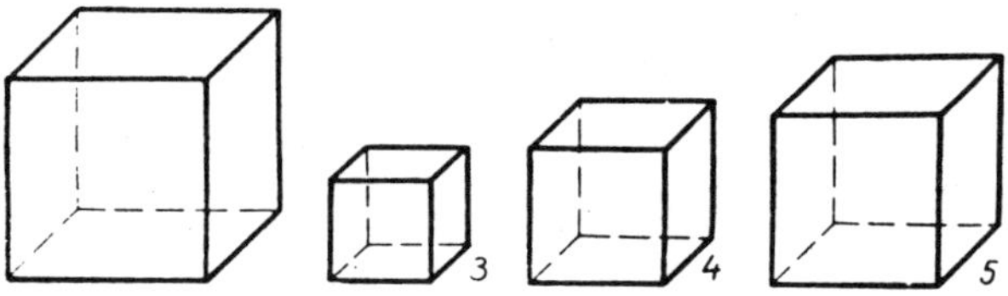

Figure 164.

Assignment 59. Solve the same problem for the cubes illustrated in Figure 165.

Answer. The edge of the first cube is _____.

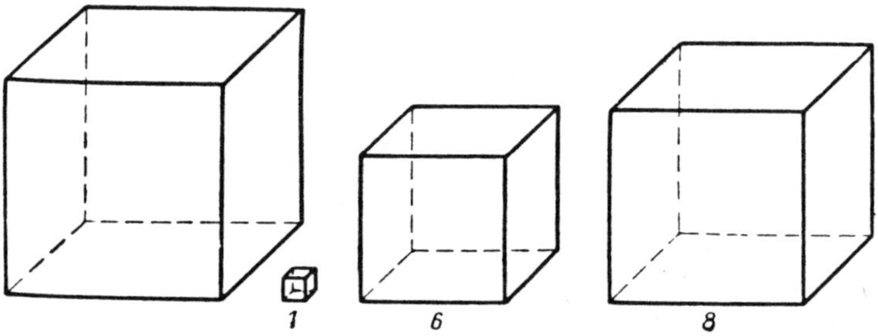

Figure 165.

Assignment 60. Here, too (Fig. 166), the volume of the first cube is equal to the sum of the volumes of the other three. But we must find the edge of the fourth cube.

Answer. _____.

Description of an Instructional Unit and Methods of Use 253

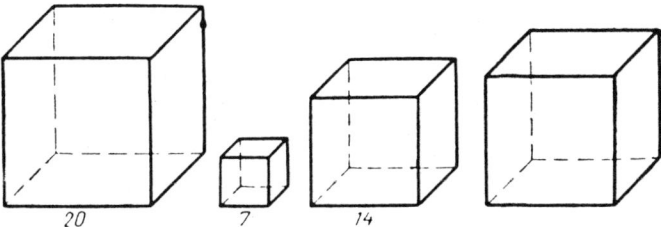

Figure 166.

Assignment 61. In this problem (Fig. 167) the sum of the volumes of the first two cubes is equal to the sum of the volumes of the other two. Find the edge of the third cube. Find its surface area. (Use the tables of squares and cubes on the workbook cover.)

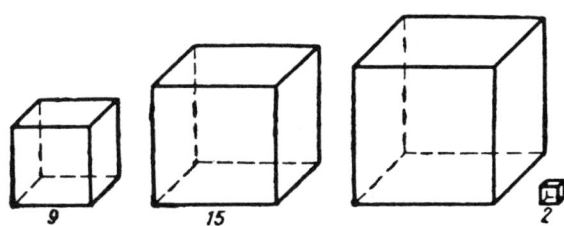

Figure 167.

Assignment 62. Find the volume of the solid shown in Figure 168.
Method 1.

This solid can be mentally divided into two parallelepipeds, as shown in Figure 169. The volume of the upper parallelepiped is _____. The dimensions of the lower parallelepiped are _____, _____, and _____, and its volume is _____. Therefore, the volume of the entire solid is equal to _____ + _____ = _____.

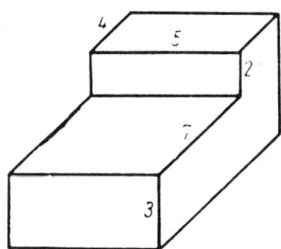

Figure 168.

Method 2.

This solid can be divided into two parallelepipeds, as shown in Figure 170. The volume of the front parallelepiped is _____. The dimensions of the rear parallelepiped are _____, _____, and _____, and its volume is equal to _____. Therefore, the volume of the entire solid is equal to _____ + _____ = _____.

Method 3.

This solid can be enlarged into a rectangular parallelepiped, as shown in Figure 171. The volume of the entire parallelepiped obtained is equal to _____ × _____ × _____, and the volume of the part added is equal to _____ × _____ × _____. Therefore, the volume of the given solid is equal to _____ - _____ = _____.

Assignment 63. Find the volume of the solid shown in Figure 172.

Assignment 64. Find the volume of the solid shown in Figure 173.

Assignment 65. Using the table of cubes, find x if $x^3 = 9^3 + 10^3 - 1^3$.

Solution. $9^3 =$ _____, $10^3 =$ _____, $1^3 =$ _____.; $x^3 =$ _____ = _____ - _____ = _____. $x =$ _____.

Answer. $x =$ _____.

Assignment 66. $x^3 = 20^3 - 15^3 - 10^3$. Between which integers does the number x lie?

Solution. $20^3 =$ _____, $15^3 =$ _____, $10^3 =$ _____, $x^3 =$ _____.

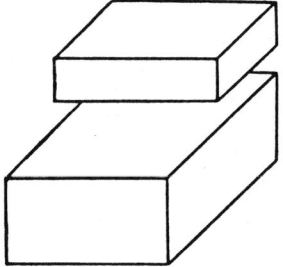

Figure 169.

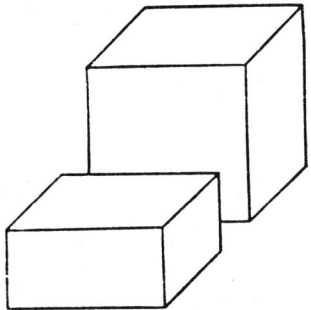

Figure 170.

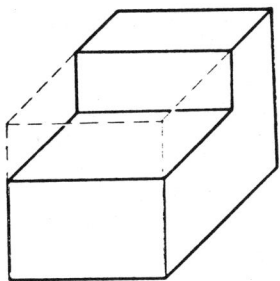

Figure 171.

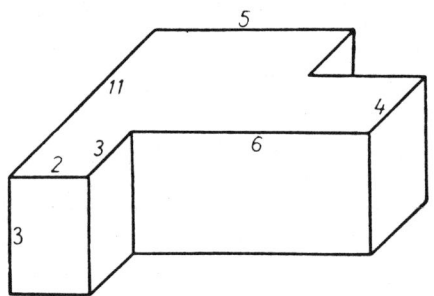

Figure 172.

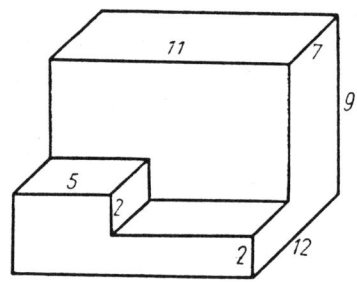

Figure 173.

But 3,625 lies between _____ and _____. Therefore, x lies between _____ and _____.
Answer. _____ x _____.
Assignment 67. Fill in the blanks.
a) $2 + 13 = 13 +$ _____ $=$ _____ [commutative law of addition].
b) $23 + (7 + 24) = (23 +$ _____ $) + 24$ [associative law of addition] $=$ _____ $+ 24 =$ _____.

Description of an Instructional Unit and Methods of Use

c) $12 + (5 + 8) = 12 + (8 + \underline{\quad})$ [commutative law of addition] $= (\underline{\quad} + \underline{\quad}) + 5$ [associative law of addition] $= \underline{\quad} + 5 = \underline{\quad}$.

d) $17 \times 2 = 2 \times \underline{\quad}$ [commutative law of multiplication] $= \underline{\quad}$.

e) $4 \times (5 \times 17) = (4 \times \underline{\quad}) \times 17$ [associative law of multiplication] $= \underline{\quad} \times 17 = \underline{\quad}$.

f) $2 \times (13 \times 5) = 2 \times (5 \times \underline{\quad})$ [commutative law of multiplication] $= (\underline{\quad} \times \underline{\quad}) \times 13$ [associative law of multiplication] $= \underline{\quad} \times 13 = \underline{\quad}$.

g) $a + b + c = (a + b) + c = a + (b + c) = (a + c) + \underline{\quad} = a + (\underline{\quad} + \underline{\quad}) = (b + \underline{\quad}) + \underline{\quad} = b + (\underline{\quad} + \underline{\quad}) = b + (\underline{\quad} + \underline{\quad}) = (b + \underline{\quad}) + \underline{\quad} = (c + \underline{\quad}) + \underline{\quad} = (\underline{\quad} + \underline{\quad}) + \underline{\quad} = \underline{\quad} + (\underline{\quad} + \underline{\quad}) = \underline{\quad}$.

Assignment 68. Fill in the blanks.

a) $5 \times 13 + 5 \times 17 = 5 \times (\underline{\quad} + \underline{\quad})$ [distributive law] $= 5 \times \underline{\quad} = \underline{\quad} + \underline{\quad} + \underline{\quad}$.

b) $2 \times (15 + 25) = 2 \times 15 + \underline{\quad} \times \underline{\quad}$ [distributive law] $= 5 \times \underline{\quad} = (\underline{\quad} + \underline{\quad}) + \underline{\quad}$.

Assignment 69. Fill in the blanks.

a) $6 \times 17 = \underline{\quad} \times \underline{\quad}$ [$\underline{\quad}$ law] $= \underline{\quad}$.

b) $12 \times 23 + 12 \times 69 + 12 \times 77 = 12 \times (23 + 69 + \underline{\quad})$ [distributive law] $= 12 \times (23 + 77 + \underline{\quad})$ [commutative law of addition] $= 12 \times (\underline{\quad} + 69)$ $12 \times \underline{\quad} = \underline{\quad}$.

Assignment 70. Fill in the blanks.

a) $5 \times 43 + 87 \times 5 + 5 \times 57 = 5 \times 43 + 5 \times 87 + \underline{\quad} \times \underline{\quad}$ [commutative law of multiplication] $= 5 \times (43 + 87 + \underline{\quad})$ [distributive law] $= 5 \times (43 + \underline{\quad} + \underline{\quad})$ [commutative law of addition] $= 5 \times (\underline{\quad} + 87) = 5 \times \underline{\quad} = \underline{\quad}$.

b) $13 + (7 + 29) = (\underline{\quad} + \underline{\quad}) + \underline{\quad}$ [$\underline{\quad}$ law] $= \underline{\quad} + \underline{\quad} = \underline{\quad}$.

Assignment 71. Fill in the blanks.

a) $5 + 7 = \underline{\quad} + \underline{\quad}$ [$\underline{\quad}$ law] $= \underline{\quad}$.

b) $17 \times 284 - 17 \times 283 = 17 \times (\underline{\quad} - \underline{\quad})$ [$\underline{\quad}$ law] $= 17 \times \underline{\quad} = \underline{\quad}$.

c) $24 \times (8 + 7) = 24 \times \underline{} + \underline{} \times \underline{} [\underline{} \text{law}] = \underline{} + \underline{} = \underline{}$.

d) $19 \times 6 + 19 \times 4 = 19 \times (\underline{} + \underline{}) [\underline{} \text{law}] = \underline{} \times \underline{} = \underline{}$.

e) $144 \times 39 - 38 \times 144 = 144 \times \underline{} - 144 \times \underline{} [\underline{} \text{law}] = 144 \times (\underline{} - \underline{}) [\underline{} \text{law}] = (\underline{}) = \underline{} \times \underline{} = \underline{}$.

f) $(a - b) \times (a + b) = (a - b) \times a + (a - b) \times b$ [distributive law] $= a^2 - ba + \underline{} - \underline{}$ [distributive law] $= a^2 - ab + ab - b^2$ [commutative law of multiplication] $= \underline{} - \underline{}$.

g) $5 \times (a + 2) = 5a + 5 \times 2$ [distributive law] $= 5a + \underline{}$.

h) $a \times (b + c) - (a + b) \times c = ab + \underline{} - ac - \underline{} [\underline{} \text{law}] = \underline{}$.

i) $3 \times 544 - 150 \times 3 + 6 \times 3 = 544 \times \underline{} - \underline{} \times \underline{} + \underline{} \times \underline{} [\underline{} \text{law}] = (\underline{} - \underline{} + \underline{}) \times 3 [\underline{} \text{law}] = (\underline{} + \underline{} - \underline{}) \times 3 [\underline{} \text{law}] = (\underline{} - \underline{}) \times 3 \underline{} = \underline{} \times \underline{} = \underline{}$.

Methodology of Using the Workbook

The workbook is a comparatively new form of educational material. Threfore it is especially important to focus on its role in the educational process and on the methodology of using it. The workbook on the topic "The Volume of a Rectangular Parallelepiped" has three goals:

1) promote the formation of the concepts in the topic, organizing the students' activity so it is adequate for these concepts;

2) indicate to the students ways to solve the principal problems (see the discussion of didactic orientation); and

3) free the students from unnecessary work.

How the workbook fulfills the first of these functions can be observed in the first assignments. Here the student must follow an algorithm for

Description of an Instructional Unit and Methods of Use

recognizing a rectangular parallelepiped. The student's activity in executing these assignments fully meets the requirements set forth earlier.

The workbook's second function can easily be understood, for example, from Assignments 4 and 5, and others. Here the student is given a rigorous sequence for doing the work, which is essential at the first stage of instruction in new types of problems. But this rigor gradually diminishes. Assignments 17, 19, 20, 23, and others serve as examples of theoretical assignments.

The third function operates in almost all the assignments. The workbook liberates the student from doing purely technical work (drawings based on the conditions of a problem, or writing out lengthy sentences). Without belittling the value of this technical work in any way, we believe that there is a disproportionate amount of it in traditional instruction. Note that use of our printed workbook does not exclude extensive use of the usual student workbook, in which the teacher can assign work as deemed necessary.

Let us focus particularly on the last assignments, which are devoted to the laws of the arithmetic operations. These assignments, as experimentation has shown, can productively be given to the students throughout the study of the topic. Careful performance of the first assignments in this cycle will enable students to proceed almost independently to the proof of the algebraic theorems in Assignment 67. By the time they reach Lesson 9, they should have solved no fewer than half of the assignments in this cycle. The workbook should be used primarily during class, although homework assignments based on it can also be given.

We recommend drawing the students' attention to the table of squares and cubes, and using it extensively while solving problems. Of course, it would be superfluous to require that this chart be memorized. But by the time they finish studying the topic, the students should know the table of linear, square and cubic measures by heart. As an example, let us consider how Assignment 1 from the workbook should look if the student has done it properly.

Assignment 1. Fill in the blanks in the following sentences.

In order to find out whether a solid is a rectangular parallelepiped, we must:

1) count to see how many faces it has (a rectangular parallelepiped has 6 faces);

2) see whether all the faces of the solid are rectangles (in a rectangular parallelepiped all the faces are rectangles).

We will give only the answers for the subsequent assignments, indicating in the necessary order what the student should write in the blanks.

Assignment 2. 4; 6; a rectangular parallelepiped.

Assignment 3. 6; 6; a rectangle; a rectangle; a rectangle; *ABFE* is not a rectangle; *CDHG* is not a rectangle; not all the faces are rectangles; is not a rectangular parallelepiped.

Assignment 4. *a, b, d, e, f; b, f, g; b, f; a, c, d, e, g.*

Assignment 5. 6; rectangle; parallelepiped; faces; 12; 8; A cube;

Assignment 6. *MD; AEHB; EHFM; EM; ABCD;* adjacent; *AD; BHFC.*

Assignment 7. opposite; adjacent; adjacent; opposite; opposite; adjacent.

Assignment 8. a rectangle; *EFGH; AEFB;* equal.

Assignment 9. *AEHD; BFGC; DMGC; EFGM;* a square.

Assignment 10. $= EF = HG$; $= EH = BC = FG$; $= DH = BF = CG$; *EFGH; C, D, E, F, G, H.*

Assignment 12. lower; equal; is equal to the back.

Assignment 16. The student can make one of the three drawings in Figure 174. It should be noted that it is sufficient for the teacher to see any one of these three drawings in the student's workbook to consider that the assignment has been done properly. Of course, if a student draws two (or even three) parallelepipeds, this is evidence of superior spatial imagination.

Assignment 17. The observations made for Assignment 16 are applicable here as well. A complete answer is shown in Figure 175.

Assignment 18. *ABFE; BFGC; AEHD; BEFC.*

Assignment 19. 2; 3; 4; 5; 6.

Assignment 20. The correct answer is shown in Figure 176.

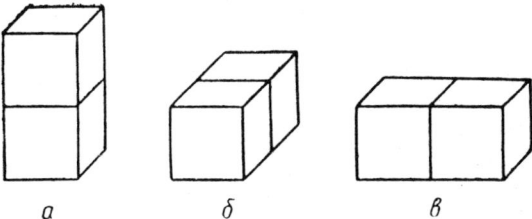

Figure 174.

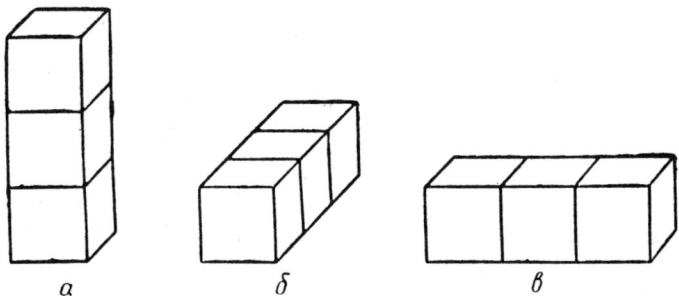

Figure 175.

Figure 176.

Assignment 21. We will give the solution in full.

Method 1. 1) It took 20 cm for the edge of the lower base; 2) 20 cm for the edge of the upper base; 3) 8 cm for the vertical edges; 4) 48 cm for the entire frame.

Method 2. 1) It took $2 + 4 + 6 = 12$ (cm) for the three unequal edges; 2) $12 \times 4 = 48$ (cm) for the entire frame.

Method 3. A rectangular parallelepiped has sets of four equal edges. 1) It took $2 \times 4 = 8$ (cm) for the edges that are equal to 2 cm; 2) $6 \times 4 = 24$ (cm) for the edges that are equal to 6 cm; 3) $4 \times 4 = 16$ (cm) for the edges that are equal to 4 cm; 4) $8 + 24 + 16 = 48$ (cm) for the entire frame.

These calculations can be written in one line:

$2 \times 4 + 2 \times 4 + 4 \times 4 = (2 + 6 + 4) \times 4$ [distributive law] $= 12 \times 4 = 48$.

Assignment 22. We cite the solution in full.

Method 1. 1) There are 4 edges of a. The sum of their lengths is $4a$ cm. 2) There are 4 edges of b cm. The sum of their lengths is $4b$ cm. 3) There are 4 edges of c cm. The sum of their lengths is $4c$ cm. 4) The sum of the lengths of all the edges is equal to $4a + 4b + 4c$ (cm).

Method 2. 1) The sum of the lengths of the three dimensions is equal to $a + b + c$ cm; 2) the sum of the lengths of all the edges is equal to $4(a + b + c)$ cm.

Assignment 23. The drawing can be done in three ways (cf. Fig. 174), and the solution is done free-form (space is left for it).

Answer. The surface area is 40 square cm; the sum of the lengths of the edges is 32 cm.

Assignment 24. The resulting rectangular parallelepiped can be represented in several different ways (Fig. 177). There is no point in asking the student to supply all of them—one is enough. The solution is free-form.

Answer. The surface is 112 square cm; the sum of the lengths of the edges is 56 cm.

Assignment 25. We need another 48 cm of wire. (Free-form solution. The teacher can recommend completing the drawing so that it represents a rectangular parallelepiped, or may say nothing about it, but then he should not require that this representation be constructed.)

Description of an Instructional Unit and Methods of Use

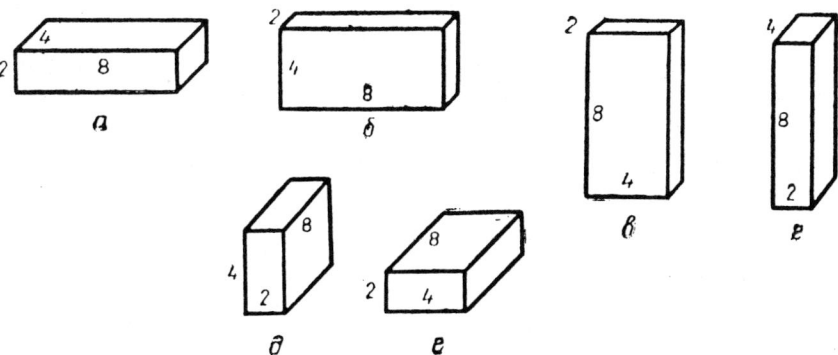

Figure 177.

Assignment 26. (a) no square faces; (b) has 2 square faces; (c) has 2 square faces; (d) and (e) have 6 square faces. Rectangular parallelepipeds (d) and (e) are cubes.

Assignment 27. The sum of the lengths of the edges of the rectangular parallelepiped has been increased by a factor of 2.

Assignment 28.

Method 1. The lengths of the edges are 4, 8, 12, 4, 8, 12, 4, 8, 12; total: 96.

Method 2. The sum of all the edges of the given parallelepiped is 48. The sum of the edges of the new parallelepiped will be equal to $48 \times 2 = 96$.

Method 3. The parallelepiped's dimensions are now equal to 4, 8, and 12. The sum of the edges of the new parallelepiped will be $12 \times 4 + 8 \times 4 + 4 \times 4 = (12 + 8 + 4) \times 4$ [distributive law] $= 96$.

Assignment 29. 6; 30; 5; 20; 6; 24.

Assignment 30. 12 square dm; 24 square dm; 40 x 60; 48 square dm; 40 x 60; 18 square dm; 30 x 60; 90 square dm; 72 square dm.

Assignment 31. The weight of the tin parallelepiped is less than the tin cube. The weight of the wire parallelepiped is equal to the weight of the wire cube.

Assignment 32. units of volume; 5; 5; 5.

Assignment 33. to see how many units of volume it contains; 2.

Assignment 34. 9; how many units of volume are contained in the solid. (Various possible ways to make the drawing are shown in Figure 178; on this subject, see the note to Assignment 24).

Assignment 35. 18; 5; 90; 90 cubic cm.

Assignment 36. 10; 40; 10; 40. (The drawing is shown in Figure 179.)

Assignment 37. 9; 9; 27. (The drawing is shown in Figure 180.)

Assignment 38. 60,000; 120.

Assignment 39. $V = a \times b \times c$.

Assignment 40. 36; how many units of volume this parallelepiped contains. (The drawing is shown in Figure 181).

Assignment 41.

V	23,000 cubic cm	9,408 cubic cm	4,560 cubic dm	320,000 cubic mm

Assignment 42.

Area of Floor	Volume
48 square m	192 cubic m
35 square m	140 cubic m
16 square m	64 cubic m

Sum of the volumes of the rooms: 396 cubic m.

Assignment 43. $S = a^2$; $V = a^3$;

a	S	V
8	64	512
17	289	4,913
25	625	15,625

Assignment 44. 8 cubic cm; 24 cubic cm; 400 cubic cm.

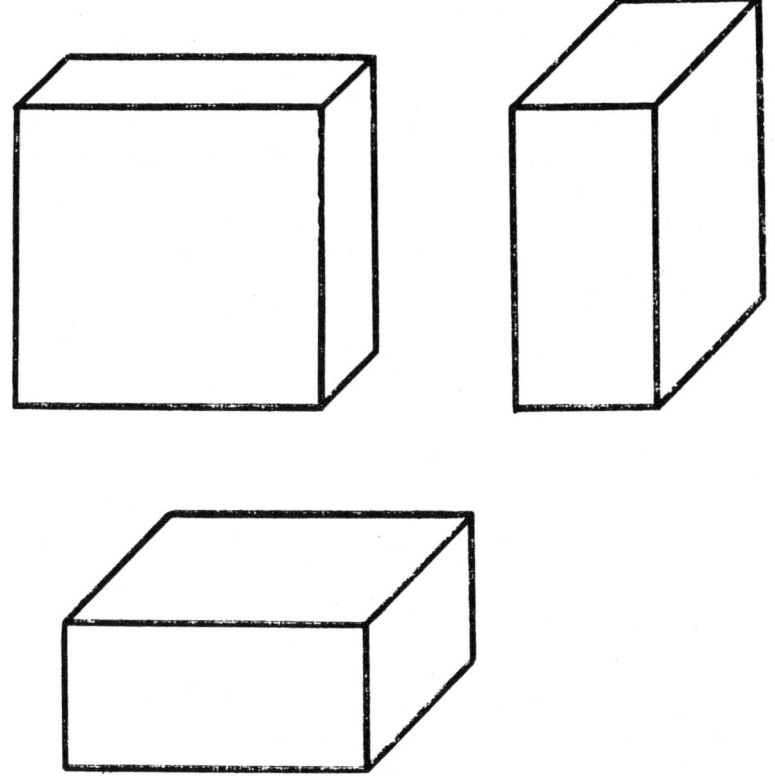

Figure 178.

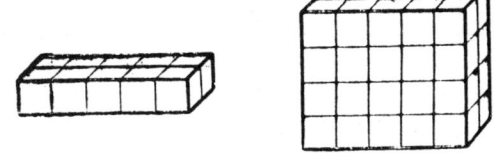

Figure 179.

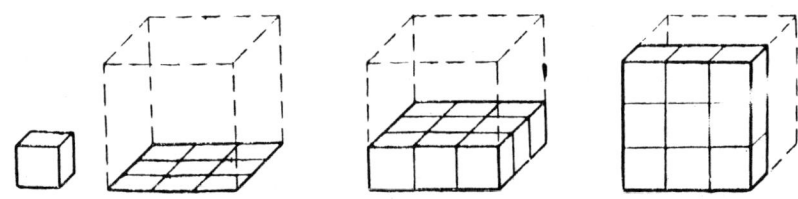

Figure 180.

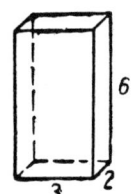

Figure 181.

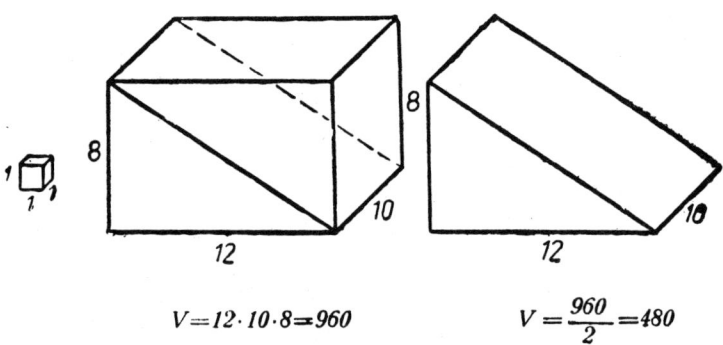

$V = 12 \cdot 10 \cdot 8 = 960$ $\qquad$ $V = \dfrac{960}{2} = 480$

Figure 182.

Description of an Instructional Unit and Methods of Use

Assignment 45. less; 96; 2; less.

Assignment 46. $V = Sh$;

S	h	V
302 square cm	10 cm	3,020 cub. cm
201 square mm	20 mm	4,020 cub. mm
15 square dm	15 dm	225 cub. dm

Assignment 47. $h = 4$ dm.
Assignment 49. 108,250.
Assignment 50. 1,000 cubic dm.
Assignment 51.

8,400 cubic dm	2,000 cubic dm	21,700 cubic cm

Assignment 52.
Method 1. $(45 + 30) \times 10 = 750$.
Method 2. $45 \times 10 + 30 \times 10 = 750$.
750; the distributive law.

Assignment 53. 700.

Assignment 54. It is best if the student fills in only the two right-hand boxes; another method is to fill in all the lower boxes.

Answer. 168 cubic m goes in the lower right-hand box in both cases.

Assignment 55. a) 3,000 and 3,000; b) 168 and 168; c) 480 and 480.

Assignment 56. The volume of the solid is equal to 480 cubic cm. (It is desirable to get an explanation in the form of the drawing in Figure 182.)

Assignment 57. 600 cubic cm.

Assignment 58. 27; 64; 125; 27 + 64 + 125 = 216; 6; 6.

Assignment 59. The edge of the first cube is 9.

Assignment 60. The edge of the fourth cube is 17.

Assignment 61. The edge of the third cube is 16; its surface area is 1,536.

Assignment 62:. Method 1: $V = 40 + 165 = 205$.
Method 2: $V = 105 + 100 = 205$.
Method 3: $V = 275 - 70 = 205$.
Assignment 63. $V = 174$ (Several variant solutions are shown in Figures 183-185.)
Assignment 64. (See the variant solutions in Figures 186-188.)
Assignment 66. Solution: $20^3 = 8,000$; $15^3 = 3,375$; $10^3 = 1,000$; $x^3 = 3,625$. But 3,625 lies between 3,375 and 4,096. Therefore, x lies between 15 and 16. *Answer:* $15 < x < 16$.
Assignment 67. We give the text in full.

a) $2 + 13 = 13 + 2$ [commutative law of addition] $= 15$.

b) $23 + (7 + 24) = (23 + 7) + 24$ [associative law of addition] $= 30 + 24 = 54$.

c) $12 + (5 + 8) = 12 + (8 + 5)$ [commutative law of addition] $= 20 + 5 = 25$ [associative law of addition].

d) $17 \times 2 = 2 \times 17$ [commutative law of multiplication] $= 34$.

e) $4 \times (5 \times 17) = (4 \times 5) \times 17$ [associative law of multiplication] $= 20 \times 17 = 340$.

f) $2 \times (13 \times 5) = 2 \times (5 \times 13)$ [commutative law of multiplication] $= 10 \times 13 = 130$ [associative law of multiplication].

g) $a + b + c = (a + b) + c = a + (b + c) = (a + c) + b = a + (c + b) = (b + a) + c = b + (a + c) = (b + c) + a = b + (c + a) = (c + a) + b = c + (a + b) = (c + b) + a = c + (b + c)$.

Assignment 68.

a) $5 \times 13 + 5 \times 17 = 5 \times (13 + 17)$ [distributive law] $= 5 \times 30 = 150$.

b) $2 \times (15 + 25) = 2 \times 15 + 2 \times 25$ [distributive law] $= 30 + 50 = 80$.

Assignment 69.

a) $6 \times 17 = 17 \times 6$ [commutative law of multiplication] $= 102$.

b) $12 \times 23 + 12 \times 69 + 12 \times 77 = 12 \times (23 + 69 + 77)$ [distributive law] $= 12 \times (100 + 69)$ [commutative law of addition].

Assignment 70.

a) $5 \times 43 + 87 \times 5 + 5 \times 57 = 5 \times 43 - 5 \times 87 + 5 \times 57$ [commutative law of multiplication] $= 5 \times (43 - 87 + 57)$ [distributive law] $= 5 \times (43 + 57 - 87)$ [commutative law of addition] $= 5 \times (100 + 87) = 5 \times 187 = 935$.

Description of an Instructional Unit and Methods of Use

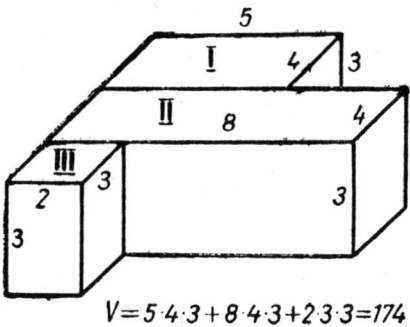

$V = 5 \cdot 4 \cdot 3 + 8 \cdot 4 \cdot 3 + 2 \cdot 3 \cdot 3 = 174$

Figure 183.

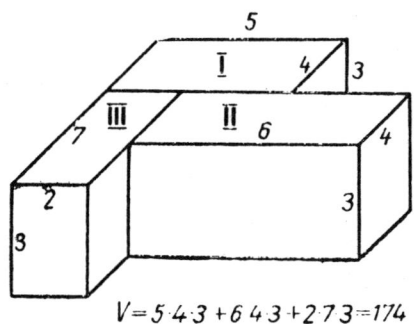

$V = 5 \cdot 4 \cdot 3 + 6 \cdot 4 \cdot 3 + 2 \cdot 7 \cdot 3 = 174$

Figure 184.

b) $13 + (7 + 29) = (13 + 7) + 29$ [associative law of addition] $= 20 + 29 = 49$.

Assignment 71.

a) $5 + 7 = 7 + 5$ [commutative law of addition] $= 12$.

b) $17 \times 284 - 17 \times 283 = 17 \times (284-283)$ [distributive law] $= 17 \times 1 = 17$.

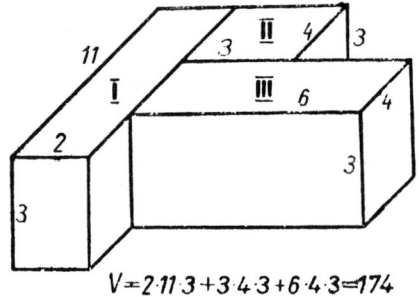

Figure 185.

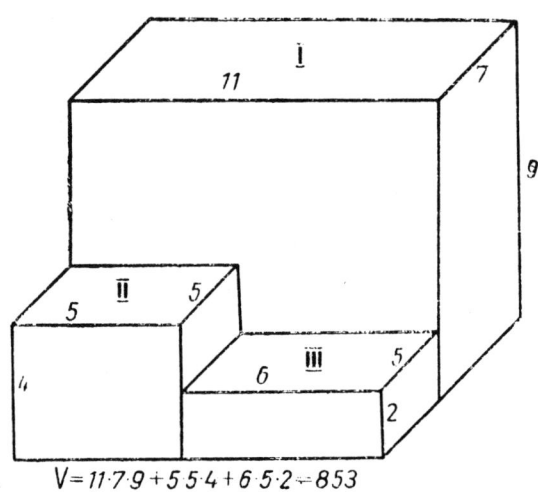

Figure 186.

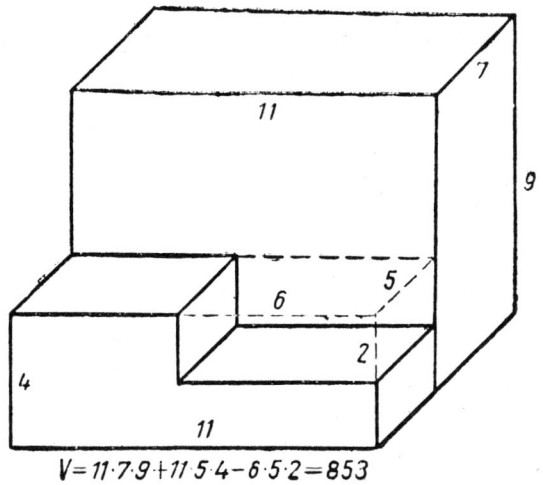

Figure 187.

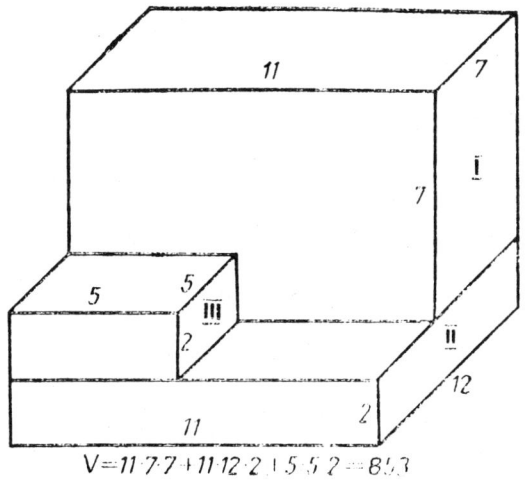

Figure 188.

c) $24 \times (8 + 7) = 24 \times 8 + 24 \times 7$ [distributive law] $= 192 + 168 + 360$.
d) $19 \times 6 + 19 \times 4 = 19 \times (6 + 4)$ [distributive law] $= 19 \times 10 = 190$.
e) $144 \times 39 - 38 \times 144 = 144 \times 39 - 144 \times 38$ [commutative law of multiplication] $= 144 \times (39 - 38)$ [distributive law] $= 144 \times 1 = 144$.
f) $(a - b) \times (a + b) = (a - b) \times a + (a - b) \times b$ [distributive law] $= a^2 - ba + ab - b^2$ [distributive law] $= a^2 - ab + ab - b^2$ [commutative law of multiplication].
g) $5 \times (a + 2) = 5a + 5 \times 2$ [distributive law] $= 5a + 10$.
h) $a \times (b + c) - (a + b) \times c = ab + ac - ac - bc = ab - bc$.
i) $3 \times 544 - 150 \times 3 + 6 \times 3 = 544 \times 3 - 150 \times 3 + 6 \times 3 = (544 - 150 + 6) \times 3 = (544 + 6 - 150) \times 3 = (550 - 150) \times 3 = 400 \times 3 = 1200$.

The Set of Problem Cards

Individual assignments can differ in form. They can be a set of 3x5 cards, each holding one or more problems addressing one facet of a topic. Or students could be given a set of pamphlets containing problems intended for the student's independent work over an extended period of time (up to a year). In our experiment we used a set of cards with one problem to a card (see Fig. 189). A total of 12 complete sets (each consisting of 180 cards) was used in the class. The methodology of using and storing the cards is discussed later.

The complete text of all the cards is given below. To save space in the book, we cite the problems in running text, rather than in the form of cards (as shown in Figure 189). Moreover, Assignments 169-180 have been subsumed under a single item.

1. Can you form a framework cube of 9, 10, 16, or 24 matches by gluing the match ends together?

2. Write down the numbers of the solids in Figure 190 which are rectangular parallelepipeds.

3. How many edges can a rectangular parallelepiped have, such that no two of them are equal?

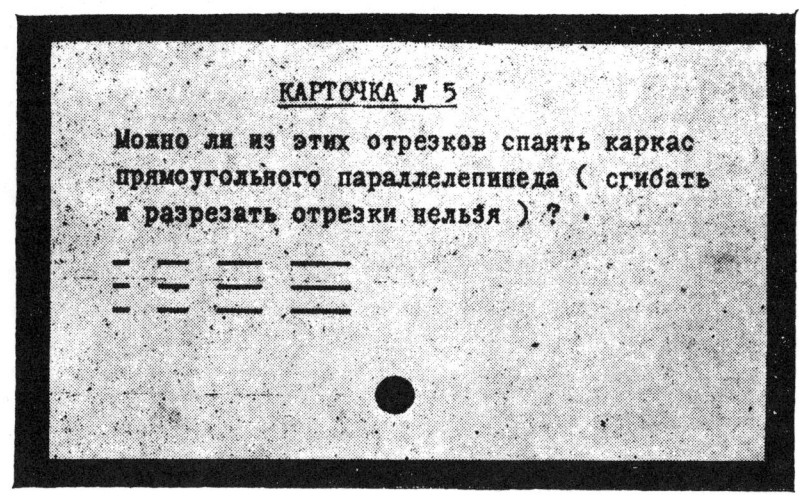

Figure 189.

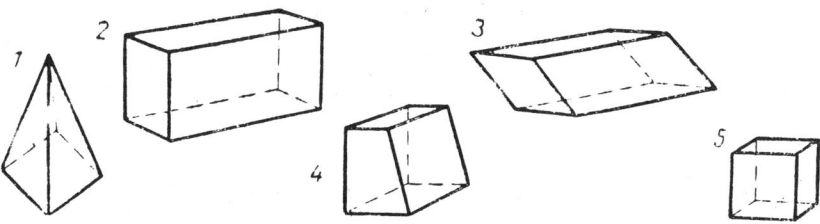

Figure 190.

4. How many colors must be used to color the faces of a rectangular parallelepiped so that each is a different color?

5. Can you fit together a rectangular parallelepiped from these segments (Fig. 191)? (You may not bend or cut the segments.)

6. Can a framework cube be formed from 10, 12, 11, or 14 matches by gluing the match ends together?

7. Write down the numbers of the solids in Figure 192 which are rectangular parallelepipeds.

8. How many edges does a rectangular parallelepiped have such that no two are parallel to each other?

9. One diagonal is drawn on each face of a rectangular parallelepiped. How many triangles is the surface divided into by these diagonals?

10. To these wires (Fig. 193) we must attach others so that a rectangular parallelepiped (framework) is obtained. How many more segments of wire are needed?

11. Can a framework cube be put together from 6, 8, 10, or 24 matches by gluing the match ends together?

12. Write down the numbers of the solids in Figure 194 which are rectangular parallelepipeds.

13. In a rectangular parallelepiped, how many faces can there be such that no two of them are congruent?

14. All the edges of a rectangular parallelepiped are painted so that the parallel edges are the same color and non-parallel edges are different colors. How many colors did it take to do this?

15. How many pieces of tape are required to tape together a framework cube made of 12 matches?

16. Can a framework cube be made from 7, 9, 12, or 20 matches by gluing the ends together?

17. Write down the numbers of the solids in Figure 195 which are rectangular parallelepipeds.

18. How many faces can a rectangular parallelepiped have such that no two of them are parallel?

19. All the edges of a rectangular parallelepiped are colored so that the equal edges are one color and unequal edges are different colors. How many colors did it take to do this?

20. How many pieces of tape are required to tape together a framework cube made of 24 matches?

Description of an Instructional Unit and Methods of Use

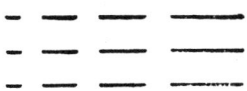

Figure 191.

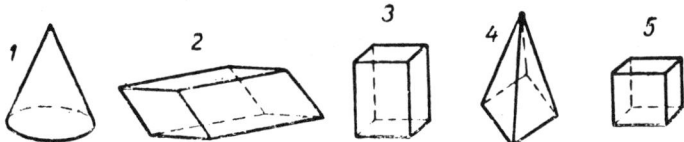

Figure 192.

Figure 193.

21. Can a rectangular parallelepiped be taped together from 20, 21, 22, 23, 24, 26, 27, 28, 29, or 30 matches? How many pieces of tape does it take to do so?

22. Is every cube a rectangular parallelepiped? Substantiate your answer.

23. Can a rectangular parallelepiped have: a) 2, 3, 4, 5, or 6 equal faces; b) 3, 4, 5, 6, 7, 8, 9, 10, 11, or 12 equal edges?

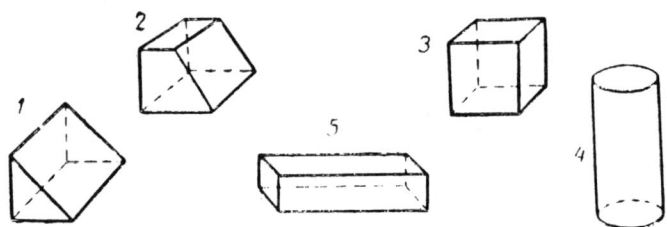

Figure 194.

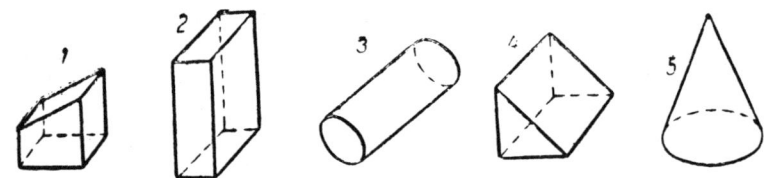

Figure 195.

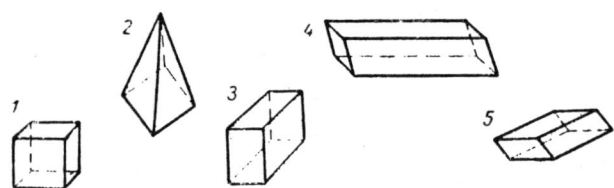

Figure 196.

24. In how many ways can faces a, b, c, d, e, and f of a rectangular parallelepiped be colored using two different colors?

25. Write down the numbers of the solids in Figure 196 which are rectangular parallelepipeds.

26. How many faces does a rectangular parallelepiped have?

27. How many edges does a rectangular parallelepiped have?

28. How many vertices does a rectangular parallelepiped have?

29. How many of a rectangular parallelepiped's edges and how many of its vertices belong to a single face?

30. It took 48 cm of wire to make a framework cube. What is the length of an edge of this cube?

31. One dimension of the rectangular parallelepiped shown in Figure 197 is increased by 5 cm. How much is the sum of the lengths of its edges increased?

32. The length of each dimension of the rectangular parallelepiped shown in Figure 198 is reduced by half. How much is the sum of the lengths of its edges diminished? How much is its area diminished?

33. It took 60 cm of wire to make a framework rectangular parallelepiped with two dimensions of 3 and 4 cm. What is its third dimension?

34. One dimension of a rectangular parallelepiped is reduced by 5 cm. How much is the sum of the lengths of its edges decreased (Fig. 199)?

35. By what factor is the sum of the lengths of the edges of a rectangular parallelepiped with edges 2, 3, and 4 cm increased if the length of each edge is increased by a factor of 3? By what factor is its surface area increased?

36. It took 17 cm of wire to form the three edges of a rectangular parallelepiped that meet at one vertex. How much wire did it take to make the entire framework?

37. One dimension of a cube has been increased by 3 cm, another has been decreased by 2 cm, and a third has been increased by 1 cm. How much has the sum of the lengths of its edges changed?

38. By what factor is the sum of the lengths of the edges of a cube increased if the length of each edge is increased by a factor of 3? By what factor is its surface area increased (Fig. 199)?

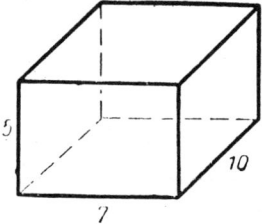

Figure 197.

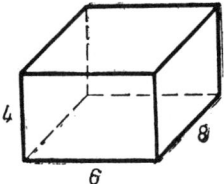

Figure 198.

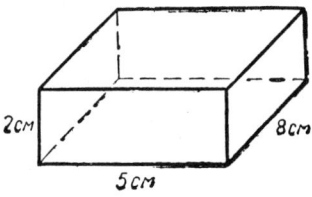

Figure 199.

39. It took 16 cm of wire to make four parallel edges of the rectangular parallelepiped shown in Figure 200. How much wire will it take to make its framework?

40. Each edge of the rectangular parallelepiped shown in Figure 201 is increased by 1 cm. How much is the sum of the lengths of its edges increased?

41. Each edge of the rectangular parallelepiped shown in Figure 202 has doubled in length. By what factor has: a) the sum of the lengths of the edges increased; b) the surface area increased?

42. It took 48 cm of wire to make the framework for one face of a cube. How much wire will the framework for the whole cube take?

43. Each edge of a rectangular parallelepiped has been increased by 3 cm. How much has the sum of the lengths of all the edges increased?

44. Each edge of a rectangular parallelepiped has been reduced by one-third. a) How much has the sum of the lengths of the edges decreased? b) How much has the surface area decreased?

45. How many centimeters of wire does it take to make a framework cube with an edge of 7 cm?

46. What is the sum of the lengths of the edges of the rectangular parallelepiped shown in Figure 203? What is its surface area?

47. A rectangular parallelepiped has dimensions of 8 cm, 6 cm, and 3 cm. The length of each of its edges is then doubled. What is the new surface area and what is the sum of the lengths of the edges of the resulting solid?

48. How many grams of paint does it take to paint a rectangular parallelepiped with dimensions of 8 cm, 2 cm, and 4 cm if it takes 16 g of paint to paint its smallest face?

49. Two dimensions of a rectangular parallelepiped have been doubled. Its dimensions were originally 5 cm, 4 cm, and 2 cm. What is the surface area of the resulting rectangular parallelepiped?

50. The edges of a rectangular parallelepiped are 17 cm, 9 cm, and 6 cm in length. One dimension is doubled. What is the surface area of the resulting rectangular parallelepiped?

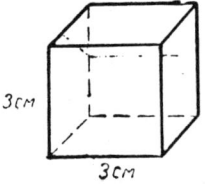

Figure 200.

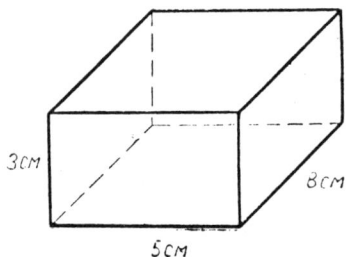

Figure 201.

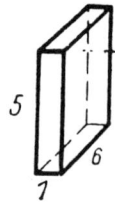

Figure 202.

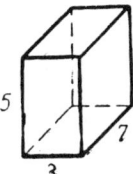

Figure 203.

51. The edges of a rectangular parallelepiped are 7 cm, 5 cm, and 2 cm in length. Each edge is increased by 2 cm. What is the surface area of the resulting rectangular parallelepiped?

52. Finish drawing the picture of the rectangular parallelepiped (Fig. 204).

53. The sum of the lengths of the edges of a rectangular parallelepiped is 56. What is the length of one edge if the lengths of the other two are 3 and 4?

54. The surface area of a rectangular parallelepiped is 20 square cm. The sum of the areas of the front and the upper faces is 7 square cm. What is the area of the left face?

55. The capacity of a box is greater than the volume of a bar. Is it possible that the bar might not fit into the box?

56. Ten unit cubes are placed in a box, and 8 boxes fit into a carton. What is the capacity of the carton?

57. Finish drawing the rectangular parallelepiped (Fig. 205).

58. The sum of the lengths of the edges of a rectangular parallelepiped is 60 cm. The length of one edge is 7 cm, and that of the other is 4 cm. What is the third dimension?

59. The area of the front face of a rectangular parallelepiped is one-fourth the total surface area. Calculate the sum of the areas of the upper and right faces if the total surface area is 20 square cm.

60. A board will not fit into a shed. Does this mean that the volume of the board is greater than the capacity of the shed?

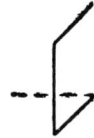

Figure 204.

Figure 205.

Figure 206.

Figure 207.

Description of an Instructional Unit and Methods of Use

61. There are 80 drops in a tablespoon, and there are 12 tablespoons in a glass. How many drops are in a glass?

62. Finish drawing the rectangular parallelepiped (Fig. 206).

63. One edge of a rectangular parallelepiped is equal to 5 cm, and the total length of all the edges is 52 cm. What are the dimensions of the rectangular parallelepiped if the second edge is 2 cm longer than the third?

64. The surface area of a rectangular parallelepiped is equal to 160 square cm. The area of the left face is one-eighth of the total area. What is the sum of the areas of the lower and the upper faces?

65. One log could fit in the cargo compartment of a truck, but another could not. Does this mean that the volume of the first log was less than the volume of the second?

66. Six unit cubes are placed in one layer on the bottom of a box; 15 such layers fill the box completely. What is the capacity of the box?

67. Finish the drawing of the rectangular parallelepiped (Fig. 207).

68. One edge of a rectangular parallelepiped is 4 cm longer than another, and the third edge is twice as long as the sum of the lengths of the first two edges. What is the sum of the lengths of all the edges if the smallest edge is 2 cm long?

69. A bar fits in a box. Does this mean that the bar's volume is less than the capacity of the box?

70. The sum of the areas of the back and lower faces of a rectangular parallelepiped is 25 square cm. Calculate the area of the right face if the total surface area of the parallelepiped is 70 square cm.

71. Fourteen units of volume can fit into a package. Exactly 10 packages fit into a suitcase. What is the capacity of the suitcase?

72. Finish drawing the rectangular parallelepiped (Fig. 208).

73. The sum of the lengths of all the edges of a rectangular parallelepiped is 20. What is the sum of the lengths of the the three edges that meet at one vertex?

74. The sum of the areas of all the faces of a rectangular parallelepiped sharing a common vertex is 14. Find the total surface area.

75. A rectangular parallelepiped has 6 faces, and there are 4 vertices for each one. Why does it not have 24 vertices?

76. A funnel can hold a liter of water (Fig. 209). Half a liter has been poured into it. Has the water reached the midpoint of the height of the funnel?

77. Finish drawing the rectangular parallelepiped (Fig. 210).

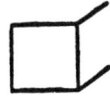

Figure 208.

Figure 209.

Figure 210.

78. One edge of a cube is 5 cm long. Find the sum of the lengths of all its edges.

79. The area of the total surface area of a cube is 54 square cm. What is the area of one face?

80. Do all the faces of a rectangular parallelepiped have the shape of a rectangle?

81. Twelve tablespoons of water exactly fill a glass. How many times greater is the glass's capacity is than that of the tablespoon?

82. Finish drawing the rectangular parallelepiped (Fig. 211).

83. The sum of the edges of a rectangular parallelepiped that meet at a vertex is 17. What is the sum of the lengths of all the edges?

84. The surface area of a rectangular parallelepiped is 18. What is the area of the faces with a common vertex?

85. A rectangular parallelepiped has 6 faces, and each one has 4 edges. Why does it have 12 edges instead of 24?

86. A funnel with a volume of 2 liters is filled with water up to half its height. How much water has been poured into the funnel: more or less than one liter?

87. Finish drawing the rectangular parallelepiped (Fig. 212).

88. The sum of the lengths of the edges of a cube is 36 cm. What is the length of one edge?

89. One face of a cube has an area of 4 square cm. What is the total surface area of the cube?

90. Do all the faces of a cube have the shape of a square?

91. A pitcher contains five glasses of water. By what factor is the pitcher's capacity greater than that of the glass?

92. 1) What is referred to as a rectangular parallelepiped?

2) How much wire does it take to make a framework cube if it takes 20 cm of wire to make the edges of one face?

3) The weight of a metal ball is twice that of a unit cube of the same metal. What is the volume of the ball?

4) Calculate $11,200 \times 4 + 4 \times 94,000 + 28,800 \times 4$, indicating the laws of the arithmetic operations that you use.

93. 1) What is referred to as a cube?

Figure 211.

Figure 212.

Figure 213.

2) How much tin will it take to make a cube if it takes 20 square cm for one face?

3) A piece of wood weighs 4 times as much as a unit cube of the same wood. What is the volume of the piece of wood?

4) Calculate $5 \times 46{,}400 + 29{,}000 \times 5 + 5 \times 23{,}600$, indicating the laws of the arithmetic operations that you use.

94. 1) Is any rectangular parallelepiped also a cube? Is any cube also a rectangular parallelepiped?

2) It took 42 cm of wire to make a framework for the faces adjoining one edge of a cube. How much wire does it take to finish constructing the cube?

3) A piece of plastic has a volume of 3 units. By what factor is its weight greater than that of a unit cube made of the same plastic?

4) Calculate $71,600 \times 3 + 3 \times 23,000 + 18,400 \times 3$, indicating the laws of the operations that you use.

95. A rectangular parallelepiped has been made of three unit cubes. Find its dimensions, the area of its base, and its volume.

96. A rectangle (Fig. 213) is divided into unit squares. How many unit cubes can fit on it in one layer; in 5 layers; in 40 layers; in 100 layers?

97. How many unit cubes can be placed together in one layer on a rectangle whose length and width are: a) 8 and 2 units; b) 20 and 21 units?

98. How many unit cubes can be placed together in a box whose length is 25, width 17, and height 2 units?

99. How many different rectangular parallelepipeds can be formed from 6 unit cubes? Calculate the surface area and the volume for each case.

100. Find the volume of a rectangular parallelepiped in cubic decimeters if its base has an area of 25 square dm and its height is 45 dm.

101. Find the volume of a rectangular parallelepiped with dimensions of $6 \times 24 \times 11$ dm.

102. A cube whose edge contains 12 units of length is formed from unit cubes. How many unit cubes are required?

103. How does the volume of a rectangular parallelepiped change if its height is increased by a factor of 3?

104. How many cubic centimeters are there in a rectangular parallelepiped in which the area of the base is 15 square cm and the height is 14 cm?

105. Find the volume of a rectangular parallelepiped with dimensions of $10 \times 91 \times 16$ cm.

106. How many unit cubes can we cut a cube into if its height is 13 units?

107. How does the volume of a rectangular parallelepiped change if the area of its base is reduced by one-half?

108. How many cubic centimeters are contained in a rectangular parallelepiped in which the area of the base is 17 square cm and the height is 26 cm?

109. Find the volume of a rectangular parallelepiped with dimensions of $8 \times 125 \times 9$ dm.

110. Calculate the volume of a cube in cubic centimeters if its edge is 120 cm.

111. How does the volume of a rectangular parallelepiped change if its height is reduced by a factor of 4?

112. Calculate the volume of a rectangular parallelepiped in cubic centimeters if the area of its base is 26 square cm and its height is 40 cm.

113. Find the volume of a rectangular parallelepiped with dimensions of $60 \times 70 \times 83$ cm.

114. How many cubic centimeters are in a cube with an edge of 11 cm?

115. How does the volume of a rectangular parallelepiped change if the area of its base is increased by a factor of 5?

116. The volume of a rectangular parallelepiped with dimensions of $16 \times a \times a$ cm is 400 cubic cm. Find the dimensions of the parallelepiped.

117. Find the height of a rectangular parallelepiped if its volume is 3,780 cubic cm and the area of its base is 108 square cm.

118. An aquarium has the shape of a cube whose edge is equal to 70 cm. It is filled with water to a height of 50 cm. How many cubic centimeters remain empty?

119. The height of a rectangular parallelepiped is 32 cm. If the area of its base is tripled, then the volume is increased by 5,120 cubic cm. Find the area of the base of this parallelepiped.

120. Find the volume of a rectangular parallelepiped in cubic centimeters if the area of its base is 5 square cm and its height is 3 cm.

121. Find the volume of a rectangular parallelepiped with dimensions of $4 \times 11 \times 6$ cm.

Description of an Instructional Unit and Methods of Use 289

122. A storeroom has the shape of a cube with an edge of 4 m. Calculate the volume of the storeroom.

123. There are two rectangular parallelepipeds with bases of 40 square cm and 80 square cm and with equal heights of 27 cm. How many cubic centimeters less is the volume of the first than that of the second?

124. Find the volume of a rectangular parallelepiped if its dimensions are:

　a) 100 cm, 10 cm, and 24 cm;
　b) 30 cm, 20 cm, and 30 cm;
　c) 80 cm, 60 cm, and 112 cm;
　d) 65 cm, 74 cm, and 340 cm.

125. A rectangular parallelepiped is made of unit cubes, with a length of 12 units, a width of 7 units, and a height of 13 units. How many cubes were required?

126. How many unit cubes can we divide a a rectangular parallelepiped into if the length, width, and height are respectively equal to: a) 20, 15, and 2; b) 7, 5, and 25?

127. A rectangular parallelepiped is made of unit cubes, and its length is 7 units, its width 6 units, and its height 11 units. How many unit cubes were required?

128. Calculate the volume of a rectangular parallelepiped in cubic decimeters if its dimensions are: a) $4 \times 27 \times 25$ dm; b) $19 \times 5 \times 40$ cm.

129. The width of a box is 3 dm, the length is three times as great as the width, and the height is 2 dm less than the width. Calculate the volume of the box.

130. In their kindergarten workshop, some students made 10 boxes of wooden cubes, with 6 cubes in each box. The edge of each cube is 4 cm. Calculate the volume of all the cubes that were made. They had 5,000 square cm of red paper. Is this enough to cover the cubes?

131. The edge of a cube is 95 dm. Find the volume of the cube.

132. There are 28 workers in a shop 21 m long, 12 m wide, and 5 m high. How many cubic meters of air are there for each worker?

133. A vault has dimensions of $8 \times 8 \times 4$ m. Three-fourths of its volume is filled with ice, which was delivered by 4 trucks. How many trips did the trucks have to make if each one could hold 4 cubic meters of ice?

134. The length of a hall is 16 m, the width is three-fourths of the length, and the height is equal to 4 m. Calculate the volume of the hall.

135. Find the edge of a cube if its volume is equal to: a) 27 cubic cm; b) 8 cubic dm; c) 64 units; d) 125 units.

136. Find the length of a rectangular parallelepiped if its volume is 78,336 cubic cm, its height is 12 cm, and its width is 34 cm.

137. What dimensions can a rectangular parallelepiped have if its volume is 12 cubic dm? (The lengths of the edges must be whole numbers.)

138. Find the length of the edge of a cube with a volume of 125 cubic dm.

139. What dimensions can a rectangular parallelepiped have if its volume is 48 cubic m? (The lengths of the edges must be whole numbers.)

140. A cube is pasted together from smaller identical cubes. Can a cube be pasted together such that it consists of: a) 26 smaller cubes; b) 27 smaller cubes; c) 28 smaller cubes?

141. The sum of the edges of a cube is 24 dm. What is its volume?

142. The sum of the areas of the faces of a cube is 24 square dm. What is its volume?

143. The volume of a rectangular parallelepiped is $6^3 = 216$ (cubic cm). Must this rectangular parallelepiped be a cube?

144. The volume of a cube is less than the volume of a rectangular parallelepiped with dimensions of $5 \times 4 \times 6$, but greater than the volume of a rectangular parallelepiped with dimensions of $3 \times 3 \times 5$. What is the volume of this cube? (The length of the cube's edge is a whole number.)

145. Why does the volume of a rectangular parallelepiped not depend on which dimensions are taken as the length, width, and height?

146. In a rectangular parallelepiped (Fig. 214) a slot with the shape of a rectangular parallelepiped is cut. Find the volume of the remaining part.

147. The area of the base of a rectangular parallelepiped is 20 square cm and the height is 6 cm. Find the volume.

Description of an Instructional Unit and Methods of Use

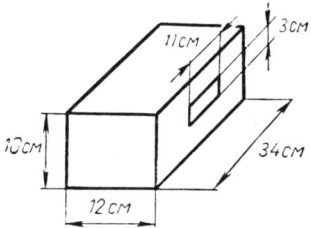

Figure 214.

148. Calculate the volume of a building in cubic meters if the area of its base is 285 square m and its height is 18 m.

149. The area of the face of a cube is expressed by the same number as is its volume. How many units does its edge contain?

150. Under what conditions is the volume of a cube expressed by the same number as its surface area?

151. How many cubic decimeters are there in one cubic meter?

152. Calculate the volume of a cube if its edge is equal to 1 m 5 dm.

153. Calculate the volume of a rectangular parallelepiped with dimensions of 5 m × (2 m 1 dm) × (4 m 8 dm).

154. How many cubic centimeters are there in one cubic meter?

155. Calculate the volume of a cube whose edge is 3 dm 2 cm long.

156. Calculate the volume of a rectangular parallelepiped in cubic meters if its dimensions are 4 m × (2 m 5 dm) × (1 m 6 dm).

157. How many cubic millimeters are there in one cubic decimeter?

158. Calculate the volume of a cube in cubic decimeters if it has an edge of 3 m 5 dm.

159. Calculate the volume of a rectangular parallelepiped with dimensions of 2 m × (3 m 6 dm) × (1 m 8 dm).

160. How many cubic millimeters are there in one cubic centimeter?

161. Calculate the volume of a cube whose edge is 4 m 5 dm long.

162. Calculate the volume of a rectangular parallelepiped with dimensions of 3 m × (1 m 7 dm) × (2 m 4 dm).

163. How many cubic millimeters are there in one cubic meter?

164. Calculate the volume of a cube whose edge is 3 m 2 dm 5 mm long.

165. One rectangular parallelepiped has dimensions of (3 m 5 dm) × (2 m 4 dm) × (1 m 6 dm), and another has dimensions of (3 m 5 dm) × 8 dm × (1 m 2 dm). How many cubic decimeters greater is the volume of the first parallelepiped? What is the fastest way to solve this problem?

166. How many cubic centimeters are there in one cubic decimeter?

167. Calculate the volume of a cube in cubic decimeters if its edge is 2 m.

168. Find the volume of a rectangular parallelepiped with dimensions of 28 × 45 × 39 dm. Write the resulting volume in cubic meters and decimeters.

169-180. Find the volume of the solids shown in Figures 215-226.

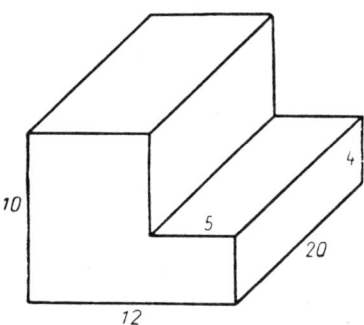

Figure 215.

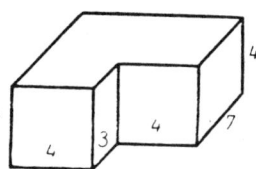

Figure 216.

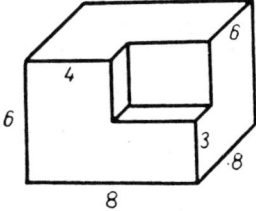

Figure 217.

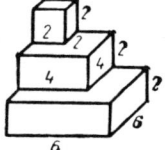

Figure 218.

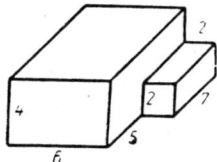

Figure 219.

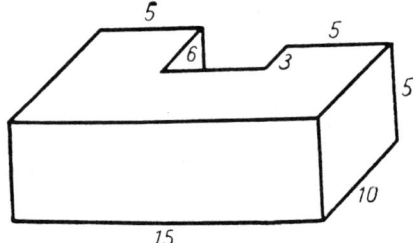

Figure 220.

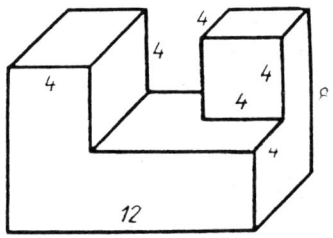

Figure 221.

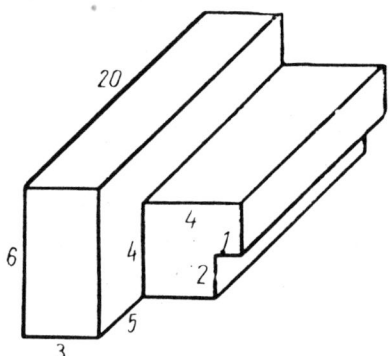

Figure 222.

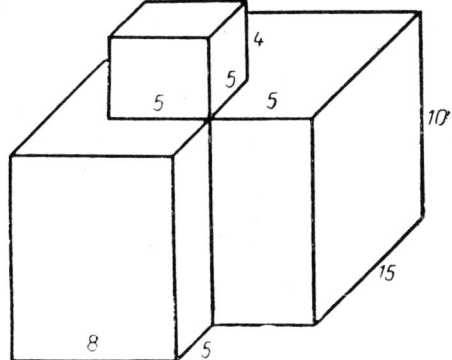

Figure 223.

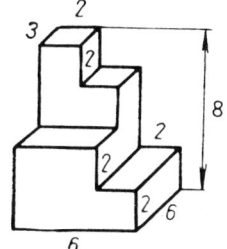

Figure 224.

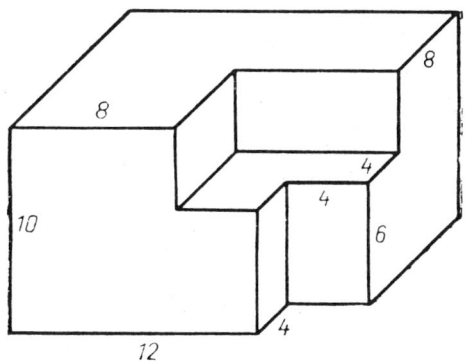

Figure 225.

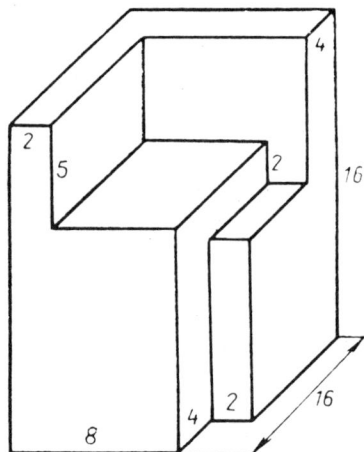

Figure 226.

Methodology of Using the Cards

The majority of the cards are grouped according by assignments, with 3 to 5 cards to each group. We think that it is advisable for the teacher to issue the student all the cards that make up one assignment at the same time. The cards are organized so that each assignment has four variants of an average level of difficulty, with one variant for especially strong students and one for weak students. We give below a sample distribution of cards according to assignments and variants.

How will a teacher use the problem cards as organized in the table? The teacher should attach cards 1-5 together to obtain the first variant of average difficulty (for Assignment 1). Since there must be 12 complete sets of problem cards for the class, the teacher puts together 12 identical copies of this variant. Combining cards 6-10 (in each of the 12 complete sets), he obtains 12 copies of the second variant. The same is done with cards 11-15 and 16-20. Then, attaching together cards 21-24, the teacher gets (again in 12 copies) a more complicated variant of Assignment No. 1 (for stronger students). Finally, cards 25-29 provide a simplified variant

Description of an Instructional Unit and Methods of Use

Assignment No.	Assignment Content	Numbers of Cards Given to Pupils						
		Assignments of Average Difficulty				Harder Assignments	Easier Assignments	Axiliary Assignments
		I	II	III	IV			
1	Defining a rectangular parallelepiped, its elements, and connection scheme	1-5	6-10	11-15	16-20	21-24	25-29	—
2	Framework, groups of 4 parallel edges, computing the sum of the lengths and surface	30-32	33-35	36-38	39-41	42-44	45-46	47-51
3	Skills in drawing a rectangular parallelepiped; more complicated problems on computing edges and surface; the concept of volume	52-56	57-61	62-66	67-71	72-76 or 82-86	77-81 or 87-91	95-99
4	The volume of a rectangular parallelpiped	100-103	104-107	108-111	112-115	116-119	120-123	124-150; 169-180
5	Changing the units for computing volume	151-153	154-156	157-159	160-162	163-165	166-168	—

(in 12 copies). Now the teacher can distribute the material and ask the students to move on to independent work. The teacher has in hand a total of 72 copies of the assignment (prepared in 6 variants), and this makes it possible to distribute the assignments so that it will be virtually impossible for students sitting close to one another to copy each other's work.

This assignment (Assignment 1) can be distributed at the second lesson devoted to this topic (see the sample lesson plans in Chapter 6). The cards for Assignment 2 (the second line in Table 4.8) can be prepared in the same way; they can be distributed in the fifth lesson on the topic; and so forth.

For convenience, the teacher need not simply put the cards together in one variant with clips (or glue), but can also designate variants by particular marks. However, under no conditions should the students know that they are working with variants of different levels of difficulty. This will lead to arrogance among the better students and feelings of inferiority among the weaker ones.

Cards 92-94 are not included in the chart; they contain assignments for written work. The variants are not fully equivalent; for example, variant 93 is somewhat harder than 92 and easier than 94. (Note that we have included here material on the laws of the arithmetic operations.)

If desired, some of the students can work independently on the cards while the other students work on other things. Then, if the students have not learned the material well enough, the same assignment can be repeated by simply exchanging variants among students. Assignment 3, which is harder than the others, has two harder and two easier variants; this makes review of the assignment (in another variant) possible for all the students. In other words, if it is necessary to reinforce the material in Assignment 3, another variant can be offered to the strong and the weak students, and the average ones exchange variants.

The question might arise whether it is advisable to print each problem on a separate card. Would it not be better to print the entire variant on a single sheet? We do not always find this to be advisable. The entire selection of problems, when printed on separate sheets, can be easily modified by the teacher. Some problems (the ones which the teacher considers the most difficult) can be eliminated; in other instances, an assignment can be made more complicated by including six or more cards. In other words, printing individual problems on cards is a more flexible arrangement, making the teacher's work more convenient. For example, if a student has not learned how to draw a rectangular parallelepiped, the teacher can fasten together cards 57, 62, 67, 72, 77, 82, 87, and 52, and give them to the student as a supplementary assignment.

Below we give the most desirable answers for some of the cards.

1. We cannot make a cube from 9 or 10 matches because that is too few (a cube has 12 edges). It is also impossible with 16 (we could form a framework cube from 12 matches, but then 4 matches would be left over). We can make a framework cube from 24 matches (with an edge 2 matches long; Fig. 227).

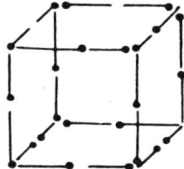

Figure 227.

2. Nos. 2 and 5.
3. Three edges (if we take four edges, two of them must be equal).
4. Six colors.
5. No, since there are groups of three equal segments, and a rectangular parallelepiped must have groups of four equal edges.
9. A diagonal divides a face into 2 triangles. There were 6 faces in all. Therefore, 12 triangles resulted.
10. There are 3 segments here, and a parallelepiped has 12 edges; thus, we need 9 more segments.
13. Three faces (Fig. 228); if we take four faces, two of them must be parallel.

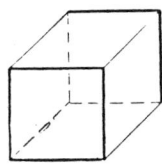

Figure 228.

14. Three colors (since a rectangular parallelepiped has three sets of four parallel edges).

15. We need just as many pieces as there are vertices in a cube—that is, 8 (Fig. 229).

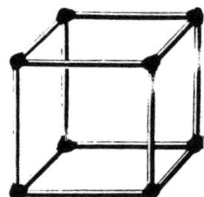

Figure 229.

19. Three colors if all the dimensions are different; two colors if two dimensions coincide (Fig. 230); one color if the parallelepiped is a cube.

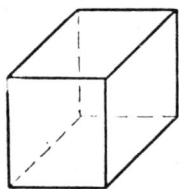

Figure 230.

20. 20 pieces (with one piece in the middle of each edge—i.e., 12—and one at each vertex—another 8; see Fig. 227).

22. Every cube is a rectangular parallelepiped (its faces are squares, and any square is a rectangle). But by no means is every rectangular parallelepiped a cube. It will be a cube only if all the edges are identical.

23. There are two equal faces (opposite ones) in any rectangular parallelepiped; there will be 4 equal faces (lateral ones) in a rectangular

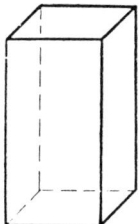

Figure 231.

parallelepiped with a square base (Fig. 231); 6 equal faces in a cube. The number of equal edges can be 4, 8, or 12 (in a cube).

24. In 64 ways.

30. 4 cm (since it took 48 cm of wire to make 12 edges).

31. 20 cm. Only 4 parallel edges are changed, each becoming 5 cm longer.

32. The sum of the lengths of the edges is cut in half, and the surface area is reduced by one-fourth.

33. 8 cm, since the three non-parallel edges (that is, the three dimensions) required 60/4 = 15 cm.

35. The sum of the lengths of the edges is increased by a factor of 3, and the surface area by a factor of 9.

36. 17 × 4 = 68 cm.

37. The sum of the lengths of the edges is increased by 8 cm.

39. 40 cm.

40. 12 cm.

41. The sum of the lengths of the edges has doubled; the surface area has increased by a factor of 4.

42. One face has 4 edges. Therefore, 48/4 = 12 cm makes one edge. Thus, the entire frame will take 12 × 12 = 144 cm.

43. 3 × 12 = 36 cm

48. The smallest face (with edges of 2 cm and 4 cm) has an area of 8 square cm. Since it took 16 g of paint, every square cm will require 16/8

= 2 g of paint. The surface area of the given rectangular parallelepiped is 112 square cm. Therefore, it takes 112 × 2 = 224 g of paint to paint it over.

49. Three answers: 1) if the edges of 5 cm and 4 cm are doubled, a parallelepiped with dimensions 10 cm, 8 cm, and 2 cm results; its surface area is 192 square cm;

2) if the edges of 5 cm and 2 cm are doubled, the result is a parallelepiped with dimensions 10 cm, 4 cm, and 4 cm; its surface area is 192 square cm;

3) if the edges of 2 cm and 4 cm are doubled, the result is a parallelepiped with dimensions of 5 cm, 8 cm, and 4 cm; its surface area is 184 square cm.

50. Three answers: 1) 1,128 square cm; 2) 1,032 square cm; 3) 930 square cm. (See the solution to Problem 49.)

51. 254 square cm.

53. The sum of the three dimensions is equal to 56/4 = 14. Therefore, the unknown dimension is equal to 14 - 3 - 4 = 7.

54. The front, the upper, and the left faces make up half the surface area of the rectangular parallelepiped. Therefore, the sum of the areas of these faces is 10 square cm. And since 7 square cm of the area goes into the front and the upper faces, the area of the left face is 3 square cm.

55. It is possible: if the bar is very long, it cannot be placed in the box; its volume may be less than the capacity of the box (if the bar is thin, that is, if it has a small crossectional area; Fig. 232).

56. 80.

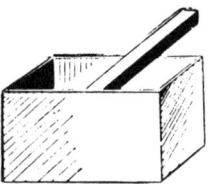

Figure 232.

59. The area of the front face is equal to 20/4 = 5 square cm. The area of the back face is the same. Therefore, 10 square cm of the area goes into the remaining 4 faces, and so 5 square cm is left for the upper and right faces.

63. The sum of the three dimensions is equal to 52/4 = 13 cm. The first dimension is 5, and so the sum of the second and third dimensions is equal to 13 - 5 = 8 cm. Since the second edge is 2 cm longer than the third, we can easily find that the second edge is 5 cm and the third is 3 cm.

66. 90.

68. The second edge is the smallest, by the conditions of the problem, since it is 2 cm. Therefore, the first edge is equal to 2 + 4 = 6 cm, and the third is equal to 2 (6 + 2) = 2 × 8 = 16 cm. The sum of the lengths of all the edges is equal to 4(6 + 2 + 16) = 4 × 24 = 96 cm.

69. It means that the volume of the bar is less than or equal to the capacity of the box: if there is room left, the bar's volume is less than the capacity of the box; if the bar fills the entire box, its volume is equal to the capacity of the box.

73. 20/4 = 5 cm.

74. 14 × 2 = 28.

75. Three faces meet at each vertex, so that if we count all the vertices by all the faces, we will count each vertex 3 times. Therefore, the number of vertices is 6 × 4/3 = 8.

76. The water has filled the funnel more than halfway, since the volume of the water that has filled the funnel to the midpoint is less than half the volume of the funnel. This is clear from Figure 233.

78. 5 × 12 = 60 cm.

79. 54/6 = 9 square cm.

80. They all do (by definition).

85. Two faces adjoin each edge, so that if we count all the edges on all the faces, we will count each edge twice. Therefore, the number of edges is equal to 6 × 4/2 = 12.

86. See the solution to Problem 76.

90. They all do (by definition).

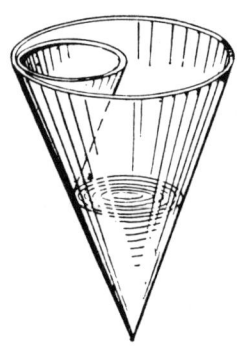

Figure 233.

92. 2) 60 cm; 3) 2; 4) 11,200 × 4 + 4 × 94,000 + 28,800 × 4 = 11,200 × 4 + 94,000 × 4 + 28,800 × 4 [commutative law of multiplication] = (11,200 + 94,000 + 28,800) × 4 [distributive law] = (11,200 + 28,800 + 94,000) × 4 [commutative law of addition] = (40,000 + 94,000) × 4 = 134,000 × 4 = 536,000.

93. 2) 120 square cm; 3) 4; 4) 5 × 46,400 + 29,000 × 5 + 5 × 23,600 = 5 × 46,400 + 5 × 29,000 + 5 × 23,600 [commutative law of multiplication] = 5 × (46,400 + 29,000 + 23,600) [distributive law] = 5 × (46,400 + 23,600 + 29,000) [commutative law of addition] = 5 × (70,000 + 29,000) = 5 × 99,000 = 495,000.

94. 2) 30 cm; 3) 3 times; 4) 71,600 × 3 + 3 × 23,000 + 18,400 × 3 = 71,600 × 3 + 23,000 × 3 + 18,400 × 3 [commutative law of multiplication] = (71,600 + 23,000 + 18,400) × 3 [distributive law] = (71,600 + 18,400 + 23,000) × 3 [commutative law of addition] = (90,000 + 23,000) × 3 = 113,000.3 = 339,000.

99. There are two different parallelepipeds (Fig. 234). To be sure, they can be drawn in different ways (Fig. 235), but there are only two different parallelepipeds in Figure 235.

106. $13^3 = 2,197$. (Given a cube, all its edges must be identical!)

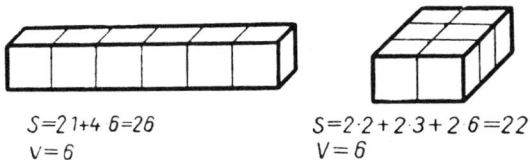

$S=2 1+4 6=26$
$V=6$

$S=2·2+2·3+2 6=22$
$V=6$

Figure 234.

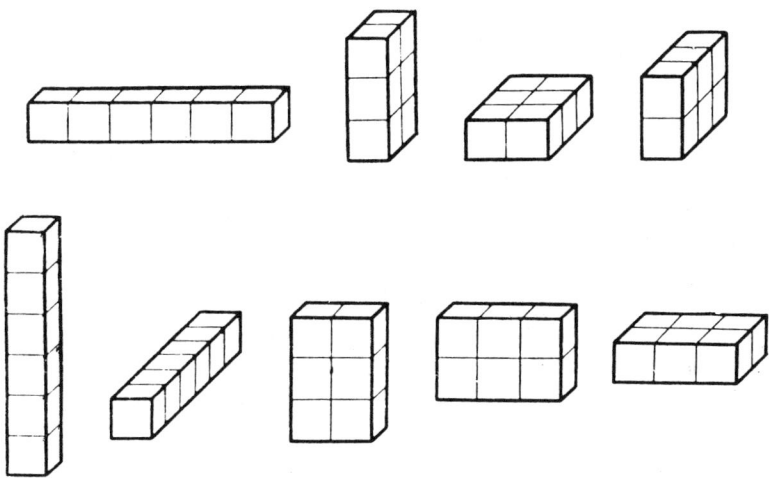

Figure 235.

107. If the height is left unchanged, the volume is also reduced by one-half.

117. If the edge of length 16 is taken as the height, and the square face of $a \times a$ as the base, then the area of the base is equal to 400/16 = 25 square cm. Therefore, the side of the base is equal to 5 cm— that is, the dimensions of the parallelepiped (in centimeters) are 16 x 5 x 5.

118. $70 \times 70 \times 20 = 98{,}000$ cubic cm.

119. When the area of the base is tripled (leaving the height unchanged), the volume is also tripled. Therefore, the volume of the parallelepiped itself is equal to 5,120/2 = 2,560 cubic cm. The area of the base is equal to 2,560/32 = 80 square cm.

129. 27 cubic dm.

130. The total volume of all the cubes is equal to $60 \times 64 = 3,840$ (cubic cm). Their total surface area is equal to $60 \times (6 \times 16) = 60 \times 96 = 5,760$ square cm, so there is not enough paper to cover them.

137. All possibilities are shown in Figure 236.

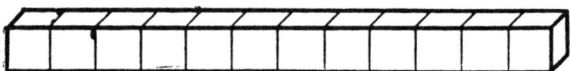

Figure 236.

139. Here are all the possibilities: (1) 48 x 1 x 1; (2) 24 x 2 x 1; (3) 24 x 2 x 1; (4) 12 x 4 x 1; (5) 8 x 6 x 1; (6) 12 x 2 x 2; (7) 8 x 3 x 2; (8) 6 x 4 x 2; (9) 4 x 4 x 3.

140. The number 26 is not a cube, and therefore no cube can be pasted together from 26 unit cubes. The same holds for 28. A cube with an edge of 3 is composed of 27 smaller cubes (its volume is equal to $3 \times 3 \times 3 = 27$ (Fig. 237)).

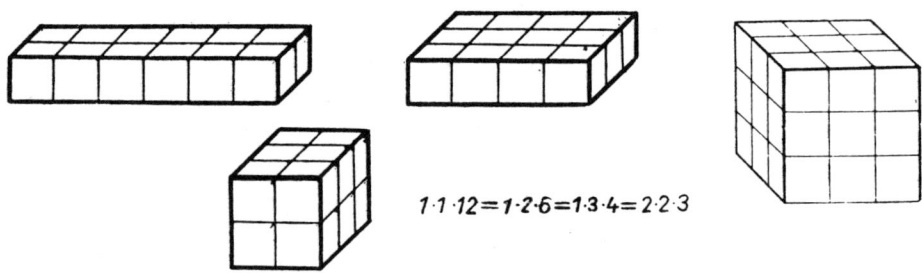

Figure 237.

Description of an Instructional Unit and Methods of Use

141. 8 cubic dm.

142. 8 cubic dm.

143. It need not be. For example, the rectangular parallelepiped can have dimensions of 2 x 3 x 36 or 18 x 12 x 1, and so forth.

144. The volume of the first parallelepiped is 120, and that of the second is 45. Therefore, the edge x of the cube we are seeking must satisfy the condition $45 < x^3 < 120$. According to the table of cubes, we find that only the number $x = 4$ satisfies this condition. Consequently, the volume of the cube is equal to $4^3 = 64$.

145. Because of the commutative and associative properties of multiplication.

146. $V = 3{,}684$ cubic cm.

149. Since $V = Sh$, we need $h = 1$ to satisfy the equality. But since the height is equal to one unit, all the edges are also equal to one unit (for this is a cube).

150. For a cube of edge a the volume is equal to a^3 and the surface area is equal to $6a^2$. If $6a^2 = a^3$, then $a = 6$.

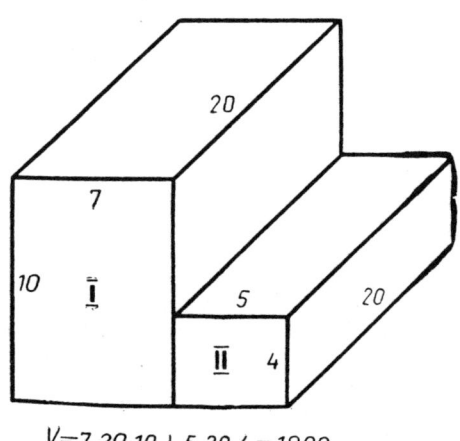

$V = 7 \cdot 20 \cdot 10 + 5 \cdot 20 \cdot 4 = 1800$

Figure 238.

165. The volume of the first cube is equal to 35 × 24 × 16; the volume of the second is equal to 35 × 8 × 12 cubic dm. We can find the difference of their volumes (without multiplying) in the following way: 35 × 24 × 16 - 35 × 8 × 12 = 35 × (24 × 16 - 8 × 12) = 35 × (48 × 8 - 8 × 12) = 35 × (8 × 48 - 8 × 12) = 35 × 8 × (48 - 12) = 35 × 8 × 36 = 35 × 2 × 4 × 36 = 70 × 144 = 10,080 cubic dm.

169-180. One variant variant division of each body into parallelepipeds is given in Figures 238-249, where the values of each volume are given as well.

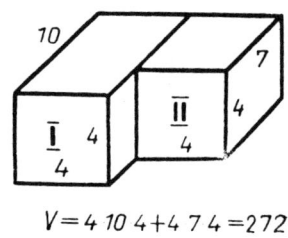

$V = 4\ 10\ 4 + 4\ 7\ 4 = 272$

Figure 239.

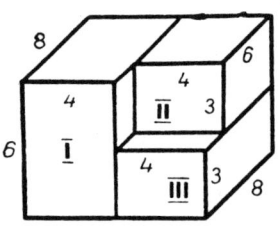

$V = 4 \cdot 8 \cdot 6 + 4 \cdot 6 \cdot 3 + 4 \cdot 8 \cdot 3 = 360$

Figure 240.

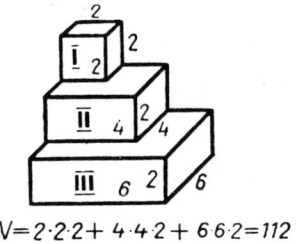

$V = 2 \cdot 2 \cdot 2 + 4 \cdot 4 \cdot 2 + 6 \cdot 6 \cdot 2 = 112$

Figure 241.

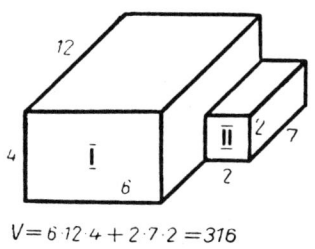

$V = 6 \cdot 12 \cdot 4 + 2 \cdot 7 \cdot 2 = 316$

Figure 242.

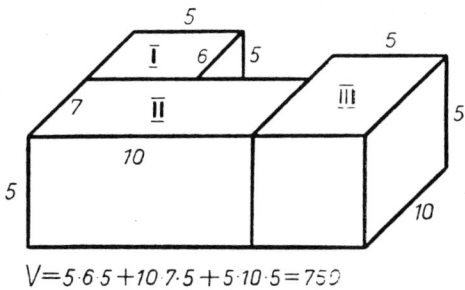

$V = 5 \cdot 6 \cdot 5 + 10 \cdot 7 \cdot 5 + 5 \cdot 10 \cdot 5 = 750$

Figure 243.

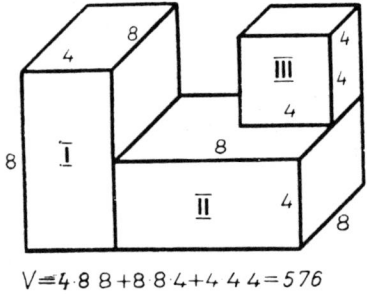

$V = 4 \cdot 8 \cdot 8 + 8 \cdot 8 \cdot 4 + 4 \cdot 4 \cdot 4 = 576$

Figure 244.

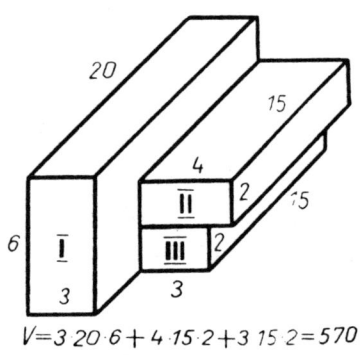

$V = 3 \cdot 20 \cdot 6 + 4 \cdot 15 \cdot 2 + 3 \cdot 15 \cdot 2 = 570$

Figure 245.

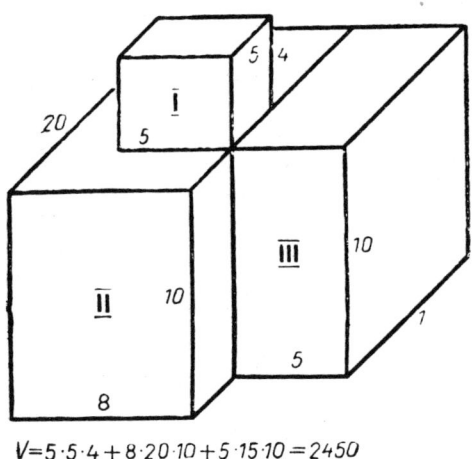

$V = 5 \cdot 5 \cdot 4 + 8 \cdot 20 \cdot 10 + 5 \cdot 15 \cdot 10 = 2450$

Figure 246.

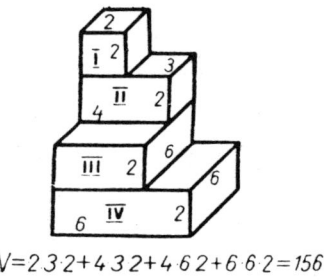

$V = 2 \cdot 3 \cdot 2 + 4 \cdot 3 \cdot 2 + 4 \cdot 6 \cdot 2 + 6 \cdot 6 \cdot 2 = 156$

Figure 247.

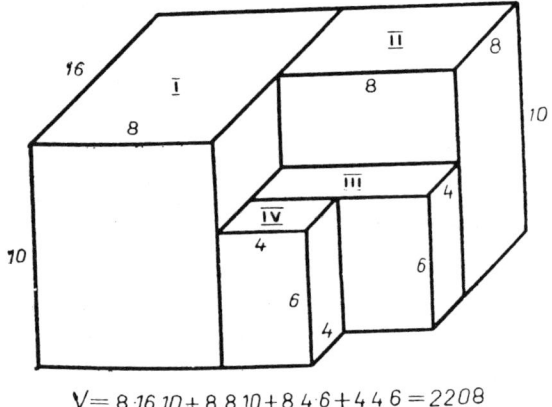

$V = 8 \cdot 16 \cdot 10 + 8 \cdot 8 \cdot 10 + 8 \cdot 4 \cdot 6 + 4 \cdot 4 \cdot 6 = 2208$

Figure 248.

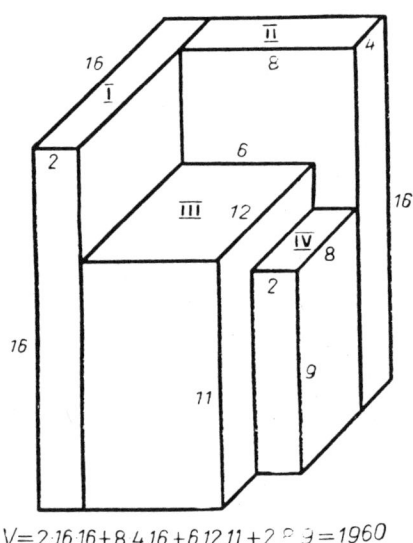

$V = 2 \cdot 16 \cdot 16 + 8 \cdot 4 \cdot 16 + 6 \cdot 12 \cdot 11 + 2 \cdot 8 \cdot 9 = 1960$

Figure 249.

Charts

The instructional unit we are describing includes the following charts: a chart of the Latin alphabet (Fig. 250); two charts on "The Laws of the Arithmetic Operations" (Figs. 251, 252); and three charts to accompany the topic "The Rectangular Parallelepiped and Its Volume" (Figs. 253-255). The chart of the Latin alphabet is intended for reference. It can be used for a number of other topics, but "The Rectangular Parallelepiped" is the first topic that requires it. The chart should be hung on a side wall in the classroom so that all the letters are easily visible from every seat in the class.

Note that in the charts on "The Laws of the Arithmetic Operations," issued by Prosveshchenie publishing house, some of the laws are given in red and others in black. These color differentiations are not needed in grade 4. They will be used in the upper grades, when considering axioms of groups, rings, and fields.

Methodology of Using the Charts

We will consider each of the charts included in the unit beginning with the chart of the Latin alphabet. As we know, foreign languages are not taught in grade 4 in most schools, and students do not learn the Latin alphabet. Many methodologists therefore advise against introducing the it in mathematics class, counseling us to limit ourselves to Russian letters, resorting if need be to the six letters that sound the same in Russian as in the Latin alphabet (these letters make up Russian word *kometa*). But this approach has little justification.

In the first place, experience has shown that fourth-graders easily learn to write and read the Latin letters. Second, the study of foreign languages violates the form of writing and pronunciation that is accepted in mathematics. The capital letters are written differently in English (*T*, *F*, and others), and almost all the letters sound different—the letters *V* and *W* in German, *C* in French, and so forth. In the Soviet school of mathematics,

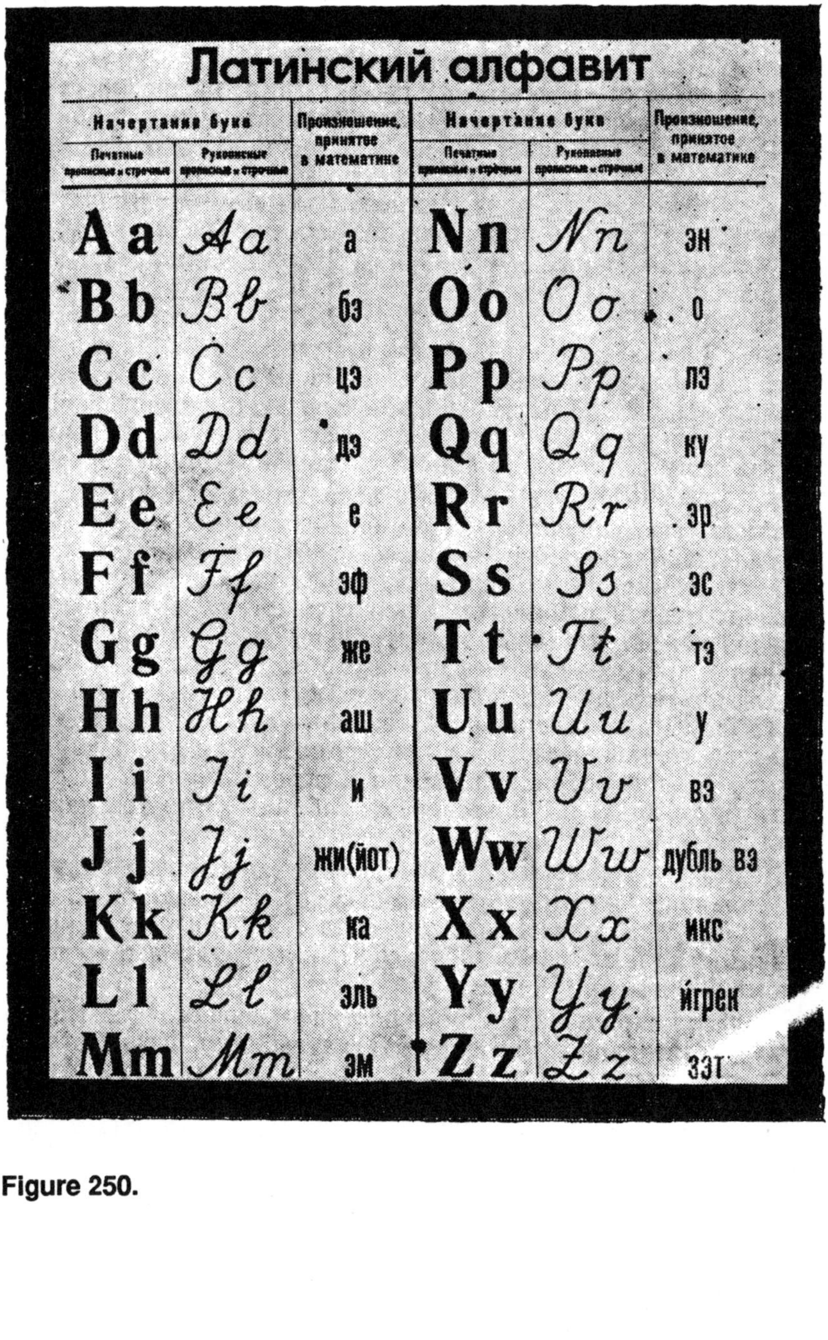

Латинский алфавит

Начертания букв: Печатные прописные и строчные	Начертания букв: Рукописные прописные и строчные	Произношение, принятое в математике	Начертания букв: Печатные прописные и строчные	Начертания букв: Рукописные прописные и строчные	Произношение, принятое в математике
A a	A a	а	N n	N n	эн
B b	B b	бэ	O o	O o	о
C c	C c	цэ	P p	P p	пэ
D d	D d	дэ	Q q	Q q	ку
E e	E e	е	R r	R r	эр
F f	F f	эф	S s	S s	эс
G g	G g	же	T t	T t	тэ
H h	H h	аш	U u	U u	у
I i	I i	и	V v	V v	вэ
J j	J j	жи(йот)	W w	W w	дубль вэ
K k	K k	ка	X x	X x	икс
L l	L l	эль	Y y	Y y	игрек
M m	M m	эм	Z z	Z z	зэт

Figure 250.

Description of an Instructional Unit and Methods of Use

The Laws of the Arithmetic Operations
(Addition)

1. $a+b=b+a$ commutativity

2. $a+(b+c)=(a+b)+c$ associativity

3. $a+0=a$

4. $a+(-a)=0$

Figure 251.

a particular Latin-French form for reading the letters of the Latin alphabet has been adopted, as shown in the chart.

The chart of the Latin alphabet should be used to teach the children how to write, read, and pronounce the letters used in mathematics—avoiding pointless cramming. The best method of achieving this is to place the chart in a visible spot in the classroom, so that it can serve as reference material for the students. Of course, the teacher, as well, should adhere to the rules of spelling and pronunciation given in the chart.

It is desirable for the chart to make its appearance in the classroom at the moment when Latin letters are first needed and remain on the wall for an extended time (possibly several years), until the students have completely mastered the Latin alphabet and the pronunciation accepted in mathematics. It would not even do any harm to regard this chart as a

> ### The Laws of the Arithmetic Operations
> ### (Multiplication)
>
> 1. $ab = ba$ commutativity
>
> 2. $a(bc) = (ab)c$ associativity
>
> 3. $a(b+c) = ab + ac$ distributivity
>
> 4. $a \cdot 1 = a$

Figure 252.

constant accessory of the mathematics classroom, wherever mathematics lessons take place.

The methodology of using the chart is extremely simple. During the first introduction with a letter needed for a lesson, the teacher asks the students to read this letter several times with the pronunciation indicated in the chart. Every time they have any difficulty writing a letter or reading it correctly, the teacher should direct their attention to the chart. For example, a student reads the letter y as "wai." The teacher points out the error: "Look at the chart. How must this letter be read?"

Of course, no work on reinforcing the skills in reading the letters needs to be done. First, the students will write and read them for many years and will get used to them on their own, as long as the teacher responds to each mistake. Second, no harm will result from incorrect pronunciation or even writing of the Latin letters in the early phases of instruction.

Description of an Instructional Unit and Methods of Use 317

Still, it makes sense to frequently ask the students to write and read the Latin letters. The topic entitled "The Volume of a Rectangular Parallelepiped" provides the teacher with many convenient opportunities. But here, too, the teacher should not carry the point too far. The Latin alphabet should never become a separate topic of instruction.

Now let us consider the methodology of using the charts on "The Laws of the Arithmetic Operations." During the topic on the volume of a rectangular parallelepiped, both charts should always be available in the classroom, except, perhaps, when the teacher wants to check for mastery of these laws, or during independent work or testing. But we do not regard these recommendations as obligatory: if the teacher so desires, the charts can be left in the classroom even during such lessons.

When the charts are first used, they should be arranged on the front wall of the classroom, and later placed prominently near the front of a side wall. At this time the charts are left as material to be memorized and for reference. Knowledge of the laws of the arithmetic operations is essential for the fourth-grader. But again, the children should not be required to memorize. The topic on "The Laws of the Arithmetic Operations" is long enough to achieve conscious and gradual mastery of these laws.

It is useful to ask questions about the laws of the arithmetic operations, forcing the student who responds not to look at the chart. When an answer is obtained, the teacher can suggest that the student look at the chart and compare his answer with what is on the chart.

If a student makes a mistake in applying the laws of the arithmetic operations, or does not use them to shorten the calculations, the teacher should suggest that the student look at the charts and analyze which available laws ought to be applied and to what numbers.

The charts also contain material not pertinent to the grade 4 curriculum, such as highlighting various elements in red and line 4 in the addition chart, $a + (-a) = 0$. This material is introduced for the study of groups and rings in the upper grades. But it cannot hurt fourth-graders. As experience has shown, they perceive the red coloring as decoration, and they pay no attention to the line $a + (-a) = 0$. If a student asks the teacher about that line, she can reply that these charts are not being studied in full and that this line will become clear when the student learns about negative numbers in another year. Of course, the line can be covered up with a strip of paper without spoiling the chart.

Current methodological literature has been increasingly willing to use the traditional mathematical names of the laws of these operations: commutative, associative, and distributive. These are the names that the charts use. Experience has shown that they are easily grasped by students in grade 4.

The chart entitled "The Rectangular Parallelepiped" (Fig. 253) is aimed at the transition from exhibiting natural models of a rectangular parallelepiped to representing it in a figure. A matchbox in three different positions is shown on the placard. The choice of a matchbox for representation is not an accident. One reason that students are familiar with matchboxes. Second, its faces have different colors. Therefore, the students have no doubt that this is a representation of a single solid, and

Figure 253.

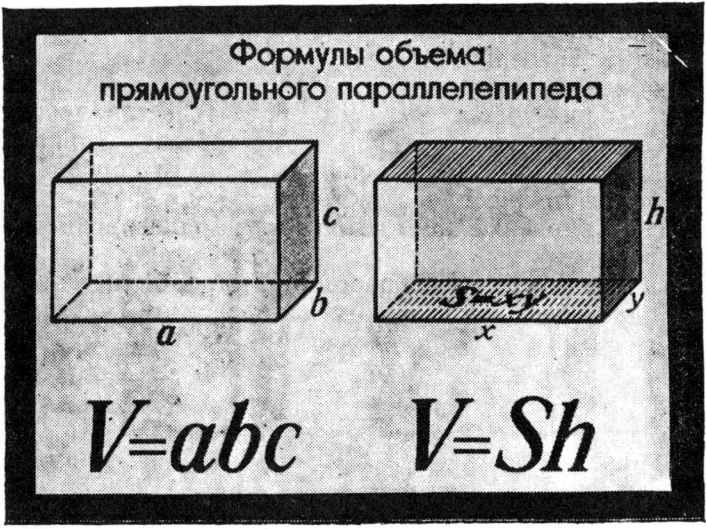

Figure 254.

these are different representations of it—representations in three different positions.

The students can use the chart from the very beginning when they are first introduced to the concepts of a *rectangular parallelepiped*, and its *face*, *edge*, *vertex*, *base*, and *height*. It is advisable to use the first models of a rectangular parallelepiped immediately after displaying the chart.

For example, the concept of a face can be introduced in this way. The teacher asks where the picture is situated on the matchbox. As the students give their imprecise answers, the teacher tells them that the picture is situated on one face of the matchbox. Then the she asks what kind of face it is (front, upper, lower, left, and so forth) in the various drawings. Next she asks what color the upper face in the third drawing is, the left face in the first drawing, and so on. The better students can be asked about the color of the hidden faces in each of the drawings.

Later the chart can be used again to give the students a notion of the distortion in shape of some of the faces of a rectangular parallelepiped when it is represented in a drawing or a figure. In addition, the chart can be used for counting visible and hidden faces, edges, and vertices, for explaining the relativie concepts of "base" and "height," and for showing how to represent a rectangular parallelepiped in a drawing. Note that the figures on the chart are executed according to the laws of perspective, while the drawings in the textbook, on the blackboard, or in the students' workbooks do not take into account distortions due to perspective (see Fig. 256). If desired, the teacher can call the students' attention to this point, directly measuring the front and back vertical and horizontal edges in each representation of the matchbox. Finally, the chart can be used to illustrate how the visible magnitude of the dimensions of a rectangular parallelepiped depends on its position. Even though only a short time is spent working with this chart, it is crucial to the development of the students' concept of the *rectangular parallelepiped.*

Now let us consider the methodology of using the charts on "The Volume of a Rectangular Parallelepiped." The first (Fig. 255) consists of three different perspectives of a rectangular parallelepiped. In one the visible faces are ruled off; another shows a layer of cubes and a column of cubes on the inside; the third is a separate picture of the layer of cubes. While explaining the material, especially when the students respond, this chart helps illustrate the account. If a student does not understand the material, then questions based on the same chart enable the teacher to determine just what he does not understand. The unclear point can then be explained. Here are some variations on these questions.

1) How many cubes are there in this layer (the picture on the right)?

2) How many of these layers are there in this parallelepiped (the lower left picture)?

3) How many cubes are there in this parallelepiped (the top picture)?

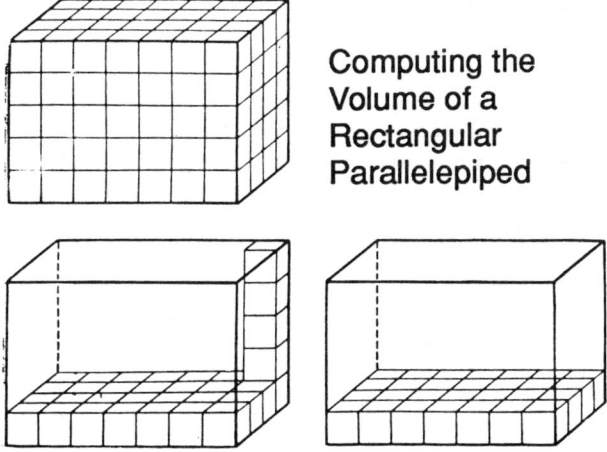

Figure 255.

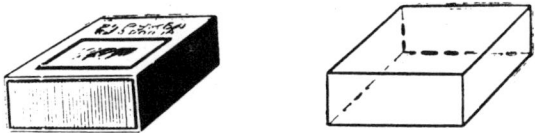

Figure 256.

It should be noted that the same chart appears as a frame in the filmstrip (see frame 39 of the filmstrip). In this case it is used only for the teacher's account. However, duplicating this frame on a separate chart strikes us as most essential, in view of the special importance of the direct calculation of volume, without formulas. This chart should be used often and in two different ways. In our version of the lesson plans it appears in the classroom during the 11th lesson and should be left on the classroom wall until the end of the topic (possibly even into the 15th lesson, during the test).

The second chart in the series (see Fig. 254) contains the formulas for volume, $V = abc$ and $V = Sh$, and serves as reference material for the first lessons on calculating volume by formulas. Of course, by the end of the topic the students should know these formulas by heart, and during the written review work the chart ought to be removed.

But the chart can also be used to reveal the meaning and interrelations among the two formulas. Thus, for the first formula, students should work along roughly the following lines for several lessons.

The teacher asks:

1) How many unit cubes are placed on the lower face if we put them in one layer? (Answer: ab.)

2) Why? (Answer: Because there will be a rows of b cubes each in a layer, or b rows of a cubes each.)

3) How many of these layers can be put into a parallelepiped? (Answer: c, since its height is equal to c.)

4) How many cubes will there be in all? (Answer: abc.)

5) What does the number abc designate? (Answer: It is the number of unit cubes in the given solid; hence, it is the volume of the solid.)

This work can be repeated by examining the layers on the left, right, upper, front, and back faces, in addition to the lower one. Thus, $V = bca$, $V = acb$, etc., are also obtained as volume formulas.

The transition from the formula $V = abc$ to the formula $V = Sh$ is best accomplished by using the first drawing and appropriate questions: How many unit cubes can be placed in one layer on the lower base? (Answer: ab.) What is the area of the lower base? (Answer: ab.) Then the area of the lower base is equal to the number of cubes that can be placed on it in one layer. Now what is the height equal to? And so forth.

Only after this idea becomes clear should the teacher focus on the second drawing. But this is not enough, either. This series of questions must be repeated and varied, contrasting the second drawing with the first. It is advisable, for example, to ask questions such as the following (focusing the students' attention on the fact that the same rectangular parallelepiped is represented both on the left and on the right):

What is the base S equal to in the second figure? (Answer: ab.)

What is the height h equal to? (Answer: $h = c$.)

Rubber Stamps, the Arithmetic Kit, and the Framework Model of a Rectangular Parallelepiped

Two kinds of stamps are used in the unit: the "Cube" and the "Rectangular Parallelepiped" (see Figure 11)—with three stamps of each kind per class. The template on the "Cube" stamp is a representation of a cube with an edge 45 mm long, corresponding to nine squares in the student's workbook. The entire planar extent of the cube is 60 mm long and 50 mm high (see Figure 12). The template on the "Rectangular Parallelepiped" stamp is a representation of a rectangular parallelepiped; the dimensions of the front face are 5x40 mm, corresponding to the 10x8 squares in the student's workbook. The entire figure is 60 mm long and 50 mm high.

It should be noted that the stamps do not produce perspective drawings—that is, they correspond to affine rather than to projec transformations. These drawings were done in so-called studio projection, in which the front face is reproduced without distortion, corresponding to the way drawings are customarily done in textbooks, on the school blackboard, and in notebooks. The projections were chosen so that the edges would be arranged most conveniently, and so that the drawing of the cubes demonstrate as clearly as possible that all its edges are equal. The two rubber stamps are inked with an ordinary ink-pad.

In contrast to the *arithmetic kit* previously issued by Uchtekhprom [Educational Technology Industries], our modernized arithmetic kit contains a *set of staircase solids*. It includes 9 varieties of staircase solids, with 5 of each kind. These solids are pictured in Figures 257-265. The simplest (Fig. 257) is composed of 3 small cubes with edges 2 cm long (more precisely, it can be broken down mentally into 3 of these small cubes). A more complicated solid (Fig. 258) is made up of 5 small cubes of the same size, and those in Figures 262-263 are composed of 6 cubes. Finally, each of the solids pictured in Figures 264 and 265 is made up of 7 small cubes. The collection also includes 45 small cubes with edges 2 cm long and 45 cubes with 1 cm edges (Fig. 266).

All the staircase solids and cubes are intended for laboratory work; they are all the same color (blue). Moreover, the arithmetic kit contains unpainted wooden cubes, bars, and disks, which were included in the previously issued arithmetic kit.

The *collapsible parallelepiped framework* (see Figure 3) has an edge with a minimum length of 235 mm, and the model is stable at up to 420 mm. The diameter of the frame's components is 6 mm. The frame is assembled from 8 fittings (Fig. 267). Four fittings consist of one steel core 225 mm long, with a diameter of 4 mm, and two tin tubes 230 mm long. These tubes have an inner diameter of 5.5 mm, and an outer diameter of 6 mm. The other four fittings consist of two cores and one tube with the same dimensions as the first set. The connection between the tubes and cores is rigid rather than hinged. The model is painted light blue.

Methods of Using the Stamps

The instructional unit includes two stamps (see Figure 11), one picturing a cube, the other a rectangular parallelepiped (see Figure 12). We recommend having 3 stamps for each of the two kinds in the classroom for a lesson, because it is a waste of time to pass the stamps from one row to another. Therefore, each of the three rows of students' tables should have its own cube and rectangular parallelepiped stamps.

It is possible to use the stamps in class before covering the subtopic "The Representation of a Rectangular Parallelepiped," as well as during and afterward. In addition, the stamps can be used by the teacher.

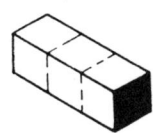

Figure 257.

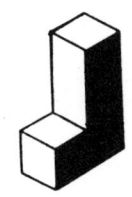

Figure 258.

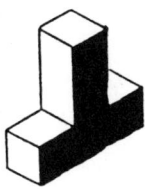

Figure 259.

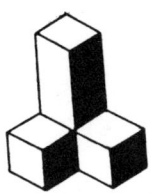

Figure 260.

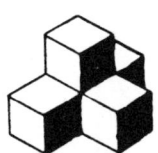

Figure 261.

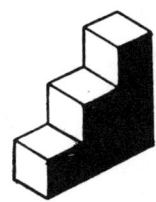

Figure 262.

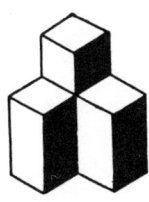

Figure 263.

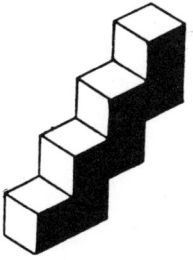

Figure 264.

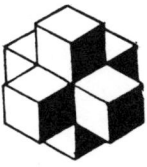

Figure 265.

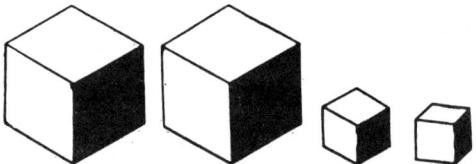

Figure 266.

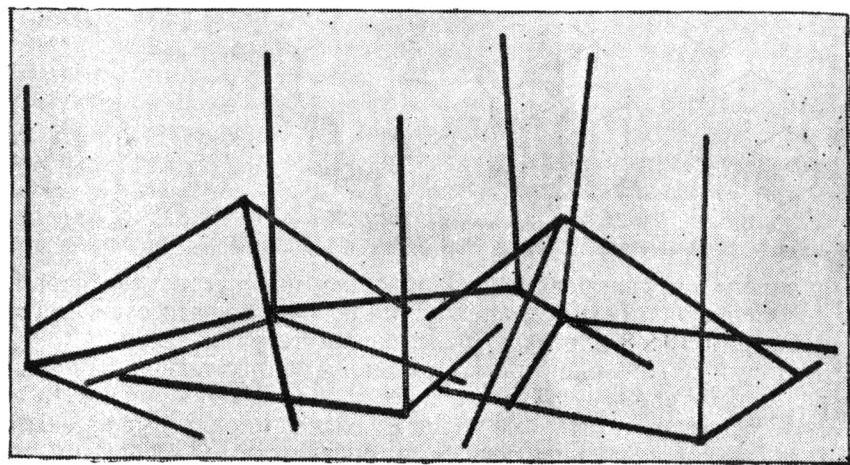

Figure 267.

Before beginning the subtopic "The Representation of a Rectangular Parallelepiped," the stamps are used if the teacher feels it necessary for the students to have an accurate drawing in their notebooks. The students of each row will pass the stamp among themselves. They gradually begin to get used to seeing an entire rectangular parallelepiped instead of this schematic representation, thus promoting the development of their spatial concepts.

Description of an Instructional Unit and Methods of Use

The teacher should decide whether stamping a picture of a rectangular parallelepiped in the students' notebooks is appropriate. The teacher may also lead the students through the process of abstracting from secondary details, as shown in the first single-concept film in "reverse order." Then, starting with a stamp representation of a rectangular parallelepiped, the student can add the secondary details, transforming it into a drawing of a television set, a building, or some other object. An example of this procedure could be shown on the blackboard (Fig. 268; compare with Fig. 12). This process of adding concrete details to an abstract parallelepiped (the reverse of the difficult process of abstraction) undoubtedly assists the students in achieving a better mastery of the concept of the *rectangular parallelepiped*. Two impressions might even be made in each students' notebook, with the suggestion that one drawing be completed to make a television set, and the other to make a suitcase, a cabinet, or some other object of roughly the same shape.

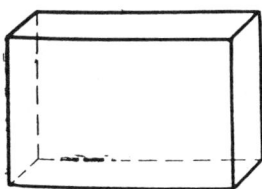 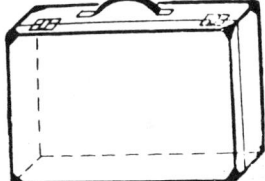

Figure 268.

While covering the subtopic "The Representation of a Rectangular Parallelepiped," the stamp impression can serve as a model, and additionally as a prompting device. For example, students who are having difficulty learning to draw a rectangular parallelepiped can be asked to approach the teacher's table, take a stamp and stamp pad, and make an impression in their notebooks. They then can be asked to do the following assignment:

1) Outline in red pencil the front face of the stamped image of a rectangular parallelepiped.

2) Outline in red pencil the edges which go "all the way back"—that is, which emanate from the vertices of the front face (here, note on which lines are continuous and which are broken).

3) Outline the remaining continuous lines, and then the broken ones.

4) Examine the resulting drawing closely and try to make a copy beside it in your notebook, performing the operations in the same order.

Of course, this work can also be done simultaneously with the entire class.

We have already discussed in detail the use of stamps after covering the subtopic on "The Representation of a Rectangular Parallelepiped" There, even though the students can make an adequate drawing, they do so slowly. It often saves time to have them use a stamp to make multiple impressions of the figures. The use of the stamps is left to the teacher's discretion. If the class is to solve 3 or 4 problems, it may be advisable for the students to draw the first figure in their notebooks and then use the stamps in subsequent problems.

Finally, several words about how the teacher can use the stamps to prepare independent work and tests. We have already discussed this. Figure 269 gives an example of independent work prepared at home by the teacher. Having first made 40 impressions, the teacher fills in the various numerical data. At the beginning of the class, the sheets are distributed among the students, and an assignment is written on the board. The content can be varied, of course, but the following tasks represent example assignments.

1) Find the sum of the lengths of the edges of the cube shown in the first picture.

Description of an Instructional Unit and Methods of Use

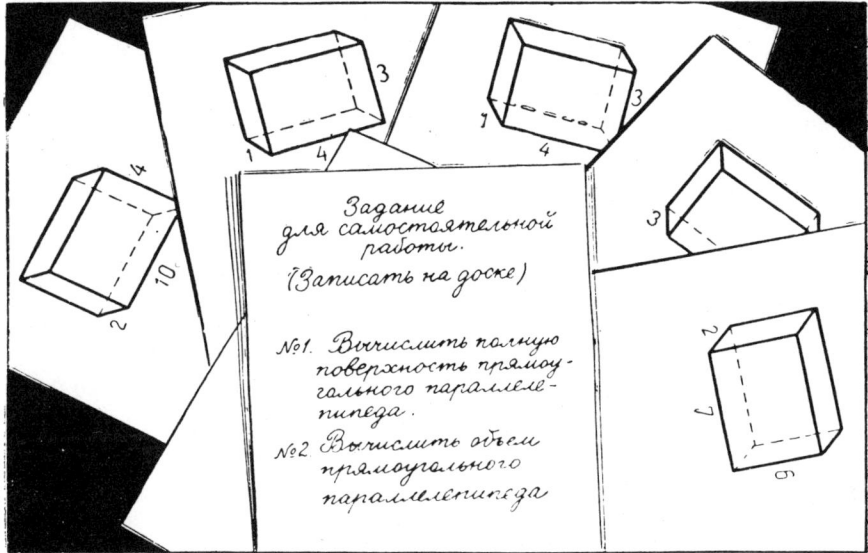

Note: The text in this figure reads "Assignment for independent work"; "(write on the board)"; "No. 1. Compute the complete surface of the rectangular parallelepiped."; "No. 2. Compute the volume of a rectangular parallelepiped."

Figure 269.

2) Find the surface area of the parallelepiped shown in the second picture.

3) Determine whether the cube or the parallelepiped has the greater volume, and how much greater.

The Methodology of Using the Arithmetic Kit

The modernized arithmetic kit is intended for various laboratory tasks: measuring the lengths of the edges, the surface area, and the volume of the staircase solids, and for mentally completing a solid to form a rectangular parallelepiped. The set includes 9 kinds of solids, which make it possible to individualize the work. The structure of the staircase solids varies in complexity, so that the complexity of the work can also be individualized. The two different types of unit cubes promotes this even further.

The basic work is designed in the following way. The students receive the solids included in the set, and each student is also given a cube with an edge of 2 cm. The teacher indicates that this cube is to be taken as a unit for measuring volume, and suggests finding the different ways of mentally decomposing a solid into unit cubes (thus obtaining a volume for the solid). The student can place the unit cube right up against his solid and find its volume by direct counting. For convenience in checking the results, it makes sense to paste numbered labels on each solid. In this case the student should write his or her name, the number of the solid, and the answer on a special slip of paper.

It is very desirable (at least for the better students) to give one more assignment to them: measuring the volume of a solid in smaller units. For this purpose the student is also given a small cube with an edge of 1 cm, and the teacher suggests finding the volume of this solid by taking the small cube as the unit of volume. Now the student can compare the small cube to the larger one, realize that its edge is half as large, estimate how many small cubes are contained in the large one (8), and multiply the earlier result by this number. It is essential here that the teacher not direct the students' attention to the length of the edges in centimeters. The student should measure the volume, not in cubic centimeters, but in the *assigned* units (the large and small cubes).

Similar work can be done in measuring the sum of the edges, as well as the surface area. It is a good idea to give both unit cubes to at least some of the students. For measuring the sum of the lengths of the edges, the students can be asked to first take an edge of the large cube as the unit length, and then the edge of the small cube. The assignment can be simplified somewhat by not indicating the unit of length, but specifying only that a cube (the large one, or in another assignment, the small one) is taken as the unit of volume. The student should know that the edge of the unit cube is the unit segment, and should use this segment for measuring lengths. In the transition to measuring with the small unit cube, the student, first determining how many times greater the edge of the large cube is than the edge of the small one (2 times), multiplies the earlier result by 2.

When the surface area is measured, two variants of the assignment can also be created. In the first (simpler) one, the face of a given cube is taken as a unit of measuring area. In the second variant, the student is again only informed that the given cube is the unit of volume. In this case it should be understood that the face of the unit cube is a unit square, the unit in which measurements should be made, and then, during the transition to the small unit cube, the previous result is multiplied by 4.

Another task using the arithmetic kit involves mentally completing a solid to form a rectangular parallelepiped. This problem can also be posed in the following way. Indicate the smallest dimensions of a box with the shape of a rectangular parallelepiped in which the given solid could be placed. But it must be pointed out that the solid must lie evenly in the box, without distortions, so that its extreme faces lie against the faces of the box. Answers to these questions are given in Figures 270-278.

Later (when the formula for the volume of a rectangular parallelepiped is derived), it is advisable to repeat this work with different solids, posing the question in a different way: What is the smallest number of cubes required to turn this solid into a rectangular parallelepiped? Some students might decide to count by placing unit cubes up against the solid. But how many unit cubes all together will it take! This method is very involved, and requires highly developed spatial concepts. In this case, it

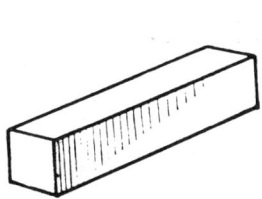
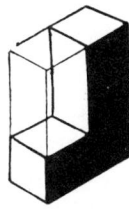
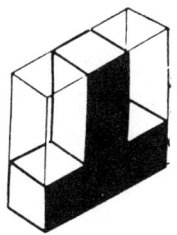

Figure 270.   **Figure 271.**   **Figure 272.**

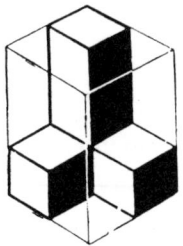

Figure 273.

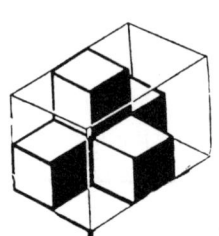

Figure 274.

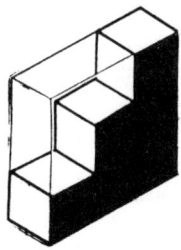

Figure 275.

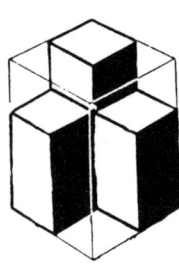

Figure 276.

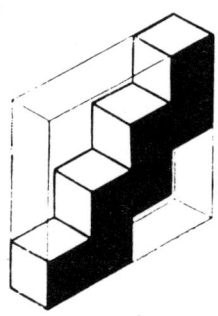

Figure 277.

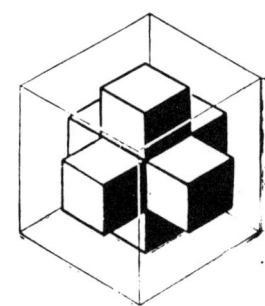

Figure 278.

is advisable to ask an additional leading question: What is the volume of the smallest box into which this solid can be placed? After this question the student gets the idea that the volume of the unfilled part of this box is equal to the difference between the volume of the entire box and the volume of the solid placed inside it. This is a very good assignment for checking how well students understand volume. It is therefore helpful not simply to do it, but also to discuss in detail in class why the difference between the volume of the box and the given solid is also the smallest number of unit cubes required to turn the solid into a rectangular parallelepiped. Again we emphasize that if the laboratory work is done before measuring the volumes in cubic centimeters, the students should not be told the dimensions of the unit cubes. The teacher should say, "The large (small) cube is taken as the unit," or "The red (white) cube is taken as the unit."

In contrast to the older arithmetic kit, this collection does not enable students to construct a cubic decimeter of cubes, columns, and layers. But we believe that such work has little use because the objects on the chart can be thoroughly examined only from the front desks and, moreover, any cube constructed is irregular and fragile, and it takes a long time to assemble and return to the box.

Laboratory work can also be designed around the worksheet.

The Methodology of Using the Framework Model of a Rectangular Parallelepiped

The framework model of a rectangular parallelepiped permits the demonstration of both general types and special cases of rectangular parallelepipeds. The cube and right square prism (rectangular parallelepiped with a square base) are two such special cases. Therefore, it is convenient to use the framework when the students are learning the concept of the equal edges and faces of a rectangular parallelepiped. For example, several pairs of equal rectangles and strips can be cut from construction paper or cardboard. Then the students can easily realize that in a rectangular parallelepiped the pairs of opposite faces are equal. If we extend the framework to such dimensions that one face is equal to a given (cardboard) rectangle, then the opposite face will also be equal to the same rectangle. It is easy to show on the framework that four or even all six faces can be equal (in a cube).

Simillar work can be done with edges using strips of paper. However, a chalk drawing on the blackboard can serve as a standard for comparing faces and edges. Thus, after drawing a rectangle on the board and extending the framework, we can easily show that the face we have chosen is equal to the opposite one. It is sufficient to turn the parallelepiped framework upside down and show that the opposite side "fits" the rectangle drawn on the blackboard.

Rectangles cut from cardboard also help develop the students' notions of the face of the framework model. The model has edges and vertices as well. But the faces are only outlined by their sides. If cardboard rectangles are attached to the frame, it can be explained to the students how a frame unambiguously represents a rectangular parallelepiped.

Furthermore, the framework can conveniently be used for forming the concept of the *surface area* of a rectangular parallelepiped, for which rectangular paper faces should be pasted onto the frame (cf. Fig. 85). The result is a "hollow" rectangular parallelepiped, yielding a visual notion of its surface area.

One of the most significant differences between the framework model and the solid rectangular parallelepiped (e.g., a wooden or plastic bar) is that the framework model clearly exhibits all the edges, their equality and parallelism, and how they are connected. Therefore, the frame is invaluable for explaining sets of four equal and parallel edges and for solving the first few problems on this topic. It is convenient to use the framework in studying how the sum of the lengths of the edges, surface area, and volume all depend upon changes in the lengths of the edges. Since the framework can be extended to almost twice its size, it can illustrate nicely, for example, the following problem: By what factor does the volume of a rectangular parallelepiped increase if one of its dimensions is doubled? If two of its dimensions are doubled? If all three of its dimensions are doubled? The teacher will easily find analogous applications for solving problems on the sum of edge lengths and the surface area.

Of course, the teacher should always remember the need for gradually eliminating visuality. Beginning with the fifth lesson, the framework should, as a rule, be used after most of the students have already solved problems. It illustrates the solution, reinforcing it visually, and prompts the weaker students, who have not yet "grasped" the solution. Of course, in difficult cases, as well as in making the transition to solving problems of a truly new type, devices involving visuality should be used (the framework, in particular). In every case, determining a reasonable proportion of visuality depends exclusively on the teacher's experience and pedagogical tact, and on the teaching methodology selected.

5

Lesson Plans for the Topic "The Rectangular Parallelepiped and Its Volume"

In addition to the educational materials included in the unit, other materials can also be used (a set of solids,[1] graduated cylinder, a slide projector, and others). The last column of Table 5.1 indicates the items in the unit, numbered following Table 1.2 (e.g., 1 designates the single-concept film "The Rectangular Parallelepiped," 7 refers to the slide series, 11 to the chart of the Latin alphabet, and so on).

Since the filmstrip, slide series, workbook, and problem cards are used throughout the lessons, Table 5.2 shows the progressive use of these instructional media (following the lesson plans given below). Let us now turn to a description of the lesson plans.

Lesson 1. The Rectangular Parallelepiped

Objectives.
1. Teach students to pick out from the solids around them the ones with the shape of a rectangular parallelepiped; teach them to pronounce and write this term; and acquaint them with models of a rectangular parallelepiped.
2. Introduce the definition of a rectangular parallelepiped. It is best not to memorize the definition, but rather recall or check it as they carry out assignments. At the same time they should learn how to establish membership in the concept of a "rectangular parallelepiped" by means of the definition.

Table 5.1 Table for Using the Objects in the Complex in Lessons (according to the Lesson Plans Cited Below)

Lesson Number	Lesson Content	Numbers of Objects in the Coplex Used
I	Rectangular parallelepiped; cube; faces, edges, vertices	1, 6, 7, 10, 11, 12, 13, 14
II	Properties of faces and edges	1, 6, 7, 10, 11, 12, 13, 14, 15
III	Representing a rectangular prallelepiped; dimensions	2, 6, 7, 10, 11, 12, 13, 14, 15
IV	Lateral surfaces, framework, surface area	6, 7, 10, 11, 12, 14
V	Solving problems. Independent work	8, 14, 15
VI	The concept of volume	3, 4, 6, 11, 12
VII	Unit cube. Measuring volume. Laboratory work.	4, 6, 9, 11, 12, 14
VIII	Solving problems. Analysis of laboratory work. Independent work.	7, 8, 9, 11, 12, 14, 15
IX	Test No. 1	15
X	Counting the number of unit cubes	6, 7, 8, 11, 12, 14, 15
XI	Computing volume of a rectangular parallelepiped	6, 7, 8, 11, 12, 13
XII	Formulas for volume. Solving problems.	5, 6, 7, 8, 11, 12, 13, 14, 15
XIII	Translation from one system of units to another	6, 7, 8, 11, 12, 13, 14, 15
XIV	Solving problems	11, 12, 13, 14, 15
XV	Test No. 2	—
XVI	Analysis of test	11, 12, 13, 15

Table 5.2 Table for the Use of the Filmstrip, Slides, Notebook Based on Printed Material, and Cards

Lesson Number	Filmstrip Frames	Slides	Notebook Assignments	Assignment Cards
I	1-5	1-3	1-5	—
II	5-7	2, 18	6-12	1-29
III	8-11	3-7, 18, 19, 20	13-20	—
IV	12-13	8-20	21-31	—
V	—	—	22-31	30-51
VI	14-29	—	—	—
VII	30-33	—	32	—
VIII	—	18-20, 41-42	33, 34	52-91
IX	—	—	—	92-94
X	34-39	21-23	35-37	52-91
XI	40	18-20, 23, 29, 35	—	—
XII	41-42	24-38, 18-20	38-49	95-99, 169-180
XIII	43-46	18-20, 34-40	50-64	100-150
XIV	—	teacher's choice	teacher's choice	151-180
XV	—	—	—	—
XVI	—	teacher's choice	—	teacher's choice

3. Introduce the students to the components of a rectangular parallelepiped: faces, edges, vertices. (They are not required to memorize the definition. It is sufficient if the students can identify the faces, edges, and vertices of various solids and relate in their own words the relations among these components—e.g., that the edges are the sides of rectangles and the vertices are the endpoints of segments that form the edges.)

4. Achieve an understanding of the cube as a special case of a parallelepiped. The student need not memorize what a cube is. It is sufficient for them, on the one hand, to include the cube in the concept of a "rectangular parallelepiped," and on the other, to know what distinguishes a cube from other rectangular parallelepipeds. The problem of the particular and the general can be raised here.

Educational Materials: models of geometric solids (see Fig. 279); framework model of a rectangular parallelepiped; frames 1-5 of the filmstrip; slides 1-3; assignments 1-5 in the workbook; the single-concept film "The Rectangular Parallelepiped"; and the charts "The Laws of the Arithmetic Operations," "The Latin Alphabet," and "The Rectangular Parallelepiped."

Procedure.

1. *Initial introduction to the concept of the rectangular parallelepiped.*

Figure 279.

a) The teacher asks the students to consider frame 2 of the filmstrip and list the common points and differences among the objects represented. (The material, function, etc., are different; the shape is common.)

b) Demonstrating one or two models of a rectangular parallelepiped (a bar, a box), the teacher asks students to name objects that have the same shape. The term "rectangular parallelepiped" is introduced for all of these objects. It should be written on the board and read in unison. Instead of writing the words "rectangular parallelepiped" on the board, the teacher can show the first frame of the filmstrip, then again turn to frame 2.

Frame 2 presents objects that are similar in shape to rectangular parallelepipeds. The students should be asked to focus on each object and state precisely which details need to be removed for the solid to become like a box or bar.[2]

c) The students are then asked to examine the chart on rectangular parallelepipeds (Fig. 253). The term "face" is introduced by exhibiting the side of a solid turned toward the class (or to the left or upwards) and saying, "This is the front (left, top) face."

d) The teacher demonstrates the model of a rectangular parallelepiped and asks the class to count to see how many faces, edges, and vertices it has. It is pointed out explicitly that the shape of each face is a rectangle. If students should doubt this, the teacher points to a similar face on the chart (the matchbox); everyone knows that these faces are rectangles, although they look different in the drawing.

e) The same assignment (counting the number of faces, edges, vertices) is done for frames 3, 4, and 5 of the filmstrip.

Frame 3 shows a solid that is free of superfluous details. It is a rectangular parallelepiped. The students can be asked what distinguishes this solid in shape from a suitcase or from a book. The students can be called to the board (or screen) and asked to point out the visible faces of the rectangular parallelepiped. The better students will point out the hidden faces.

When frame 4 is shown, the work on counting the faces is repeated. Work on understanding the concepts of an edge and a vertex proceeds by the same method. It is best to show this frame, not immediately after frame 3, but after a break, during which work is done with the chart "The Rectangular Parallelepiped." (It is a waste of time to demonstrate the edges on models, since the students in the back rows will see very little.)

Frame 5 drills all the terms introduced in the lesson. In narrating this frame, the student should articulate the word "parallelepiped" distinctly, and should point to and count the number of faces, edges, and vertices with assurance.

2. *Defining the concept of a rectangular parallelepiped.*

a) The teacher exhibits and discusses the set of solids, including a generalized rectangular parallelepiped, a rectangular parallelepiped with a square cross-section, a cube, an oblique quadrangular prism, a truncated quadrangular pyramid, a pentagonal pyramid, a hexagonal prism, and a "spatial cross." Each solid bears a numbered label. The students are asked to write in their notebooks the numbers of the solids that they think are rectangular parallelepipeds, and, separately, the numbers of those which are not.

In checking the assignment, the teacher divides the solids into three individual groups: 1) solids that everyone has correctly identified as rectangular parallelepipeds; 2) solids that everyone has correctly identified as not rectangular parallelepipeds; and 3) solids that at least some students have identified incorrectly.

Then the teacher selects one solid from the first group. The students are asked to explain why it is a rectangular parallelepiped. Then they work in the workbook—the students read the definition and do assignments 1, 2, 3, and 4. It is helpful to check assignment 4 using slide 2 (see Fig 119). After doing an assignment by the model given in the workbook, the students are asked to determine whether any solids in group 3 are rectangular parallelepipeds.

3. *The cube as a special case of a rectangular parallelepiped.*

a) The teacher asks the students to establish whether a cube is a rectangular parallelepiped.

b) Then the students are asked to consider whether there can be a cube that is not a rectangular parallelepiped. Can there be a rectangular parallelepiped that is not a cube?

Conclusion: A cube is always a rectangular parallelepiped. But it is a special case in which all the faces are squares.

c) The students do assignment 5 in the workbook. Slides 1 and 3 can be used to reinforce this material (see Fig. 119).

At the conclusion of this lesson it is useful to show the single-concept film, "The Rectangular Parallelepiped" in its entirety.

Lesson 2. Properties of the Faces and Edges of a Rectangular Parallelepiped.

Objectives.

1. Develop the concepts of adjacent faces and opposite faces. (The students should be able to point out a common edge to establish that faces are adjacent, and cite the lack of a common edge as proof that two faces are opposite. Definitions need not be memorized.)

2. Learn the following properties:

a) Opposite faces of a rectangular parallelepiped are equal.

b) Every four parallel edges of a rectangular parallelepiped are equal.

The students can "discover" these properties by superimposing a rectangle, cut to match one face, onto other faces, and by superimposing sticks or paper strips equal to a given edge onto other edges. The students should be able to identify pairs of opposite faces and sets of four equal edges in any rectangular parallelepiped they are shown, and solve problems involving these properties.

Educational Materials: models of rectangular parallelepipeds; framework model of a rectangular parallelepiped; the single-concept film "The Rectangular Parallelepiped"; frames 5-7 of the filmstrip; assignments 6-12 in the workbook; assignment cards 1-29; the charts "The Latin Alphabet," "The Rectangular Parallelepiped," and "The Laws of the Arithmetic Operations"; and slides 2 and 18.

Lesson Plans on Rectangular Parallelepipeds and Volume

Procedure.

1. *Review the definition of the concept of a rectangular parallelepiped.*

a) The teacher exhibits models or shows slide 2 and asks the students to establish whether any of the solids shown is a rectangular parallelepiped. The students should substantiate their answer by means of the definition. Frame 5 of the filmstrip can again be used. The single-concept film "The Rectangular Parallelepiped" can be used for review with or without sound.

b) The teacher shows a rectangular parallelepiped or frame 6 of the filmstrip, stating, "This is a rectangular parallelepiped." Students are asked, "Tell everything that you know about this solid." (There are 6 faces; all the faces are rectangles; there are 12 edges; there are 8 vertices.)

2. *The common edge of two faces.*

The teacher tells the class:

a) You have listed several properties of rectangular parallelepipeds. Today let's learn about the other properties. How many edges are there for each face? (Four.) How many are there faces in all? (Six.) Why are there only 12 edges and not 6 × 4 = 24? (Because some faces have common edges, and we do not count these edges more than once.)

b) Do the two given faces have common edges? (The students point to the common edges of two indicated faces on the model and in filmstrip frames 5-7, or indicate that there are no common edges.)

c) The teacher gives a definition: The faces of a rectangular parallelepiped that have a common edge are said to be *adjacent*. What must we check in order to establish whether the two given faces are adjacent or not? (Whether the faces have a common edge.)

d) The teacher projects slide 18 on the blackboard and labels the vertices with letters. Are these two faces adjacent? (The students should explain their answers: "Yes, they have a common edge," or "No, they have no common edge.")

e) Faces that have no common edges are said to be *opposite*. Opposite edges of a parallelepiped are demonstrated on the chart and on models, with slides and filmstrip frames. The students are asked to establish on their own whether certain given faces are adjacent or opposite. For this purpose they do assignments 6-7 in the workbook.

3. *The property of opposite faces.*

a) The teacher shows a model of a rectangular parallelepiped on which one face is covered by a rectangle cut to match this face. The students are asked to check whether the faces in a rectangular parallelepiped are equal to the given face. After stating the hypothesis, the cut rectangle is superimposed onto the faces that seem equal to the given face. It is useful each time to specify exactly which faces are equal—the adjacent or opposite faces.

Conclusion: Opposite faces are equal.

b) This work is repeated for all opposite faces of the given parallelepiped and for one or two more parallelepipeds. Then the teacher asks the students to do assignments 8-9 in the workbook.

Conclusion: In any rectangular parallelepiped opposite faces are equal.

4. *Properties of edges.*

a) The teacher shows a parallelepiped, fastens a stick to one edge, and asks the students to hypothesize which edge is equal to the given one. The stick can be used to verify the hypothesis when it is placed along the indicated edges. Each time the teacher should emphasize that parallel edges turn out to be equal.

b) The teacher asks several questions: "How many edges equal to the given edge does the rectangular parallelepiped have?" (Three—not counting the original edge itself.) "How many edges equal to one another are there in all?" (Four.) "What can we say about the four equal edges?" (They are all parallel.) "Does this parallelepiped have another set of four equal edges?" "How many sets of four equal edges are there in all?" This work should be repeated for the sets of four edges in several parallelepipeds.

Conclusion: In any rectangular parallelepiped, the sets of four parallel edges are equal.

This conclusion can be reinforced by performing assignments 10-12 in the workbook. The properties of the faces and edges of a rectangular parallelepiped can also be reinforced by frames 5 and 6 of the filmstrip. There the students are asked to indicate which faces are equal, and which edges are equal. The teacher should not ask one type of question that we heard during experimental trials of the unit: "How are the faces equal? How are the edges equal?" (meaning by pairs or by fours).

5. *Assignment cards.*

Cards 1-29 can be used in this lesson. If the students do not complete the assignments successfully, they can be offered for homework. If, on the other hand, there is time left over, the results can be discussed.

Lesson 3. Dimensions of a Rectangular Parallelepiped. Drawing a Rectangular Parallelepiped.

Objectives.

1. Introduce the students to the concepts of the dimensions and height of a rectangular parallelepiped. The dimensions are the "representatives" of each set of 4 equal edges. Each student should be able to identify the dimensions of a given parallelepiped and understand that any dimension can serve as the height.

2. Teach the students to finish an incomplete drawing of a rectangular parallelepiped and construct a representation on their own.

Educational Materials: framework rectangular parallelepiped; the single-concept film "Representing a Rectangular Parallelepiped"; frames 8-11 of the filmstrip; slides 3-7 and 18-20; the charts "The Latin Alphabet," "The Rectangular Parallelepiped," and "The Laws of the Arithmetic Operations"; and assignments 13-20 of the workbook.

Procedure.

1. *Review the properties of the faces and edges of a rectangular parallelepiped.*

a) The teacher exhibits a model or a representation (for example, in slide 18) of a rectangular parallelepiped and asks the students to tell what they know about the faces of this solid. (There are 6 of them, all are rectangles, and the opposite faces are equal.)

b) A similar assignment can be done dealing with the properties of edges. (There are 12 of them, there are parallel and non-parallel edges, and every four parallel edges must be equal.)

c) Showing slide 18, which illustrates a rectangular parallelepiped without numbers, the teacher indicates the length of one edge and asks them to summarize what they know about the length of the edges of this parallelepiped (we know the length of each of the parallel edges).

d) In the same frame, the lengths of two edges can be indicated, and the students can be asked to tell what they know about the length of the edges of this rectangular parallelepiped.

e) The same frame is shown. The teacher names the lengths of three edges (in numbers). The dimensions of the remaining edges should be written in on the drawing.

f) Slide 20 (a cube) is shown. The teacher states that it is a cube, indicates the length of an edge, and asks what must be true about the other edges.

2. *Dimensions*.

a) After considering possible variant solutions to the assignment in frame 18, it can be concluded that it is necessary to take edges belonging to the three different groups of four, and that it is most convenient to take three edges that intersect at one vertex. The term "dimension" is introduced.

b) The teacher asks the students to find the dimensions of a model of a rectangular parallelepiped using a ruler.

c) The teacher states that the dimensions are usually referred to as the *length*, *width*, and *height*. The length and width represent the dimensions of the base, and the height is the third dimension. The students are asked to show the height of a rectangular parallelepiped when it is placed differently (using the chart, "The Rectangular Parallelepiped").

d) The teacher poses an oral problem: In a rectangular parallelepiped 5 edges are 3 cm, and one edge is 5 cm (these conditions should be written on the board). What do we know about the dimensions of this parallelepiped? (The students should reason in roughly the following way: There are 3 groups of four equal edges, and therefore there must be 4 edges of

5 cm, 4 edges of 3 cm, and another 4 edges of 3 cm.) The three given dimensions should be filled in on the picture in slide 19 (a rectangular parallelepiped with a square cross-section).

e) A similar problem: 9 edges of a rectangular parallelepiped are each 12 cm long. What are the dimensions of this parallelepiped? (It is a cube.) A picture of it should be shown (slide 20), and it should be stressed that only one dimension is given on the diagram, since we know that it is a cube.

3. *Representing a rectangular parallelepiped.*

The teacher shows the single-concept film "Representing a Rectangular Parallelepiped," and then reviews the construction of the figure. Filmstrip frames 8-11 can be used at this point.

Frame 8 shows the familiar translucent parallelepiped, along with a diagram of it. The teacher tells the students that they must learn to draw a rectangular parallelepiped on paper, and that she will now show them how to do it. Frame 9 shows the front face of a rectangular parallelepiped. It should be stressed that we see the front face best and that it is represented without distortion in the shape of a rectangle. Before showing frame 10, the lights can (but need not) be turned on and the students' attention directed to the picture of the matchbox on the chart. There, only the front face has the shape of a rectangle, and the left and the upper faces are distorted.

Frame 10 shows the edges originating from the vertices of the front face. The teacher should emphasize that they are parallel and point out the dotted lines for the hidden edge. The construction is completed in frame 11. This frame is an exact copy of frame 8. The teacher notes that the hidden edges are represented by dotted lines.

Note that this sequence of drawing need not be required (first the front face, then the edges originating from its vertices, and finally the back face). This would contradict the materials in the slide series and the workbook, but above all, it would be a typical example of a totally unnecessary new "rule." The indicated sequence is just one possible method of construction, but it may be the most convenient.

If the teacher has time, she can make the work more complicated. Frame 8-11 can be projected directly onto the blackboard. When frame 9 is shown, a student is asked to come to the blackboard and draw the edges originating from the vertices of the front face. When the drawing is complete, the frame is changed. These edges are already included in frame 10 so the projected picture should coincide with the chalk drawing. If it does not, the chalk drawing is corrected. Then the students complete the drawing of the rectangular parallelepiped in frame 10 and, when frame 11 is shown, they either realize that the drawing is correct or find mistakes in it.

The students can complete a diagram of a rectangular parallelepiped (slides 3-7 are projected onto the blackboard). The students draw rectangular parallelepipeds in their workbook (assignment 13). Assignments 14- 20 can be given for homework.

Lesson 4. The Framework, Surface, and Two-Dimensional Cutout Pattern of a Rectangular Parallelepiped

Objectives.
1. Check the students' mastery of previous material.
2. Acquaint the students with the term "framework" and reinforce the properties of edges.
3. Give students a notion of the surface and reinforce the properties of faces.
4. Give students a notion of a two-dimensional cutout pattern for a rectangular parallelepiped.

Educational Materials: framework rectangular parallelepiped; filmstrip frames 12-13; slides 8-20; assignments 21-31 in the workbook; the charts "The Latin Alphabet" and "The Laws of the Arithmetic Operations"; a bar; an empty box; a cardboard two-dimensional pattern.[3]

Procedure.
1. The teacher checks whether the students have learned to see the hidden and visible faces and edges in a picture of a rectangular parallel-

epiped. Here slide 20 is projected four times on the blackboard, with the picture turned 90° each time. The students are told that assignment 18 in the workbook is being checked and are asked to determine which cube in Figure 136 corresponds to the projected picture. They are asked to use the workbook to read which face is in front in the pictures. At the same time, they can be asked to name either the back or the lower face or the face opposite an indicated one on the projected figure. The teacher can check whether assignments 19-20 in the workbook have been done correctly through questioning.

2. *The framework of a rectangular parallelepiped.*

a) The teacher shows a bar and explains to the class: "You know that a rectangular parallelepiped is a solid. It is as if it were filled up inside. We call this (showing the framework to the class) a rectangular parallelepiped as well. How can a rectangular parallelepiped be obtained (holding up the framework) from this (holding up the bar)?" (The first is obtained from the second if we take all the edges of the second.)

b) The teacher asks the students to do assignments 21 and 22 in the workbook, pointing out that they can use the charts "The Laws of the Arithmetic Operations," which are already hanging in the classroom. The solution to problems 21 and 22 must be checked.

3. *The surface of a parallelepiped.*

a) The teacher again exhibits a bar and an empty box. The class is asked to point out how these parallelepipeds differ. (The box is hollow.)

b) The teacher states that the box will give them an idea of the outer casing of a rectangular parallelepiped, that is, its surface.[4]

c) The students tell what the surface of a rectangular parallelepiped consists of. (6 rectangles)

d) The class reviews the rule for calculating the area of a rectangle, and solves problems on calculating surface area (workbook assignments 29-31; assignments 23-28 can also be used). While checking, it is useful to return to the properties studied, and, in particular, to emphasize that opposite faces are equal.

It should be mentioned that we have indicated all the workbook assignments that can be used in Lesson 4. Do not forget, however, that the same problems are taken up in the next lesson as well. Therefore, the teacher can give them assignment 29, for example, and then introduce the students to the material described in points 3 and 4. Finally, if there is any time left, the teacher can give other assignments.

4. *The two-dimensional pattern.*

a) The teacher shows a cardboard pattern of a rectangular parallelepiped (folded into a parallelepiped) and states that this little box is made up of rectangles fastened together. What will happen if this rectangular parallelepiped is cut along the edges? (It falls apart into 6 rectangles.)

b) The teacher tells the class that the box can be cut so that the rectangles do not fall apart, and shows them frames 12 and 13 of the filmstrip. She then uses the cardboard cutout to show the same thing.

5. *Problem solving* based on slides 8-17. Problems composed by the teacher based on frames 18-20 can also be used.

Lesson 5. Problem Solving. Independent Work.

Objectives.

1. Review how the area of a rectangle is calculated.

2. Reinforce the properties of the edges and faces of a rectangular parallelepiped.

3. Show the students how the laws of the operations can be used to solve problems on the length of the edges and the area of the faces.

Educational Materials: assignments 22-31 in the printed workbook; problem cards 30-51.

Procedure.

The students are asked to do all the workbook assignments from 22-31 that they have not yet done. The work is done on their own. They consult with the teacher only if necessary. At the lesson's end the workbooks are collected for checking. As the assignments are done, the students receive cards 151-168.

Lesson Plans on Rectangular Parallelepipeds and Volume

Lesson 6. Basic Concept of Volume.

Objectives.
1. Eliminate gaps in knowledge noted by the teacher when checking the students' independent work.
2. Demonstrate that every solid occupies space, and introduce the concept of the "volume of a solid."
3. Show that volume is always measured in terms of certain measures; develop the concept of a unit of volume.

Educational Materials: the single-concept films "The Concept of Volume" and "The Volume of a Solid"; filmstrip frames 14-29; the charts "The Latin Alphabet" and "The Laws of the Arithmetic Operations."

Procedure.
1. *Analysis of independent work.*
2. *A rudimentary notion of volume.*

"All the objects around us occupy space. All of them have volume." The students repeat this conclusion after watching the single-concept film "The Concept of Volume" and frames 14-19 of the filmstrip. After showing the single-concept film, the teacher asks what conclusion the students can draw. After the conclusion is stated, the class reviews it using the material in the filmstrip frames. This can done in the following way.

The teacher shows frame 14, which represents a decanter and glasses. The students are asked to compare the amount of water in the decanter and in a glass. The teacher summarizes: There is room for more water in the decanter than in the glass; we say that the capacity or the cubic content of the decanter is greater than that of the glass. We also say that the volume of the water that will fit into the decanter is greater than the volume of the water that will fit into a glass.

Frame 15 is shown. The teacher summarizes: We can say that the capacity of the decanter in frame 14 is equal to the volume of 5 glasses.

Frame 16 is shown. With help from the students, the teacher establishes that salt, like water, also occupies space—it has volume. The volume occupied by the salt that fills the jar is greater than the volume of the salt that fills the glass.

Filmstrip frame 17 is shown. All the molds represented in the drawing have the same volume. This can be established by filling one mold with water and pouring the water into another mold.

Filmstrip frame 18 is shown. This frame makes it possible to consider the fact that different objects can occupy the same amount of space. For the students to draw such a conclusion, the teacher tells them beforehand that one of the molds was filled with clay; when the clay dried up, it was removed, and water was poured into the vacated space. Like the clay, the water filled the mold.

The class returns to frame 17, with the molds. The teacher exhibits an empty mold and asks whether the air that fills the empty mold has volume. The teacher summarizes: The air that fills the empty mold does have volume. The volume of air in the mold is equal to the volume of the water or clay. If we pour water or put clay into an empty mold, it will displace the air and will occupy the same amount of space.

The teacher concludes: Water occupies space and therefore has volume. What are some other objects around us that have volume? After hearing the students' ideas, the teacher leads them to the conclusion that every object in our surroundings has volume. After the conclusion has been stated, frame 19 (with caption) is projected. One student reads the conclusion aloud.

The teacher moves to frame 20 and comments on it. The clay that was removed from the mold is dropped into a jar filled to the brim with water. What will happen then? (The clay will occupy the space formerly occupied by the water, and the water will overflow.) After hearing the answers, the teacher asks what will happen if the water that overflows the jar is collected and poured into the mold from which the clay was removed (frame 21). (The water will fill the mold). If a cube is dropped into a full jar and the overflowing water is collected, will the water fill a mold? It is important to analyze each possible case in detail.

1) The water fills part of the mold. Then the volume of the cube is less than the volume of the clay, since the cube has displaced less water.

2) The water fills the entire mold and does not overflow. Here the cube's volume is equal to that of the clay.

Lesson Plans on Rectangular Parallelepipeds and Volume

3) The water fills the entire mold, and part of the water overflows. This means that the cube has displaced more water than the clay did. The cube's volume is greater than the volume of the clay.

The teacher summarizes: Every solid immersed in a liquid displaces some of the liquid; the volume of the displaced liquid is equal to the volume of the solid.

Frame 22 (with caption) is shown. One student reads the conclusion aloud. The teacher shows frame 23. The students are asked to tell what has happened there. (A solid was dropped into a jar containing a liquid, displacing some of it. The volume of the displaced liquid—and therefore the volume of the solid—is shown to be equal to the volume of the empty part of the jar. Thus, the jar was filled to the brim with water.)

3. *Methods of comparing and measuring volume.*

The teacher can show the single-concept film "The Volume of a Solid," which discusses various ways to measure volume. However, if reloading the equipment is inconvenient, the explanation can be given with using the filmstrip. In this case the single-concept film "The Volume of a Solid" can be shown at the next lesson. Without showing the film, the exposition can be organized as follows:

a) The students are asked to think of a way to compare the volume of the water in the decanter and in the teapot. The water can be measured again with glasses. If, for example, there are 5 glasses in the decanter and 6 in the teapot, the volume of the teapot is clearly greater than that of the decanter. (But here it is essential that the measurement involve identical glasses.)

The teacher shows frame 24 (2 glasses). "You see, the glasses are not equal. We have poured water from the full thick-walled glass into the thin one, and it did not fill it. If the decanter is measured by thin glasses and the teapot by thick ones, then we will not know whether more water will go into the teapot or into the decanter."

Frame 25 is shown (a glass and a jar). The teacher says that the volume of dry substances like sugar or sand, as well as liquids, can be measured in glasses. The students are asked to tell and to show how to measure the volume of sand using a glass. (Pour sand from the jar into the glass. If it turns out that the glass has been filled 5 times, the volume of the jar is equal to 5 glasses. But it is again important to indicate precisely which kind of glass—thin- or thick-walled—was used to measure the volume.)

The students can be asked to find in the workbook a drawing for assignment 30, which poses the following problem: "An aquarium without any fish in it is filled halfway with water. We need to put a light in the aquarium to illuminate and heat the water. Can we find the volume of this light using a glass? (Yes, we can. It is sufficient to note the level of the water before we put the light in. Then we drop in the light and scoop water out in glasses until the remaining water is lowered to its original mark. The volume of the water displaced by the light is equal to the volume of the light. For example, if the light displaced 3 glasses of water, then its volume is equal to 3 glasses of water.)

b) The teacher asks the students to list various ways of measuring volume. (The volume of liquid and dry substances can be measured in glasses, spoons, medicine droppers, etc.)

c) Frame 26 is shown. The teacher states that in ancient Russia material was measured in cubits, or "elbows." "In your opinion, how did a person know in advance how many cubits of material he had to buy to make a coat?" "He didn't know, unless he knew what kind of cubit the person he was buying it from had.") The teacher concludes that it is inconvenient to use indefinite units of measure, and asks what measures are used to measure length today.

d) The teacher shows frame 27 and reads the accompanying text.

e) The teacher asks the class to think about whether a graduated cylinder can be used to establish the volume of hard solids. Frames 28 and 29 are shown. With the teacher's help, the students tell how to find the volume of the ball and express the volume in milliliters. The teacher concludes that not only can the volume of a liquid be measured in milliliters, but also the volume of a hard solid. The teacher stresses that it is not always handy to measure the volume of hard solids in liters and milliliters since a large stone or a house would hardly fit into a graduated cylinder.

Lesson Plans on Rectangular Parallelepipeds and Volume

At the end of the lesson the teacher tells the class that in the next lesson the students will learn about another unit that is more frequently used to measure the volume of hard solids.

Lesson 7. The Notion of Measuring Volume in Cubic Units. Laboratory Work.

Objectives.

1. Provide a notion of cubic units (by analogy with the volumes discussed earlier, volume is measured in "cubes" rather than glasses).

2. Learn the definition of volume: Volume is a number that shows how many units of volume are contained in a given solid. (The students should learn the definition in the course of doing the assignments; they need not memorize it.)

Educational Materials: the single-concept film "The Volume of a Solid"; frames 30-33 of the filmstrip; assignment 32 in the workbook; the charts "The Latin Alphabet" and "The Laws of the Arithmetic Operations"; the arithmetic kit (modernized).

Procedure.

1. *Review* (how volume can be measured).

The students are asked to list several methods of measuring volume (mugs, cups, spoons, a graduated cylinder, etc.). Here it is established explicitly that a liter and its parts are used as units for measuring volume. In conclusion, the teacher asks what is meant by "the capacity of a 3-liter vessel (a 5-liter vessel, a half-liter vessel)." (Three 1-liter tankards will fit into it, or 5 tankards, or half a tankard.) The single-concept film "The Volume of a Solid" is shown.

2. *The unit cube.*

a) The teacher shows frame 30 of the filmstrip (a picture of a box with small cubes). She observes that these cubes can be placed in the box and no space will be left over. The students are asked to characterize the capacity of the box (the capacity of the box is equal to 6 cubes).

The teacher reminds them of the earlier discussion, that the capacity of the decanter was equal to 6 glasses. The glass was the unit of volume. If the capacity of a jar was equal to 6 liters, it has been clearly indicated what unit of volume was used: the liter tankard.

In the new problem (with the little cubes), the cube plays the role of the measuring cup. The volume of the box is equal to 6 cubes. In this case the cubes are called "unit cubes" (or units of volume).

The teacher draws a conclusion: Whenever we measure volume, we establish how many units of volume are contained in the given solid. The students are asked to think about what the volume of a solid is. To sum up, filmstrip frame 31 (with caption) is shown. One student reads it aloud.

b) The teacher shows frame 32, with the unit cube, and comments: "A unit cube has an edge—the unit of length. This can be an arbitrary unit (since the volume of liquids or dry substances is often measured by an arbitrary cup or spoon).

In many cases, including this one, length is measured in metric units: meters (m), centimeters (cm), millimeters (mm), and others. Accordingly, cubes with an edge of 1 cm, 1 m, etc., are most often taken as units. In these instances the unit cubes have a special name. A cube whose edge is equal to 1 m is called a "cubic meter." What is a cube called if its edge is equal to 1 mm, 1 cm, 1 inch (about 2.5 cm)?

3. *Determining volume* (by counting unit cubes).

a) The teacher shows frame 33—a staircase solid. The students are asked to tell what must be done to find the volume of this solid. In summary, the teacher states that the class previously counted the number of tankards, glasses, spoons, and so on, which served as units of volume. Now, when a cube is taken as the unit of volume, we need to find out how many of these cubes are contained in a given solid. On the blackboard (after counting) is written:

$$V = 5 \text{ (cubic units)}.$$

b) The teacher leads the class to the conclusion that 5 is the number that shows how many units of volume are contained in the given solid.

Lesson Plans on Rectangular Parallelepipeds and Volume

The students are asked to open the workbook, read the definition, and do assignment 32. The solutions are checked by the whole class.

4. *Laboratory work.*

Objective: Reinforce the definition of the concept of "volume."

The students receive one staircase solid from the arithmetic kit and two cubes—a large one and a small one. They are to fill in a worksheet. (Only assignment 1 should be regarded as compulsory; the other assignments are given at the teacher's discretion.) The worksheet takes the following form:

Solid No. _____ Pupil_____ Grade _____

1) Find the volume of the solid, taking the large cube as the unit.

The volume of a solid is _____, which shows how many _____ are contained in the given solid. This solid contains _____ units of volume.

Answer. The volume of the solid is _____.

2) Find the volume of the same solid, taking the small cube as the unit.

Answer. The volume of the solid is _____.

3) Find the sum of the lengths of the edges of the solid, taking the large cube as the unit.

Answer. The sum of the lengths of the edges is _____.

4) Find the sum of the lengths of the edges of the same solid, taking the small cube as the unit.

Answer. The sum of the lengths of the edges is _____.

5) Find the area of the surface of the given solid, taking the large cube as the unit.

Answer. The surface area of the solid is _____.

6) Find the surface area of the same solid, taking the small cube as the unit.

Answer. The surface area of the solid is _____.

7) How many large cubes must be added to obtain a rectangular parallelepiped from the given staircase solid. What are the volume, the sum of the lengths of the edges, and the surface area of the resulting rectangular parallelepiped, if the large cube is taken as the unit of measure?

Answer. To construct a rectangular parallelepiped from a given staircase solid, we must add _____. For the resulting rectangular parallelepiped the volume is _____; the sum of the lengths of the edges is _____; and the surface area is _____.

8) Count to see how many large cubes must be added to obtain a cube from the given staircase solid. What are the volume, the sum of the lengths of the edges, and the surface area of the resulting cube, if the large cube is taken as the unit of measure?

Answer. To construct a cube from the given staircase solid, _____ must be added. For the resulting cube, the sum of the lengths of the edges is _____ ; the volume is _____ ; and the surface area is _____.

Lesson 8. Problem Solving, Analysis of Laboratory Work, Independent Work.

Educational Materials: slides 18-20, 41, 42; assignments 33 and 34 of the workbook; cards 52-91; the charts "The Latin Alphabet" and "The Laws of the Arithmetic Operations"; rubber stamps; arithmetic kit.

Procedure.

1. *Analysis of laboratory work.*

a) Showing slides 41 and 42, the teacher assigns the questions on the laboratory worksheet.

b) The teacher asks the students how they determined the volume of the solid when the small cube was the unit of volume, noting the students who guessed, without counting, that they had to multiply the number of large cubes by 8.

c) For students who do not quite understand why they need to multiply by 8, the teacher shows how the large cube can be formed from small ones. (Four small cubes can be placed on the face of the large cube. The height of the resulting parallelepiped is less than the height of the cube. To get the large cube, we have to put on one more layer. There are 4 cubes in one layer, and twice as many in two layers.) Assignments 33 and 34 in the workbook can be assigned.

Lesson Plans on Rectangular Parallelepipeds and Volume

2. *Independent work on cards 52-91.*

Lesson 9. Test No. 1.

Educational Material: cards 92-94.
Procedure.
At the beginning of the lesson the teacher makes a brief analysis of the independent work and goes over the most common errors. The cards with the text of the test are then distributed to the students.

Lesson 10. Counting the Number of Unit Cubes

Objective.
Make the transition from simply counting the units of volume to rational calculation of the number of units.

Educational Materials: filmstrip frames 34-39; slides 21-23; assignments 35-37 in the workbook ; cards 52-91; the charts "The Latin Alphabet" and "The Laws of the Arithmetic Operations"; rubber stamps.

Procedure.
1. *Analysis of the test and oral questioning.*
The teacher calls attention to the properties of a rectangular parallelepiped and to establishing inclusion in the concept of a "rectangular parallelepiped," reviewing with the students how to find the volume of a staircase solid by counting the unit cubes.

2. *Practice in calculating the number of objects placed in a definite order.*
a) The teacher discusses the importance of learning how to determine the number of objects precisely, without counting them. The students calculate the number of objects in filmstrip frames 34-37.

The teacher uses frames 38-39 to explain how to calculate the number of cubes that make up a parallelepiped. For example, the students can be asked to calculate how many cubes can be placed on the area represented in frame 38 in one, two, three, etc., layers. Then the teacher can move to frame 39 and ask them to calculate the number of cubes that could be placed in one layer on the lateral or the front face, in two, three, etc., layers on this face, or in the given solid.

b) The students do assignments 35 and 36 in the workbook. Assignment 37 is given for homework.

c) Slides 21-23 are shown.

d) The students work with cards 52-91.

Lesson 11. Calculating the Volume of a Rectangular parallelepiped.

Objective.

Make the transition from counting units of volume to calculation by multiplying the dimensions. The transition should be organized such that at any moment the students can "see" and "show" the number of volume units represented by the product of dimensions.

Educational Materials: filmstrip frame 40; slides 18-20, 23, 29, 35; the charts "The Latin Alphabet," "The Laws of the Arithmetic Operations," and "The Volume of a Rectangular Parallelepiped"; rubber stamps.

Procedure.

Calculating units of volume from the dimensions alone.

a) To check the students work on assignment 37 in the workbook, slide 20 (a cube) is projected onto the blackboard. The teacher identifies each of the three dimensions, whereupon one student is called upon to repeat all the constructions made in assignment 37. However, work on assignment 37 may also be organized at the same time as the same problem is solved on the board (slide 20).

b) In filmstrip frame 35, the class is asked to calculate the number of unit cubes that can be placed inside a given solid. The teacher emphasizes that the calculation can begin with any face. The students are asked to calculate how many unit cubes can be placed on one specified face (which is ruled off into squares). Then they are asked to calculate how many of these layers can be stacked up. Finally, they calculate the volume of the solid.

c) The teacher directs the students' attention to the fact that the number of cubes that are placed on a face is equal to the number of squares into which the given face is divided—that is, the volume of one layer is equal to the area of the face. The number of layers is equal to the third dimension. Thus, the volume is equal to the product of the height and the area of a face taken as the base. (The conclusion is formulated orally. All the arguments are repeated for the three different bases and their corresponding heights. This reasoning is followed through with examples of concrete numerical dimensions. It is useful to show slide 18 on the board, label the vertices, and drill the class in solving problems analogous to the one given in slide 23.)

d) Slide 18 is shown—a parallelepiped whose dimensions are indicated by the teacher (e.g., 2, 3, and 4). The teacher asks the class to calculate the volume of this solid.

First it is established what it means to calculate the volume (finding a number that shows how many unit cubes are contained in a solid). Then it is established that if we know the lengths of the edges, we can reason as in the previous problem. However, to do so we must divide the edges into individual linear units. It is helpful to project the filmstrip frame onto the board and mark off the lengths with chalk to show the number of cubes that go into this face and the number of layers.

e) The volume of several other solids is determined (slides 19 and 20). Each time the students should be asked to calculate the number of cubes that will go into the base and calculate the number of layers. Slide 29 can also be shown; there the lengths of the edges are numerically small. Therefore, it is easy to break down a face into squares, calculate how many cubes can be placed on the face, and calculate the number of layers.

Lesson 12. Formulas for the Volume of a Rectangular Parallelepiped.

Objective.

Demonstrate simple methods of calculating the volume of a rectangular parallelepiped by formulas. Here, if necessary, the students should be able to calculate unit volumes (mentally breaking down a parallelepiped into its component unit cubes).

Educational Materials: filmstrip frames 41, 42; the single-concept film "The Volume of a Rectangular Parallelepiped"; slides 24-33, 18-20; assignments 38-49 in the workbook; cards 95-99; all charts in the unit; rubber stamps.

Procedure.

1. *Review the material in the previous lesson.*

a) A rectangular parallelepiped (slide 18) is projected onto the blackboard. The teacher indicates the dimensions. A student is asked to tell how to calculate the number of units of volume.

b) For the same problem, another student is asked to take other dimensions and repeat the calculations.

2. *Calculating units of volume when the dimensions are expressed in letters.*

a) Slide 18 is shown—a parallelepiped without numbers. The teacher recalls that many problems have been solved using this picture, taking different numbers each time. But, regardless of the numbers, the number of cubes that could be placed on one of the bases was calculated in each case. This number is equal to the area of the base. Then the number of layers that would fill the rectangular parallelepiped was calculated. The number of layers was always equal to the height of the rectangular parallelepiped.

b) The same frame is shown. The teacher says that the dimensions of the rectangular parallelepiped are known. But it makes no difference what they are. Using letters is suggested as a way of representing the lengths. On the blackboard, near three edges meeting at a vertex, the teacher writes the letters a, b, and c.

c) The students are asked to repeat the arguments they already know, and calculate the volume of the parallelepiped, taking different faces as the bases. Each time the teacher emphasizes that they are finding the area of the base and multiplying it by the height.

d) Slide 24, depicting the volume formulas and the faces divided into squares, is shown. The teacher explains how the number of unit cubes is calculated by multiplying the dimensions. For example, the students are asked to tell how to calculate the volume if they begin with a lateral face. It is explained that they should calculate the number of squares that can be placed on the lateral face. This number is equal to the area of the lateral face. After the students have told how to calculate the number of squares, their attention is directed to the notation on the left: $S = a \times b$.

Next, it is explained that the number of unit cubes placed on a lateral face is equal to the area of the face. The students' attention is directed to the fact that the layer of cubes is not shown. All that remains of the layer are one cube in the middle of the face and another in the column of cubes at edge c. Then they should determine how many layers of cubes can be stacked up. (The number of layers is equal to the third dimension.) After the students have told how to calculate the volume, their attention is directed to the brief notation on the left: $V = a \times b \times c$. Similar work is done with the two remaining pictures. The students must be encouraged to ask why the notation $V = a \times b \times c$ is possible in all three cases. The students can be required to explain why $a \times b \times c$ is written instead of $a \times c \times b$ or $c \times b \times a$.

e) Using examples, the teacher explains how to substitute numbers for letters in the volume formulas. Here a chart or filmstrip frames can be used.

f) To wrap up this part of the lesson, the single-concept film "The Volume of a Rectangular Parallelepiped" is shown.

3. *Calculation by formulas.*

Problems are solved using slides 25-33. The teacher periodically directs the students to calculate the number of unit cubes. Such questions as the following are posed: "What does the number obtained after multiplying the dimensions mean?" "Why, when we calculate the volume of a rectangular parallelepiped, do we multiply the area of the base by the height?" "What do we find out when we multiply two dimensions?" (We find the area of a face, and thus how many cubes can be placed on that face.)

If there are any difficulties, slide 24 should be shown. Assignments 38-49 in the workbook can also be assigned. Of course, some of these problems can be used in other lessons as well. It is desirable for assignment 43 in the workbook to be checked during the lesson. Slide 24 can be used here. The students show that a^2 means: 1) the number of unit squares placed on a given face; and 2) the number of unit cubes placed in a single layer on these squares. If we again multiply by a, we find out how many unit cubes there are in all the layers—that is, we find the volume of a cube of edge a.

Lesson 13. Converting from One Unit to Another.

Objectives.

1. Show that a change in all the dimensions of a parallelepiped by a factor of a entails a change in the volume of the parallelepiped by a factor of a^3.

2. Teach the students how to convert from one cubic unit to others.

Educational Materials: filmstrip frames 43-46; slides 18-20, 34-40; assignments 50-64 in the workbook; cards 100-150; all the charts in the unit; the rubber stamps.

Procedure.

1. *Review* the volume formulas and the effect on the volume if each dimension of a parallelepiped is changed by an identical factor.

a) The students do an assignment based on slides 18-20. The teacher supplies the numbers.

b) The teacher chooses three students to stamp (with the rubber stamps) two rectangular parallelepipeds in each student's workbook. Then the teacher says: "Label the dimensions in the first picture $2a$, $2b$,

2c, and find the volume of the parallelepiped with these dimensions." Filmstrip frame 43 is shown when the assignment is checked.

c) The teacher then asks them to label the dimensions $3a$, $3b$, and $3c$ for the the second picture and find that parallelepiped's volume. Filmstrip frame 44 is shown during checking.

d) The teacher asks the students to think about how the volume of a cube will change if its edges are doubled. (It will be 8 times as large). During the check, 8 small and 1 large cube from the collection can again be used. The small ones are placed on one face of the large one, and the number of layers is calculated.

e) How does the volume of a cube change if each edge is tripled? (The cube stamps can be used analogously to steps (b) and (c).) Filmstrip frame 45 is shown during the check.

2. *Converting from one unit to others.*

The teacher asks questions in approximately the following sequence:

a) A cube has an edge of 1 dm. What is its volume in cubic centimeters?

b) A solid has a volume of 6 cubic dm. What is its volume in cubic centimeters?

A clear explanation must be given in response to this question. For example, "The solid is made up of 6 cubes with an edge of 1 dm, and in every such cube there are 1,000 smaller cubes with an edge of 1 cm; therefore, the solid is made up of 6,000 smaller cubes with an edge of 1 cm—that is, it has a volume of 6000 cub. cm."

c) Several numerical assignments of the same type are repeated. Slides 41 and 42, showing staircase solids, can be used while they are being done. The question is posed in the following way: "The unit cube shown here has an edge of 1 dm. What is the volume of the staircase solid in cubic decimeters? in cubic centimeters?"

d) After the preparatory work has been done, the teacher asks: "A solid has a volume of a cubic decimeters. What is its volume in cubic centimeters?" Then (possibly, with preliminary numerical examples) she asks questions about the conversion from cubic centimeters into cubic millimeters, from cubic meters into cubic centimeters, and so forth.

e) In conclusion, problems are considered on calculating the volume of parallelepipeds for which the edges are expressed in different units, say, 2 m x 3 m x 8 dm. But the solution should be obtained not merely by multiplying out the dimensions in decimeters (20 x 30 x 8); it should be explained geometrically. The solution might take the following form: "The length of the rectangular parallelepiped is 2 m, which means that 20 cubes of one decimeter can be placed along this edge; the width is 3 m, which means that 30 cubes of one decimeter can be placed along this edge. There will be $20 \times 30 = 600$ cubes in one layer. The rectangular parallelepiped's height is 8 dm, and therefore there will be 8 of these layers. The volume is equal to $600 \times 8 = 4{,}800$ cubic dm."

It is a good idea to conclude the problem with the question: "The dimensions of a rectangular parallelepiped are a meters, b meters, and c decimeters. What is its volume in cubic decimeters?"

f) The students do independent work using assignments 50-64 in the workbook and cards 100-150.

Lesson 14. Review. Preparation for Unit Test.

Educational Materials: all charts in the unit; the workbook; assignment cards 151-180; the filmstrip; the slides (selected by the teacher).

After any topic has been studied, the basic facts studied in the topic should be summarized. By long-standing tradition, this work consists of three stages: a) preparation for a test; b) taking the test; and c) analyzing the test.

The first stage includes an explicit statement of what the students have learned in the given topic. In the course of the discussion the teacher corrects misconceptions, poses problems, and determines how the students should prepare at home for the next lesson. The second stage (the test itself) is the students' accounting of what they have learned. During the third stage the entire topic is summarized, including a discussion of the answers as given by the students on the test. Lesson 14 is devoted to the first of these three stages.

Procedure.

Independent problem solving (cards 151-180) should be organized during the lesson, but the main idea is to conduct a discussion. It must be determined whether the students remember:

a) what concepts were studied in class during the topic "The Rectangular Parallelepiped and Its Volume";

b) how these concepts were defined;

c) what facts based on these concepts were learned; and,

d) what fundamental problems were solved in class.

The students should recall (points (a) and (b)) what is meant by rectangular parallelepiped, cube, edge, face, vertex, base, height, volume, unit of volume, cubic meter, cubic decimeter (liter), and cubic centimeter (millimeter). This is best done by questioning the entire class. The teacher can show appropriate filmstrip frames, asking the students to comment briefly on them.

The students should be able to (point (c)): name the number of faces, edges, and vertices of a rectangular parallelepiped, and note that opposite faces and the edges connecting them are equal; indicate every object around us has volume; and write or read the formulas for the volume of a rectangular parallelepiped, indicating the relations between the units of volume. The entire class can also be questioned here, using the filmstrip.

In accordance with point (d), the student must recall problems on: representing and completing an unfinished picture of a rectangular parallelepiped; finding the sums of the lengths of its edges and its surface area; measuring the volume of hard solids by immersing them in liquids; measuring the volume of a solid by calculating its component unit cubes; calculating the volume of a rectangular parallelepiped by formulas; converting the volume from certain units into others; and using the tables of squares and cubes. It is also useful to review problems on calculating the volume of a more complicated solid, which can be mentally broken down into two rectangular parallelepipeds (the last assignments in the workbook). If any time remains, it is useful to conclude by analyzing one problem from cards 169-180 (which are meant, by and large, for the better students).

As these kinds of problems and others are reviewed, the students should be asked to give examples of problems of a specific type. Then the teacher can have them solve the problems that they were unable to solve in the previous lessons. Here it is advisable to use the remaining undiscussed slides and assignment cards, as well as to analyze with the class the problems from the workbook that they have already solved. This will refresh their memory, not only of the text of the problems, but also of the methods used to solving them.

Lesson 15. Unit Test.

The teacher makes up the test. We will give one possible variant as an example.

Problem 1. The dimensions of a hayloft are 15 m x 20 m x 40 dm. Hay is kept in the loft. There are 60 kg of hay for every cubic meter of the loft's capacity. One cow will eat 16 kg of hay in a day. How many days will the hay feed 40 cows?

Problem 2. What must be verified to establish that a given solid is a rectangular parallelepiped?

Problem 3. The volume of a cube is 343 cubic cm. One dimension is doubled. Find the sum of the lengths of the edges, the surface area, and the volume of the resulting rectangular parallelepiped.

A set of assignments of this kind will address the problem material that has been established. Indeed, the first problem breaks down into the following more elementary problems:

a) conversion from one measure to others;

b) calculating the volume of a rectangular parallelepiped; and,

c) solving familiar types of problems.

Problem 2 addresses the necessary prerequisites for membership in the concept of a rectangular parallelepiped, and requires that students work with the definition.

The solution to problem 3 requires:

Lesson Plans on Rectangular Parallelepipeds and Volume

a) solving an inverse problem (finding x from x^3) using the table of cubes;

b) drawing a rectangular parallelepiped to go with the problem; and

c) finding the sum of the lengths of the edges, the surface area, and the volume of the rectangular parallelepiped.

Thus, the basic logical and computational problems in this topic are covered. Note that the last problem (which is related, in particular, to calculating the sum of the lengths of the edges) yields the following beautiful solution,

$$7 \times 8 + 14 \times 4 = 2 \times 7 \times 8 = 112 \text{ cm},$$

so that good students can especially distinguish themselves.

Lesson 16. Analysis of the Test. Problem Solving

In analyzing the test it is essential to analyze the errors related to students' direct calculations, mastery of the concept of volume, understanding of methods of calculating the volume of a rectangular parallelepiped, and so forth. Even if obvious errors in the principal concepts are not detected, the teacher should summarize the entire topic, focusing in particular on the concept of volume and how to calculate the volume of a rectangular parallelepiped.

In connection with measuring the sum of the lengths of the edges, the surface area, and the volume of a rectangular parallelepiped, the teacher should emphasize the importance of the guidelines by which calculation in mathematics is done. Archimedes and Lebesgue, who studied the theory of measurement, can be brought in here. The very existence of such a branch of mathematics, and the fact that only in the past century have fundamental discoveries been made in this area, are interesting for the students.

In analyzing methods of calculating the volume of a rectangular parallelepiped, it is a good idea to point out that the formula $V = Sh$ holds not only for a rectangular parallelepiped, but also for any cylinder (including one that is not circular) and or prism (including an oblique one). This enables the students to better understand how what they have learned fits into the general system of mathematical knowledge.

Notes

Notes to Chapter 1

1. Pestalozzi, J.H. (1963). *Selected Pedagogical Works* [*Izbrannye pedagogicheskie sochineniya*], v. 3. Moscow: Izdatelstvo APN RSFSR, p. 217.
2. *In Memory of P. F. Lesgaft* [*Pamyati P.F. Lesgafta*]. Collection of articles. Moscow: Uchpedgiz, 1947.
3. Lenin, V.I. *Complete Collected Works* [*Polnoe sobranie sochinenii*], v. 25, pp. 152-153.
4. Ushinskii, K.D. (1945). *Collected Works* [*Sobranie sochinenii*]. Moscow: Publishing House of the RSFSR Academy of Pedagogical Sciences, v. 6, p. 265.
5. The Russian words contrasted here are *naglyadnost* ('visuality') and *glyadet'* (literally 'to look')—Translator.
6. Atutov, P.R. (1967). "Several Questions Involving the Use of Visuality in Instruction" ["Nekotorye voprosy ispolzovaniya naglyadnosti v obuchenii"]. *Soviet Pedagogy* [*Sovetskaya pedagogika*], no. 5.
7. Gromov, A.P. (1960). *Film-Strips and Movies in Secondary School Mathematics Lessons* [*Diafilmy i kino na urokakh matematiki v srednei shkole*]. Moscow: Uchpedgiz.
8. Zankov, L.V. (1960). *Visuality and the Motivation of Pupils in Instruction* [*Naglvadnost i aktivizatsiya uchashchikhsya v obuchenii*]. Moscow: Uchpedgiz.
9. Shapovalenko, S.G. (1967). "Creating a System of Modern Materials for the General-Education Secondary School" ["O sozdanii sistemy sovremennogo oborudovaniya dlya srednei obshcheobrazovatelnoi shkoly"]. *Soviet Pedagogy* [*Sovetskaya pedagogika*], no. 5.
10. Konobeevskii, N.P. (1964). "School Table" ["Tablitsa uchebnaya"]. *Pedagogical Encyclopedia* [*Pedagogicheskaga entsiklopediya*]. Moscow: Sovietskaya Entsiklopediya, v. 4.
11. Rozenblat, G.G. (1955). "On the Theoretical Foundations and Principles of Visuality" ["K voprosu o teoreticheskikh osnovakh i printsipakh naglyadnosti"]. *Scholarly Proceedings of the Herzen Leningrad State Pedagogical Institute* [*Uchenve zapiski LGPI im. Gertsena*], v. 105, p. 98.
12. See the Notes to the Introduction.
13. This "pure mathematical" interpretation of a model does not contradict its traditional interpretation.

14. For a more detailed discussion of entropy in an information theory context see W. Parry, *Topics in Ergodic Theory*. Cambridge: Cambridge University Press, 1981; or Martin & England, *Mathematical Theory of Entropy*, Encyclopedia of Mathematics and Its Applications, Vo. 12, Reading, MA: Addison-Wesley, 1981. (Ed.)

15. Boltyanskii, V.G. (1967). "What is Programmed Instruction?" ["Chto takoe programmirovannoe obuchenie"], *Mathematics in the School* [*Matematika v shkole*], no. 5.

16. Ibid.

17. It would be more correct to speak of instructional media with magnetic fastenings. However, the term "magnetic media" has taken firm root.

18. Strezikozin, V.P. (1968) "Several Didactic Requirements for Instructional Films" ["O nekotorykh didakticheskikh trebovaniyakh k uchebnym filmam"], in *Symposium on the Theory of Educational Cinema* [*Simpozium po teorii uchebnogo kino*]. Moscow.

Notes to Chapter 2

1. See A.N. Kolmogorov's preface to Lebesgue, H. (1960). *On the Measurement of Quantities* [*Ob izmerenii velichin*]. Moscow: Uchpedgiz, p. 11.

2. The new mathematics curriculum devotes somewhat fewer hours to this topic.

3. Galperin, P.Ya. (1965). *The Basic Results of Research on the Problem "The Formation of Mental Operations and Concepts"* [*Osnovnye rezultaty issledovanii po probleme "Formirovanie umstvennykh deistvii i ponyatii"*]. Moscow: Moscow State University Publishing House.

4. The reader has undoubtedly noted that here we are regarding a rectangular parallelepiped not as the result of two-level abstraction (i.e., abstraction by identification from a previously formed abstract mathematical concept of a "polyhedron"), but as the result of direct abstraction by identification from real objects (bars, boxes, etc.). Such a "leap" over one step in abstraction is entirely appropriate here—all the more so because only this method is possible in grade 4, because the abstract mathematical concept of a polyhedron has not yet been formed.

5. Properly speaking, the *general* case in this conjunctive context would involve a finite collection of properties $T = \{\alpha_k\}$ for which x is in P if the statement $\wedge_T \alpha_\kappa$ *is* true (Ed.)

6. There is some dispute over this definition of trapezoid. Presently, the most often accepted definition requires a trapezoid to have exactly one pair of parallel sides. (Ed.)

7. Here the logical connective "or" designated by the sign $\vee$ is distinguished from the conjunction "or" in ordinary speech (*either* this *or* that, but not both together).

8. Presumably one might ascertain this without actually testing each number; e.g., one need only check primes up to the square root of the number. (Ed.)

9. Galperin, P.Ya. (1965). *The Basic Results of Research on the Problem "The Formation of Mental Operations and Concepts"* [*Osnovnye rezultaty issledovanii po*

probleme "Formirovanie umstvennykh deistvii i ponyatii"]. Moscow: Moscow State University Publishing House.

10. The calculations are done as in Problem 1, and will not be given in detail.

11. Zykova, V.I. (1950). "Operirovanie ponyatiyami pri reshenii geometricheskikh zadach" ["Operating with Concepts in Solving Geometry Problems"]. *Proceedings of the RSFSR Academy of Pedagogical Sciences [Izvestiya APN RSFSR*, v. 28. Moscow: RSFSR Academy of Pedagogical Sciences Publishing House; Zykova, V.I. (1965). *Essays on the Psychology of Mastering Elementary Geometric Knowledge [Ocherki o psikhologii usvoeniya nachalnykh geometricheskikh znanii]*. Moscow: Uchpedgiz.

12. Talyzina, N.F. (1957). "Mental Conclusions in Solving Geometry Problems" ["Osobennosti umozaklyuchenii pri reshenii geometricheskikh zadach"]. *Proceedings of the RSFSR Academy of Pedagogical Sciences [Izvestiya APN RSFSR]*, v. 80. Moscow: RSFSR Academy of Pedagogical Sciences Publishing House.

13. Such a set will be referred to as an instructional unit. (Ed.)

15. Khinchin, A.Ya. (1963). *Pedagogical articles [Pedagogicheskie stati]*. Moscow: RSFSR Academy of Pedagogical Sciences Publishing House.

16. This may contrast with the experiences of teachers elsewhere. Many students do not have significant informal experiences with negative numbers prior to their introduction in the classroom. (Ed.)

17. Four hundred years ago a number of famous mathematicians refused to acknowledge negative numbers, calling them absurd, "less than nothing."

18. Kabanova-Meller, E.N. (1955). "On the Role of Visual Material in the Process of Abstraction and Generalization in Schoolchildren" ["O roli naglyadnogo materiala v protsesse abstraktsii i obobshcheniya u shkolnikov"]. *Issues in Psychology [Voprosy psikhologii]*, No. 2; Kabanova- Meller, E.N. (1962). *The Psychology of the Formation of Knowledge and Skills in Schoolchildren [Psikhologiya formirovaniya znanii i navvkov u shkolnikov]*. Moscow: RSFSR Academy of Pedagogical Sciences Publishing House; Menchinskaya, N.A. (1950). *The Psychology of Mastering Concepts [Psikhologiya usvoeniya ponyatii]*. *Proceedings of the RSFSR Academy of Pedagogical Sciences [Izvestiya APN RSFSR]*, v. 28.

Notes to Chapter 3

1. Presumably, by the standard isometric transformations: translations, rotations, and reflections. (Ed.)

2. Lebesgue, H. (1960). *On the Measurement of Quantities [Ob izmerenii velichin]*. Moscow: Uchpedgiz.

3. More precisely, for classes D and E, we require only that $A \cap B$ be a set of measure 0. (Ed.)

4. Rokhlin, V.A. (1966). "Area and Volume" ["Ploshchad i obem"]. *Encyclopedia of Elementary Mathematics [Entsiklopediya elementarnoi matematiki]*. Moscow: Nauka, v. 5, pp. 7-88.

5. Khadviger, G. (1966). *Lectures on Volume, Surface Area, and Isoperimetry* [*Lektsii ob ob'eme, ploshchadi poverkhnosti i isoperimetrii*]. Moscow: Nauka.

6. For details of the proof, see Khadviger, G. (1966). *Lectures on Volume, Surface Area, and Isoperimetry* [*Lektsii ob obeme, ploshchadi poverkhnosti i isoperimetrii*]. Moscow: Nauka; or Rokhlin, V.A. (1966). "Area and Volume" ["Ploshchad i obem"]. *Encyclopedia of Elementary Mathematics* [*Entsiklopediya elementarnoi matematiki*]. Moscow: Nauka, v. 5, pp. 7-88.

7. Khadviger, G. (1966). *Lectures on Volume, Surface Area, and Isoperimetry* [*Lektsii ob ob'eme, ploshchadi poverkhnosti i isoperimetrii*]. Moscow: Nauka, p. 105.

8. The theory of volume is treated in this way in Rokhlin, V.A. (1966). "Area and Volume" ["Ploshchad i obem"]. *Encyclopedia of Elementary Mathematics* [*Entsiklopediya elementarnoi matematiki*]. Moscow: Nauka, v. 5, pp. 7-88.

9. Here we use property (3)—invariance.

10. This is property (1)—standardization.

11. This is property (4)—additivity.

12. This is a separate problem, of course, which the students have already solved.

Notes to Chapter 5

1. The (Fig. 279) is available commercially; it can be supplemented by homemade solids.

2. The first part of the single-concept film "The Rectangular Parallelepiped" can be demonstrated as one variant. The students can also turn impressions from rubber stamps into completed drawings.

3. Models of these cut-outs are available commercially or can be easily made independently.

4. The possibilities for using the framework for an account of the surface are discussed earlier.

References

1. Atutov, P.R. (1967). "Several Questions Involving the Use of Visuality in Instruction" ["Nekotorye voprosy ispolzovaniya naglyadnosti v obuchenii"]. *Soviet Pedagogy* [*Sovetskaya pedagogika*], no. 5.

2. Boltyanskii, V.G. (1967). "What is Programmed Instruction?" ["Chto takoe programmirovannoe obuchenie"], *Mathematics in the School* [*Matematika v shkole*], no. 5.

3. Galperin, P.Ya. (1965). *The Basic Results of Research on the Problem "The Formation of Mental Operations and Concepts"* [*Osnovnye resultaty issledovanii po probleme "Formirovanie umstvennykh deistvii i ponyatii"*]. Moscow: Moscow State University Publishing House.

4. Gromov, A.P. (1960). *Film-Strips and Movies in Secondary School Mathematics Lessons* [*Diafilmy i kino na urokakh matematiki v srednei shkole*]. Moscow: Uchpedgiz.

5. Kabanova-Meller, E.N. (1955). "On the Role of Visual Material in the Process of Abstraction and Generalization in Schoolchildren" ["O roli naglyadnogo materiala v protsesse abstraktsii i obobshcheniya u shkolnikov"]. *Issues in Psychology* [*Voprosy psikhologii*], no. 2.

6. Kabanova-Meller, E.N. (1962). *The Psychology of the Formation of Knowledge and Skills in Schoolchildren* [*Psikhologiya formirovaniya znanii i navvkov u shkolnikov*]. Moscow: RSFSR Academy of Pedagogical Sciences Publishing House.

7. Khadviger, G. (1966). *Lectures on Volume, Surface Area, and Isoperimetry* [*Lektsii ob ob'eme, ploshchadi poverkhnosti i isoperimetrii*]. Moscow: Nauka.

8. Khinchin, A.Ya. (1963). *Pedagogical articles* [*Pedagogicheskie stati*]. Moscow: RSFSR Academy of Pedagogical Sciences Publishing House.

9. Konobeevskii, N.P. (1964). "School Table" ["Tablitsa uchebnaya"]. *Pedagogical Encyclopedia* [*Pedagogicheskaga entsiklopediya*]. Moscow: Sovietskaya Entsiklopediya, v. 4.

10. Lebesgue, H. (1960). *On the Measurement of Quantities* [*Ob izmerenii velichin*]. Moscow: Uchpedgiz.
11. Lenin, V.I. *Complete Collected Works* [*Polnoe sobranie sochinenii*], v. 25.
12. Menchinskaya, N.A. (1950). *The Psychology of Mastering Concepts* [*Psikhologiya usvoeniya ponyatii*]. *Proceedings of the RSFSR Academy of Pedagogical Sciences* [*Izvestiya APN RSFSR*], v. 28.
13. *Pamyati P.F. Lesgafta* [*In Memory of P. F. Lesgaft*]. Collection of articles. Moscow: Uchpedgiz, 1947.
14. Pestalozzi, J.H. (1963). *Selected Pedagogical Works* [*Izbrannye pedagogicheskie sochineniya*], v. 3. Moscow: Izdatelstvo APN RSFSR.
15. Rokhlin, V.A. (1966). "Area and Volume" ["Ploshchad i obem"]. *Encyclopedia of Elementary Mathematics* [*Entsiklopediya elementarnoi matematiki*]. Moscow: Nauka, v. 5.
16. Rozenblat, G.G. (1955). "On the Theoretical Foundations and Principles of Visuality" ["K voprosu o teoreticheskikh osnovakh i printsipakh naglyadnosti"]. *Scholarly Proceedings of the Herzen Leningrad State Pedagogical Institute* [*Uchenve zapiski LGPI im. Gertsena*], v. 105.
17. Shapovalenko, S.G. (1967). "Creating a System of Modern Materials for the General-Education Secondary School" ["O sozdanii sistemy sovremennogo oborudovaniya dlya srednei obshcheobrazovatelnoi shkoly"]. *Soviet Pedagogy* [*Sovetskaya pedagogika*], no. 5.
18. Strezikozin, V.P. (1968) "Several Didactic Requirements for Instructional Films" ["O nekotorykh didakticheskikh trebovaniyakh k uchebnym filmam"], in *Symposium on the Theory of Educational Cinema* [*Simpozium po teorii uchebnogo kino*]. Moscow.
19. Talyzina, N.F. (1957). "Mental Conclusions in Solving Geometry Problems" ["Osobennosti umozaklyuchenii pri reshenii geometricheskikh zadach"]. *Proceedings of the RSFSR Academy of Pedagogical Sciences* [*Izvestiya APN RSFSR*], v. 80. Moscow: RSFSR Academy of Pedagogical Sciences Publishing House.
20. Ushinskii, K.D. (1945). *Collected Works* [*Sobranie sochinenii*]. Moscow: Publishing House of the RSFSR Academy of Pedagogical Sciences, v. 6.
21. Zankov, L.V. (1960). *Visuality and the Motivation of Pupils in Instruction* [*Naglvadnost i aktivizatsiya uchashchikhsya v obuchenii*]. Moscow: Uchpedgiz.
22. Zykova, V.I. (1950). "Operirovanie ponyatiyami pri reshenii geometricheskikh zadach" ["Operating with Concepts in Solving Geometry Problems"]. *Proceedings of the RSFSR Academy of Pedagogical Sciences* [*Izvestiya APN RSFSR*, v. 28. Moscow: RSFSR Academy of Pedagogical Sciences Publishing House.

23. Zykova, V.I. (1965). *Essays on the Psychology of Mastering Elementary Geometric Knowledge* [*Ocherki o psikhologii usvoeniya nachalnykh geometricheskikh znanii*]. Moscow: Uchpedgiz.